D0042212

More Than Victims

MORALITY AND SOCIETY
A Series Edited by Alan Wolfe

More Than Victims

BATTERED WOMEN, THE SYNDROME SOCIETY, AND THE LAW

DONALD ALEXANDER DOWNS

The University of Chicago Press
Chicago and London

DONALD ALEXANDER DOWNS is a professor of political science at the University of
Wisconsin, Madison. He is the author of *Nazis in Skokie*, which won the 1986 Anisfield-
Wolf Book Award in Race Relations, and *The New Politics of Pornography* (published by
the University of Chicago Press), which won the Gladys M. Kammerer Award of the
American Political Science Association.

The University of Chicago Press, Chicago 60637
The University of Chicago Press, Ltd., London
© 1996 by The University of Chicago
All rights reserved. Published 1996
Printed in the United States of America
05 04 03 02 01 00 99 98 97 96 1 2 3 4 5

ISBN: 0-226-16159-5

Library of Congress Cataloging-in Publication Data

Downs, Donald Alexander.
    More than victims : battered women, the syndrome society, and the
law / Donald Alexander Downs.
        p.   cm.—(Morality and society)
    Includes bibliographical references and index.
    ISBN 0-226-16159-5 (cloth : alk. paper)
    1. Self-defense (Law)   2. Abused women—Legal status, laws, etc.
3. Criminal liability.   4. Battered women syndrome.   I. Title.
II. Series.
K5087.S4D69   1996
345′.025553—dc20
[342.525553]   96-16427
                                                         CIP

∞ The paper used in this publication meets the minimum requirements of the American National
Standard for Information Sciences—Permanence of Paper for Printed Library Materials, ANSI-
Z39.48-1984.

To the memory of my mother, Mary Jane Downs

Things become clear . . . if, following Hegel, we find in consciousness itself a fundamental hostility toward every other consciousness; the subject can be posed only in being opposed—he sets himself up as the essential, as opposed to the other, the inessential, the object. . . . But the other consciousness, the other ego, sets up a reciprocal claim. . . .

It is nonsense to assert that revelry, vice, ecstasy, passion, would become impossible if man and woman were equal in concrete matters; the contradictions that put flesh in opposition to the spirit, the instant to time, the swoon of immanence to the challenge of transcendence, the absolute of pleasure to the nothingness of forgetting, will never be resolved; in sexuality will always be materialized the tension, the anguish, the joy, the frustration, and the triumph of existence . . . mutually recognizing each other as subject, each [man and woman] will yet remain for the other an *other*. The reciprocity of their relations will not do away with the miracles—desire, possession, love, dream, adventure—worked by the division of human beings into two separate categories; and the words that move us—giving, conquering, uniting—will not lose their meaning.

— SIMONE DE BEAUVOIR, *The Second Sex*

CONTENTS

ACKNOWLEDGMENTS

I am indebted to many individuals and colleagues for the assistance they provided me in writing this book. Although many no doubt will not agree with my conclusions, I value the contributions and intellectual companionship they offered. Our interactions were small but meaningful examples of how intellectual and normative disagreements can foster mutual respect and learning.

My initial thanks go to those who consented to being interviewed, especially to women who have been battered. I appreciate your contributions, and hope that the policies I recommend will bring justice to cases of battered women who use lethal force without falling into the trap of the present legal approach that portrays them as presumptively mentally incapable. I owe special thanks to Ronda Richardson, whom I interviewed, and on whose case I participated as a consultant. Ronda's case provides many insights, and I use it many times as an illustration.

For direct assistance with the research, which included conducting interviews, literature and case research, and discussions with me about the substantive issues of the work, I owe special thanks to several graduate and law students who always went the extra mile for me: Chris Taylor, Claudia Obermueller, Dan Levin, Michael Gauger, Evan Gerstmann, and Ann Jacobs. Each of these individuals contributed in his or her distinctive way. Chris and Claudia helped me interview prison inmates with great ability, and taught me a lot about how to approach domestic violence. Dan offered me characteristically intelligent insights about social theory and law, and gave me some excellent research ideas. Mike gave me superb editorial advice that was sorely needed, and has helped me with his general, all-purpose wisdom.

Evan and Ann deserve special mention because they have contributed to the manuscript itself and have assisted me throughout the project. Each is as compassionate and thoughtful as he or she is hardheaded. Evan conducted many interviews for me and has been foremost in discussing the book with me. I am deeply indebted to his assistance. Appropriately, Evan is also my co-author for chapter 8, in which we lay out our alternative to the battered woman syndrome. Ann conducted massive research on syndrome cases for me. She was also my connection to the *Richardson* case, which I discuss often in this book. Ann wrote a short manuscript on the battered woman's syndrome based on her case investigations, and I cite and quote this work in the text itself. Ann served as co-chair of the legal defense team in charge of the retrial of the *Richardson* case. Both Ann and Evan embody the qualities the book endorses: hardheadedness balanced with informed compassion.

I owe further special thanks to three people. First, my sister, Jane Downs, gave me exceptionally helpful ideas and insights, especially concerning literary examples and the relationship between society and conceptions of mental health. Jane's probing intelligence, unmatched humor, erudition, and joy in thinking encouraged me to connect the syndrome phenomenon to broader issues in society. Second, I want to acknowledge Kate Ross, an intellectual ally and challenger whose thinking and actions have compelled me to take the notions of reason and personal responsibility seriously. Steadfast to what is formidable, Kate is immune to intellectual and moral fads and sloppy thinking. Third, Gerald Mueller, the chair of the original *Richardson* defense team, also gave me great assistance. Gerry allowed me to be a consultant to the defense; and my interviews with him illuminated issues surrounding defense strategy. Gerry's legal expertise, professional dedication, and passion for justice made a big impression on me.

Undergraduate students also added to my thinking about the problem of domestic violence and the issue of syndrome defenses, and some conducted case and literature research for me. First, students in my large lecture course, Criminal Law and Justice, and my seminar course on criminal law and legal theory have inspired me over the years to struggle with the conundrums of criminal culpability. Political Science 452 and 695 at Madison have never failed to renew the spirit of inquiry and the desire to think about difficult normative and legal questions. Second, a few undergraduates have done serious research for me on this project and discussed its controversies, especially Anat Hakim, Martin Sweet, and Lisa Rechsteiner, all, like Ann Jacobs, refugees of 695. Though I stand in the debt of all 695 students, these students merit special mention.

I have also benefited from discussions with colleagues at Madison and elsewhere, especially Len Kaplan, Marc Galanter, Herman Goldstein, and Walter Dickey at the University of Wisconsin Law School. Marc has encouraged this project from its inception, and given me several incisive ideas about the social meaning of syndrome defenses, while Len has taught me much about the connections and tensions among law, psychology, and society. Each man is devoted to the life of the mind in his unique way. In my own department, Marion Smiley, Booth Fowler, Virginia Sapiro, Charles Anderson, and Bernard Yack have helped to widen and provoke my understanding of such important issues as responsibility, politics, gender, and community. Katherine Hendley, Joel Grossman, and Herbert Kritzer remain influential colleagues in public law, and have contributed to my understanding of law and politics in too many ways to recount. Elsewhere, Timothy Litton of Capital Law School and Robert Kagan of Berkeley have given me very helpful ideas about the issue of syndrome defenses. And Alan Wolfe of Boston University gave me superlative advice about organization at a crucial point in the development of the manuscript, saving it from the plight of irretrievable disorder.

I am grateful to the University of Wisconsin for bestowing a Vilas Fellowship upon me, which purchased me enough time and financial support in 1992 and 1993 to pursue the research upon which this book is based. Dennis Dresang, chair of the Department of Political Science at the time, was responsible for initiating my nomination for the Vilas, and I thank him for the confidence he placed in me. I am also grateful to the department for continuing to maintain an environment conducive to intellectual, ideological, and methodological diversity. We are committed to the First Amendment maxim that "debate on public issues should be uninhibited, robust, and wide-open." I value this increasingly unusual environment.

PART **I** *The Syndrome Society*

CHAPTER ONE

The Syndrome Society:
Justice or Illegitimate Excuse?

This is a book about the uses and abuses of the new type of "syndrome" excuses for criminal actions that have gripped criminal law and justice for better than a decade. Dramatized in 1993 by the famous Menendez brothers murder trial in Beverly Hills and in 1994 by the Lorena Bobbitt trial in Virginia, which relied, respectively, on battered child syndrome (BCS) and battered woman syndrome (BWS), victimization syndrome defenses promise new ways of considering the legal responsibility and culpability of individuals who lash out against their abusers in contexts that do not always conform to the traditional standards of self-defense or duress.

The law of self-defense is based on a rather strict presence of necessity: it requires that the defender use deadly force only if the threat of death or great bodily harm is imminent or presently impending, and that the response be reasonable, apportioned to the extent or quality of the threat. In addition, the intent must be to defend oneself, not to inflict retribution or gain a personal victory or advantage over the other.[1] Duress (or coercion) arises when a victimizer forces a victim to commit a crime by threats to the safety of the victim or someone else. It involves a "person's unlawful threat (1) which causes the defendant reasonably to believe that the only way to avoid imminent death or serious bodily injury to himself or to another is to engage in conduct which violates the literal terms of the criminal law, and (2) which causes the defendant to engage in that conduct."[2]

Such victimization syndromes as BCS and BWS are designed to account for the omnipresent pressures and dangers that plague oppressive domestic environments—dangers that can defy the relatively narrow confines of the traditional laws of self-defense and duress, which were formulated without knowledge or recognition of such situations of captivity and abuse.[3] Advocates of syndrome defenses maintain that because of power differences, victims of domestic abuse often need to use defensive force outside the state of imminent danger, such as when the oppressor is sleeping or when a lull in the violence exists.[4] I will call such situations "nonconfrontational" cases of deadly force.

Since human victimization is unjust, victimization syndromes by their very nature signal the justice of using deadly force outside the confines of traditional self-defense law. At the same time, the new syndromes also embody evidence of mental states caused by psychological stress and trauma that differ from more traditional or established notions of mental disorder or incapacity: trauma induced by specifiable human oppression. As Judith Herman remarks in *Trauma and Recovery*, a work to which I will often refer, "The syndrome that follows upon prolonged, repeated trauma needs its own name."[5] Consequently, victimization syndromes have also been used to show insanity and diminished capacity. Legal insanity, a complete defense, normally means that the defendant lacked the mental capacity (in terms of cognitive and/or volitional capacity) to conform his or her behavior to the law.[6] Diminished capacity is a partial defense. It can be used to negate the "specific" intent element of a crime (usually premeditation or deliberation), especially in murder cases, in which it can reduce the charge to manslaughter. In battered woman cases, for example, the defendant could use diminished capacity to argue that all the years of abuse have made her mentally unstable, if not "insane," thereby rendering her incapable of forming the specific intent required to make her fully legally responsible. A Missouri court has recognized this claim in a case involving a battered woman who claimed to suffer from BWS.[7] As we proceed, I will call such excuses as insanity and diminished capacity "incapacity excuses."

Victimization syndromes in criminal law also include Vietnam War veteran syndrome (VS), rape-trauma syndrome (RTS, used more by the prosecution than the defense), and hostage syndrome (afflicted in situations of violent captivity and kidnapping). All these victimization syndromes are, essentially, species of post-traumatic stress disorder (PTSD), which the American Psychiatric Association designated an official disorder in the third edition of its Diagnostic and Statistical Manual in 1980.[8] Such organically based conditions as gambler's and premenstrual syndrome have also arisen, but they do not deal with victimization at human hands.

Syndrome logic represents a new way of thinking—a new worldview—that has contributed to understanding and justice in ways I will explore as we proceed. But it is also ridden with pitfalls that call for examination. On the positive side, the syndrome defenses make us aware of the special fears and anxieties of individuals subjected to violence and related forms of abuse on a sustained basis. They shake us out of our states of denial, and compel us to construe the needs of self-defense in a new light. In addition, they foster a more complex or subtle understanding of the psychological ramifications of domestic violence. Individuals subjected to such abuse do suffer trauma and psychic wounds. Any adequate and just accounting of criminal responsibility must take the mental states engendered by such abuse into consideration.

On the negative side, syndromes are formulaic and politicized in ways that pay insufficient heed in their own rights to the subtleties of reality and individual cases, and unnecessarily compromise the presumption of individual responsibility upon which legal justice and equal citizenship rest. The *Menendez* case represents the *coup de grâce* of syndrome logic in these regards: nonculpability regardless of the absence of any conceivably meaningful presence of danger to the defendants when the two brothers killed their mother and father. I will show below that justice in domestic violence cases can be achieved without sacrificing the presumptions of reason and responsibility, and without ignoring important factual differences that distinguish individual cases. Even though victims of domestic violence often suffer psychic wounds, they also often know precisely what is going on with their oppressors, and when they resort to deadly force, there is often good reason to do so.

Surprisingly, trauma and reason can coexist. Much of the literature concerning battered women depicts this coexistence, explicitly or implicitly. But confusion surrounds the understanding of the relationship between these mental states, confusion that has befogged the entire debate. On the one hand, psychologists highlight the mental strains and defects battered women suffer. Lenore Walker, the creator of the term "battered woman syndrome," states, "The process of learned helplessness [a key component of BWS] results in a state with deficits in three specific areas: in the area where battered women think, in how they feel, and in the way they behave."[9] This trauma and associated incapacity is potentially relevant to certain behaviors of the victims of domestic violence, including the inability to liberate themselves from their tormentors.

On the other hand, the literature is replete with a counterassumption: *that when it comes to the key issue in self-defense law, the presence of imminent or impending danger, the victims of domestic violence often discern their mates' readiness to inflict violence with acute perceptive powers—powers forged out of the painful and intense experiences that characterize many relationships in this context.* Far from blunting the mind, fear and trauma sharpen it in this domain. Julie Blackman, an honored researcher and scholar in the field of domestic violence, maintains that testimony about the situations and dangers battered women confront will help jurors and society to fathom the *heightened reason* with which battered women perceive impending danger:

> [These sources] explain the reasonableness of a battered woman's perception of danger as an alternative form of reasonableness. That is, battered women are construed as reasonable in a relational framework and with a sense of history that is quite explicitly different from the traditional, legal standard of reasonableness. . . . Careful attention to the battered woman's past experiences with her husband's or partner's violence enhances one's capacity to understand her attack against him as reasonable or not. A true

standard of reason is best approximated when all relevant factors that bear on good judgment are considered.[10]

Blackman's point about battered women's reason will prove to be Archimedean for my analysis. It receives support from other well-known advocates of battered women. For example, in *When Battered Women Kill,* Angela Browne wondered if the relationships of battered women who resorted to deadly force against their mates differed from the relationships of other battered women. Comparing samples of the two groups, she found that the abusers of battered women who kill are more likely than the mates of other battered women to have abused drugs and alcohol, to have used deadly or dangerous violence, threats, and sexual assault more frequently, and to have threatened children. "As the assaults became more brutal and the abusers seemed increasingly unconcerned about the harm they were inflicting, the women's focus shifted from attempts to understand to an emphasis on survival."[11] This logic, like Blackman's, points toward situational factors and accurate perceptions of danger rather than to psychological incapacity in the form of a syndrome. In other words, it seems to fit the standards of self-defense rather than the logic of psychological incapacity. Indeed, I will show below that syndrome logic in the form of BWS actually undercuts battered women's self-defense claims at many turns.

One of my interviewees, Nora Cashen, a former victim of domestic violence who has worked closely with battered women in Wisconsin, provided the clearest statement about the presence of situational reason within an environment of trauma. She depicted battered women as exhibiting

> [a] lot of hyper-vigilant behavior, monitoring his behavior to know all the time what he is up to. They become experts of his cues, very externally motivated, they don't think of themselves. They monitor their own behavior to see what they can do to maintain control over the situation . . .
>
> I wouldn't phrase it as diminished capacity. It is someone whose survival has been so focused on maintaining peace, their energy is so channeled, they lose their ability to have perspective. It's like anything else— a job with long hours, you lose your social skills. So there is diminished capacity in this sense.[12]

If so, the key to justice in domestic violence self-defense cases lies in applying the standards of self-defense with an understanding of the special circumstances and pressures that battered women confront. Such practical reasoning differs from relying on a "syndrome," which signals incapacity to employ reason, and which fails to draw lines concerning responsibility based on the facts of cases. Battered women are victims, but they normally do not surrender reason in their desperation, at least when it comes to the single most important issue in self-defense cases: the

reasonable perception of imminent danger. Many commentators we will encounter in our inquiry leave no doubt about their commitments to giving battered women justice, yet express deep reservations about the "syndrome connection" as the preferred way to deal with battered women's defense claims. The syndrome connection portrays the victims of abuse as incapable of exercising reason and responsibility. Can we not achieve justice in this domain without asking these victims to shed the very attributes that make equal citizenship possible?

We will see that the battering relationship can be very complex, and that battered women develop distinct mental states concerning different aspects of the relationship. Trauma can compromise mental competence or functionality when it comes to such things as assessing the destiny of the relationship or the feasibility of extricating oneself from the clutches of violence. But trauma often has the opposite effect on other perceptions, including discerning the inclinations, needs, and potential violence of the batterer to whom the woman is "traumatically bonded" (see below). The more we understand the intersubjectivity of such bonding, the more we come to appreciate the counterintuitive link between trauma and heightened rationality concerning the need for self-defensive maneuvers.

In the end, the main problem with syndrome logic is that it ineluctably undermines the logic of self-defense, which is a logic of reason. This shortfall gives rise to the central thesis of this book: *that the reality of domestic violence requires the criminal law to pay great heed to the defense claims of battered women and children, but that the syndrome connection is a problematic way to accomplish this task.*

Syndrome defenses pose related problems as well, each of which extends from the confusion of reason and unreason just discussed. To begin, I must stress a very general point. More and more people are growing disenchanted with the proliferation of "syndromes" and "abuse excuses" in society. In the next chapter I will portray this proliferation, which goes way beyond the prominent syndromes mentioned above. In the early 1980s social and political pressures led to serious limitations of the insanity defense, especially after the verdict of "not guilty by reason of insanity" in John Hinckley's trial for attempting to assassinate President Reagan. If a backlash against syndrome and abuse defenses were to arise, it would be a great injustice if the valid self-defense claims of the victims of domestic abuse were to go down with the syndrome ship. Relying upon the syndrome connection as the key to legal defenses in such cases threatens this very result. It is time to consider prying such legal defenses away from the already leaky syndrome connection.

Next, syndromes' rigidity is often intellectually disingenuous, and it can compromise the prospects of defendants who do not fit the stereotype of the syndrome. The very term "syndrome" denotes uniformity rather than difference. Webster's International Dictionary defines syndrome as "a group of signs and symptoms that occur together, and characterize a disease."[13] This problem is exacerbated when the syndrome is construed in medical or pathological terms as a form of mental disorder.[14]

We will see that many women's characters, situations, and reactions to stress simply do not fit the BWS mold, especially if the women do not conform to images of womanhood prevalent in the white middle class; but this lack of fit should not in any way compromise their right to defend themselves from danger. Sharon Angella Allard contends that BWS encourages unprincipled racial stereotyping: "The theory incorporates stereotypes of limited applicability concerning how a woman would and, indeed, should react to battering. To successfully defend herself, a battered woman needs to convince a jury that she is a 'normal' woman—weak, passive, and fearful. . . . Race certainly plays a role in the cultural distinction between 'good' and 'bad' woman. The passive, gentle white woman is automatically more like the 'good' fairy princess stereotype than a [b]lack woman, who as the 'other' may be seen as the 'bad' witch."[15]

Along these same lines, by signifying mental incapacity, syndrome logic ineluctably "labels" its recipients as unable to bear the obligations of citizenship. Being found "mentally ill" has consequences for how one is perceived by others. As many of those who have reflected on the legal issues surrounding victimization excuses have observed, the forms in which we legally construct defendants have consequences for equal citizenship.[16]

The concept of responsibility is in many important respects indivisible.[17] If a person is labeled (or officially pronounced) incapable of being responsible in one context, that person will often surrender the benefits that accrue to bearing responsibility in another context. Below we will encounter a telling example: battered women found to have been afflicted by BWS have fared badly in hearings concerning custody of children. Courts have rendered justice in such cases only by *abandoning* BWS in favor of a logic that considers battered women's trying circumstances rather than their psychological syndromes. Once again, situational analysis proves preferable to syndromic speculation.

BWS presumes that most or all battered women react in similar fashion to their victimization; they lack the *will* that characterizes distinctive individuals. We will look at many cases below in which Lenore Walker testified that battered women defendants were "women without wills," and we will see that there *are* generalities that characterize battering relationships, but that battered women also often salvage heroic capacities to cope. Patti Seeger, spokeswoman for the nationally recognized Dane County Advocates for Battered Women, located in Madison, Wisconsin, denounced the theory of "learned helplessness" in an interview which I will draw on in a later chapter. Seeger proclaimed that she "disagreed totally" with this theory. "Rather than being helpless, battered women adopt survival skills."[18]

Hence, battered women embody a paradox: they *are* victimized, but they also often possess more capacity for judgment than a defense based on learned helplessness acknowledges. Seeger's "survivor" logic, which is now the predominant logic in the literature outside of the judicial system (which relies on BWS), is consistent with the norms of situational reason defended by Blackman and Browne above, not with the standards of incapacity excuse. In addition, we will see that each case must still be dealt with on its own merits because of individual variance. We will also see that the manner in which this tension is resolved has powerful implications for political theory and citizenship.

Accordingly, syndromes' formulaic quality also obscures the diversity of situations in which victims resort to violence or commit allegedly criminal acts. Some kill in response to imminent danger, while others strike back at their tormentor while he is asleep or otherwise indisposed. Others hire third parties to kill the batterer at an indefinite time in the future. In addition, many victims suffer greater abuse than other sufferers do. In some cases abuse is directly related to the resort to lethal force, whereas in other cases it is an important background fact rather than a precipitating factor. Though abuse is always unjustifiable, the relevance of being victimized to the standards of self-defense law varies in each of these situations. Adjudication of self-defense cases vindicates the maxim that "God lies in the details." But syndrome logic ignores erstwhile important details. It provides no means by which to draw distinctions that are usually important in the criminal law. *And unlike the insanity defense, which by its very nature applies only in rare cases, syndrome incapacity is presumed to be "typical" of individuals who are exposed to the wide continuum of oppressive harms at issue.* PTSD is premised on this assumption. The syndrome defenses stake out a territory of unprecedented scope.

Another problem stems from the fact that in criminal trials victimization syndromes use inconsistent claims of excuse based on mental incapacity and justification. Generally speaking, criminal acts are "justified" in law if self-defense or defense of others is involved or if the larger social good would be promoted more by committing the act than by not committing it (for example, trespassing to save a baby from crawling into a swimming pool). Criminal acts are "excused" if the defendant is under "duress" or lacks the mental or emotional capacity to be blameworthy. Though the lines that distinguish justification and excuse are not always clear (as I will show later in the book), justification "speaks to the rightness of the act; an excuse to whether the actor is accountable for a concededly wicked act."[19] Thus, self-defense is considered a right thing to do because of the defensive rights of the original target and the wickedness of the original aggressor. Excused acts are wrong in themselves, but we deem the perpetrator less blameworthy because of the extraordinary situational pressures he or she confronted (duress) or because of mental or related impairment (insanity). Self-defense and duress also involve a standard of reason that is lacking in incapacity excuses.

Unlike other defenses, syndrome defenses often juxtapose incapacity excuse and justification or rely alternately on one or the other. On the one hand, this juxtaposition reflects the paradox of reason and unreason to which I have already alluded. On the other hand, it suggests that these defenses are more result-oriented than principled (a form of group "advocacy science" according to one source).[20] And on the level of citizenship, it suggests that courts and society are still unsure of the legal status of such victims. For example, to the extent that BWS signifies excuse as a kind of incapacity or helplessness, it supports notions of incapacity for reason and responsibility. To the extent that BWS supports justification, it acknowledges the ability to be responsible under trying circumstances. But we will see that BWS's connection to justification and reason is tenuous, at best.

The points just raised indicate that syndrome logic provides questionable means by which to distinguish the culpable from the nonculpable. In a similar vein, syndromes allow juries and society to rely on sometimes questionable scientific evidence in assessing legal responsibility, a move that constitutes a retreat from the burden of exercising normative and communal judgment in difficult cases of self-defense. But accepting this burden is crucial to political freedom and citizenship. As Hannah Arendt (following Kant) has shown, discriminating judgment involves a "community sense" that emerges out of the process of thinking and forging community standards. Community standards, in turn, are based on refining the dialectical relationship between particular cases and more general standards which are themselves subject to ongoing dispute and reconsideration. Judgment "is 'the faculty of thinking the particular'; but to *think* means to generalize, hence it is the faculty of mysteriously combining the particular and the general."[21] That is, judgment consists of weighing relevant factors in relation to a framework of standards, and striving to make the right choices in the face of complexity and openness to the contingency of all decisions. Making such choices often requires being able to risk being wrong and bearing the existential and political burden of responsibility for the result. It is a form of deliberate political action in its own right. As Mary Midgley remarks concerning judgment:

> *Judging* is not in general simply accepting one or two ready-made alternatives as the right one. It cannot be done by tossing up. It is seeing reason to think and act in a particular way. It is a comprehensive function, involving our whole nature, by which we direct ourselves and find our way through a whole forest of possibilities. No science rules here; there is no given system of facts which will map our whole route for us. We are always moving into new territory.[22]

Community standards of legal judgment are essential attributes of political community and citizenship. Although psychological science educates public judgments, such judgments are not reducible to psychological science per se. Judgments involve notions of appropriate behavior and conduct in particular contexts, not scientific or therapeutic fact; their acceptance requires persuasion and appeals to reason and common sense. Accordingly, the status of judgment reflects the integrity of the political community as a whole.

In a related sense, the theory of learned helplessness that lurks at the center of BWS envisions women in a manner that compromises their equal citizenship by portraying them as "women without wills." Learned helplessness depicts them, in Simone de Beauvoir's words, as "immanent," which means lacking in meaningful agency and individuation. De Beauvoir contrasts immanence with "transcendence," which entails the capacity for agency, individuation, and judgment.[23] We will see later that the most sophisticated accounts of battering relationships defy simplistic portrayals of battered women as immanent (the will is never relinquished, finding often ingenious new ways to express itself), and that the logic surrounding immanence is not the logic of citizenship. Indeed, de Beauvoir was acutely aware of the implications of her key concepts for citizenship.

An approach superior to BWS would address battered women as equal citizens entitled to the same protections of the law as anyone else. Empathy and equal protection are crucial. But syndromization inhibits the cultivation of the "common ground" upon which meaningful inclusion and citizenship grow. Rather than opening the door to include battered women in the discourse of equal justice, BWS reinforces the battered woman as "other." As Shirley Sagaw states, "While the recognition of the battered woman's syndrome revised the law of self-defense for a limited class of women . . . a new stereotype of the battered woman is created, once again placing women outside the purview of the reasonable. Thus battered women have been placed in a double bind of two stereotypes: if an abused woman's responses in the relationship did not conform exactly to the legal stereotype of a woman suffering from battered woman syndrome, courts could find her, by definition, to be neither battered nor reasonable."[24]

The dialectical relationship between rights and responsibilities reinforces this conclusion. Constitutional freedom is made up of equal protection of the law (the legal form of equal respect) and the capacity of citizens to govern themselves, to be presumptively responsible for their acts. From this vantage point, what makes us responsible is not necessarily some universal feature of human beings but the specific requirements of action and citizenship in a society which values constitutional freedoms. Constitutional freedom is ultimately unthinkable and undoable without the presumption of self-governance. We need to take the presumption of personal responsibility seriously, but we also need to fathom the reality of domestic violence and provide its victims with justice. In the broadest sense, this book must come to terms with the following dilemma: *how to serve the demands of responsibility and empathy at the same time.* This is a difficult task. But justice, which is never easy, demands nothing less.

Rather than contributing to this task, syndrome logic provides easy answers. Reliance upon it signifies a growing failure to exercise considered judgment about right and wrong, especially in cases like *Menendez,* where the brothers killed their parents despite the lack of any kind of impending danger being present. The "syndrome connection" compromises judgment and political community by redefining self-defense (which has traditionally been based on the jury's perception of the reasonableness or appropriateness of the defender's use of lethal force) as a psychological and therapeutic issue, and by undermining the connection between self-defense and personal responsibility. We will see that the discourse of BWS (and the syndrome connection of which it ineluctably comprises a part) makes no room for the discourse of responsibility. The proof is in the pudding: Walker and other advocates of BWS and related victimization syndromes have provided us with no meaningful way by which to distinguish the culpable from the nonculpable. One searches Walker's many works in vain for counterexamples to BWS and nonculpability.

Another troubling aspect of treating self-defense in domestic violence contexts with a therapeutic concept is that this method deflects attention from the responsibility of the abusers to the mental states of the victims of battering. As many advocates of battered women claim, "psychologizing" the issue diverts our attention from the political aspect of battering, which is based on the batterer's need to control and dominate his mate, and the uncomfortable fact that domestic violence is prevalent. Kathleen Kreneck, policy coordinator of the Wisconsin Coalition against Domestic Violence, remarked, "[BWS has penetrated the legal system so much] because we are a victim-oriented society. It is easier to deal with this than real social change. It is a therapeutic concept, Walker [the creator of BWS] is a therapist. We easily blame victims, we find fault in them. But domestic violence is political, an oppression of women, an expression of sexism."[25] Hence, reliance on the syndrome connection as the key to justice in self-defense situations represents society's failure to protect victims of domestic abuse in the first place. We "pay them back" for our original omission (cover our original transgression) by giving them a syndrome defense at trial. The key to justice from this perspective is to punish abusers for their violence and to enact measures to prevent domestic violence.

This book seeks to find the best way to accept and deal with the knowledge that has been generated by the new studies of victimization without falling prey to the traps set by the syndrome connection. In treating syndrome defenses, we must be careful to avoid a Manichean approach that views victimization syndromes and related forms of knowledge as purely wrong or purely right. Victimization syndromes are embedded in a new field of knowledge concerning victimization that has brought startling, dark truths to light. In this light, the syndromes have contributed to moral and intellectual responsibility. If we design to move beyond the syndrome approach concerning criminal law defenses to what I consider a better method, we must do so dialectically, not dismissively. We should strive to listen to the new knowledge as we question and criticize it. As we proceed, the reader will note that I rely on and utilize BWS, post-traumatic stress disorder (PTSD), and other forms of victimization syndrome as evidence in portraying and analyzing the problems associated with domestic violence and the criminal law. This critical reliance is necessary in order to preserve what I consider valid in the pioneering work that made domestic violence an issue in the first place; and there is much that is valid. The pioneers of domestic violence research and the law have done heroic work. But it is time to reassess the new paradigm they have developed, and to see how well it stands up to the norms of the larger body politic and the principles embedded in the criminal law. In the end, I will attempt to show how defenses can use victimization knowledge to support the norms and discourse of reason and responsibility. This book is meant to be a step in that dialectical process.

In this respect, my analysis both resembles and differs from the critiques of the "recovery movement" in psychology that have arisen in very recent years in works by Frederick Crews, Elizabeth Loftus, Katherine Ketcham, Lawrence Wright, Richard Ofshe, Ethan Watters, and others.[26] The recovery movement maintains that trauma often induces victims of child sexual abuse to repress their memories or recollections of the abuse, which can be retrieved later in life by the proper psychological method (psychotherapy, hypnosis, the interview with administration of sodium amytal). Advocates deem such recovery sufficient evidence of the actuality of abuse. The recovery movement is a companion of the syndrome connection, for both movements are concerned with the psychological implications of domestic violence and sexual abuse, and both movements have been supported by similar political movements and similar intellectual horizons and authorities. They share the same intellectual *gestalt*. The work of Judith Herman, a founder of the recovery movement and author of the award-winning *Trauma and Recovery* published in 1992, is a primary example of this link between recovery and syndrome logic.[27] In *Trauma and Recovery*, Herman relies extensively upon work about BWS and other syndromes.

Crews, Loftus, Wright, and Ofshe raise serious questions about the validity of recovered memory evidence. Among other things, the concept of repression upon which the movement is based is questionable, and it is doubtful that such selective repression is consistent with what we know about how the mind and memory work. And professionals can induce symptoms and recollections by the mechanism of suggestion. In the next chapter, I will show that such suggestibility has consistently accompanied the development of modern psychology. These problems have led to many false accusations and a new form of "witch-hunt," as revealed in recent works that have exposed the fraudulence of the child abuse prosecutions in the famous McMartin and Amirault cases in California and Massachusetts. As this book goes to press, a similar wave of demonstrably false accusation has broken out in Wenatchee, Washington, as chronicled by Dorothy Rabinowitz for the *Wall Street Journal*.[28]

The problem, as we will discover below and in many of the legal cases I will analyze throughout the book, is that evidence of child abuse is also extensive. Consequently, we must be careful to avoid the "category mistake" that disingenuously links the fate of the child abuse movement to the fate of the memory recovery movement. These are two separate issues. The following proposition confronts us: whereas child abuse is indeed a major problem, the method of memory recovery is suspect. In the longer run, the credibility of the movement against child abuse might depend upon severing itself from the recovery connection, under the sway of which it is increasingly difficult to distinguish fact from fantasy.

My approach resembles that of the recovery movement's critics to the extent that I seek to pry the criminal defenses of battered women who use deadly force away from the syndrome connection. But my approach differs from these critics in that I am far less skeptical of the underlying reality of abuse toward which the psychological theory at stake is directed. To be sure, some defendants have "manufactured" abuse in criminal trials, as I will recount below. But defendants have always been tempted to fit the facts to the frameworks of defense law. More importantly, I will document abundant evidence of abuse of women in domestic contexts, and show how such abuse engenders real fear and danger. And battered women do not forget or repress their abuse, as the children of the recovery movement allegedly do. Battered women are acutely aware of the abuse and the dangers it poses. The real question in criminal cases is the relationship between the abuse and the act of self-defense. Accordingly, I draw on the insights and evidence of Walker and Herman (as well as on many other sources) at the same time that I criticize their work.

What I question is the syndrome model for dealing with the problem in criminal trials.

The book will focus on BWS because it is the most successful syndrome, and because it is deeply implicated in the conflicts concerning equality, justice, and citizenship that animate the syndrome debate. Examining BWS provides the best way to illuminate the implications for criminal law and political theory of the "syndromizing" of the problem of victimization. The multiple themes of violence, abuse, power and powerlessness, citizenship, justice, and political and legal constructions of the self emerge most prominently in the consideration of this syndrome. In addition, BWS has emerged as the predominant means of defending battered women who kill or commit other serious crimes. As noted above, BWS as a term is the creation of Lenore Walker, a psychologist who at one time was slated to testify on behalf of O. J. Simpson in his trial for killing Nicole Brown and Ron Goldman. In his opening statement to the jury, defense attorney Johnnie L. Cochran Jr. described Walker to the Simpson jury as "the world's most renowned expert on battered woman syndrome."[29]

BWS and the knowledge field of which it is a part undoubtedly have a lot to teach us about gender justice. But at what point is it advisable to abandon BWS in favor of standards of responsibility that provide justice for women (not just those who fit the syndrome) and apply equally to all citizens? Recognizing this tension, Kathleen O'Donovan portrays the Canadian use of BWS as a necessary step in the legal system's incorporation of women's voices and experiences (she speaks of "the battered woman and her syndrome"), then insinuates that this usage is a step in a dialectical process that points toward surpassing BWS:

> The reader may ask why self-defence and provocation law can be readily used by an embodied male, whilst expert witnesses are required to testify to a 'syndrome' in order to fit abused women into these defenses. Answers given earlier used ideas of gendered fear, physical [ab]uses of the body, legal history, the legal construction of the reasonable man. Nevertheless, the questions are pertinent in strategic terms. Why can't women's experiences be accommodated by law without resort to experts? Canadian law provides answers on a number of levels. In summary, myths about, and stereotypes of battered women must first be displaced. Then the experiences of such women can be introduced. To accomplish both of these tasks experts are required.[30]

This book will consider O'Donovan's question: Why can't women's experiences be accommodated by law without resort to experts carrying syndromes in their bags?

I will treat the issue in distinct sections. In the following chapter, I will lay out the growth of syndrome logic in culture, politics, psychology, and the law. In part 2, I will portray and discuss the nature of domestic violence, theories of battering relationships (including BWS and more subtle, complex models), and the major substantive problems that accrue to BWS as a form of knowledge and criminal defense. In part 3, I will turn to a more specifically legal analysis, depicting the positive and negative uses of BWS in relevant case law. In this part I will also discuss the implications of syndrome logic for political theory and citizenship, an analysis which supports defenses that appeal to the potential rationality of defendants rather than victim ideology and syndromic forms of incapacity excuse. Finally, in part 4, Evan Gerstmann and I will provide a positive legal policy alternative to a syndrome approach to the defense of battered women who kill.

I will draw on interviews with major actors in the domestic violence and syndrome fields in the Madison, Wisconsin, area and other areas, including twenty interviews conducted in July 1993 with women incarcerated for homicide at Taycheedah Correctional Institution in Fond du Lac, Wisconsin, whose crimes were influenced by battering. I use these interviews largely for illustrative purposes, not for statistical reasons or the like. Domestic violence is now a complex field, involving shelters, therapists, police departments, district attorneys, defense lawyers, and researchers. The interviews we conducted enabled me and my assistants to gain a grasp of the nature of this field of practice and knowledge, and to appreciate its overt and more subtle interconnections. I also served as a consultant to the defense in a battered woman murder case in Kenosha, Wisconsin, and observed and contributed to the defense at the trial. I will refer to this case (*State v. Richardson*, 1993) often for illustrations. In this case, the jury found Ronda Richardson guilty of second degree reckless homicide (the lowest level of culpability for homicide). The appeal led to a major ruling by the Wisconsin Supreme Court in late 1994: that the trial court erred in not allowing the expert psychologist called by the defense to give her own opinion concerning whether the defendant's behavior and characteristics were consistent with the profile of the battered woman. The Wisconsin Supreme Court ruled, however, that the trial court properly refused to let the expert offer an opinion as to Ronda's state of mind at the time of the killing (the legal "ultimate issue").[31]

As stressed, the logic of BWS is connected to the broader development of victimization syndromes. Thus, we need to understand the knowledge field within which BWS is embedded in order to properly evaluate BWS as a legal and psychological concept. The next chapter deals with the "syndrome revolution" from legal, political, and social perspectives.

CHAPTER TWO

The Rise of the Syndrome Society:
A New Perspective on Criminal Culpability

In our time the politics and law of abuse are omnipresent, especially in the areas of gender and the family. Cases of battered and sexually abused women and children who strike out against their oppressors captivate the public's imagination. Reasonable citizens want the law to prosecute the abusers and render simple justice. Society no longer tolerates the notion that such abuse lies beyond the law on the ground that the man "owns" the victims or that the acts are protected by the sanctity of the domestic realm. But cases of victim retaliation are often more problematic, unless the retaliatory act fits an accepted criminal law defense like self-defense or duress, where danger to the self or others is imminent. We want the law to lead us to justice in such cases, yet justice is not always easy to achieve.

A recent homicide case in a small town in southern Wisconsin illustrates the dilemma. Jeffrey Thrasher shot his father point-blank because he could no longer endure the brutalization and domination that Douglas Thrasher inflicted upon him, his mother, and his sister. As the unsuspecting Douglas entered the house one day, Jeffrey unloaded years of moral rage into his father's body and what was left of his father's soul. The act did not amount to self-defense, at least not as the law defines it, because Douglas at that moment did not confront Jeffrey with deadly harm. During the sentencing hearing, the judge's voice shook with emotion, and he cried at pivotal points. After the jury rendered its sentence, the teary prosecutor hugged the defense attorney. Only an eyewitness can bear proper witness:

> "Douglas Thrasher deserved to be punished, but he didn't deserve to be killed," Green County Circuit Judge John Callahan said Friday before sentencing Jeffrey Thrasher, 21, to nine years in state prison for the November 7 [1992] shotgun killing of his father, Douglas.
>
> The sentence, which Callahan called "a very difficult one to make," shocked those in the courtroom who had listened to witnesses describe years of abuse by Douglas Thrasher against members of his family-including his wife, Rose, son Jeffrey, and daughter Christine Colvin, in-

cluding shooting at them, shooting the youngsters' pets, and beating all of them with belt buckles and his fists.

Rose Thrasher broke down crying and nearly collapsed after hearing the sentence. So did Christine. Other family members filled the quiet, ornate courtroom with sobs of pain after Callahan closed the three-day sentencing hearing. They had all hoped for leniency. They had hoped against Jeffrey being sent to prison.

Thrasher faced up to 20 years in prison on the charge of second-degree intentional homicide in the killing. According to his attorneys, his earliest chance for parole will be in 28 months . . .

Defense attorney Paul Merkle Jr., who also was visibly shaken by the sentence, said he would urge the more than 750 county residents who signed petitions asking Callahan to give Thrasher probation, to "continue to fight for justice for Jeffrey and ask Gov. Thompson to grant him clemency or a pardon." . . .

Merkle, a Beloit public defender, called Friday's sentencing the "most heartbreaking of my 19 years of law practice." He and his partner, Roger Sturdevant, of the Monroe public defender's office, spent hundreds of hours gathering research in their attempt to show that Jeffrey Thrasher and his family were victims of battered woman and child abuse syndrome and to show the young man's action of killing his father was his only defense to that abuse.

"This is not like any other case I have ever had," said Merkle. "This is the best example this state has had of a pure defense of child abuse syndrome, abuse that led to killing as the only way out."[1]

The *Thrasher* case exemplifies several important issues in the kind of cases that give rise to this book. First, legal authorities had not intervened to prevent or deter Douglas Thrasher's reign of brutality. This not unusual state of affairs exacerbated the desperation of Jeffrey's act.

Second, Jeffrey Thrasher did not suffer insanity or diminished capacity, the traditional excuses for criminal behavior in such situations, for he fathomed the nature and consequences of his act all too well. Child abuse syndrome stood in lieu of these defenses as a quasi-*justification* for Jeffrey's act, not simply an excuse. In other words, Jeffrey claimed that his act was somehow the right thing to do under the circumstances. But how can one justify a deadly act when one is not acting to defend oneself from an equally deadly encounter? Should the ancient sense of justice be stretched to include cases of retribution in which the former victim kills because he or she "can't take it anymore?"

Third, Jeffrey Thrasher's attorneys used evidence pertaining to "battered child syndrome" (BCS) in an attempt to make up for these legal deficiencies. This syndrome is, as indicated in chapter 1, part of a larger proliferation of the new "victimization" syndromes[2] that are considered part of a broader psychiatric disorder, post-traumatic stress disorder (PTSD), which attained official status as a disorder in the American Psychiatric Association's Diagnostic Statistical Manual in 1980 (DSM-III).[3] The syndromes capture the psychological effects of long-lasting oppression in the context of the family or of violent acts against the self (war or rape). In important ways they fill the gaps in the traditional defenses provided by criminal law, and their very content addresses the travails of powerlessness and oppression that have gained currency in the law and politics of our time. They are part of a new Weltanschauung of victimization, a new form of consciousness that, in turn, construes cases of retaliatory justice in a different light.

In a fourth sense raised by the *Thrasher* case, we can see that the new syndrome evidence differs from traditional psychiatric evidence because it more precisely delineates a cause of psychological disorder or trauma. Freudian psychoanalytic theory (the major predecessor) posits that trauma is the product of the deeply rooted psychodynamics that develop over one's life, especially those forged in childhood. In a nutshell, we can establish blame for one's mental difficulties in only a generic, diffuse sense: parents typically "are to blame" because of the general way they brought up their children, or because they did not fully appreciate the sensitivity of their child. As epitomized in the famous case of Dora, Freud alleges that most thoughts or images of sexual and physical abuse in children are a function of fantasy and desire.[4] Among other things, this understanding blurs the lines of responsibility for trauma. Seldom does psychoanalytic theory provide a basis for saying "you induced the illness or trauma because you beat your child or actually seduced your child." In a typical case, the blame for the trauma an individual suffers is diffused to the human condition.

Critics have accused Freud of hiding sexual abuse behind the facade of fantasy. Following the leads of a handful of predecessors, Freud at one time understood that sexual abuse of children was more widespread than conventional wisdom acknowledged. In "The Aetiology of Hysteria," a paper read before the Society for Psychiatry and Neurology in 1896, Freud maintained that such abuse lay at the heart of hysteria. The psychiatric world greeted this pioneering paper with ostracizing silence. Jeffrey Moussaieff Masson, Alice Miller, and others have revealed how and why Freud eventually altered course. Miller unveils child abuse at the heart of virtually all adult disorders, detecting its influence lurking within great art, including the works of Picasso, Buster Keaton, and Nietzsche. She began targeting Freud and similar deniers in an onslaught of works published during and after the 1970s.[5]

Masson "exposes" Freud in his 1984 book, *The Assault on Truth: Freud's Suppression of the Seduction Theory.* Masson contends that Freud feared the psychoanalytic movement's demise in its infancy if it clung to the theory of actual abuse, for the patriarchal powers in society would not brook such a claim. Consequently, Freud reconstructed psychoanalysis's foundation on the fantasy theory.[6] Masson probably overstates the case against Freud, for there is reason to believe that fantasy can cause trauma and later recollections; and Allen Esterson has recently shown that Freud might have exaggerated the original seduction theory, only to replace it with an equally overstated fantasy theory, because of Freud's inveterate tendency to find "total" or "absolute" causes of trauma. One's status as the great pioneer (or "conquistador," to use the word Freud applied to himself) destined to uncover the secret of all trauma (the riddle of psychology's sphinx) would be compromised if trauma actually arose from many sources rather than from a single constellation associated with the discoverer's name. Child abuse accounts for virtually all of trauma or none of it.[7]

But even if Freud is less culpable than Masson charges, Masson's critique represents the rise of a new mindset or paradigm shift that is essential to the new victimization syndromes. Trauma and emotional disorders might indeed stem from actual, nonfantasized abuse. The presumption concerning the origin of trauma and its link to behavior has shifted in a profound way. Since the mid-1970s, when Congress, in response to the budding child abuse movement, pressured states to prosecute child abuse and to pass mandatory reporting laws concerning child abuse (the Mondale Act of 1974, followed by amendments in the 1980s), knowledge of the prevalence of child abuse has grabbed public notice. Soon such statutes loomed in all fifty states.[8]

The recent surge of the "recovery movement" in psychology is but the latest incarnation of this *epistēmē* or paradigm shift.[9] Under the sway of hypnosis (some say of the suggestion of therapists), patients in psychotherapy "remember" abuse they suffered as children, abuse which they have repressed for years, sometimes decades. Although it is relatively easy to substantiate claims of rape or battering by listening to victims' accounts or by considering corroborating evidence, this, unfortunately, is not often the case for "recovery" of memories of childhood abuse. Questions naturally arise concerning the validity of "recovered" memories in the context of highly suggestive therapy and the fact that all our memories are interpretations, not hard facts (our imperfect relationship to the past is hermeneutical, not positivistic). Lawrence Wright chronicles the rise of the recovery movement concerning satanic cults in America, and how this movement culminated in a veritable witch-hunt of false accusation and confession in Olympia, Washington, in the late 1980s.[10] As of today, no law enforcement agency (including the FBI) has managed to find concrete evidence to support claims regarding satanic cults. And such prominent scholars of cults and memory as Ofshe, Loftus, and others have recently published devastating critiques, as mentioned above.[11] Perhaps predictably, some individuals who assert that they are victims of false accusations (including the parents of Roseanne Barr) established a foundation in Philadelphia in 1992 based on the new "syndrome," the False Memory Syndrome Foundation.[12] Debate rages over whether the recovery movement is a blessing or a new form of witch-hunt, especially in the wake of prominent cases that appear suspicious.[13] But we do know that many forms of child abuse have indeed taken place. For every false accusation against a Cardinal Joseph Bernadine (falsely accused in 1994), an accurate one seems to surface.

Although some major figures grasped the extent of child abuse in the nineteenth century, society chose not to face this hard truth until the 1960s. The term "child abuse syndrome" appeared in an article in the *Journal of the American Medical Association* in 1962, and Murray Straus and his colleagues remark in their path-breaking book *Behind Closed Doors* that researchers coined the term "child abuse" in the early 1960s to encompass the growing awareness of this form of domestic violence.[14] By the late 1970s, the child abuse movement had gained headway by deploying, along with "medicalization" of the issue whereby child abusers were defined by mental health professionals as "sick," the tools of all successful social movements: the development of research and the rise of key figures dedicated to fostering awareness and acceptance of the disorder, and the growth of (feminist and children's) movements which pressured for public attention and recognition in psychiatry.[15] And during the 1970s psychiatry "discovered" a new disorder that embodied the most nightmarish effects of child abuse (especially sexual abuse): "multiple personality disorder" (MPD). By 1980 the American Psychiatric Association officially recognized MPD as a disorder in DSM-III. MPD is considered a severe (yet not atypical) manifestation of child sexual abuse. A victim becomes afflicted with MPD because overwhelming trauma stemming from child abuse causes the mind to create alternative identities or fragments in order to protect or shield the psyche from the pain and terror.[16] The MPD movement is an integral part of the development of the new paradigm of victimization. Its sensationalistic qualities guarantee societal interest, and it serves as a rallying point for advocates. "The real politicking [for MPD] came in the late seventies, when elaborate preparations were made for the third edition of the *Diagnostic and Statistical Manual* of the American Psychiatric Association. . . . With *DSM-III* the movement had legitimated itself."[17] In DSM-IV, published in 1994, the APA changed the name of the disorder to "Dissociative Identity Disorder" (DID) and added amnesia as one of its conditions (in the wake of a decade of debate over the role of amnesia). DSM-IV's list of criteria for the disorder ends with a "note," which stresses that the disorder's symptoms in children are "not attributable to imaginary playmates or other fantasy play." According to Ian Hacking, "The final 'note' has a subtext. Many advocates wanted a new diagnostic category of childhood multiple personality disorder. They did not succeed but got their foot in the door. They hope to open the door wider in DSM-V."[18]

The first person found not guilty of serious crimes (rape, kidnapping, robbery) by virtue of being "insane" due to multiple personality was Billy Milligan in the late 1970s. Books that renewed modern interest in multiple personality include Corbett H. Thigpen's and Hervey M. Cleckey's *The Three Faces of Eve*, published in 1957, and Flora Rheta Schreiber's legendary *Sybil*.[19]

MPD and DID are controversial and contested disorders that cover the most extreme psychological adjustments due to child abuse. Few question that severe child abuse inflicts trauma and psychic wounds (though Hacking points out that the evidence of long-term negative effects is surprisingly lacking. Claims in this domain rest on faith rather than demonstration).[20] But as of the late 1980s, psychologists had not reached consensus on the exact nature of the characteristics of child abuse, and it is very difficult to differentiate symptoms of child abuse from symptoms related to the emotional strains that inevitably accompany childhood (various fears, sense of helplessness, nightmares, etc.).[21] Nonetheless, Ronald Summit's development of a five-stage syndrome that parallels the stages of BWS has attained acceptance in the field: secrecy (a "shared secrecy" bonds abuser and abused); helplessness (in which resistance is seen as futile); entrapment and accommodation; delayed, conflicted, and unconvincing disclosure; and retraction.[22] Symptoms include high anxiety, nightmares, eating disorders, depression, and low self-esteem. The special or separate reality forged by abusive families creates a different background for the consideration of criminal defenses, as Joelle Moreno explains:

> Battered and sexually abused children live in a world that is strikingly different from the safe and nurturing home depicted by traditional values and social expectations. Instead of being protected and cared for, these children are "thrown into conflict, confusion, insecurity, and anguish."
>
> This is the background against which parricide often occurs. Over the past 25 years, efforts to understand the dynamics of intrafamily abuse have led to attempts to identify common characteristics of both the violent family and the abused child. . . . Research in this area now enables experts to offer the uninitiated a glimpse into the world of the abused child.[23]

Psychoanalysis has traditionally been attacked by the right because it putatively supplants traditional moral discourse with therapeutic logic. Now it is under attack from the left, as a new politics, psychology, and law emerge, unveiling more specific, ascertainable causes of abuse that make legal and moral attribution of blame more feasible in the area of domestic abuse.[24] The victimization syndromes attempt to attain a Grail that eluded psychoanalysis: *finding the Archimedean point or fountainhead in the genesis of trauma and mental "illness,"* the origin of the universe of psychoanalysis. Whereas Freudian psychodynamic theory laid the ultimate responsibility for illness on Oedipus's mythical lap, victimization syndromes take names by identifying real perpetrators. Victimization bears a human face.

In a related sense, victimization syndromes represent an attempt to reinstate the sanity of individuals who commit acts that previously labeled them indelibly as "insane," especially in cases involving battered women, abused children, and rape victims. In this interesting and propitious sense, syndrome defenses provide a logic that might empower defendants to assume the status of equal citizenship once they surmount the oppressive condition that has defined them. In her book about her forensic mission in defense of battered women who kill, *Terrifying Love,* Lenore Walker remarks, "Contrary to myth, a battered woman, once out of the battering relationship, is unlikely to become involved with another batterer. . . . On the contrary: once free of abuse and terror, their lives can be very good indeed." [25]

Jeffrey Thrasher hoped that his act would lead to a "not guilty" verdict. Victimization syndromes provide evidence to support this claim: *the individual's reaction to the victimizing condition he or she confronted was normal under the circumstances.* BWS, BCS, and other syndromes straddle a fence in law and psychology between rationality and abnormal psychology; hence, battered women who kill are portrayed at trial as rational under the circumstances and as suffering trauma which reduces their rationality in other respects. On the one hand, this coexistence of A and not-A seems disingenuous or in bad faith. On the other hand, it might reflect the true state of things (depending on the case), and it serves the political point of maintaining the possibility of recovery and entry to the status of equal citizenship. We will have to decide below whether this promise has merit.

Another important implication of the *Thrasher* case derives from the fact that while the use of syndrome evidence assisted in the understanding of the broader facts, it did not eliminate the difficulty of judging. Can we give vent to compassion without sacrificing the reason and responsibility that are pillars of liberal justice? As with many cases of battered wives who kill their husbands, the trial became a cathartic symbol of deep cultural and legal divisions and the painful effort to reconcile these differences in common judgment under the rule of law.

For the most part, the new victimization syndromes and the understanding that accompanies them *complicate* the attribution of responsibility by shifting the focus from the defendant to the person responsible for the victimization. According to the traditional extreme, the defendant bears full responsibility absent a context of self-defense or duress. Prosecutors in many trials even today (especially in more conservative jurisdictions beyond the frontiers of progressive change) belittle evidence of victimization in the name of upholding traditional notions of responsibility and power relationships which they associate with these notions. For the new extreme, the defendant's victim (the victim of the victim, as it were) is responsible because the new syndromes trace concrete causal blame for trauma to his shoulders in a manner that lessens the defendant's responsibility. Up to and including the fateful act, the defendant is defined as an extension of the oppressor; only after this act is he or she an independent self capable of self-determination. Defendants hope this transference will shift responsibility fully to the victim. As James Acker and Hans Toch remark in a critical article on BWS:

> We are concerned . . . with the exculpatory deployment of a "syndrome" as a psychological condition which motivates violence in lieu of—or as a constraint to—volition. Used this way, the "syndrome" not only draws attention to the victim (the husband) as the aggressor but assigns to the victim (the husband) attributes that are so constraining as to make him the cause of his own homicide.[26]

Syndromes and the New Attribution of Blame

A full transference of causation boils down to the proposition that the initial victim has no agency or independent selfhood. He or she is pure immanence. Such thinking reflects a major reorientation in the attribution of responsibility that has occurred over the last twenty years. In 1970 William Ryan published a famous book in which he decried the tendency to "blame the victim" in the area of welfare research. Ryan devotes the first edition of this book to discussing the plight of blacks and the poor. In the preface to the revised edition published in 1976, however, he surrenders to the temptations of intellectual imperialism. Ryan charges that victimization is widespread in our society, and that vulnerability includes "catastrophic illness," the "deliberate manipulation of inflation," "grossly unfair taxes," and "pollution."[27] Ryan's intellectual expansionism occasions Christopher Lasch to comment that "the victim has come to enjoy a certain moral superiority in our society; this moral elevation of the victim helps to account for the inflation of political rhetoric that characterizes the discourse of survivalism."[28]

In a Lexis search Marc Galanter of the University of Wisconsin Law School discovers no use of the phrase "blaming the victim" before 1970. After that, usage of the phrase began to grow slowly, until it mushroomed after 1985. Galanter finds this trend: from January 1, 1970, to January 1, 1975, one reference; 1975–1980, four references; 1980–1985, seventy-nine references; 1985–1990, 325 references; January 1, 1990, to December 30, 1993, one thousand references (Lexis stops giving the number of citations once a thousand has been reached).[29]

In addition to the expansion of Ryan's phrase, the term "syndrome" has proliferated in recent years. "Syndrome" is now part of our national public vocabulary. Seemingly every trend that involves conflict or potential emotional stress is designated a "syndrome." Recent examples include "post Cold War syndrome," which relates to the policy dilemmas the United States faces in the wake of the collapse of that major foreign policy paradigm; NFL (National Football League) syndrome, which afflicted the Los Angeles Raiders defensive lineman Bob Golic after he retired from playing football; "Little League Parent syndrome"; and "Here We Go Again syndrome," suffered by the hapless Buffalo Bills, who keep losing Super Bowls with record-breaking frequency.[30] Our database search of contemporary patterns and uses of the term "syndrome" in law reviews found that roughly half of such articles dealt with AIDS or Down's syndrome; the other half pertained to more socially constructed varieties of the term. With BWS, RTS, and the like, we found: "advocacy scholarship syndrome" (the tendency for scholarship to serve politics rather than intellectual integrity); "editorial syndrome" (the effect of being an editor on how one views the news); "twelve angry men syndrome" (becoming too involved and losing objectivity); "racial hatred syndrome" (proffered as a defense for racists who commit racist-inspired violence);[31] "Cravath syndrome" (everybody seems to have a lot of knowledge about what life as a lawyer is like); and "failure syndrome" (the tendency for young black males not to succeed). In 1950, 1960, and 1970 not a single law review article used the word "syndrome." In 1980, one article used the word. Then the word takes off: 1985, 86 articles; 1988, 114 articles; 1990, 146 articles.

A similar search spanned newspapers and periodicals. In December 1993 alone, more than one thousand (the highest number the search will designate) articles used the term "syndrome," though most referred to Down's syndrome or AIDS. But a generous sprinkling of other references included "Polish syndrome" (reluctance to vote); "IUD syndrome" (letting children spend too much time in front of computers; "Al Saunders syndrome" (a football coach worrying about too many things at once); "hope-deficiency syndrome" (loss of hope); "Chicken Little syndrome" (uninformed debate about the environment); "SOTSH syndrome" (shock and horror due to sex on television); "never-let- anything-go-wrong syndrome" (the tendency to under-tolerate risk on a cutting-edge scientific and engineering project); "man-in-the-white-coat syndrome" (why the company doctor never gets audited).[32]

The expansion of the term "syndrome" could reflect how deeply the logic of therapeutic psychology and psychiatry have permeated the culture. Along similar lines, psychiatry's notion of "disorder" has exploded in recent decades. The "bible" of the profession, the Diagnostic Statistical Manual (DSM) has grown in leaps and bounds since its first version in 1952. Today it covers "disorders" such as sexual unhappiness, hyperactivity or attention disorder, "adjustment disorder," and the like. As one commentator remarks, "As Yale psychiatry professor Jay Katz conceded several years ago, 'If you look at [the diagnostic manual], you can classify all of us under one rubric or another of mental disorder.' The National Institute of Mental Health (NIMH) claims that it has determined through interviews by 'lay interviewers' that more than 25 percent of adults in America have at least one 'psychiatric disorder' within any one-year period."[33] The sometimes virulent debate surrounding Attention Deficit Disorder (ADD, which joined the Diagnostic Statistical Manual along with PTSD in 1980) epitomizes this trend, for ADD is a vaguely defined disorder implicated in a broad set of behaviors often typical of children and young people, with no defined medical basis (it is easy to imagine this term being integrated into Dissociative Identity Disorder down the line). The disorder appears to be highly socially constructed; and practitioners are currently bent on expanding its application to adults, even though no solid evidence supports this extension. Richard Vatz states that "because ADD is so vaguely defined, even for a psychiatric disorder, it is tailor-made for bogus claims."[34]

These developments have been accompanied by the explosion of psychiatry as a multilevel institution with widening reach and effects. Once again, Nietzsche's cultural antennas were exceptionally prescient when he sensed in the late 1880s (*The Genealogy of Morals*) that as the ethic of health and happiness replaced the ethics of responsibility and achievement, the West stood on the verge of becoming one big hospital (though not even Nietzsche could foresee the health industry one day becoming one-seventh of the American economy). Stuart A. Kirk and Herb Kutchins point out in a book on the making of DSM-III that from 1975 to 1990, the total number of psychiatrists, clinical psychologists, clinical social workers, and marriage counselors increased from 72,000 to 98,000 in the United States.

> The new diagnostic manual provides the official justification for psychiatry's expanding control over what some have labeled the "medicalization of deviance." . . . Psychiatrists even claim that tobacco use falls within their purview. Furthermore, psychiatric classification affects how society allocates millions of dollars of health funds.[35]

On a related plane, the concept of "battering" has expanded over the years. Elizabeth Schneider remarks, "Over the last ten years, the focus on abuse as primarily physical has shifted and broadened. This broader description has several dimensions but is premised primarily on an understanding of coercive behavior and power and control, rather than 'number of hits,' as the critical definition of battering relationships. As the battered women's movement continues to develop, practical experience is blurring the distinction between physical abuse and other aspects of the battering relationship."[36] We will see later that psychological and other forms of abuse can be powerful indeed; yet the law requires greater precision in its concepts, especially when justifying the deployment of deadly force. Though abusive relationships are sealed by psychological and emotional abuse, only physical preservation can justify the use of deadly force. In fathoming the issue of self-defense in domestic violence cases, we must proceed with analytical and conceptual caution. Acknowledging a particular type of abuse is not the same thing as justifying deadly force to prevent it.

Finally, these syndromes represent a new type of scientific psychological evidence that is tied to broader legal, scientific, and social developments. David McCord, a leading scholar on their evidentiary status, remarked in the late 1980s:

> Before the mid-70s, cases discussing the admissibility of nontraditional psychological evidence were few and far between. During the last decade, however, a flood of nontraditional psychological evidence has inundated the courts in criminal cases. Several of these types of evidence are known as "syndromes." Examples include rape trauma syndrome, battered woman (or wife) syndrome, and pathological gambler's syndrome. Some of the types of evidence are characterized as "profiles." The battering parent profile, the child sexual abuser profile, and the profile of the defendant as incompatible with the commission of the crime charged are examples. Other types of evidence are not denominated either "syndrome" or "profile" but are nonetheless nontraditional. Examples include diminished capacity, the psychology of child sexual abuse, the fallibility of eyewitness identification, psychological testimony regarding witness credibility, and other miscellaneous types of testimony.
>
> Our current legal system is ill-equipped to deal with this deluge.[37]

The general law of evidence assisted the growth of syndrome defenses in the 1970s and 1980s by lowering the threshold for the admission of "soft" (less quantitative) scientific evidence. The admission of expert testimony has been governed primarily by a three-part test set forth in *Dyas v. United States* (1977): 1) the subject matter to which the testimony pertains "must be so distinctly related to some science, profession, business or occupation as to be beyond the ken of the average juror" (experts must have special knowledge jurors lack); 2) "the witness must have sufficient skill, knowledge, or experience in that field or calling as to make it appear that his opinion or inference will probably aid the trier in his search for truth"; and 3) expert testimony will not be admitted if "the state of the pertinent art or scientific knowledge does not permit a reasonable opinion to be asserted even by an expert."[38]

The second and third parts deal with reliability of the expert testimony. The second addresses the qualification of the expert, and the third pertains to the status of the field about which he or she is testifying. In the past, courts relied on the 1923 *Frye* test to decide whether new or novel scientific evidence is reliable enough to qualify. In *Frye v. United States*, the federal court excluded lie-detector evidence because it was not "generally accepted" in its field of expertise.[39] Evidence standards reflect judgments about the relationship between experts and other citizens, the autonomy of science, and the relationship between expertise and legal responsibility. Changes in the law of evidence reflect the sociological and political condition of knowledge in addition to knowledge's purely scientific status.

Then in the 1970s Congress passed the new Federal Rules of Evidence—about the same time that it had promulgated the Mondale Act to protect children from domestic abuse. These rules adopted a more flexible and liberal approach than *Frye* and even *Dyas* by stressing simply the *relevance* of the evidence to the legal issues in the case and whether admission would "assist" the trier of fact (the jury) in reaching a just decision. Under this approach, the first important question is whether the evidence's relevance (Rule 402) outweighs its possible prejudicial effect (Rule 403). Relevance is established simply by showing that the evidence makes an element of culpability more or less likely (however slightly).[40] This "assist" test is flexible, and it implies that the court will be less concerned with the limits the *Frye* test placed on expert testimony. Finally, the rules abolished the "ultimate issue" rule, which held that no expert could express an opinion as to the ultimate issue in the case (e.g., did the defendant actually possess the disorder or show characteristics of the disorder, and did this mental state negate culpability for the act?).

The lower courts have tended to follow a mixed approach between *Dyas* and the new rules. Then in 1993 the Supreme Court officially adopted the Federal Rules for the federal courts in *Daubert v. Merrell Dow Pharmaceuticals,* and declared *Frye* obsolete in a case involving a lawsuit against Merrell Dow Pharmaceuticals, Inc., for birth defects the plaintiffs claimed were caused by prenatal ingestion of Bendictin. In softening the standards of admission, the Court stated,

> "Science is not an encyclopedic body of knowledge about the universe. Instead, it represents a *process* for proposing and refining theoretical explanations about the world that are subject to further testing and refinement." [Quoting a brief for American Association for the Advancement of Science and the National Academy of Sciences as amici curiae 7–8.]
>
> The inquiry envisioned by Rule 702 is, we emphasize, a flexible one.[41]

The Court's logic in *Daubert* seemed to endorse the balanced, flexible approach to the admission of expert testimony and evidence that a growing number of writers have advocated in recent years for the admission of syndrome evidence. But recent evidence suggests that courts have applied *Daubert* in a restrictive fashion, especially because syndrome evidence is not readily subject to falsification.[42]

Overview of Other Major Syndromes Other than BWS

So the *Thrasher* case drew on the new victimization worldview that furnishes the intellectual background of the emergence of syndrome defenses. In order to properly understand this background, let us take a peek at the major syndromes in criminal law. Because BWS is the central focus of this book, I will postpone discussion of BWS until chapter 3, where we can give it special attention.

Battered Child and Child Abuse Syndromes [43]

The American Humane Association estimates that 132,000 children were victimized by sexual abuse in 1986, and the number could be higher owing to underreporting. But only about three hundred children a year retaliate by killing their abuser or cajoling someone else to do the job for them.[44] As with rape-trauma syndrome, prosecutors of child abusers have used child abuse syndrome (CAS) and child sexual abuse accommodation syndrome (CSAAS) to show that the victim possesses the profile characteristics of children who have been sexually or otherwise seriously abused. "Battered child syndrome" (BCS) is a more recent incarnation of the syndrome which deals more with battering than with sexual abuse. Accordingly, most of the cases dealing with CAS pertain to prosecutions of child abusers rather than of children using the syndrome to buttress a justification or excuse defense, though this situation has recently begun to change. Courts have split over the admissibility of expert testimony by the prosecution in child abuse cases, but they have virtually unanimously allowed experts to testify about the general nature of the syndrome to counter claims raised by the defense that the child did not behave as one would expect a victim of such abuse to behave.[45] One of the most propitious uses of syndrome evidence is to counter such stereotyping.

In the most prominent early cases involving children defendants accused of killing a parent, the courts did not admit CSAAS evidence because the facts did not indicate plausible self-defense claims and because CSAAS was not accepted as a scientific theory.[46] But a trend has developed toward allowing expert testimony dealing with the syndrome in order to apprise the jury of the profile of a sexually abused child. This trend has led to convictions of lesser offenses in two cases, and the first known acquittal in such a case in 1986.[47] In April 1993, the Washington State Supreme Court became the first in the nation officially to recognize BCS in ruling that the trial court should have admitted evidence of the syndrome to support the self-defense claim of Andrew Janes, who killed his abusive stepfather in 1988.[48] The year before, a jury in Tyler, Texas, acquitted a seventeen-year-old girl in a highly publicized case in which the judge allowed her to introduce evidence of prior abuse and an expert's testimony on the psychology of battered victims.[49]

As a result of these and other noteworthy cases that attracted substantial publicity in 1992 and 1993, writers perceive major shifts in public opinion about child abuse, BCS, and justifiable homicide. A writer in *Time* magazine has declared:

> A few years ago, such sympathy would have been unheard of. Children who killed their parents were the ultimate pariahs. Regarded as evil or mentally ill "bad seeds," they virtually always earned the harshest judgment of the public and the courts . . .
>
> That attitude is slowly starting to change. Today youngsters who slay

abusive parents are drawing more understanding from a public that has wakened to the national nightmare of child abuse.[50]

The evidence suggests that BCS could be poised to "take off" in the mid-1990s as BWS did in the 1980s. As a reporter remarked in a June 1993 show on BCS and the Janes case, "There are strong parallels in the Janes case to a similar Washington decision over battered women who kill their abusive partners. Following that ruling, courts in other states began to look more sympathetically on the plight of those women."[51]

Rape-Trauma Syndrome

Rape-trauma syndrome (RTS) originated in a key article in 1974 by Ann Burgess and Linda Holstrom.[52] RTS indicates that victims experience an initial shock reaction, which is followed by major reorientations of consciousness and lifestyle. Victims feel guilt, fear, and depression, and often undergo changes in their work and social habits, their sleep patterns, and their sexual desires.[53] RTS differs from BWS because RTS testimony is used as circumstantial evidence that a rape occurred. Because the standards of proof in criminal law are necessarily slanted in favor of the defense, the typical use of RTS poses problems of due process and fairness that BWS often avoids. (But we will see that BWS's use in self-defense raises a host of questions that do not haunt RTS.)

Women often react to being raped in ways that nonvictimized people will not understand, such as delaying reporting of the crime or downplaying the anguish at first. RTS testimony helps to show that such reactions may be normal under the circumstances, thereby rehabilitating the victim's credibility at trial. *In this use, RTS reinforces the individuation of justice by checking stereotypes that reify victims.*

Other courts have expressed caution about prosecution use of RTS because it leads to its own form of stereotyping that deindividualizes the case from the opposite direction. In *State v. Saldana,* for example, the Minnesota Supreme Court ruled that RTS displaces the jury's function because it influences the jury to focus on typical symptoms rather than on the specific facts of the case; RTS testimony "unfairly prejudices the [defendant] by creating an aura of special reliability and trustworthiness."[54] Along these lines, some academic critics hold that the response of each victim varies according to age, personality, family support, life situation, and related factors.[55] Furthermore, RTS testimony might prejudice the jury against the defendant by blinding the jury to other evidence, so some courts have limited its admissibility on grounds of prejudice, while others have questioned its validity in showing the absence or presence of consent (the major rape defense).[56]

RTS can create its own stereotype based on the logic of the syndrome: the alleged victim behaved like a rape victim typically behaves, therefore she must have been raped. The landmark California Supreme Court decision in *People v. Bledsoe* (1984) strikes a balance that serves individuation while checking syndromic stereotype in the other direction. *Bledsoe* ruled that RTS evidence is admissible only in cases in which the alleged rapist suggests or claims that the plaintiff's conduct after the incident is not consistent with what a rape victim would do. The court commented: "[I]n such a context expert testimony on rape trauma syndrome may play a particularly useful role by disabusing the jury of some widely held misconceptions about rape and rape victims, so that it may evaluate the evidence free of the constraints of popular myths." Many courts have followed this approach in subsequent years.[57] The key goal is to check against stereotyping in either direction.

Vietnam Veteran's Syndrome and PTSD

As DSM-IIIR describes PTSD, it arises from stressors "outside the realm of usual human experience," stressors other than chronic illness, bereavement, marital conflict, and the like. But most people who experience such stressors presumably will be affected by the same fear, sense of helplessness, and such symptoms as flashbacks concerning the event, numbness, increased emotional arousal, and avoidance of things reminiscent of the event. DSM-III designates these symptoms "intrusion," "avoidance," and "arousal."[58] In *In the Shadow of War*, Israeli clinical psychologist Menachem Student reflects on the nature of the two perceptual realities for the many "survivors" of Israeli war:

> War is a totally different reality from that of everyday life. One cannot understand it through the use of the tools appropriate to everyday reality. The transition from one reality, whose only rule is survival by any means, to another, everyday reality where care, love, and hope can take place, is a central concern of my book . . .
>
> War hollows out a desolate central core which, sooner or later, threatens each of its victims with an inability to function, with a breakdown in relatedness . . . [59]

A Vietnam veteran we interviewed, T. M., still experiences panic attacks. He told us that these symptoms (technically PTSD-related) stem from the hypervigilance and excitation brought about by war conditions. He related a combat encounter on his twentieth birthday. "I hit the ground. I had to get the damned gun [M-16]. I had an adrenaline, out of body experience. I could almost see the bullet coming into my head. It's all so surreal. . . . It's so irrational, it's frustrating. It's atavistic. Like you're back in a state of nature. And you just live in a primal existence."[60] Along the same lines, Nora Cashen, a former battered woman and a longtime participant in Advocates for Battered Women and other women's causes in Madison, spoke to us about the special reality that battered women often confront:

> I've been thinking about this a lot in moral and religious terms. Give me a different ear and you'll get a different story. It's a combination of being forced and choosing to strike back. Many battered women have liminal

experiences outside the realm of ordinary experience. It's not meditative, but it's a sense of being outside of ordinary experience. Women talk about abusive relationships in extraordinarily metaphysical terms, very religious terms. It's some kind of extremity for them, making them confront their own mortality, their children's lives, what it means to be a human being, to be a victim, to be responsible for children's' well-being—extraordinary questions. Then these culturally facilitated things about how you behave normally don't have much meaning, reinforcing their whole experience that cultural niceties don't have much meaning because they have been so persecuted.[61]

PTSD has emerged as the umbrella concept that connects RTS, BWS, war trauma, and CSAAS/BCS. Psychiatrist Judith Herman, a leader in the field of victimization syndrome, postulates that these syndromes add up to "the rediscovery of the syndrome of psychological trauma." She states,

Only after 1980, when the efforts of combat veterans had legitimated the concept of post-traumatic stress disorder, did it become clear that the psychological syndrome seen in survivors of rape, domestic battery, and incest was essentially the same as the syndrome seen in survivors of war.[62]

Several approaches to PTSD hold sway. Mardi Jon Horowitz has created a cognitive information-processing model of PTSD based on psychodynamic theory and cognitive dissonance theory. Constant and obsessive nightmares, flashbacks, and other forms of intrusion are products of the psychological tendency to repeat traumatic events that we have survived, and/or the need to reprocess traumatic experience to reconcile it with the expectations and values harbored before the stressor erupted. Traumatic events disrupt antecedent assumptions about the world and personal invulnerability.[63] Mary Ann Dutton holds that researchers "suggest that PTSD is more likely to develop when the trauma occurs in a previously safe environment, which might be expected to be the case for many battered women."[64] Other researchers understand PTSD as a product of both cognitive dissonance or stress and biological factors which include high physiological arousal owing to the stress. The latter can lead to either great anxiety and activity or emotional withdrawal.[65]

Vietnam veteran's syndrome represents a new approach to the old problem of war trauma. Soldiers who experience morally shocking and/or dangerous, threatening events in wartime often become traumatized and undergo various forms of extreme anxiety and stress that can persist a long time. Vet syndrome defenses usually proffer claims that the defendant committed violent acts in a dissociative state akin to insanity, during which he believed he was embroiled in a combat situation all over again.[66] John Wilson and Sheldon Ziglebaum found three major types of reaction to war stress in veterans they encountered: a dissociative reaction in which the veteran acts as if he or she were back in combat; a compulsive "living on the edge" in which the veteran strives to act in dangerous situations that stimulate excitement; a deep "survivor guilt" which engenders depression and despair, often to the point of suicide or engaging in criminal conduct in order to get caught.[67]

In response to the explosion of commentary about PTSD and the exertions of veterans, Congress passed Public Law 98–160 in 1983, directing that a comprehensive study be conducted of the mental health status of Vietnam veterans. The study concluded that 829,000 of 3.14 million Vietnam vets suffered from PTSD at the time of the investigation, and that the severity of PTSD was associated with the exposure to traumatic and morally disruptive actions and phenomena in the theater of war.[68] The establishment in the early 1980s of special Community Center units within the Veterans Administration to deal with the mental health aspects of vets furthered the application of PTSD logic to veterans, and vets began to use PTSD-related defenses in criminal trials and in cases involving claims for government benefits.[69]

Before DSM-III in 1980, the symptoms associated with PTSD were not included in a single diagnostic classification. According to Peter Erlinder, "the lack of a recognized definition of these symptoms diminished the validity of the theory that reactions to combat could influence behavior long after the war."[70] Previous concepts of war stress either located the cause of trauma in physical lesions in the brain (as in Mott's notion of "shell shock" in 1919) or portrayed war trauma as a form of Freudian neurosis ("war neurosis") which follows the typical etiology of the neuroses.[71]

Veterans who raised "shell shock" claims after World War I did not fare well very often. In one 1925 appeal of a conviction for committing a lewd and lascivious act on a minor, the Supreme Court of California spoke disparagingly of "so-called 'shell shock.' "[72] Such skepticism also prevailed after World War II, though media and the movies presented sympathetic portrayals of war trauma and adjustment to civilian life (*The Man in the Gray Flannel Suit*, *The Best Years of Our Lives*, etc.). Erlinder remarks that "veterans were largely unsuccessful in proving a causal relationship between their war experience and subsequent conduct which resulted in criminal proceedings."[73] *People v. Walker* (1948) is a noteworthy and perhaps indicative murder case. While on duty in the Pacific in 1941 Walker encountered many demoralizing and dangerous situations, including finding "some thousand dismembered, decomposed Japanese bodies strewn over the area. The stench affected the men's ability to rest, to sleep, and eat. The practice prevailed for a while among the enlisted men of preparing the heads of Japanese so that the skulls could be shellacked and used for desk ornaments." After the war, Walker (who also had a family history of insanity and suicide) was morose, brooding, melancholy—all consistent with war-induced trauma. In his trial for murder, the court refused to let his war experiences and trauma affect the verdict or the sentence absent a clear showing of insanity. It sentenced Walker to death. The trial court relied on traditional normative assumptions about moral and legal responsibility. The Supreme Court of California quoted the trial court judge's sentencing logic approvingly:

> I recognize the defendant's war service and the disturbing effect it may have had upon him; but as I also said yesterday, his service was shared by millions of other boys who have come back home and who are leading normal lives. I recognize the fact that defendant has what may be classified as an unstable personality; that he may be disturbed emotionally, but I think it would be true that most persons who choose for themselves a life of violent crime are unstable and disturbed. I believe that that cannot enter into our deliberations.[74]

After World War II the psychiatric community and the Veterans Administration decided to systematize classifications of psychiatric disorders and develop a more reliable and coherent nomenclature system for the military. In 1951 the American Psychiatric Association published DSM-I, which was based partly on the classification system William Menninger developed for the VA. This system included "Gross Stress Reaction" resulting from exposure to significant stressors like war. When the APA published DSM-II in 1968, it relegated war trauma to a subset of a larger category called "transient situational disturbances" because trauma induced by World War II and Korea had faded to memories.[75] But as the psychological casualties of Vietnam returned home during the 1970s, psychiatry would revisit the issue of war trauma. The result was PTSD.

Like some other psychiatric disorders today, PTSD was forged by politically active psychiatrists who strove to give medical expression to their experiences with trauma induced by human caprice or action. In particular, such activist antiwar psychiatrists as Robert Lifton and Chaim Shatan worked hard within the APA to win official recognition of PTSD.[76] Their efforts resemble the pressures exerted by Judith Herman, homosexuals, and other activists who have shaped the writing of the DSM over recent years. Indeed, the APA's 1973 shift on homosexuality (in which the APA officially rescinded its designation of homosexuality as a disease) opened the door to other reforms, including the move toward adoption of PTSD as an official disorder.[77] Lifton is among the best known of American psychiatrists. He has written pioneering works on the psychological effects of the atom bomb at Hiroshima and exposure to significant stressors in war. Two close associates of Shatan also helped in the movement toward PTSD: William Niederland and Henry Krystal, who pioneered research on "survivor syndrome" in survivors of Hitler's death camps.[78]

By the early 1990s, a major knowledge industry had sprouted around PTSD. In early 1993 lawyers held the first annual national meeting on PTSD and the law in Colorado; and several state mental health associations had created special units to study and promulgate knowledge about PTSD.[79] Such knowledge fields tend to expand as knowledge opens new frontiers and new groups gain a stake in gaining scientific recognition. We saw above that the children's movement has claimed there should be a special dissociative disorder for children, and that the "subtext" of dissociative identity disorder in DSM-IV speaks to this claim. The same applies to PTSD. Herman and others have contended that persons who witness deadly harm or threats to others constitute a special PTSD group. Accordingly, the new DSM-IV provides a new disorder concerning this type of terror that follows PTSD in the manual: "acute stress disorder." [80]

PTSD did appear to provide a relatively more successful concept to use in defending veterans against criminal charges. As of 1984, at least twenty-one states and five federal districts recognized PTSD; and many courts criticized trial courts for not taking it seriously enough.[81] *Early evidence* of surprising successes in trial courts abounds. Among the most illustrative cases is *State v. Heads* (1981), which involved a violent veteran who killed his sister-in-law's husband while hunting down his estranged wife (it is not unusual for vet-syndrome cases to involve wife battering or male domination of spouses or girlfriends).[82] He was convicted and sentenced to life in prison in a first trial in 1978, but an appeals court reversed his conviction for reasons unrelated to psychiatric issues. By the time of his second trial in 1981, the APA had promulgated PTSD. I quote Erlinder's commentary on this trial because it highlights the ways in which PTSD and related victimization syndromes can provide new evidentiary opportunities that help the defense:

> The effect of the new knowledge provided by the diagnostic criteria in DSM-III aided the presentation of the Heads case in two significant ways. *First, DSM-III's description of PTSD helped explain Mr. Heads' previously unexplained behavior. Second, because PTSD is caused by a traumatic event in the defendant's past and because comparisons in a defendant's life before and after the traumatic event help identify the effects of the traumatic event, PTSD provided a theory of admissibility for virtually the entirety of Charles Heads' life.* These factors were essential to enable the jury to understand the psychologically devastating effects of combat. In addition, DSM-III's requirement that the original traumatic event "evoke[s] significant symptoms of distress in most people" provided a basis for admitting testimony of those who had shared the Vietnam experience. The language in DSM-III, therefore, provided the theory of legal relevance for admitting into evidence testimony of Mr. Heads' childhood, his work history, his Vietnam experiences, his difficulties with adjustment on return and the fact that he had no serious criminal record, as well as the testimony of others regarding their Vietnam experiences and reactions.[83]

A jury found Heads not guilty by reason of insanity. The use of PTSD was emblematic of the use of BWS in battered woman cases, because it broadened and deepened the portrayal of the defendant's plight and trauma. But in this case the PTSD was a chronic condition, not something that disappeared when the stressor went away. While such opening serves the defense, this style of justice comes with a price. Heads escaped a murder conviction because the psychiatric strategy of the defense took the focus off the victim and put it on the sorry plight of the defendant. Erlinder endorses this result, but in so doing he does not bother to consider the plight of Heads's victimized wife and the man Heads killed. *Heads* shows that cases can involve multiple victims, especially when the defendant is a veteran.[84]

Despite these early successes, it is not at all clear that veteran PTSD cases have proved as successful for the defense as BWS cases. Few major successes have been reported or commented on since the early 1980s, and the case law on such defenses deals with them in a markedly less sympathetic manner than the BWS cases of the 1980s. War veteran cases illustrate the normative, political, and pragmatic factors that influence judgments about legal responsibility, though it is difficult to generate definitive conclusions. Discussions with practitioners and a look at state high court case law since the early 1980s suggest that defendants are encountering difficulty in winning acquittals on the grounds that war-related PTSD diminishes responsibility. Many of these cases involve horrendous crimes associated with combat reenactments or war backgrounds. Though the path of BWS has also been checkered (see below), this trend is clearly more favorable than Vietnam veteran's syndrome (PTSD), as reading dozens of cases between 1980 and 1990 shows. In one recent Milwaukee case, a Vietnam veteran suffering substantial emotional effects from the war flew into an abandonment-type panic after his wife left him. He sought her out with a shotgun and killed her. A jury convicted him of murder. Among other things, the jury thought that the victim was without blame in provoking the violence. *Unlike BWS cases, the victims in cases of veteran-inflicted violence have usually done nothing to implicate themselves in the crime.*[85] Though the psychological states of veterans and battered women are allegedly similar (Herman), social judgments of blameworthiness differ based on the normative complicity of the victim.

The case law of many state high courts reflects this trend. For example, in *People v. Babbitt* (1988), the Supreme Court of California upheld the conviction of Babbitt for counts of murder, rape, burglary, and robbery. The jury had listened to his tales of war-induced trauma, and sentenced him to death. Normally, defendants' death penalty appeals receive optimal consideration by state high courts. Babbitt had imbibed alcohol and pot all day, and allegedly could not remember the assaults. He proffered three psychological theories in his defense: a bicycle accident when he was twelve years old had impaired his ability to think clearly under stress; he had PTSD as a result of Vietnam; he may have had psychomotor epilepsy that made him unconscious during the two attacks. The court ruled that very hostile comments by the prosecutor about psychiatric logic were not prejudicial to the defense.[86] More importantly, the court upheld the trial court's exclusion of some combat evidence because Babbitt's victims were not associated in a clear enough way with Vietnam stimuli. *"[I]n the absence of any evidence supportive of a connection between defendant's reaction to symbols of Vietnam and his attacks on Leah Schendel and Marvis W., the trial court's ruling was not error."*[87] We should note that the California Supreme Court also refused to consider Babbitt's Vietnam experience as a grounds for mitigation of sentence, even though the sentence was death.[88]

Premenstrual Syndrome and Gambler's Syndrome

Other syndromes that have gained attention have fared less well in criminal trials than BWS. The reasons for the different results appear to be based on political and normative factors rather than those based on psychological science. Strong professional and political constituencies have buttressed BWS. And in BWS criminal cases the victim has often incited the violence, so he shares in the blame. Premenstrual syndrome (PMS), on the other hand, has perhaps more scientific validity as a concept than BWS, but it lacks these advantages.[89] Whereas BWS is caused by a human abuser, PMS arises from a biological condition which renders transference of blame for behavior less feasible. PMS defenses have proved "successful" in a handful of unusual cases in Britain and Canada, but no major trend has developed.[90] Dershowitz, however, does cite (and criticize) a 1991 case in which a woman orthopedic surgeon used PMS as a defense to a drunken driving charge. The defendant flew into a rage when the police officer stopped her. Dershowitz comments that this case "is the first known instance of a PMS acquittal in this country and may serve as a precedent for future cases. The doctor and her lawyer were ecstatic over their victory."[91]

Organized women's groups fear the use of the syndrome will boomerang on the equal citizenship and status of women in society. In 1985 Joann D'Emilio argued in St. John's Law Review that PMS had greater scientific status than BWS, and that courts should consider it as a defense in criminal cases.[92] The next year Elizabeth Holtzman, then district attorney for Kings County, New York, responded with a scathing critique of D'Emilio's alleged inaccuracies, concluding with a political argument. "The mistaken notion of premenstrual symptoms as a cause of violence by women could seriously undermine women's progress in the workplace and elsewhere."[93]

Other reasons for PMS's rough going include the difficulty of fitting it into such defenses as insanity, diminished capacity, and autonomism, and the fact that society is less willing to countenance a defense based on a biological condition that all women share.[94] PMS is too general and diffuse to allow for the type of individuation that is most conducive to the excusing of criminal acts. BWS, on the other hand, points to a specific, identifiable oppressor, and many citizens have placed consideration of battered women's plights high on their agendas. As one of the leading attorneys in the defense of battered women told me, "BWS taught me and teaches juries that she's the victim, not him!"[95]

Gambler's syndrome has suffered the same fate as PMS. Though medical scientists have established its existence as an addictive condition, it is not a prominent criminal defense (though it has influenced sentencing).[96] DSM-III classifies pathological gambling as a disorder of impulse control.[97] In *U.S. v. Lewellyn*, for example, the court refused to reverse the district court's preclusion of an insanity defense in a trial of a pathological gambler for embezzlement, mail fraud, and making false statements. Applying *Frye*'s general acceptance test, the court stated that pathological gambler's disorder was a newly discovered disorder, and that the field had yet to establish that "some pathological gamblers lack substantial capacity to conform their conduct to the requirements of laws prohibiting embezzlement and similar offenses."[98] In one rather incredible case, the IRS ruled that a pathological gambler owed it taxes on "cancellation of indebtedness income" of $2,935,000 because of a settlement the gambler made with a casino (he owed $3,435,000, but the casino settled for $500,000). The tax court upheld this ruling.[99]

The disorder has also failed to excuse lawyers from disbarment in cases in which they have misappropriated clients' funds to pay off gambling debts or to fund their habit. In one representative case the court pointed to the need to take responsibility seriously, to the lack of evidence that the respondent had an "uncontrollable urge" to misappropriate funds, and to the social need to control lawyers' temptations in this area of such ethical significance to the profession. "The attorney's ready access to funds poses a special danger for clients."[100]

The Question of Predisposition

We must address a final point before we look at the broader implications of the new syndromization. A major concern of advocates of both battered women and traumatized veterans has been to demonstrate that the specific incidents of war and spouse beating give rise to psychological disorder rather than being symptoms of preexisting disorder. The reasons for this insistence are both empirical and political. Empirically, it is simply a fact that war or domestic incidents can cause traumatic disorder in their own rights. PTSD is often correlated with the degree of exposure to significant stress in the theater of war. Politically, an emphasis on prior disorder downplays the responsibility of the stressors of war or of domestic violence, shifting "blame" from these enormities to the battered woman (a "masochist") or the veteran ("he was messed up anyway"). As a result, research in these fields is politically charged, especially because funding sources pay attention to the implications of such findings.[101]

But other studies suggest that predisposition is not irrelevant, *especially when it comes to determining the connection between war-induced trauma and subsequent vio-*

lent behavior.[102] Some studies show that once we control for those factors that typically predispose one to commit antisocial acts in our society (low education, low economic status, family history, substance abuse, etc.), Vietnam veterans might not commit violent crimes with greater frequency than non–veterans who possess the same characteristics. Bruce Boman agrees that exposure to combat definitely predisposes toward PTSD and deep psychological adjustment problems. No one disputes this fact today, just as no one disputes that rape causes deep trauma. *What is at issue in Boman's article is whether PTSD and combat exposure make one more likely to commit violent crimes.* Boman shows that the few studies completed so far have not demonstrated such tendencies whatsoever. "Once again, when the question of violence, criminality, and suicide is addressed, controlled studies have dispelled the prevailing image of the antisocial Vietnam veteran with a hair-trigger control over his explosively violent impulses."[103] Students of the new forms of trauma commit a category mistake when they conflate the fact that traumatic experiences cause deep stress disorders with the claim that such stress causes or determines criminal conduct. Erlinder's comment above that PTSD reveals the "causal relationship" between war experiences and subsequent behavior proves to be too much. I will build on the distinctions among trauma, mental disorder, and criminal conduct in the critique of BWS and the syndrome mindset below.

The reality of predisposition is probably mixed. There is no doubt that battering, child abuse, and war experiences can produce significant trauma in their own rights. But some individuals are more predisposed than others, and sometimes the effects of this trauma are accompanied by other factors such as drug or alcohol abuse and violent dispositions and activities. Although predisposition should not be presumed, it should not be automatically precluded.[104] And, of course, this idea does not have any logical or demonstrated connection to criminal conduct.

The Syndromes as New Forms of Evidence: The Frontier between Politics, Science, and Law

Syndromes represent the advent of a form of "expert" testimony that builds its house on the frontier between professional psychology as a discipline and experiences once considered to be understandable by the lay citizenry. For example, BWS involves an unusual form of expert testimony, based on the new sciences of victimization, as Sanford Kadish and Stephen Schulhofer observe in comparing an important BWS case (*State v. Kelly*) with an earlier case (*State v. Wanrow*) that required self-defense law to take the gender of the defendant into consideration:

> *Kelly* represents a greater challenge to the traditional criminal law of self-defense than *Wanrow:* The issue in *Kelly* is not simply testimony on the past relationships between the defendant and the deceased in order to judge the plausibility of the defendant's claim of reasonable apprehen-

sion of attack (this much of *Wanrow* is widely accepted), but whether to permit experts to testify on what are traditionally regarded as common sense matters within the province of the jury (that is, did the defendant actually fear for her life at the time, and if so, was her fear reasonably grounded?).[105]

Previous expert psychiatric testimony has attempted to assist the jury in understanding the nature of psychological functioning and disorder, realities that experts are trained to fathom better than lay persons (such knowledge is "beyond the ken" of the jury). In self-defense trials, however, BWS and other syndromes only partly deal with specialized fields of knowledge and scientific processes; they also deal with judgments about people's perceptual mental states and how these mental states affected the defendant's behavior—judgments traditionally assumed to be within the province of jurors.[106] People more readily understand what it means to be traumatized by battering and rape; after all, fear is a primordial emotion that visits us often. So the connections between the "disorder," the cause of the trauma, and the act are clearer than in other cases because the oppressive condition behind the act bears a human face. The main difference in self-defense cases involving domestic violence is the presence of fear in the context of the home and of one the defendant loves or has loved. In the end, the jury must be willing to fathom fear in a context that traditionally has been a "haven in a heartless world."

In addition, victimization syndrome–based defenses encompass a wider set of defendants than typical insanity defenses. Traditional insanity cases are rare, with only the most disordered individuals qualifying. But syndrome trauma is considered typical of all those who are victimized. When applied to insanity or related incapacity defenses, syndrome evidence expands the domain of the potentially insane. In the end, however, syndromes are about trauma, not insanity per se. The link between trauma and insanity or diminished capacity is assumed, yet quite unclarified.

This expansion of expertise into the domain of common sense (the province of the jury) can contribute to the attainment of justice, especially because it makes the jury aware of unusually oppressive circumstances that often compel human beings to react in ways the jury would not anticipate. Susan Murphy contends that exclusion of expert testimony in such cases can distort the jury's perception of reality. "For a defendant whose perceptions truly are different from the norm, affected by a history of battering, the exclusion of expert testimony prevents validation of her perceptions."[107]

Still, courts have properly worried about such scientific estimations because they have a tendency to posit psychological or environmental determinism which negates the normative concepts of free will and responsibility that make ordered society possible. As a federal judge declared in a BWS case we will return to in a later chapter, "It is not psychology which establishes the norm for determining whether someone has a will—it is society which enforces its collective judgment through its legal system."[108]

Syndrome evidence is "soft" science, not "hard," making it more accessible and therefore permeable to the emerging paradigm shift of victimization that surrounds it.[109] By lowering the wall between expert and layperson understandings, syndrome evidence extends the therapeutic ethic's reformulation of self and responsibility. Arthur Kleinman depicts the process of "medicalization" in *The Illness Narratives:*

> Relabeling alcoholism as an illness and child abuse as a symptom of family pathology are further examples of the widespread process of medicalization in Western societies, whereby problems previously labeled and managed as moral, religious, or criminal are redefined as disorder and dealt with through therapeutic technology. These problems open a window on Western society, showing its chief cultural concerns and conflicts . . .
>
> The cultural meanings of illness shape suffering as a distinctive moral or spiritual form of distress. . . . [L]ocal culture systems provide both the theoretical framework of myth and the established script for ritual behavior that transform an individual's affliction into a sanctioned symbolic form for the group.[110]

In his major work on the new syndromes, McCord compares them to more traditional scientific testimony, finding that they provide comparison of an individual's behavior with that of others in similar situations; present excuses that differ from such traditional mental excuses as incapacity and insanity; entail injection of expert testimony where it has historically not been allowed or injected; might have a strong influence on the jury; and are hard to contain in terms of their applications to particular aspects of the case at hand. These factors reveal a lack of defined boundaries to the new form of incapacity excuse.[111]

We should consider the formulation of BWS and the other syndromes as an advance in understanding the impact of interpersonal victimization and how reason in such contexts differs from reason in nonvictimization contexts. But like all scientific constructs in the area of human relations and psychology, such constructs are tentative by their very nature. If Thomas Kuhn is right that even "hard" science is based on ultimately contingent "paradigms" consisting of theoretical suppositions, then such contingency applies *a fortiori* to the science of human nature.[112]

The New Victimization Syndromes and Political Culture: The Making of a New Truth

Trials that showcase the new syndromes also reflect conflicts deep in the heart of culture. Plato and the Greek tragic poets were the first to recognize the relationship between the psychology of public law and the status of culture and the family; Shakespeare's tragic plays carried this understanding to even higher levels in the sixteenth century, with their penetrating portrayals of the links between legal conflict and cultural and familial disorder. In our time, arguments over the status of the family fuel the "culture wars." Much of this debate stems from new knowledge about the prevalence of child and wife abuse.[113]

At the same time, institutional, professional, and cultural pressures that envelop the issue shape assessments of the scope of the problem. Foucault's teachings about the links between truth and power apply to such progressive movements as readily as they pertain to traditional claims to truth.[114] Charles Krauthammer, in a recent article on the contemporary psychology and politicization of the family, writes,

> The new psychology is rooted in and reinforces current notions about the pathology of family life. Rather than believing, as we did for a hundred years under the influence of Freud, that adult neurosis results from the inevitable psychological traumas of sexual maturation, compounded by parental error and crystalized in the (literally) fantastic memories of the patient, today there is a new dispensation. Nowadays neurosis is the outcome not of innocent errors but of criminal acts occurring in the very bosom of the ordinary-looking family. Seek and ye shall find: the sins of the fathers are visible in the miserable lives of the children. Child abuse is the crime waiting only to be discovered.[115]

A large literature exists on the relationships between the science of psychology, the framing of mental disorder (or "disease"), and social, cultural, and political judgments. We will see later that the attribution of responsibility itself is also strongly influenced by political and social judgments. A similar set of relationships influence the way social problems are conceived, and the factors that determine whether a problem becomes a "social problem" in the first place. For a long time, society simply ignored domestic violence or defined it in euphemistic terms of avoidance as a "mere domestic matter." Focus on the harm domestic violence causes women came about only because resurgent feminism thrust this understanding into public consciousness and politics.[116]

Joseph Gusfield portrays how the public formation of issues worthy of attention is based on the "culture of public problems" or the "sociology of social problems." The factors that influence this formation include the relevant power of those affected by the problem at hand; how the problem is defined (partly a function of available knowledge and power); which individuals or institutions are seen as central to causing or resolving the problem; and whether the problem is viewed as best solved by public or private choice:

Human problems do not spring up, full blown and announced, into the consciousness of bystanders. Even to recognize a situation as painful requires a system for categorizing and defining events . . .

The sociologist has come to recognize that many human situations and problems have histories; they have not always been construed and recognized as they are today or will be in the future. What is now labeled and seen as "mental disorder" has a history in which the same behavior was accorded different status in different historical periods.[117]

Gusfield suggests that the very attributions of responsibility and causality are, at least to some important extent, socially shaped and value laden. Such moral judgments are deeply embedded in social and political practices and in assessments that cannot help being historically and socially influenced, even if they are not totally contingent upon such judgments: social forces interact with our moral judgments and sentiments in a dialectical manner. In a classic work on causation, H. L. A. Hart and A. M. Honoré maintain that we attribute responsibility not solely on the basis of facts and purely objective factors, but on value judgments about who should be held accountable:

Usually in discussions of law and occasionally in morals . . . the expression "responsible for" does not refer to a factual connection between the person held responsible and the harm but simply to his liability under the rules to be blamed, punished or made to pay. . . . There is no implication that the person held responsible actually did or caused the harm.[118]

During the nineteenth century, the law of property, nuisance, torts, and eminent domain undervalued certain forms of suffering inflicted by entrepreneurial capitalism (e.g., damage to property or body caused by trains, dams, and the like) in order to facilitate economic growth.[119] But the twentieth century has been characterized by an increasing sensitivity to suffering and the plights of various "victims" around the world. This sensitivity stems from several phenomena, including the legacy of the Enlightenment promise of happiness and escape from oppression and suffering; the legacy of the Romantic movement's cult of sensibility to suffering; the death and destruction wrought by war, tyranny, and industrialism; the growth of ideologies of victimhood, antidiscrimination, and rights in the last few decades; the expansion of knowledge about the effects of various activities on human beings around the world.[120] Politics accompanies the attribution of victimhood, as Joseph A. Amato explains:

Paradoxically, our era, which proclaims happiness as a universal goal, not only preoccupies itself with—even invites despair over—certain forms of suffering, but also on an ever escalating scale it recognizes, ideologizes, and politicizes some forms of suffering and victims, making them valid, fashionable, and even official. At the same time, other forms of suffering, sacrifice, and victims are disregarded and even negated. Indeed, if the central contention of this work is correct, the conflicting claims of suffering increasingly have come to threaten identity, conscience, and public discourse in recent history . . . [121]

One way in which one set of victims can corral more public attention than other victims is to attain scientific authorization or validation. Syndromes as psychological science have served this function for many victims of abuse. Pointing out this effort hardly compromises such victims' claims for justice: it simply shows why these particular just claims grab society's attention rather than other just claims.

Political power and social values also influence the development of psychological science. Because of the vagueness and mystery surrounding psychological states, psychiatry and psychology (forms of "soft science") are much more vulnerable to the influences of social and political forces than are other forms of science that have more verifiable empirical foundations. This does not mean that psychiatry has not made significant advances and that all claims to scientific status are mere pretension (after all, science is a process of methodical doubt and testing, which affects psychiatry as well as any knowledge endeavor); it means only that the subject matter of psychiatry, the mind, the emotions, consciousness, the *psyche*, the soul—depending on the school of thought—is less amenable to exactitude and certitude than is the subject matter of many other scientific disciplines. As Aristotle contends in the *Nichomachean Ethics*, "[I]t is the mark of the educated man to look for precision in each class of things just so far as the nature of the subject admits." [122]

In a related sense, the self can be explained in terms of a duality that both enchants and bedevils human nature: "form" or "function." "Form" pertains to the laws governing nonmental or material processes; it comprises the realm of determinism. "Function" designates the actual (phenomenal) experiences of consciousness and choice; it is the realm of agency and individual uniqueness. Some thinkers such as the great existentialist and psychiatrist Karl Jaspers interpret this tension as the difference between "understanding" and "explanation." [123] Such diverse intellectual endeavors as the philosophy of mind, existentialism, the philosophy of science's distinction between science and metaphysics, and Kantian epistemology and ethics pivot on this distinction as well. The recent resurgence of the debate between biological approaches to psychiatry and nonbiological approaches that stress understanding and psychodynamics epitomizes this tension, as does the reinvigorated movement toward a psychiatry based on drug or pharmaceutical therapy. [124] The historical development of psychiatry has swung between "spiritual" (psychodynamic) and biological emphases since modern psychiatry's inception, so these new developments join a historical dialectic.[125]

Paul McHugh and Phillip Slavney build their analysis of psychiatric classification and practice on the subtleties of the distinction between form and function:

> [I]t is clear that this domain [consciousness] is not only a place where events (forms, experiences) occur but also a realm in which purpose (function, intentions) reigns. Forms and functions, events and purposes, obviously interrelate, but it is difficult if not impossible to view a mental event in these two ways simultaneously . . .
>
> Thus, the dialectic we are discussing is inherent in the domain of consciousness. This duality of forms and functions, events and purposes, is found in no other medical discipline. The focus of special attention in dermatology, cardiology, neurology, and so on is on a bodily structure and its capacity for pathological change. Only in psychiatry do practitioners face such a dual set of expressions, and face them right from the start of the examination of the patient.[126]

As "function," psychiatry is often as much art as science, at least in clinical and personal contexts. Psychiatry is preeminently an interpretive science because it deals with that ultimate mysterious text, the mind. "Since consciousness is viewed as a text with a hidden meaning, the thoughts and behaviors of the patient are symbols to be interpreted."[127] Paul Ricoeur elucidates this understanding in his brilliant analysis of the interplay between the "economic" (physical/instinctual) and the hermeneutical aspects of Freud's thought. Ricoeur speaks of psychoanalysis as a "hermeneutics of suspicion" and builds his analysis on the tensions between form and function, between hermeneutics and economics: "Psychoanalysis never confronts one with bare forces, but always with forces in search of meaning; this link between force and meaning makes instinct a psychical reality, or, more exactly, the limit concept at the frontier between the organic and the psychical."[128] We will see in chapter 7 that political freedom and citizenship depend in profound ways on the primacy of human function over form, and that this dependence is crucial to the criminal law.

Thus, psychiatry is often an interpretive science and art that pursues the links between what Ricoeur calls the "individual secret" and the "universal destiny."[129] This understanding weds psychiatry to institutions and society. Feminist works and other works on psychiatric classification go further and show important connections between psychiatric classification, cultural values, and political power. We saw above how the psychiatric recognition and formulation of multiple personality disorder (now dissociative identity disorder) was indebted to a mixture of research, politics, and social trends. In *Trauma and Recovery*, Judith Herman takes this understanding further in discussing the ways in which power shapes psychiatric understanding, and how feminism has supported new ways of understanding trauma in relation to gender oppression:

> The study of psychological trauma has a curious history—one of episodic amnesia. Periods of active investigation have alternated with periods of oblivion . . .
>
> Three times over the past century, a particular form of psychological trauma has surfaced into public consciousness. Each time, the investigation of that trauma has flourished in affiliation with a political movement. The first to emerge was hysteria, the archetypal psychological disorder of women. Its study grew out of the republican, anticlerical political movement of the late nineteenth century in France. The second was shell shock or combat neurosis. Its study began in England and the United States after the First World War and reached a peak after the Vietnam War. Its political context was the collapse of a cult of war and the growth of an antiwar movement. The last and most recent trauma to come into public awareness is sexual and domestic violence. Its political context is the feminist movement in Western Europe and North America.[130]

Herman's insight is consistent with what we know about the social construction or framing of "disease," though perhaps she provides a more explicitly political emphasis. Different cultures define, interpret, and treat even physical diseases in different ways. Lynn Payer, for example, has shown that German medicine traces many diseases to the heart because the heart plays a major role in Germany's romantic notion of the self; Payer contrasts this approach to that of the Americans, who engage in more interventionist and mechanical medical procedures (she finds automobile metaphors and metaphors about "attacking" problems in many interviews with American doctors) and to that of the English, who are more stoic than the Germans and less attacking than the Americans. Payer attributes many of these differences to culture and the different developmental paths of medical practice in the societies.[131] Along these lines, whereas American psychiatry has recognized multiple personality as a disorder, European psychiatry's diagnostic manual (the International Classification of Diseases, ICD-10) does not—an omission that angers leading MPD movement practioners. ICD-10 does include a long classification of forms of dissociation, however.[132]

In 1980 the American Psychiatric Association reformulated the entire edifice of classification of all disorders with the publication of DSM-III (more on this in chapter 6). Earlier, owing to astute and strong political pressure by gay activists and key allies in the psychiatric profession (including Robert Spitzer, who pioneered the conceptual revolution of DSM-III as well as PTSD), the APA dropped homosexuality as a disorder in 1973, replacing it with a more benign classification that emphasized trauma due to unwanted sexual desires.[133]

The case of homosexuality reveals how homosexuals considered negative psychiatric labels normatively inappropriate forms of labeling, and how political and moral pressures can succeed in challenging these labels and the attendant psychological theories.[134] Some of the groups that pioneered these changes wanted others to view their members as responsible, self-determining individuals who are as capable of equal citizenship as anyone else. Some psychiatrists, however, still bemoan what they deem the "politicization" of psychiatry, which they believe has contributed to the delegitimation of psychiatry as a science.[135] But homosexuals wanted to be seen and treated as free, responsible citizens, and the advocates of battered women wanted society to understand that victims' subjugation was not due to a voluntary surrender of their wills. Their oppressors impose the victimization. Thus, each case involved the politics of equal citizenship.[136]

Edward Shorter has recently shown how the packaging of psychosomatic illnesses has been shaped historically by reliance on "symptom pools" that consist of factors derived from the psychological *Weltgeist.* Yet symptom pools must seem consistent with available scientific knowledge and serve the conscious and unconscious interests of doctors, patients, and society.[137] For example, hysteria dropped out of the picture in the twentieth century when its symptoms no longer served the interests of women and doctors, and as doubts about the nature of the "disease" grew in a changing social and scientific environment. (Much of the contemporary "recovery movement" might suffer the same fate.) Shorter fashions similar arguments about forms of "dissociation," "central nervous disease," and "multiple personality," which have risen, fallen, and been repackaged in the annals of mental medicine and psychological culture:

> For students of psychosomatic illness, the point about multiple personality disorder is that a climate of suggestion can elicit not merely physical symptoms such as paralysis, but fashionable mental symptoms as well. What particular mental and physical symptoms appear in a given period depends not at all on the underlying characteristics of a purportedly immutable "disease entity," but on the climate of suggestion prevailing at the time.[138]

Another theme recurs throughout Shorter's analysis of the historical complicity between patient and doctor in the framing of psychosomatic disease: such framings might serve women's needs in oppressive social contexts, but they invariably perpetuate victimization and compromise women's prospects of equal respect and citizenship.

Thus, the very framing of mental disorders is shaped by the sociology of knowledge and cultural influences. Conversely, society is affected by developments in psychiatry and psychology. We find suggestive evidence of this influence in the way groups have extended the logic of the syndrome to other fields, issues, and discourses. Consider, for instance, a recent controversy that arose out of a feminist class at the University of Washington in Seattle on the nature of the family. A team of instructors taught the course with an aggressively antifamily ideology. When some students challenged this approach, the instructors (the course had a major instructor as well as "course facilitators" who maintained ideological order) attempted to squelch competing discourse. One male student (who was raised in an alternative style of family that the instructors were normally prone to praise) refused to be cowed and persisted in questioning the tenets of the course. This resistance led to a confrontation, which culminated in the student's expulsion from the class. After further hearings, the university lived up to the reputation of contemporary universities by succumbing to compromise: it gave the student credit for the course and maintained the ban on his attendance. What is interesting for our purposes is that some of the course facilitators were so traumatized by the publicity the case attracted that they fled Seattle. The main instructor related that the episode triggered "post-traumatic stress disorder" in the defectors, and that their psychological condition was akin to rape-trauma syndrome.[139] This remarkable claim indicates how the discourse of victimization syndromes has permeated the political culture. And the theme of the class portrays connections between the concept of victimization syndrome and political ideology surrounding the family. It also shows how activists may drape ultimately political claims in the garb of scientific legitimacy.

Beyond the specifics of each syndrome, the concept of "survivorship" underlay the various syndromes, tying the victimization syndromes to broader cultural developments. "Survivor syndrome" had gained currency in the studies of survivors of World War II concentration camps and death camps, and the victims of the atomic bombings of Hiroshima and Nagasaki.[140] The notions of "survival" and individuals as "survivors" played pivotal roles in the development of research on the nature of trauma stemming from disaster, human cruelty and oppression. As knowledge of domestic violence, sexual assault, related forms of domination, and the effects of technological accidents gained currency through the interplay of research and politics, America began to define itself, at least in part, as a nation of "survivors." By the 1990s, more and more individuals had "come out" as survivors of various forms of child abuse, including television talk-show host Oprah Winfrey and comedian Roseanne Arnold Barr (whose parents have since contested this claim and formed the False Memory Syndrome Foundation in Philadelphia). In the fall of 1992, Winfrey narrated an extraordinary documentary show on incest that networks CBS, ABC, NBC, and TBS aired simultaneously—the first time networks ever reached out to such a vast audience except for such single events as presidential addresses or major political hearings.

Survivorship emerged as a major theme in the works of such popular writers as John Irving and Joyce Carol Oates. At the point in *Hotel New Hampshire* when

Irving is moved to define the character of his fictitious autobiographical family, he designates them a band of "survivors." And anyone who reads *The World According to Garp* cannot help but remark on its similarity to the growing literature on PTSD, which illustrates the trauma that grips us in the wake of unforeseen accidents in a topsy-turvy (postmodern) world that plays cruel games with our congenital need for order and security. Irving's novels, of course, transcend one-dimensional survivalism by wrestling profoundly with the tensions between danger and freedom, fear and hope. Irving is perhaps the novelist of our time because his art grapples with the themes of victimization and hope, immanence and transcendence. In describing Hope Standish, one of T. S. Garp's woman characters, Irving remarks "Hope is seen as a strong survivor of a weak man's world." Like the music of Bruce Springsteen, Irving's art is both dark and redemptive, teaching that redemption and joy depend on creativity that comes to terms with suffering rather than dwelling on it. Irving's treatment of sexuality (also like Springsteen's) celebrates sexuality while also embodying these tensions, setting him in opposition to Andrea Dworkin, who views male sexuality as simply exploitative aggression. In 1992, Irving and Dworkin went at each other with these competing worldviews in a debate over the relationship between pornography and art in the *New York Times Book Review*. A similar tension and movement is seen in rock music. Whereas Springsteen's music in the 1970s and 1980s offered hope and redemption in the face of suffering, the music of such contemporary X-generation groups as Pearl Jam has forsaken the message of hope in favor of a message of hopelessness.[141]

In the 1970s and 1980s, many survivor-oriented productions or events captured the nation's fascination, including several "disaster" movies (*Earthquake, The Poseidon Adventure, Fire, The China Syndrome*, etc.), the spectacular weeklong television docudrama "Holocaust," and the Skokie free speech controversy, in which Holocaust survivors heroically resisted a demonstration by a Nazi group in their community. At this same time, books about the psychological consequences of being raised by Holocaust survivors gained national attention.[142] The logic of a politics of survivorism swelled into the 1980s, especially in the revival of fatalistic religious views on the right and the new politics surrounding the First Amendment, in which groups rose to claim the need for laws against forms of expression that harmed their self-esteem and emotional security. The new forms of "progressive" censorship fit nicely with the dawning age of new forms of self and psychological defense. Catharine MacKinnon, the leading feminist antipornography activist, claims that pornography is "women's Skokie."[143]

The new syndromes, then, were consistent with emerging political movements, consciousness, and new knowledge about the brutality of relationships. Moreover, they were in tune with the more general psychological tenor of society. In Joseph A. Amato's terms, the syndromes drew energy and meaning from the advent in recent decades of the concept of "universal victims": the idea that individuals in the late twentieth century presumptively suffer victimization by a variety of forces, including the legacies of death and destruction left in the wake of war, oppression, industrialism, and imperialism. What Nietzsche portended at the turn of the century, Amato beholds as a reality: a condition in which the ethic of suffering replaces an ethic of achievement as the dominant intellectual and moral verity.[144]

Conclusion

The portrayal of the syndrome society in this chapter wove a rather complex tapestry that included revelation of hidden truths, social and political construction of truth, and both promising and questionable ways of construing the self and society. As we proceed, it will be our task to draw on knowledge in this field that is conducive to the just adjudication of cases and to constitutional citizenship. We will see that the syndrome connection poses sufficient problems for criminal law and citizenship to justify looking elsewhere for the key to justice in cases of battered women who kill.

Now let us look at the nature of domestic violence and BWS in detail.

PART **II** *Domestic Violence and Battered Woman Syndrome (BWS)*

CHAPTER THREE

The Nature of Domestic Abuse

Criminal cases involving battered women often deal with complex, nuanced factual situations that vex the desire to generalize. Battered woman cases are symbolically and politically rich, fertile grounds for competing interpretations that serve a variety of ends. So once a particular image of battered women gains currency, it is not always easy to control its use. For example, men have often commandeered symbols relating to women, modifying them for their own purposes (a process Caroline Bynum calls "symbolic reversal").[1] And other groups have pounced on battered woman cases and appropriated them for their causes, as we will see below. But we may conclude that the issue of battered women who kill or attempt to kill is emblematic of women's struggle to achieve autonomy, self-determination, and equal respect in the presence of conspicuous subjugators. These cases revive notions of Hegel's portrayal of the ultimate encounter between master and slave, waged on a stage constructed with domination, subjugation, and the fear of death.[2]

In the next two chapters we will look at the nature of domestic violence against women in some detail, including the psychology of battering relationships and the effects of battering on the victims of abuse. It is important to get a grasp of these facts, for we can generate responsible legal policy only from an adequate apprehension of the reality that battered women confront. Also, we will see that this reality involves a delicate balance of trauma and heightened rationality concerning one's status vis-à-vis the batterer.

Domestic abuse is a serious problem. In 1984, for example, 4,408 homicides occurred within the family, with 48 percent of these involving a spouse. Of these, 1,310 were women killed by husbands, 806 were men killed by wives.[3] In 1993, 1,530 women were killed by their husbands or companions, according to the FBI.[4] In his famous study on homicide in Philadelphia, Martin Wolfgang finds that 60 percent of the husbands killed by their wives had "precipitated" their deaths by threats or acts of violence, whereas only 9 percent of the wives had precipitated their deaths.[5] And in the important 1992 abortion rights case *Planned Parenthood of Southeastern Pennsylvania v. Casey,* the United States Supreme Court struck down Pennsylvania's spousal notification requirement on the basis of the plurality's understanding of battered women's plights. The Court relied on a report by the American Medical Association which estimates that male spouses severely assault four million women each year, or about eleven thousand each day. The Court also cited recent FBI statistics disclosing that 8.8 percent of all homicide victims are killed by their spouse, and that 30 percent of women who are homicide victims are killed by their male partners.[6]

Gendered Versus Non-Gendered Perspectives

Scholars debate the extent to which domestic violence should be construed as a gender issue that focuses on the prevalence of male domination, or whether it should be considered as a form of interpersonal violence for which males and females bear equal responsibility. The resolution of this issue affects the presumptions one brings to court cases and the viability of syndrome logic in general. An exchange in the 1990 *Journal of Interpersonal Violence* addresses the problem. Introducing the debate, moderator Lucy Berliner remarks,

> [S]ignificant controversy exists about the explanations for [violent behavior in families]. In particular, professionals disagree about the extent to which gender and unequal distribution of power between men and women should be the organizing principle for understanding the phenomenon. This debate is most acute in theoretical discussions about violence between adult partners. The issue is crucial, because strategies for intervention and prevention in individual situations and on the societal level are strongly influenced by the conceptual framework that is adopted.[7]

The non-gendered perspective, which is associated with positivistic survey research, asserts that domestic violence is a problem for men and women, and that men and women are equally culpable for its perpetration. In their classic work, *Behind Closed Doors*, Murray Straus, David Gelles, and Susan Steinmetz establish the paradigm for the non-gendered approach. They look at families as systems of interaction (a "general systems" approach) and ask questions about violence based on the now famous "Conflict Tactics Scales" (CTS), which included questions about the use of force within the family. The authors find that violence was perpetrated as often by women as by men. In another famous (or infamous) essay published in 1977 and based on a similar methodology, Steinmetz concludes that there are many "battered husbands" whose plights have been ignored in the new era of feminist consciousness.[8] These two works provoked a storm of controversy, and Steinmetz's work led to political hearings, which resulted in temporary cutbacks in funding for battered women's shelters.[9] Powerful tensions can erupt between causes and scholarship.[10]

In support of the non-gendered approach, R. I. McNeely and Coramae Mann contend that more husbands are victimized by wives' violent acts than vice versa (2.2 million versus 1.8 million in 1975, for example); that studies of dating show equal use of shoving, pushing, and grabbing; that some studies show that women who kill their spouses have prior records for violence; that women in court who kill their children often fare better than men who kill their children; and that women are more likely than men to use dangerous weapons against their mates. Researchers have shown that some battered women have criminal records for violence (which are not all due to retaliation against men who initiate the aggression) and are adept at "being tough." [11] An interviewee serving life for killing her abuser's new girlfriend told us that she was accustomed to "pushing around and manipulating men who were soft. I'd take advantage of them if they were too soft." [12] In 1992, San Diego socialite Betty Broderich stalked and harassed her ex-husband before she murdered him and his new wife in their bed. [13] Mann and McNeely declare, "[T]he average man's size and strength are neutralized by guns and knives, boiling water, bricks, fireplace pokers, and baseball bats. Many fail to realize that domestic assaults do not involve pugilistic fair play, or to consider that attacks occur when males are asleep, or incapacitated by alcohol, age, or infirmities." [14]

Critics charged that Straus, Gelles, and Steinmetz did not consider the issue of self-defense and retaliation in their 1980 study that found a lot of mutual combat; [15] but they and other researchers have recently controlled for retaliation and still concluded that violence is evenly distributed along gender lines and that much female-generated violence is not defensive in nature. In addressing the question "Are woman as violent as men?" Straus and Jan E. Stets conclude: "Turning to the question of whether the rates are misleading because violence by women is largely self-defensive, we find that women initiate violence about as often as men. These results cast doubt on the notion that assaults by women on their partners primarily are acts of self-defense or retaliation." [16]

Other classic works from the later 1970s challenge this perspective by framing the problem as a function of the social and historical sanctioning of violence against women in the home, and the difficulty women as a group confront in gaining the independence that would allow them to escape their bondage. Del Martin's *Battered Wives* and Dobash's and Dobash's *Violence against Wives* show the historical collaboration between law and men to deprive women of equality, property, and rights, and how batterers' controls over women have been backed up by the legal system in the past. Dobash and Dobash maintain that "In order to understand and explain violence between husbands and wives we must go beyond the interacting couple, the isolated and abstracted social relationship, and place the violent behavior in its proper historical and contemporary setting." [17]

More importantly, the gender perspective also emphasizes and seeks to understand the disproportionate impact of *severe* domestic violence on women, as exhibited by the statistics cited at the beginning of this chapter. Cases in which women are "subordinated" by men into committing drug crimes present further evidence of the gendered nature of severe threats. (We will look at several such cases in later chapters.) The case law is virtually void of similar subordination of men by women. One public defender told me that his participation in a battered woman murder case led him to suspect battering in nonhomicide cases, so he began to ask his clients in jail, "He was beating on you, wasn't he?" To his astonishment, several women began to cry and confessed that this was indeed the case. Once one looks beyond the surface of things, the world no longer looks the same.[18]

Furthermore, violent domination of one's spouse as a systemic practice is undoubtedly more prevalent among men than vice versa. For example, Shawn Sullivan, writing in the *Wall Street Journal,* descries the battering of each of his sisters in the inner city and the general intensification of the battering ideology among growing numbers of inner-city residents (a phenomenon that our interviews in prison also revealed in startling detail): "Specifically, I mean an atmosphere in which young men are 'taught' by their fathers, if they have one, and older brothers to refer to women as 'ho's' (whores) who need abuse; where physical violence is a common means of ending verbal disputes; and where women are mistrusted and detested."[19]

Batterers are often unbelievably brutal. They instill a real fear. The case law is replete with murder convictions of men who have killed or attempted to kill their estranged women, and we encountered several in our interviews. One of my interviewees was in love with a woman who had managed to escape her battering boyfriend temporarily. Months later he sought her out and shot her to death. (My source requested anonymity because he fears retaliation by this man, even though the man languishes in prison with a life sentence.) In October 1994, Wisconsin state records disclosed that eight women had been murdered by men over a three-year period despite the presence of court orders requiring the men to stay away from them.[20] In a North Carolina case, *State v. Simpson,* Simpson hunted down his ex-girlfriend months after he had stabbed her during an argument, and blew her head off with a shotgun. An assistant district attorney from Milwaukee told us about a case she prosecuted in which a Vietnam veteran drove to his estranged wife's home and shot her dead. The list goes on and on.[21] One prison interviewee's portrayal of the reign of fear that has not ceased even with her abuser's death suffices to make the point: "He threatened to kill me and told me I would never get rid of him, and he would always haunt me for the rest of my life . . . and if he couldn't have me, no one else could have me. . . . He said he'd torment me for the rest of my life, and even though he's dead and I'm here, he still torments me. And he's right. I'll never get rid of him because he's always in my mind."[22]

Findings about female-generated violence counsel us to exercise caution in the face of pressures to think of abuse as one-sided in terms of gender. *But there is no evidence that shows men living in the same fear for their lives as battered women,* at least in anything approaching a systematic sense. On the contrary, the shelters and jails are full of such women. In her study of more than four hundred battered women, Lenore Walker finds that "[t]he women believed the batterer could or would kill them in three-quarters of those relationships. Only 11% said they had ever tried to kill the batterer, and 87% believe that they (the woman) would be the one to die if someone was killed." [23] Several of our interviewees were also threatened with death and believed in the plausibility of the threats. And women endure another fear which men almost never confront: *the fear of rape.* Fear of rape is a background to the lives of women from which they can never escape. It obviously contributes to the gendered nature of fear of violence. Indeed, Stets and Straus concede in the article just quoted that "[t]hough women may be as violent as men within the home, we found that there is a tendency for women victims to sustain more physical injury than men victims." [24]

On the other side of the coin, however, we must guard against jumping to conclusions based on this reality. Only real deadly harm or serious bodily injury (including rape) justifies reacting with lethal force. Group-based critiques of battering based on patriarchy (Dobash and Dobash) are valuable as explanations of battering, but they cannot, in themselves, provide justifications for using lethal force to retaliate against batterers. Possessing patriarchal attitudes per se hardly qualifies one to be a target of a self-defensive act, and patriarchal men who batter are no more eligible to be such targets than are men who batter for other reasons. Motive explains an act, but the law of self-defense can concern itself only with situations of objective danger. Thus, even if patriarchal belief systems and forms of power help to explain woman-battering and the more general suppression of women, they are not as relevant to the key perception of danger that qualifies one for self-defense. [25] A danger of the new victimization worldview is that it threatens to blur the distinction between sexism and lethal situations that justify self-defense, especially as notions of the vulnerability of the self proliferate in the syndrome society. And, as we will also see, making character or motive irrelevant also serves the rights of those who defend themselves against deadly harm, including battered women. One of the primary reasons BWS arose in the first place was to counter illegitimate bias against the rights of battered women to defend themselves against lethal danger. *Battered women's characters or their reasons for staying in the relationship are legally irrelevant to the right to defend themselves.* This point highlights the criminal law's necessary preoccupation with individual culpability, and the constitutional premise that one's character, thoughts, and beliefs do not in themselves constitute criminal culpability.

In *Toward Feminist Jurisprudence,* Catharine MacKinnon advocates a group-based notion of gender justice; nonetheless, her essay seems as much a treatise on the dilemmas of feminist jurisprudence as it is an advocacy of such. MacKinnon depicts the assumptions of gender-based justice in her portrayal of the distinction between excuse and justification. Excuse points to the individual circumstance, while justification deals with universally right action:

> Feminism tends to collapse the distinction itself by telescoping the universal and the individual into the mediate, group-defined, social dimension of gender . . .
>
> In such a view, *a man never attacks a women as an individual, nor does she ever respond as such.* Nor are the same responses justified for a man as for a woman, at least not for the same reasons.[26]

Two implications to MacKinnon's famous thesis stand out. First, a model of law that ignores broader gender differences is inadequate because empirically grounded gender differences make for different stresses and dangers in contexts like self-defense. Treatment of individual cases must be mediated or balanced with this understanding. Second, justice should be predominantly dual and group based: "[A] man *never* attacks a women as an individual, nor does she *ever* respond as such" (emphasis added). Although the first implication is justified to grasp fully the meaning of battering, the latter threatens to lead to a new form of injustice. What if the woman in the case happens to be more violent than the man? And should John Doe's slapping his wife be construed in terms of Jerry Doe's potentially lethal attacks? What happens to the gender equation in these cases? In the name of individuating criminal justice, MacKinnon ends up substituting one nonindividuated generalization for another. A new form of stereotyping and scapegoating rises out of the ashes of its predecessor.[27] *Although the fear of death and rape is gendered in the sense I articulated, we risk imposing a reality in the individual case if we accept MacKinnon's dualistic logic.* Of course, MacKinnon's dualistic systemic view would be justified if domination were as one-way and universal as she presumes. But we will see as we proceed that this portrayal of gender relations goes too far. In addition, we will see in the critique of BWS below that some defendants and others have exaggerated claims about battering in trials and other contexts. Though there is no reason to believe that such exaggeration is widespread, such findings counsel us to pay scrupulous attention to the facts of each case at the same time that we acknowledge the gendered nature of the fear of death and rape.

The answer to our conundrum lies between the poles of making battering irrelevant and making it a defense in itself, an answer that feminist Katharine Bartlett suggests in her theory of "feminist jurisprudence." Bartlett accepts that historical circumstances and social status influence perceptions and attitudes, but she carefully avoids the kind of victim-status epistemological reductionism that thwarts independent and objective thinking. Bartlett also rejects the Manichean dichotomy between male and female power and reasoning that prevails in some feminist jurisprudence, advocating a form of practical reason in its stead.[28] "Practical reasoning approaches problems not as dichotomized conflicts, but as dilemmas with multiple perspectives, contradictions, and inconsistencies. These dilemmas, ideally, do not call for the choice of one principle over another, but rather 'imaginative integrations and reconciliations,' which require attention to particular context."[29]

As we proceed I will show that the syndrome approach to the problem of battered women who kill creates its own kinds of stereotypes and "dichotomized conflicts" that compromise the tenets of individualized justice and practical reasoning.

Battering's Basic Nature and Effects

Battering often incites fear and a powerful sense of degradation which transforms one's consciousness. One of our prison interviewees attempted to commit suicide and ended up murdering an elderly woman who ran a grocery store. She confided,

> He told me if I ever turned him in, he would kill me. . . . I believed it very much. . . . I didn't even feel safe one hundred and some miles from this man. . . . I got so bad that I said the only way out is suicide. I became very suicidal, very depressed. Started self-abusing. . . . Every other week in the psych unit. I got so bad that I says, "Well, Reggy's [her son] not going to grow up knowing his mother is going to commit suicide, I'm taking him with me." So I threatened to kill him, too. . . . I accepted his [her husband's] rules because I was scared half to death. . . . I was like a robot, a puppet. I didn't even feel like I had a heart that was beating. I'd pinch myself to see if I was human. The only time I felt I had control over what I did. . . . I bought a gun.[30]

Faced with terror, battered women often develop understandings and coping skills that are reasonable under the circumstances. In summarizing her discussion of three "severely battered women" in New York City who resorted to violence, Julie Blackman, who possesses one of the keener appreciations of the reality governing severe battering relationships, declares, "The psychological consequences they displayed varied, but were unified by the central role of the fear produced by their partner's violence and domination, the intensity of their reactions, and the fact that their psyches were fully products of the violence they endured. It is as if there was nothing left—no part of them had been shielded from the ravages of the violence."[31]

But fear plays different roles in different relationships, and women handle it in a variety of ways because of their different personalities, psychological makeups, and economic and communal resources. Traumatic events are mediated by our values, experiences, and expectations, which are composed of cultural and individual factors.[32] Nonetheless, although relationships vary, it is nonetheless true that individual relationships might be characterized by patterns, as Mary Ann Dutton explains:

> [T]he battered woman is exposed to more than discrete violent episodes; rather, the abuse is characterized by continual occurrences of various behaviors by her partner that function to exert power and control over her, often for an extended period of months or years . . .
>
> [A] husband's loud voice or a raised fist may signal danger when these behaviors are associated with his actual use of violence in the past or the reasonable expectation that he might use violence in the future . . .
>
> Many women describe a certain "look in the eye" that signals extreme danger. For a number of women, it was that look that triggered a self-defensive reaction. They had come to know that the look meant violence was inevitable and imminent. Unless one were to understand the patterning within previous incidents, when "that look" preceded the violent rape, the choking to unconsciousness, or the severe beating, it would make little sense why a woman might respond with such terror at simply "a look in the eye."[33]

This observation is crucial, and has led many advocates to endorse BWS because of its emphasis on a pattern. *But we will see that the presence of the type of pattern Dutton describes is not the same thing as the syndrome logic of BWS.* BWS stresses the similarity of all women's responses to violence. Dutton's pattern pertains to the woman's insights into the behavior and emotional signals of her abuser. Different relationships develop different patterns and cues.

Battering disempowers its victims and prevents them from living full lives with self-determination. It creates economic and related forms of dependency, sometimes to pathetic extents. Dobash and Dobash remark, "Pizzey recounted the story of a woman who got on a bus without a penny in her pocket to pay the fare, and Eisenberg and Micklow described the predicament of a woman who spent a long time saving $1.70 with which to escape. Martin told a story of a woman who found it impossible to get ahold of just $5.00, and there were numerous cases in our own research."[34]

Battering also wreaks psychological damage related to trauma.[35] Many battered women are ridden with fear and anxiety. One of our prison interviewees avoided men as much as possible; when I walked into the room while she was being interviewed by one of my women research assistants, this inmate froze and was unable to talk. She told my assistant that she avoided being around men because they instilled fear in her.[36] Victims often suffer symptoms related to PTSD, including intrusive thoughts, avoidance responses, difficulty sleeping and concentrating, hypervigilance, depression, suicidal inclinations, substance abuse, and somatic problems associated with trauma. The extent of these symptoms is mediated or affected by such factors as the response of the legal system to one's victimization, the presence or absence of support by family, friends, or others, and one's character and background.[37]

Elaine Hilberman and Kit Munson, who interviewed sixty badly battered women, state, "They remained vigilant, unable to relax or sleep. Sleep, when it came, brought no relief. Nightmares were universal, with undisguised themes of violence and danger." The trauma makes one obsessively focused on how to cope. This affects the arousal system, since one is always on the alert to deal with (guard against or avoid) the stressor and trauma. Thus, concentration on other issues or tasks is difficult. This state appears to diminish one's capacity to deal with some matters, but it heightens capacity to deal with batterers and anticipate their intentions. Autonomic arousal and fear lead to obsessive hypervigilance. *Dutton points out that although this behavior resembles paranoia, it is based on a rational assessment of reality.*[38]

Forty-eight percent of the women in Angela Browne's homicide group had talked about killing themselves, compared to 31 percent of the comparison group. One study has found that battering is a "catalyst event" in one of four suicide attempts by women. Several of our prison interviewees reported suicide attempts or thoughts. One stated that she "felt evil. Everything I ever loved went away. I felt dead inside, just going through the motions for a long time, no feelings." The day she decided to kill herself, she felt happy for the first time in years, "like a little kid, tingly, floating, like weights had been lifted off my shoulders." Another attempted suicide twice and threatened it eight times.[39]

Battered women often feel shame associated with degradation and defilement. Martin Symonds states that many victims of violence "have lost their self-respect when they view their compliant behavior with shame, and they have gained the unenviable status of being a victim." One of our prison interviewees said she had no self-esteem, and felt "dirty, like trash."[40] Many commentators maintain that battered women suffer lower self-esteem than other women, and court cases abound with this assumption. Battered women blame themselves for what happens, as they come to accept their batterers' view of them. Interviewees remarked that prison had given them the opportunity to develop self-esteem because it freed them from their oppressive circumstances. One is "just now discovering myself"; another said, "I now realize I was a fool. I wouldn't take this today. I'll never be abused by a man again."[41] Nonetheless, the situation might be more complex than this portrayal suggests. Many battered women maintain a sense of worth and agency. Even Walker found in her survey (based on a Likert-style semantic differential scale) that her battered women scored much *higher* on the self-esteem scale than she had predicted. I will discuss the implications of this finding below.

Dutton also reports "changes in cognitive schema," and "relational distur-bances." *Cognitive schema disturbances* include the loss of the sense of safety, that it is a "safe world." As writers from the time of Hobbes to Czeslaw Milosz have fathomed, human beings naturally seek a sense of personal safety and security. The sense of security evaporates in the case of battered women because the man who should love them victimizes them, and often the community which is supposed to protect them does not.[42] We have seen that cognitive frameworks affect the nature of trauma, so part of the trauma associated with domestic violence stems from the disruption of normative assumptions about the nature of reality. Three reports of dreams replete with telling symbolism by women to Hilberman and Munson reveal the impact of this disruption in agonizing form. "My husband was chasing me up the stairs. . . . I was trying to escape but I kept falling backwards." "There was a man breaking in the house . . . trying to kill me." "Snakes were after me . . . in my bed."[43]

We asked Nora Cashen, who worked for many years as a counselor for battered women in Madison, about what distinguishes women who kill from women who do not. Her answer offered a remarkable observation about the tearing of the sense of law, order, and community:

> They have to confront whatever it is for them: their own mortality, their children's lives, what it means to be a human being, to be a victim, to be responsible for children's well-being. These are extraordinary questions. Then, these culturally facilitated things about how you behave normally don't have as much meaning. Reinforced by their whole experience, cul-tural niceties don't have much meaning. They have been so persecuted. It appears to them that there is no more justice in the world. The rules of the world don't work. What they thought was real, their whole map of reality, is thrown into question. To expect them to behave in a way that is in accord with our sense of reality is ridiculous.[44]

This overwhelming sense of fear and betrayal can destroy the sense of the "*world as meaningful*," since the relationship violates every notion of what a rela-tionship should be. In his discussion of positive versus negative self-identity, Anthony Giddens illustrates how a constructive narrative requires a sense of continuity in time. When fear or anxiety gain ascendency, this continuity unravels. Giddens describes this effect in words reminiscent of many observations of bat-tered women.

> Time may be comprehended as a series of discrete moments, each of which severs prior experiences from subsequent ones in such a way that no continuous 'narrative' can be sustained. Anxiety about obliteration, of being engulfed, crushed or overwhelmed by externally impinging events,

is frequently the correlate of such feelings. . . . [T]he individual experiences what Laing calls an 'inner deadness' deriving from an inability to block off impinging dangers—an incapacity to sustain the protective cocoon.[45]

Gerry Mueller, Ronda Richardson's defense attorney, stressed that Ronda lacked a sense of a continuum of time to such an extent that the defense team had to work hard to instill one in order for her testimony of abuse to have credibility. Mueller explicitly linked this lack to Ronda's general inability (at that period of her life) to show emotion and a sense of injustice about the abuse she suffered. When Ronda took the stand, Mueller had to carefully walk her through each point of time.[46]

Along these lines, a battered woman may develop a "*continuum of tolerance*" in which, like Job, she puts up with what other women would never think of enduring. The "social judgment theory" of Sherif and Hovland is suggestive along these lines. They posit a "latitude of acceptance," within which people exposed to significant ongoing hardship come to accept what most people would never tolerate.[47]

Battering: Forms and Motivations

For us to appreciate and assess battered women's situations, we, too, need to know something about batterers. Battering is often rooted so deeply in the self that it is unrealistic to expect the behavior of habitual batterers to change.[48] Acknowledging this intractability helps us to grasp the desperate reality many battered women experience.

What are batterers like and why do they batter their women? In his key chapter on "The Anatomy of Violence" in *Violent Men*, Hans Toch envisions violence proneness as a combination of self-assertion and self-doubt.

> We have suggested that two types of orientation are especially likely to produce violence: One of these is that of the person who sees other people as tools designed to serve his needs; the second is that of the individual who feels vulnerable to diminishment. . . . Both rest on the premise that human relationships are power-centered, one-way affairs; both involve efforts at self-assertion with a desperate, feverish quality that suggests self-doubt.
>
> Of course, this description does not fit all cases.[49]

First and foremost, battering is an exercise of control and domination. Battering gives the batterer maximum control over the woman. We need to emphasize *the act* of battering over the potential psychopathology of the batterer because this focus illuminates the impact on the victim and the responsibility of the batterer. To exert control, one interviewee's batterer even injected her with drugs while she slept. "He was a controlling person. One time he tied me up because he thought I was going to leave him. He wanted me to stay, always stay under him." Of our twenty prison interviewees, virtually every one spoke time and again of her abuser's obsession with control. "Once he fell in love with me, he became very possessive. If I wasn't at home and he couldn't find out where I was, and even if I talked to him, if I talked to him in a negative way or raised my voice, you would get hit. . . . He wanted to have control over everything I did. . . . Anything would set him off." [50]

For some men, battering is an extension of the violence they deploy against everyone as a *modus operandi* to get what they want (the focus of Toch's book); others inflict it only on their spouses. One prison interviewee remarked, "He would hit me like it was nothing. Like you were a dog. But he wasn't like that with a man. He couldn't hit a man like that. Now, I know he was a real wimpy guy, he could only do this to a woman." [51]

Leaders in Advocates for Battered Women told us that they avoid using psychological terms for battered women as much as possible. Seeger declared, "I don't like the application of mental health terms to the victims of domestic violence, as each victim's circumstances are unique. There is always a danger of applying one theory to everybody. . . . In our area, we seldom use words like that ['syndrome'] because we recognize the problem of pigeonholing. . . . What I use is a theory of power and control. . . . [The psychological approach] may be useful in trial, but it misses the political issue, which is about sexism. . . . [B]attered women and sexual assault clearly stem from sexism, as does sexual harassment." As Kathleen Kreneck of the Wisconsin Coalition against Domestic Violence remarked, "Men batter to control. Sexism is very political. The use of violence is an extension of this. Historically, it has been accepted. For decades, we believed that men owned women and children. This is why we have worked so hard to keep it in the home." [52]

Abuse can be physical and psychological (this use of the term "psychological" differs from the use above, since it deals with mental manipulation rather than psychopathology). All physical abuse has a psychological impact, but some abuse is designed to manipulate the psyche. [53] Physical abuse varies in terms of its frequency and severity. One notorious example arose in the 1989 North Carolina case *State v. Norman*, which I will build on in the concluding chapter. Judy and Thomas Norman had been married for almost twenty-five years, since she was fourteen. Thomas grew very abusive after the fifth year, especially when he drank, which was often. According to the North Carolina Supreme Court,

> His physical abuse of her consisted of frequent assaults that included slapping, punching, and kicking her, striking her with various objects, and throwing glasses, beer bottles, and other objects at her . . . putting her cigarettes out on her, throwing hot coffee on her, breaking glass against her face and crushing food on her face. . . . [H]er husband did not work

and forced her to make money by prostitution, and . . . he made humor of that fact to family and friends. He would beat her if she resisted going out to prostitute herself or if he was unsatisfied with the amounts of money she made. He routinely called the defendant "dog," "bitch," and "whore," and on a few occasions made her eat pet food out of the pet's bowls and bark like a dog. He often made her sleep on the floor. At times, he deprived her of food and refused to let her get food for the family. During those years of abuse, the defendant's husband threatened numerous times to kill her and to maim her in various ways.[54]

Judy Norman shot and killed her sleeping husband when the abuse took a deadly turn that included escalating threats and Thomas telling a medical team to "let her die" while they revived her after a suicide attempt. Asked why she killed him, she replied: "Because I was scared of him and I knowed when he woke up, it was going to be the same thing, and I was scared when he took me to the truck stop that night it was going to be worse than he had ever been. I just couldn't take it no more. . . . That's worse hell than anything."[55]

Abusers often force their spouses and/or children to act like "dogs." This is not happenstance, for dogs symbolize obedience and dehumanization: they walk on all fours like babies or our ancestors in the evolutionary scale, and their accentuated sense of smell represents an earlier stage of human evolution that we look back on with disdain. Treatment as a dog catalyzed one of our prison interviewees to arrange the murder of her husband by a third party. "He started talking about getting another dog. He used to force me to have sex with animals, dogs. He read a lot of pornography, and would make me have sex with a dog at gunpoint. I couldn't do that again." Another interviewee reported about her stepfather, "A lot of abuse was mental. He'd make us kids bark like dogs to get dinner. Even as kids we knew this was humiliating."[56]

Food is another symbol often encountered in battering cases. In cultural terms, men have often associated women with food, in a manner that is ambivalent for the male psyche, for food preparation represents the division of labor in patriarchal orders governed by the public/private split: women are the providers of food in the domestic realm. Food also represents our connection to the earth, the mysteries of nature, and death, since nature is the realm of nonindividuation. And our love of food embraces our desire and our dependency, since our fragile existences depend on food. As Camille Paglia and Simone de Beauvoir demonstrate in their different ways, men have associated women with nature and its powerful mysteries. But men are riveted with ambivalence about this realm because they have putatively transcended nature, and they subliminally associate longing for women with absorption into the realm of passion and death.[57]

The tantrum that ignited the famous "burning bed" case in Michigan in 1977 presents a classic example of food and dog symbolism. Mickey Hughes was outraged that his wife Francine had begun to achieve independence by going back to school; unlike a dog, she was empowering her mind. One evening, her school work prevented her from preparing what Mickey considered an acceptable meal. He flew into a tantrum-driven rage, destroyed Francine's books (the symbols and vehicles of her transcendence), and rubbed food all over her face and hair after having dumped it on the floor. Mickey then raped Francine and passed out, during which time she burned him to death in his bed.[58]

Mickey Hughes inflicted psychological as well as physical abuse. Many abusers are masters of psychological manipulation and cruelty; by creating doubts in their spouses' minds about their own sanity, they gain an edge in control and power. Darald Hanusa, a clinical psychologist in Madison, related a chilling tale of an abuser who deployed psychological abuse as his *modus operandi* against Hanusa's patient. The abuser had had a long relationship with his first wife and won custody of their child after divorce by convincing the court that his ex-wife was "crazy." He then began to abuse his new partner psychologically. This woman's isolation made it harder for her to apply a "reality test" to the things he did to make her doubt her sanity. As in the movie *Sleeping with the Enemy,* everything had to be in its place in this man's house. (Hanusa described him as "obsessive compulsive.") He would yell at her for not putting the toilet paper in the right place, though she knew that he had moved it. He would hide items he told her to buy, claiming she had forgotten to buy them. When she produced the sales slips to prove her innocence, he refused to believe her. Once she caught him urinating in the coffee machine. She told him, "You drink it." He said, "Go ahead and tell, no one in the family will believe you." She told others in the family, only to confront disbelief. And one morning, she heard a ticking sound in the bedroom and discovered a tape recorder playing a tape of a tremendous argument she and the abuser had had the previous night. She was yelling and making threats on the tape, while he remained nice and calm. She figured he was trying to set her up for something, so she took the tape and put it in the glove compartment of her car. He broke into the glove compartment and stole the tape, revealing that he had been watching her throughout this episode. When she asked him what happened to the tape, he said, "What tape?"[59]

Jealousy and possessiveness often trigger abusive incidents, and abusers often isolate their spouses as much as possible, eliminating their connections to the outer world. In our interviews we encountered several such situations. One prison interviewee said, "I didn't have friends. Once married, Robert told me that I would have to choose between him and my friends." Another prison interviewee (who eventually killed her abuser's new lover in a jealous rage) was beaten the first time she went alone to a friend's bar. "He hit me because I was at somebody else's house.

I fell down and he kicked me. He just beat my ass. He was choking me, and it all became a blur. We went somewhere else, I don't know where. [He] told me to take off my clothes because 'I'm going to whip you with this hanger.' I tried to talk rationally with him but he kept hitting me. It was like whips." Another prison interviewee pointed out that her "marriage was a nightmare. The guy was a truck driver, and when he would leave, he would put screws in the door to our home so I couldn't leave. . . . He made sure we didn't have a telephone. We lived out in a trailer by his mom." Another interviewee, Ronda Richardson, told us about how her boyfriend beat a potential suitor to shreds, and how he kept a padlock on their bedroom door. When they returned to his parents' house before the night she killed him, he conducted several "vagina checks" for evidence of intercourse with other men.[60]

One prison interviewee produced perhaps the most revealing portrayal of jealousy and rage. She eventually shot and killed her abusive boyfriend during a ritual of brinksmanship with the gun he often "played with." The batterer would point the gun at her, threaten to kill her, then put the gun in her hands, and threaten to kill himself. Under his direction, they would pass the gun back and forth. One night after he had abused her, the gun went off "by accident." He died two days later. She is now serving an eighteen-year sentence for first-degree reckless homicide. She described one incident in the relationship:

> I had come home from shopping one night with a friend of mine. We had snuck off and didn't come back while he was at work. I was doing some birthday shopping. . . . I walked in the house and it was dark. So I turned on the light, and there he was sitting over in the corner right by the window. He was just sitting there. He had the gun in his hand. And I said, "You're home early," and he said, "I guess I am." And he just sat there playing with the gun and looking at me. And then after a while he got up and started getting rowdy with me. Where had I been, why was I gone, who had I been with, if I'd been drinking. Swearing up and down that I had been drinking. . . . Then after a while, he calmed down and went to sleep after he handcuffed me to the bed.[61]

Sometimes jealousy compels a batterer to kill pets. Angela Browne reports on a battered woman who sought solace and affection in her cats, only to witness their brutal destruction by her partner.[62]

Batterers will also abuse or threaten to abuse the children as a way to control or inflict revenge on their mates. One interviewee told us,

> [B]ut see, he knew how to get me [to come back]. If I walked out, he had the kids to turn to. So, of course, I was too scared. I couldn't let him hurt

the kids, so I would come back and take the abuse myself. . . . And one time he came in [to the psychiatric unit at a hospital] and I told him I wanted a divorce. . . . And soon as he left the thing [psychiatric unit] he called on the phone, and got ahold of me, and threatened me right away. "If you go through with this divorce, I have the kids. I'll make sure something happens to them." So, right away, I backed down.[63]

Jealousy, possessiveness, and control point to the dangers that confront women when they attempt to escape the relationship. One interviewee spoke of the reign of fear that has not ceased even with her abuser's death. "He threatened to kill me and told me I would never get rid of him and he would always haunt me for the rest of my life . . . and if he couldn't have me, no one else could have me. . . . He said he'd torment me for the rest of my life, and even though he's dead and I'm here, he still torments me. And he's right. I'll never get rid of him because he's always in my mind."[64] Analogously, many cases of women who kill their abusers arise in the context of attacks over separation. (Women also kill their spouses out of anger over the batterer's proclamation of separation; these women are bound by the paradoxical "bonds of love" we will discuss.)[65] Martha Mahoney captures the problem of separation in a noted article:

Case law and the popular consciousness that grows from it have submerged the question of control by psychologizing the recipient of the violence or by equating women's experience of violence with men's experience. We urgently need to develop legal and social explanations of women's experience that illuminate the issue of violence as part of the issue of power, rather than perpetuating or exacerbating the images that now conceal questions of domination and control . . .

The question "why didn't she leave" shapes both social and legal inquiry on battering; much of the legal reliance on academic expertise on battered women has developed in order to address this question. At the moment of separation or attempted separation—for many women, the first encounter with the authority of law—the batterer's quest for control often becomes most acutely violent and potentially lethal.[66]

Hanusa told us that only about 3 percent of his batterer patients are "mentally ill," though an additional 15 percent suffer from depression. "Most of what I see is that men who batter have learned it as a response to conflict situations."[67] But many batterers are extremely jealous and, paradoxically, dependent on their women. The concept of separation attack signals desire to control and psychological weakness, characterizing a batterer who cannot brook the woman having independent selfhood. He leans on the woman he persecutes.[68]

Yet psychological understandings should not support denials of responsibility. As Hanusa claims, few batterers are insane; the cases show they know precisely what they are doing. And many men who have suffered similar pasts and psychological states have not indulged in battering. If we excuse those who batter because of psychological state, we undermine the moral credit of those who resist. Psychological pathology and ingenuity in the strategies of domination are intrinsically compatible. Batterers can become masters of manipulation and control because they invest an inordinate amount of psychic energy in their domination. As Thomas Szasz observes, what the criminal law denotes as "diminished capacity" often amounts to "heightened capacity" in psychological terms. "Indeed, if we paid more attention to the circumstances of sensational crimes, and less to the expert opinions of psychiatrists, then many such crimes—for example, that of John Hinckley, Jr.—would seem to be the acts of agents possessing increased, rather than diminished, capacity for committing criminal acts."[69]

Ken Streit, director of Wisconsin's Legal Assistance for Institutionalized Persons program, acquired a similar impression of many batterers he has encountered. Many are able to ferret out women whom they can control. "They can sense, pick up the clues, about a woman just by meeting her. They don't go after women who aren't like this. They can sense who is easy to victimize, and they prey on her. They can tell who is vulnerable, and who is not. It's a special kind of intelligence that they develop."[70]

James Ptacek and other researchers find that many batterers experience uncontrollable, explosive outbursts of rage, which suggests psychological stress. Yet they employ several strategies to excuse or justify their abuse, including many "diminished capacity" arguments: alcohol and/or drugs; an accumulation of uncontrollable rage that exerts "a hydraulic type of inevitability" (a variation of frustration-aggression); victim blaming (if only she would do what I want, if only she did not make me jealous, etc.); and denials of injury and harm caused by their battering.[71] Rage undoubtedly ignites many battering incidents, but it does not explain why batterers single out their spouses. And rage is not a valid excuse, especially if it is accompanied, as it often is, by other forms of controlling behavior. Ptacek convincingly argues that "[a]ppeals to loss of control and victim-blaming are the most common ways that these men sought to escape responsibility for their violence."[72] Furthermore, "uncontrollable" rage offers a tool to *control others*, because it instills fear in the hearts of its targets. Thomas Schelling calls this strategy of conflict the "paradox of irrationality," which amounts to the incontestable proposition that strategic displays of irrationality (especially in the form of violence and cruelty) can get people to do things they would otherwise resist.[73]

Psychologists and psychiatrists have discovered several "psychopathologies" or mental "problems" associated with batterers. I will treat these "disorders" as descriptive of behavior, attitudes, and motives rather than as evidence of "mental illness" or "disease," for the concept of mental illness is not always accurate or coherent.

Degrees of Psychopathology and Violence

Studies of the psychological traits of men who batter are of surprisingly recent vintage, for this particular question did not arouse research interest until the later 1980s.[74] Researchers are wary of developing a profile for batterers because they do not believe that batterers have one specific personality structure. But they have found several characteristics that battering men appear to possess in excess, including chronic alcoholism or substance abuse; a low threshold for anger or hostility, especially concerning women; depression; dependency; higher anxiety; low self-esteem; paranoia; dissociation from their own feelings; poor impulse control and rigidity; and antisocial tendencies, including a heightened need for control and dominance. One study linked these tendencies to such DSM-III disorders as borderline personality, narcissism or antisocial personality, dependent or compulsive personality, and psychopathic personality.[75]

More important for our purposes, researchers have constructed typologies of batterers that are associated with the degrees of violence they perpetrate. Edward Gondolf used a cluster analysis of interviews with more than five hundred battered women, and discerned four basic types of batterers in terms of psychological characteristics and quality of violence. Type I, the "sociopathic," comprised about 5 percent of the survey. The sociopathic type inflicts the most severe injury, batters and/or sexually violates his spouse and children, abuses alcohol or drugs severely, and generally has a long arrest record. Type II (32 percent), the "antisocial batterer," is severely abusive physically, but he inflicts less vicious abuse than the Type I sociopath (though he is more likely to have used weapons). Type III is the "chronic batterer" (30 percent) who subjects his victims to significant abuse, but less injuriously than Types I and II, and he is less likely to have used weapons in his assaults. Type IV, the "sporadic batterer," made up 33 percent of the total. This type wreaks the least severe verbal and physical abuse, and does so the least frequently. He often apologizes after his abuse episodes. His victims seek the police the least and are most likely to return after leaving the abusive relationship.[76]

Life with the worst abusers must be pure hell and a constant struggle to survive, especially if such men will not suffer their victims leaving them. One prison interviewee admitted, "[H]e had me so fearful I didn't even dare to breathe. Half the time it was like this."[77]

Alexandra Symonds distinguishes two types of violent (physically and psychological) spouse relationships in her critique of the theory that female masochism is responsible for woman beating: relationships based on the intrinsic violence of the man, and those shaped by the neurotic interactions that can arise in the marriage. In the latter case it is more feasible to talk about a subtle, equally shared form of masochism, but this concept should not be gendered, because both parties feed on their own and the other's suffering. The former cases are "tragic situations where the women are usually beaten over a period of years, often requiring hospitalization and sometimes losing their lives as a result of the beatings. They are terrorized victims of a situation where society has given tacit permission for a disturbed individual to vent his disturbance essentially without interference and without offering the victim protection or safety." [78]

In contrast to the psychopathically violent batterer who defines the reality of the relationship, in "neurotic interaction" violence represents a last resort or a byproduct of ongoing psychological jousting and conflict, as in Edward Albee's play *Who's Afraid of Virginia Woolf.* "Occasionally the husband strikes the wife in desperation," Symonds writes. "In other similar marriages there are outbursts of more serious violence. Both parties in such a marriage are neurotically bound to each other and each, in some important way, is insensitive to the other's needs." [79] In the latest research, Stets and Straus find that, controlling for self-defensive acts, that men and women initiate violence about one-quarter of the time each, and "that among couples where violence occurred, both partners are violent in about half the cases." [80] The gender-neutral approach of the Conflict Tactics Scale (Straus et al.) appears to be most valid in this type of context, which involves more equality between the parties. [81]

Dark Hearts

Violent relationships are often psychologically complex and dynamic, for the batterer's anger and abuse stem from emotional ambivalence about love objects. (He has trouble with "basic trust," according to Susan Hanks, and the couple often develops "psychological fusion" in which the woman "is emphatically attuned to the man in spite of the battering." See the discussion of "traumatic bonding" in the next chapter.) Both partners in this type of relationship fall prey to mutual dependency and isolation from others. [82]

Emotional ambivalence and emotional bonding can prevail in violent relationships. Researchers' work is replete with comments by women that they love their abuser, even after they have taken his life. Several of our prison interviewees expressed love for the man who was responsible for their plights. One interviewee, serving time for killing her husband while *she* was attempting to commit suicide, said, "I still love him very much. I still feel married to him. This may change in twenty to forty years." [83] Another confessed that she stayed in the abusive relationship because she was afraid to leave, but also because "I loved him. I'm still fighting that. Even though we're divorced, I still want to be with him. But yet, I can sit here and look and see what he does, and know it's not right, but yet there's a part of me that still wants to be in that relationship because that's what I know and grew up with . . . and I feel like I can change him."[84]

Such women can contribute to their entrapment by virtue of their romanticized vision of what the marriage can become and their refusal to face the difficult truth of the relationship's destiny. Caught in this contradiction, they oscillate between faith and hopelessness, a sense of power and a sense of powerlessness, self-esteem and depression (see below).[85] I quote Hanks's most salient observations that convey the tortuous path of torturous love:

> The man's experience of the woman's real or imagined withdrawal triggers his long-standing, unconscious fears of separation and abandonment against which he defends through the primitive mechanisms of splitting, projection, and projective identification. He splits off and projects his abandoned bad self—full of self-destructiveness, self-hate and self-derision—into the woman, whom he then batters in a desperate attempt to reestablish psychological fusion within the relationship and to mitigate his abandonment fears. In a reversal of his childhood role, he becomes the external abusive object battering his denigrated, hateful bad self.
>
> Violence may also express the rage resulting from the man's pathological belief that the woman has failed in her perceived role of shielding him from a terrorizing feeling of aloneness and consequent fears of psychological disintegration. He depends on her comforting, nurturing, and soothing functions to feel whole and good. . . . He batters her in a paradoxical attempt to "get her to stop withholding." The violent behavior is reinforced if, in fact, the battering results in a restoration of the woman's emotional attunement during the reconciliation stage of the repetitive cycle of violence . . .
>
> The woman also participates in the projective identification by introjecting and identifying with the split-off projections of the battering man. She experiences herself as hateful and bad. She believes the man's false accusations that she has failed in her emphatic role of adequately soothing him . . .
>
> As a consequence, the woman introjects and identifies with the man's projected hate and derision. She feels angry, ashamed, and embarrassed about the violence—but not outraged. . . . She is vulnerable to developing the battered woman's syndrome.[86]

The type of batterer Hanks describes exhibits emotional ambivalence toward women and the failure to construct a balanced and harmonious masculinity. I will call this the theory of "dark hearts," after a book of that title by Loren E. Pedersen. This theory integrates Toch's analysis of the defensive machismo mentality of violent men with psychoanalytic understandings of emotional ambivalence in relation to the feminine, and new feminist theory on the conflicts men have with object relations.[87]

Such psychoanalytic and feminist theorists as Alexander Mitscherlich, Nancy Chodorow, Camille Paglia, Jessica Benjamin, and de Beauvoir have depicted the way in which cultures premised on male "transcendence" vis-à-vis the feminine create deeply rooted tensions in the male psyche concerning gender identity. Public culture has been built by male transcendence from the mysteries and conditions of nature (symbolized by the feminine) and female nurturing; consequently, anxiety and ambivalence toward feminine qualities comprise part of the condition of masculinity. Chodorow unveils the travails of masculine identity in an order in which mothers are the primal objects of desire but male fear of the feminine is prevalent. The absence of fathers as integrated personalities accentuates the tendency toward negative identity:

> A boy, in his attempt to gain an elusive masculine identification, often comes to define this masculinity largely in negative terms, as that which is not feminine or involved with women. . . . Internally, the boy tries to reject his mother and deny his attachment to her and the strong dependence upon her that he still feels. He also tries to deny the deep personal identification with her that has developed during his early years. He does this by repressing whatever he takes to be the feminine inside himself, and, importantly, by denigrating and devaluing whatever he considers to be feminine in the outside world . . .
>
> Masculinity becomes and remains a problematic issue for a boy. . . . It involves denial of attachment or relationship, particularly of what the boy takes to be dependence or need for another, and differentiation of himself from another.[88]

Studies of batterers display such ambivalence repeatedly, and the presence of ambivalence propels both rage and Walker's cycle theory (see below).[89] The woman is seduced by the batterer's paradoxical need for love. The case of interviewee Ronda Richardson in Kenosha, Wisconsin, provides a key example of this type of personality. By all accounts, David Miller, the lifelong lover whom Ronda killed, was consumed by the need to assert his masculinity through violence and aggression. Ronda told her attorney, Gerry Mueller, that David's father had informed him that "I don't mind if you come home beaten up, so long as you put up a good fight. But I won't let you in the house if you ran like a coward." Ronda desired David and enjoyed being seen with him in public. In her interview with me, Ronda portrayed the relationship in a language of wonder. She had longed for his love since she was a little girl, and she admired his "cool" and swaggering demeanor.[90]

Psychopaths or men with other emotional problems can be very appealing, at least in the short run.[91] The fact of some sort of appeal poses a challenge to psychologies and theories of human nature that do not grasp the depths and intricacies of the human heart.[92] Earlier I quoted the head of Wisconsin's program of Legal Assistance for Institutionalized Persons (LAIP), who observed that some batterers possess an uncanny ability to select and control women who are vulnerable to their appeals. Even Walker provides accounts of battered women who felt "excited" about their abusers, though not the abuse. Some women stay out of fear or necessity, although "[o]thers believe that if they leave this marriage, they will never again find such sexual excitement. They may stay in the marriage until the brutality becomes more aversive than the reinforcement of sexual pleasure."[93] One of our interviewees described how the magnetic excitement generated by her father held her mother and others captive. A. V. W.'s father loved his children and wife but beat them severely. It took her mother years to pry herself away from him, not because he threatened to kill her if she left him, but because she loved him and found him so exciting. Though they split and divorced in 1986–88, her mother misses him and loves him "more than ever." Later, she could not bring herself to marry a secure, loving middle-class man because he would have condemned her to boredom in comparison to her ex-husband. Like Odysseus coping with the Sirens, A. V. W.'s mother takes precautions to avoid encountering her former husband whenever she picks up the children at his residence because she knows she will succumb to his spell:

> He's like Jekyll and Hyde. He can be so great, then turn. He was a tyrant. It wasn't a gender thing. It was ownership. He owned us. It was like a leader who is tyrannical but also takes care of you. Words that describe my father are "transcendence," "mystical," " magical," "captivating." When you are with him, he takes 100 percent of your attention. You forget about the rest of the world, about what is going on in the world, about the bad times. Everybody who meets him thinks this about him. He has real animal magnetism. We lived out in the country alone, isolated, totally self-sufficient, and we were never bored. For some it is addictive, like playing with fire. You think you can control it, but you can't.[94]

A. V. W.'s observations of her mother and father bring to mind Dorothy Allison's autobiographical literary portrayal of a mother's choice between the daughter she loves and the wounded, abusive man she loves. At the end of *Bastard out of Carolina*, Anney ("Mama") leaves her daughter Bone with her extended family to go off with Daddy Glen, whom the family has ostracized because of the way he has physically and sexually abused Bone. Mama confesses to Bone before she departs at the end of the prize-winning novel that "I just loved him." When Bone thinks of Daddy Glen, she feels his "black despair whose only relief would be death."[95]

But like Walker's clients, A. V. W.'s mother wanted the excitement without the abuse and left when the costs of the relationship exceeded the benefits. And Richardson killed her lover when (in her estimation) imminent deadly harm shone out of the darkness of his eyes. One can account for the psychological complexity of the bonds of love without making the "category mistake" of justifying or excusing battering, and without limiting a woman's right to defend herself from danger.

Theories of Battering Relationships

In this chapter we will look at battering relationships in terms of the responses of women, though we must bear in mind that the relationship is ultimately interactive. As a leading authority on the intersubjectivity involved in hypnosis remarks, "As in any intense relationship the motivations of the individuals involved are extremely complex and the behavior of each with regard to the other must be understood in the context of the total relationship. An explanation which purports to account for such behavior by singling out one aspect of the relationship—i.e., hypnosis—must be viewed with skepticism."[1] I will discuss three basic models or frameworks of battering relationships that are the most prominent and powerful. Battered women develop distinct mental states concerning different aspects of the relationship—distinctions that will prove important to constructing an appropriate legal policy based on the norms and standards of self-defense. BWS treats these mental states in a manner that obfuscates rather than clarifies the distinct issues at stake.

Walker and Learned Helplessness:
The Battered Woman as the Helpless Victim of a Cycle of Deceit

BWS in the Courts

Lenore Walker is the psychologist who published the Ur-book on BWS entitled *The Battered Woman* in 1979.[2] Although she did not testify, Walker recently gained further fame by being slated for a while as an expert witness for the defense in the O. J. Simpson case. She has developed a "cycle theory of violence" that explains the patterns of belief and behavior of allegedly typical battered women, and has been an extraordinarily successful activist and legal entrepreneur. By far the most prominent and authoritative source for the use of BWS in criminal trials, she heads Walker and Associates, a group of psychologists and advocates of battered women which deals with research and forensic practices concerning battered women. Probably 80 to 90 percent of the references in the case law refer to her and her work.

BWS arose in the late 1970s as part of the Weltanschauung of feminism and related political and legal movements. The first major work in the United States on the social problem of battered wives or spouses per se was Del Martin's *Battered Wives*, published in 1976, which followed the first work in Britain, Erin Pizzey's *Scream Quietly or the Neighbors Will Hear You*, published in 1974.[3] These and related works sprouted out of new knowledge of the prevalence of battering generated by the "shelter movements" in America and Britain, which burgeoned in the early 1970s with Pizzey's work in London.[4]

Early in the 1980s, courts were generally inhospitable to the new form of evidence, questioning its relevance to self-defense, whether it would assist the jury in its decision, and the reliability of the expert testimony. In 1981, the Supreme Court of Wyoming held in *Buhrle v. Wyoming* that BWS is inadmissible because of the undeveloped nature of BWS as a concept and the court's perception that most of the research on BWS was by advocates with a stake in the outcome of cases.[5] Perhaps the tenuous status of the self-defense claim in that case (see chapter 6) influenced the court's decision. In another 1981 case, *State v. Thomas*, the Ohio Supreme Court refused to admit BWS expert testimony because it concluded that self-defense issues are not beyond the comprehension (ken) of average jurors, and that BWS had not achieved "general acceptance" in the relevant scientific community.[6] But things would change.

In the late 1970s two major murder trials dealing with battered women defendants gained national attention: the Francine Hughes "burning bed" case, and the Jennifer Patri "burning corpse" case in Wisconsin (see below).[7] Within a year or two of these trials, pathbreaking research was reported on the psychology and sociology of battering. By the end of the 1980s, numerous organizations and institutes dealing with the legal defense of battered women had been founded, including the National Clearinghouse for the Defense of Battered Women in Philadelphia.

Just before Walker's *The Battered Woman* appeared, the Washington State Supreme Court furnished a harbinger of things to come by promulgating a gendered notion of self-defense in *State v. Wanrow* (1977). The Washington court held that courts should use a "reasonable woman" test which recognizes the actual beliefs of the defendant at the time of the attack. "The respondent was entitled to have the jury consider her actions in the light of her own perceptions of the situation, including those perceptions which were the product of our nation's 'long and unfortunate history of sex discrimination.' "[8] *Wanrow* spawned a series of cases that stressed the need to make the test for self-defense more gender-based and individualized.[9] This case set the stage for the widespread (if not total) acceptance of BWS in the 1980s. Seldom has a new brand of defense been so successful so quickly in terms of gaining admission as evidence in criminal trials. Stephen Schulhofer, a leading criminal law scholar, declares that "[t]he Walker approach has won extraordinarily rapid and widespread acceptance in the courts. Testimony on battered wife syndrome is now widely admitted, even in cases in which the abusive spouse was killed while sleeping, or ambushed by a hired killer."[10]

In 1979, the federal court of appeals for the District of Columbia in *Ibn-Tamas v. U.S.* became the first appellate court to deal directly with BWS testimony in the trial of a battered woman who killed her husband during an attack. The expert was none other than Walker herself. The court did not require that such testimony be admitted per se. It remanded the case to the lower court for a hearing on admissibility on the grounds that the testimony could be relevant to the defendant's perceptions of danger; at this hearing the lower court decided not to admit BWS.[11] But the call for a hearing opened the door to evidentiary considerations of BWS in subsequent cases. Since that time, literature and litigation dealing with the syndrome have mushroomed, and courts have considered BWS in a variety of contexts, including cases involving homicide or attempted homicide (usually linked to self-defense), duress (more recently), child custody, the validity of confessions, child abuse, and parties to crime.

In 1981, Maine's Supreme Court cited *Ibn-Tamas* in ruling that BWS was admissible in support of a self-defense claim on the grounds that it would have assisted the jury in understanding the woman's perceptions at the time of the fatal act. In the trial, the prosecution argued that the jury should not have taken the beatings seriously because the defendant could have left the relationship. The trial court had excluded BWS on the grounds that it would be irrelevant, prejudicial, and confusing to the jury. The BWS self-defense bus began to roll.[12] Other jurisdictions followed suit, including (in chronological order) courts in West Virginia,[13] New Hampshire,[14] Georgia,[15] Washington,[16] North Dakota,[17] Illinois,[18] New Jersey,[19] Florida,[20] Kansas,[21] California,[22] Kentucky,[23] Missouri,[24] and Canada.[25] Jurisdictions that had not admitted BWS in key cases by the early 1990s included: Wyoming (on grounds of the undeveloped state of BWS and the lack of evidence in the case at hand to support the need to resort to self-defense);[26] Louisiana (because the defendant in the case at hand did not plead insanity, the defense amounted to diminished capacity or partial responsibility, which the state did not recognize);[27] Missouri (BWS is irrelevant given lack of evidence in the case to sustain a self-defense plea);[28] and Oregon.[29] Though courts in these states had not admitted BWS, the legislatures in Louisiana and Missouri, as well as other states, have recently passed (or are considering) legislation designed to accommodate battered women's self-defense claims and BWS, and to create uniformity in state law.[30]

The Ohio Supreme Court's reversal of *Thomas* in *State v. Koss* brings into relief the transformation of legal doctrine and understanding that transpired during the 1980s. *Thomas* and *Koss* bracket a decade of profound change. Written by a woman justice, Alice Robie Resnick, *Koss* embraces many of the social, political, scientific, and legal changes that had taken place in the decade since the same court had handed down *Thomas*. Paying special attention to Walker's work, Resnick refers to legislative and case law changes in the intervening years, and to the growing acceptance of BWS expertise. "[S]ince 1981 several books and articles have been written on this subject. In jurisdictions which have been confronted with this issue, most have allowed expert testimony on the battered woman syndrome."[31] The *Koss* court then quoted Walker and *State v. Kelly:*

> "[The testimony] is aimed at an area where the purported common knowledge of the jury may be very much mistaken, an area where jurors' logic, drawn from their own experience, may lead to a wholly incorrect conclusion, an area where expert knowledge would enable the jurors to disregard their prior conclusions as being common myths rather than common knowledge." [Quotation from *Kelly*.]
>
> Thus, admission of expert testimony regarding the battered woman syndrome does not establish a new defense or justification. Rather it is to assist the trier of fact in determining whether the defendant acted out of an honest belief that she was in imminent danger or great bodily harm and that the use of such force was her only means of escape.[32]

Generally, expert testimony on BWS is admitted to dispel the common misconception that a normal or reasonable person would not remain in such an abusive relationship; to bolster the defendant's position by rehabilitating her credibility as a witness and/or lending credibility to her version of the facts; and to substantiate her belief that she was in imminent peril of death or serious bodily harm.[33] The objectives are crucial—the issue is whether BWS's psychological profile is the best means to achieve them.

Walker and others have advocated testimony on BWS for other reasons as well. First, they believe that women often kill their tormentors in nonconfrontational, "nontraditional" situations that do not fit the standards of self-defense (contract murders, killing while he is asleep or in a similar state of relaxation, or during a lull in the violence when the danger is not exactly imminent). This lack of fit leads to injustice because battered women often reasonably feel fear even in nonconfrontational settings, and postponing the deployment of defensive force until the moment of imminence imperils those who are weaker than their adversaries. Battered women feel "cumulative terror" because of the constant state of fear that pervades the relationship.[34]

Several cases deal with women who kill spouses who are asleep or otherwise incapacitated.[35] But the courts are divided on the use of self-defense instructions and the use of BWS in such cases that involve nonimminent danger. Several courts have declared BWS inadmissible in cases that do not involve self-defense as a matter of law.[36] Some states simply allow BWS expert evidence if the defendant establishes that she is a battered woman. In *Commonwealth v. Stonehouse*, the Supreme Court of Pennsylvania ruled that BWS was relevant to showing justification in the use of deadly force where the defendant had been shown to be a victim of psychological and physical abuse.[37] In *Chapman v. State*, the Supreme Court of Georgia held that BWS "is not a separate defense. Rather, evidence of the syndrome is admissible in an attempt to show that the defendant had a mental state necessary for the defense of justification although the actual threat of harm does not immediately precede the homicide."[38] And in *Fielder v. State*, the Texas Court of Appeals framed BWS along classic Walker lines, and then proceeded to hold that BWS is more relevant in nonconfrontational cases than in confrontational ones:

> Where the defendant acts in the absence of provocation it is obvious that testimony on the battered woman syndrome would be relevant to show the reasonableness of the defendant's fears and of the perceptions that such acts were necessary to protect herself under the circumstances. In the first situation, however, where the defendant acts in direct response to physical aggression by the batterer, the necessity of such testimony becomes more attenuated to the issue of the reasonableness of her fears as the extent of the provocation increases. As the level of the attack by the deceased batterer increases in intensity, the reasonableness of the defendant's fears becomes more obvious to the trier of fact.[39]

Other courts have tied BWS more strictly to the traditional parameters of self-defense. In *State v. Anderson*, for example, the Missouri Court of Appeals stated that "[i]n the case at bar the defendant did not make a *prima facie* showing from the evidence of the elements of self-defense justifying the use of deadly force. . . . The literal reading of [the state evidence statute] prohibits the battered woman syndrome where the defendant has not been able to raise the issue of self-defense. This is consistent with the law in other states."[40] *State v. Norman* took this approach to an extreme. The court held that Judy Norman merited no self-defense instruction despite her desperate situation because "[t]he imminence requirement ensures that deadly force will be used only where it is necessary as a last resort in the exercise of the inherent right of self-preservation."[41] In *State v. Manning*, an Ohio defendant explicitly linked BWS to mental states spawned by PTSD. She argued that courts should admit BWS "whenever a battered woman experiences a sudden flashback triggering an immediate fear of danger causing her to respond instinctively in self-defense." The court rejected this argument in ruling that BWS is designed to assist the trier of fact in determining whether the defendant acted out of an honest belief that she was in imminent danger and needed to resort to deadly force.[42] Again, this holding was shaped by the way in which Ohio frames self-defense law.

The second reason advocates support BWS is that they contend that BWS is necessary to counter myths about the way battered women behave, as well as prejudices that juries entertain because they "blame the victim." Recently courts have continued to use this logic of "disputing myths" as a rationale for admission of BWS testimony.[43]

Third, some feminists believe that women tend to think in terms of relationships and patterns more than men, so a theory that encapsulates patterns not only captures the nature of the fear and danger that bedevil the battered woman, but gives voice to "woman's way of knowing." Walker asseverates in *Terrifying Love*, "Women seem to see events as occurring in patterns rather than in discrete individual increments or incidents. . . . Patterns may be perceived, but usually they are not interwoven in the male mind with discrete individual incidents. Men, therefore, can more easily tell their stories using the rules of the legal system." [44]

The Key Tenets of BWS

The "cycle theory" and the theory of "learned helplessness" attempt to address these issues. Walker depicts three distinct phases to the cycle of violence that characterizes many relationships: the buildup of tension, the acute battering incident actuated by uncontrollable rage, and loving contrition. Battering reduces the victim to a state of fear and anxiety during the first two phases, stretching her perception of fear beyond the time frame of the battering episode. Cumulative terror grips the entire relationship. Thus, the imminence prong of self-defense doctrine is problematic because it purportedly envisions danger as divisible, recognizing danger and terror only in the face of specific acts. In addition, the woman's relative lack of power makes the proportionality requirement of self-defense a problem. The contrition stage reveals why a woman will stay after being beaten; her abuser fools her into believing it will not happen again. *The cycle theory is key to arguments of self-defense based on justification, for it explains what happens and why it is reasonable from the vantage point of the battered woman to feel danger outside the state of imminent harm and why it is reasonable for her to stay in the relationship.*

Later, with repetitions of the cycle, a battered woman's disbelief may vanish or wane, but by now she has fallen into learned helplessness. Learned helplessness and the dysfunctions that accompany it explain why she does not leave after it is unreasonable to believe he will improve. *Accordingly, the theory of learned helplessness is key to incapacity defenses.* In the end, *Walker's two theories are ingenious efforts to blend the logics of justification and incapacity excuse.*

As seen, the cycle theory explains the typical environmental cues of abuse and psychological states that a battered woman experiences and that make her reactions differ from those that nonbattered individuals would expect.[45] The theory of "learned helplessness" is crucial for reasons Walker pinpoints:

> In applying the learned helplessness concept to battered women, the process of how the battered woman becomes victimized grows clearer. Re-

peated batterings, like electrical shocks (in animal experiments), diminish the woman's motivation to respond. *She becomes passive.* Secondly, her cognitive ability to perceive success is changed. She does not believe her response will result in a favorable outcome, whether or not it might. Next, having generalized her helplessness, the battered woman does not believe anything she does will alter any outcome, not just the specific situation that has occurred. She says, "No matter what I do, I have no influence." She cannot think of alternatives. She says, "I am incapable and too stupid to learn how to change things." Finally, her sense of emotional well-being becomes precarious. She is more prone to depression and anxiety.[46]

Walker derives learned helplessness from the noted work of the behavioral psychologist Martin Seligman. Seligman administered electric shocks to dogs in cages from which they could not escape. Once it sank in that they could not escape, the hapless animals ceased making any effort to escape when the shocks commenced, even after the doors were opened. The animals "unlearned" this response (or nonresponse) only after being repeatedly dragged to the doors.

Seligman, then Walker, found that their human subjects reacted similarly to the dogs. Walker remarks:

> With people, Seligman found that it was the cognitive aspect of this syndrome, that is, the individual's thoughts, that proved all-important. In other words, even if a person has control over a situation, but believes that she does not, she will be more likely to respond to that situation with coping responses rather than trying to escape, similar to the way Seligman's dogs responded once they had "learned" helplessness. Thus, when people are involved, the truth or facts of the situation turn out to be less important than the individual's set of beliefs or perceptions concerning the situation. Battered women don't attempt to leave the battering situation, even when it may seem to outsiders that escape is possible, because they cannot predict their own safety; they believe that nothing they or anyone else does will alter their terrible circumstance.[47]

We will see that this statement is enlightening and problematic (not an unusual condition in reading Walker). The theory of learned helplessness helps capture the battered woman's plight, but in this statement Walker psychologizes it to such an extent (the "truth or facts of a situation turn out to be less important than the individual's set of beliefs") that she undermines battered women's capacities to be objective and reasonable. Although Walker and some courts have argued that because BWS is a form of PTSD it does not constitute a "mental illness," we will see *that PTSD defenses in other contexts almost always entail the absence of rationality and objectivity on the part of the defendant,* thereby posing difficulties for self-defense claims based on precisely these states or qualities.[48]

In 1984 Walker published her most scientific work, *The Battered Woman Syndrome,* which presents the results of her survey of several hundred battered women who responded to requests to be interviewed. The surveys showed that evidence of tension-building prior to battering existed in 65 percent of the cases, and that loving contrition existed in 58 percent of the cases.[49] In addition, Walker and her associates found high levels of substance abuse in batterers and abused women (more in batterers), and personality disorders associated with depression and threatened self-esteem. Walker's treatment of these issues is interesting.

Walker found in her major survey (using the CES-D scale) that battered women suffered depression at higher rates than her nonbattered control group, though women in battering relationships were less depressed than women who had left them, and women who had employment and other forms of activity and support suffered depression less than those without these opportunities. These results show that depression is a function of more than one variable, even in battering situations. But, as we have seen, battering as a *modus operandi* is often accompanied by the elimination or weakening of these opportunities that assuage the depressive effects of battering.[50]

Walker refers to Levinsohn's "behavior reinforcement theory" to explain why depression afflicts battered women more severely after leaving violent relationships. Reinforcement theory postulates that depression follows a sharp reduction in the quality and amount of positive reinforcements. Women leave when the negative reinforcement in such relationships outweighs the positive, and they return when life outside the relationship is unlivable—a classic example of Hobson's choice. "[C]linical reports consistently refer to battered women who return to their abuse because they were too lonely, too frightened, too overwhelmed, and too depressed to continue on their own."[51] Walker also refers to work in cognitive psychology that links depression to the sad realization that one cannot reach a desired goal, such as a decent marriage. Battered women often abandon hope.[52]

Walker and many other sources contend that battered women suffer lower self-esteem than other women, and court cases abound with this assumption. Nonetheless, the situation might be more complex than this portrayal suggests. Many battered women keep a flame of self-worth and agency going. As mentioned in chapter 3, Walker herself found that her battered women scored noticeably *higher* on the self-esteem scale than expected! Walker states,

> It was predicted that battered women's self-esteem would be quite low and our results, surprisingly, show the opposite. The women reported that they saw themselves in a more positive way than they perceived either

other women or men in general. Surprisingly, they perceived themselves as stronger, more independent, and more sensitive than other women or men. This finding of a positive self-image is unusual and inconsistent with current theories about battered women.[53]

Walker speculates that the battered women interviewees might have sought to please their interviewers by appearing to possess self-esteem, and that approval-seeking is consistent with BWS.[54] But interviewers might be more pleased by showings of lack of self-esteem, for that would comport with the theory of help-lessness they profess. Walker's fallback position is more convincing, though she acknowledges that it stands in tension with the findings concerning depression: "An alternative and more likely explanation is that battered women develop a positive sense of self from having survived in a violent relationship and that causes them to believe they are equal to or better than others. However, there is incompatibility between these high self-esteem findings and the reports of depression as reported in the CES-D results."[55]

Walker received another surprise in her findings concerning "locus of control." This concept relates to the issues of power and domination. Levinsohn's locus-of-control scale measures three types: "internal control," which deals with one's capacity to be in control of one's life; "powerful others," which concerns others' control over one's life; and one's belief in the role of "chance," which indicates how much influence one has over the course of one's life. Walker predicted that battered women would score "significantly higher" on the powerful-others scale and lower on the internal-control scale. Instead she found that

> Battered women, both in and out of the relationship, saw themselves as having a great deal of control over what happens to them.
>
> It may be that battered women do believe they control their own lives. Battered women often manipulate the environment in order to minimize the opportunity for the batterer to find a reason to be angry. Most of our sample indicated that to avoid getting the batterer angry they would, on a day-to-day basis, keep the kids quiet so as not to disturb him (84%); make sure the house was clean when he came home (84%); cook something they knew he would like (87%); avoid subjects they knew he did not like to discuss (91%); and avoid starting conversations with him, waiting instead until he began talking to them (70%). In addition, 40% of the women thought that they could sometimes control the batterer's behavior. It may be this sense of internal control that is the hope which allows the battered woman to believe she will be able to change the batterer or the environment in such a way that things will get better.[56]

Correlatively, Walker discovered, battered women scored no higher than the norm on the "powerful others" scale; that is, they did not view their lives as being controlled or dominated by others more than other women.[57] Walker surmises that battered women might not be able to admit that they suffer domination because that would compel them to admit the essential hopelessness of their situation.

Herman's "Complex Post-Traumatic Stress Disorder" and Captivity

In *Trauma and Recovery,* psychiatrist Judith Herman conceptualizes these effects of sustained abuse more within the logic of PTSD. However, she constructs a new notion of DSM categories and PTSD that takes more explicit account of the more complex symptomology in "survivors of prolonged, repeated trauma," such as victims of domestic sexual abuse or violence:

> The somatic symptoms of survivors are not the same as ordinary psycho-somatic disorders. Their depression is not the same as ordinary depression. And the degradation of their identity and relational life is not the same as ordinary personality disorder . . .
>
> The syndrome that follows upon prolonged, repeated trauma needs its own name. I propose to call it "complex post-traumatic stress disorder."[58]

Herman's symptom chart covering "CPTSD" includes specific references to the mental states engendered by interpersonal abuse and intersubjective relations, including: "sense of helplessness or paralysis of initiative"; "sense of defilement or stigma"; "sense of complete difference from others"; "preoccupation with relationship with perpetrator"; "unrealistic attribution of total power to perpetrator"; "sense of special or supernatural relationship"; "acceptance of belief system or rationalizations of perpetrator"; "loss of sustaining faith"; "sense of hopelessness and despair."[59]

Herman's construction of CPTSD addresses the totalistic control of battered women, which she captures in the central chapter of her book, on "captivity":

> Some battered women speak of entering a kind of exclusive, almost delusional world, embracing the grandiose belief system of their mates and voluntarily suppressing their own doubts as a proof of loyalty and submission. . . . Prolonged captivity also produces profound alterations in the victim's identity. All the psychological structures of the self—the image of the body, the internalized images of others, and the values and ideals that lend a person a sense of coherence and purpose—have been invaded and systematically broken down.[60]

DSM-IV (1994) provides an answer to Herman's plea with the new disorder "acute stress disorder," which follows PTSD in the manual and embodies terms drawn from the new psychology of violent victimization. This disorder deals with the traumatic consequences of experiencing, witnessing, or confronting "events that involved actual or threatened death or serious injury, or a threat to the physical integrity of self and others," and the victim's response "involved intense fear, help-lessness, or horror." [61]

Battered Women as "Survivors"

Many theorists and activists have challenged Walker's model of BWS, even though it still enjoys predominance in the criminal law. Women with criminal records or women who are not uncomfortable with using violence or other forms of aggression fall outside Walker's profile, and not all batterers are "contrite" along the lines of Walker's model. A new paradigm of battered women has gained currency in the fields of research and advocacy, though the first case I have encountered that discusses it was decided in 1992. This is the paradigm of battered women as "survivors." [62] Gondolf published *Battered Women as Survivors* in 1988. He and his associates gathered the largest samples of battered women ever taken (more than six thousand from Texas shelters), and learned that many women exerted positive efforts to deal with a difficult situation. Gondolf's studies indicated that "rather than being passive recipients of the violence," the women "appear instead as active participants in the definition of the relationship and of themselves. If anything, the battered women learn, as the abuse escalates, that the self-blame associated with learned helplessness is inappropriate." Battered women start seeking help as the overall context of the relationship becomes less caring and more dangerous. "[T[his survivor model implies more of a 'system failure' than a failure on the part of the battered woman." In this model learned helplessness might be a function of the trauma and anxiety a woman feels by separating from her mate when she arrives at the shelter. [63]

At this point many begin to look for help with police, shelters, or other forms of intervention. If these efforts fail, learned helplessness might set in and women might lose a sense of the "observing self," which is an attribute of reflective judgment and autonomy. With appropriate shelter or related help, however, *a new definition of self* can arise, phoenix-like: *the transition from helpless victim to survivor.* Many of our interviewees expressed the positivity of this "recovery" or transformation. A prison interviewee said that "I was a victim; now I am a survivor." [64] But she said this only from the vantage point of prison, not from within the relationship.

Masochism, Traumatic Bonding, Bonds of Love, etc.

Other approaches address the intersubjectivity of the battering relationship. These theories cast light on certain aspects of the battered woman's behavior and the relationship that the theories above leave in relative darkness, including the unwelcome fact that women are sometimes complicit in their own victimization. As Jessica Benjamin declares:

Even the more sophisticated feminist thinkers frequently shy away from the analysis of submission, for fear that in admitting woman's participation in the relationship of domination, the onus of responsibility will appear to shift from men to women, and the moral victory from women to men. More generally, this has been a weakness of radical politics: to idealize the oppressed, as if their politics and culture were untouched by the system of domination, as if people did not participate in their own submission. To reduce domination to a simple relation of doer and done-to is to substitute moral outrage for analysis. Such a simplification, moreover, reproduces the structure of gender polarity under the guise of attacking it.[65]

Benjamin's point reminds one that true equal respect is secured only by intellectual integrity and commitment to the truth (however entangled or ambiguous that truth might be), not by acknowledging only what is emotionally comfortable or politically expedient. Furthermore, acknowledging and fathoming the dialectical nature of battering relationships (and gender relations in general) does not begin to excuse batterers for their attacks. Nor does it compromise battered women's legal defense claims, which in the end should have nothing to do with the roles they play in sustaining the spousal relationship.

Masochism Reconsidered

Masochism is a dreaded theory that psychiatry has endorsed. The Freudian understanding professed that females are predestined to be masochistic because of psychodynamic factors peculiar to women's psychological development. Feminist theory and criticism have supplanted this theory with evidence that women are often *made* "masochistic" by experience. And masochism is no stranger to men. But the sadism/masochism binary opposition reflects the male/female opposition in Western culture. However unjustly, masochism is perceived as a feminine quality because it represents the "done to" and qualities of immanence.[66]

Although self-destructive behavior and emotions govern many cases of both male and female behavior, the reasons for the behavior are more social and political than the Freudian model stipulates. In *Sweet Suffering: Woman as Victim*, Natalie Shaines reformulates the psychoanalytical understanding of female masochism by emphasizing that women learn it culturally and developmentally (hence those who grow up in abusive homes are more likely to behave as their gender role models did).[67] Contemporary feminist theorists who accept revised notions of masochism provide a political and social interpretation by interpreting masochistic behavior as a way in which disempowered individuals can salvage a degree of control and influence in their lives. In a recent brilliant work that integrates literary, social, and psychoanalytical theory, Michelle A. Masse shows how gender relations in Gothic novels reflect the variety of avenues by which women of the time struggled to achieve recognition, power, and respect in a world dominated by men. Masse demonstrates how masochism is ultimately a destructive way to achieve a measure of control and recognition. Sadism is masochism's flip side, the mentality of the doer as opposed to the done-to. But sadism and masochism are bound by the same premise. In a logic that links depth psychology and social analysis to notions of "survivorship" (as well as an implicit critique of learned helplessness), Masse pursues the ways in which gender relations embody reciprocal forms of domination, even if one partner is the more powerful:

> In discussing masochism, I do not want to emphasize what is done *to* women without also examining what they are *doing*—the ways in which they use masochism as a strategy to create and maintain identity, not solely as a sad acknowledgement of absence. In trying to avoid either/or options of active/passive, agent/victim, I am arguing against a polarization that simply switches who's on top (but always assumes that one must be) and in favor of mutual and deeply problematic regulation through which both sadist and masochist define self and other . . .
>
> It is a basic coping strategy to defend the ego, one internalized by oppressed women and others . . .
>
> Thus, even within the confines of masochism, the girl simultaneously seeks security *and* freedom, and will continue to do so as best she can. The seeming passivity of masochism disappears the more we consider: its passivity is primarily that of means, while its end remains the activity refused the girl by her culture . . .
>
> The masochist attempts to bypass what Benjamin calls "the core conflict between assertion and recognition" by demanding that others recognize and love her precisely for her *non*assertion. Her silent suffering becomes her claim to fame. . . . Her appreciation and applause exonerate and exalt the noble victim . . .
>
> The masochist, then, can rework her enforced helplessness and pain so that, at least in fantasy, she gets the present she was promised for being a "good girl": recognition and love . . .
>
> The masochist seeks affirmation of her existence.[68]

Thus, masochism reflects the intersection of social situation and mental state. Like hysteria in the nineteenth century, it is a product of environment as mediated by the human need for recognition and power.[69] More broadly, masochism serves not only as a form of control and power for the weak (through the sanctification of suffering, as in Christianity, or by compelling the attention of the inflictor), but as a universal desire to escape the tensions of public and private relationships and responsibilities toward others. It offers relief from the extreme tensions that characterize love (and battering relations are often very tense and "wired").[70]

The discussion of masochism reveals that learned helplessness can itself be a form of survivalism, since such helplessness might partially assuage the tormentor by offering a sacrifice of the victim to satisfy the batterer's unquenchable inner need for violence or control. In *Violence and the Sacred*, Rene Girard portrays many forms of violence, including punishment, as a function of the need to sacrifice in the name of justice and retribution, to inflict suffering on a sacrificial victim (hence, the infliction of the criminal sanction is ultimately a form of sacrifice).[71] A batterer may be enacting an endless ritual of sacrifice and retribution for wounds inflicted in the morning of his life. His concrete victim is a substitute for a more ancient object of retribution. Attentive to his needs, the battered woman senses this pathological form of being an object of need. But this move by the battered woman is ironically a manifestation of agency, not passivity. Battered women might find solace and justification for their suffering through religion and comparison of their plights to religious martyrdom. Again, many of our and other researchers' interviewees have been very religious.

Walker holds that traditionalism disposes women and men to accept male superiority and, concomitantly, battering by males. But the role of traditionalism can be more complex and subtle than Walker fathoms. It can support a sense of self-worth based on preserving the marriage in the face of great stress and travail. Many battered women report feeling that they are the ones who hold their mate together, that their suffering provides a kind of redemption. Battered women normally long for the battering to disappear, yet the ways of the psyche can compel them to turn defeat into a twisted form of victory based on the rewards of suffering and the self-respect that can come from enduring such hardship. Job proved himself worthy of God. Is this one reason that Walker's sample reported higher self-esteem and locus of control than expected?

In the end, however, we must approach even the revised theory of masochism with great care. Although masochism can serve deep psychological functions in relation to oppressive or anxiety-ridden circumstances, it generates meaningful pleasure only when it is a freely chosen form of behavior, not when it is merely a desperate grasp at satisfaction in a tormenting environment. The psychology of masochism is complex, assuming idiosyncratic form in different relationships and in different contexts of power. Freely chosen masochism obviously differs from the significance some battered women might reluctantly adopt out of the necessity to retrieve a measure of meaning and significance in hellish circumstances. The latter is another sign of the will to power's refusal to die and the pleasure principle's cunning ability to adapt itself to any condition. Ultimately, the potential presence of "masochism" in battering relationships is but a rather curious signification of the treaties weakness enters into with oppression.

The discussion of "masochism" indicates that the will to power is amazingly pro-tean. Under the sway of the will to power, passivity (learned helplessness) is a weak form of agency. Pure passivity is an impossibility.[72] Thus, battering relationships can involve interdependencies. Batterers, as we have seen, are often desperately, if ironically, dependent upon their spouses. Dependency of a similar and different kind can characterize battered women. First, many feel responsible for their men because of their views about appropriate women's roles. Second, fear can seal the relationship in surprising ways. The batterer needs the victim for recognition and control, and the victim needs the batterer because he becomes the center of her existence. As Don Dutton and Susan Lee Painter remark, "The strength of the emotional ties between a woman and her battering partner is well-known to those who work with battered women. Lawyers, therapists, family court counsellors, judges and police are often surprised and frustrated by the apparent loyalty of women towards the men who beat them."[73] Several of our prison interviewees spoke hauntingly about their psychological bonding with their men. One was often handcuffed by her jealous boyfriend, who made credible threats to kill her if she left. She remarked that "I was in love with him, as crazy as it seems. People would ask me, 'How can you love someone who does that to you?' How *do* you explain it? I mean, I don't understand it because after my first ex-husband, I always said I'll never get in a violent relationship again."[74]

Dutton and Painter point to a number of reasons that battered women stay with their abusers, including exposure to domestic violence as children, psycho-logical factors involving self-destructive behavior, psychological dependency, and lack of access to social/economic resources. But not all battered women possess these characteristics or backgrounds. Consequently, Dutton and Painter look at the "dynamics of the relationship." They expostulate a theory of "traumatic bonding" in which the cycle of counterdependency begins with the man's assaults and severe dependency needs. Thus, the batterer bears responsibility for the dynamics of the relationship, especially for the physical abuse. But the woman enters a partnership as the relationship develops over time:

> The man attempts to restrict his partner's independent existence, which is a constant threat to his security; the woman, in hopes of avoiding ar-guments and reducing the accompanying violence, begins to organize her life completely around her partner and his demands. Her compliance le-gitimizes his demands, builds up a store of repressed anger and frustra-tion on her part (which may surface in her goading him or fighting back during an argument, leading to escalated violence), and systematically eliminates opportunities for her to build up a supportive network which would eventually assist her in leaving the relationship. Her compliance

makes her counter-dependent upon her partner, as she devotes herself completely to fulfilling his needs . . .

The dynamics of counter-dependency within the couple's relationship may contribute to the woman's inability to extricate herself from the relationship by creating a situation in which her moves toward separation are accompanied by increasing feelings of distress at losing a relationship upon which she is psychologically dependent.[75]

The bonding needs engendered by trauma cement the codependency. Captivity in situations of extreme power imbalance often compels the captive to bond more closely to the captor to gain as much control and sense of power as possible from the situation. Psychology now recognizes this phenomenon as the "Stockholm syndrome." The D.C. Circuit Court of Appeals, in the pathbreaking *Ibn-Tamas* case in 1979, based its decision to remand for a hearing on the admissibility of BWS expert testimony in part on the analogy between such testimony and psychiatric testimony in the Patricia Hearst case in 1976. The court deemed knowledge of psychological effects of beating and captivity to lie beyond the ken of the average juror.[76]

Four basic conditions spawn Stockholm syndrome: the captive believes the captor is capable of killing her; the captive cannot escape, so the captor holds the captive's life in his hands; the captor isolates the captive from outsiders; and the captor exhibits intermittent kindness toward the captive. The Sixth Circuit Court of Appeals discussed the hostage or Stockholm syndrome in 1987 in *U.S. v. Kozminski* and declared that the syndrome requires ten elements of severe deprivation and threats, mainly dealing with prolonged, vigilantly monitored captivity, withdrawal of emotional supports, and isolation.[77] Note the strictness of these standards.

As we have seen, battered women often confront such situations, though their cases are complicated (or dissimilar) because they have normally married or entered the relationship with the abuser voluntarily, so their love antedates the abuse. Also, the captivity analogy applies only to the more extreme forms of abuse and isolation. In such cases, the captive's personality changes, and a curious symbiosis can develop between man and woman, compelling the captive to forge an emotional bond with the captor, secured by the fear of death.

Anna Freud coined the concept "identification with the aggressor" to describe the basic form of ego defense against anxiety in traumatic situations.[78] Through such identification the ego attains a needed yet ultimately illusory sense of security and control. If severe abuse wreaks a form of "psychological murder," reaction by resorting to traumatic bonding enlists a first line of "psychological self-defense."

Anna Freud delineates the defense mechanisms of the ego as largely fantastical schemes that attempt to protect the ego from anxiety by virtue of ultimate denials of reality. In children and even adults, such mechanisms can be useful devices to help people through difficult times. But the danger of embarking upon too radical a denial of reality looms over this psychological maneuver, especially in such captive situations. Battered women in the more severe cases of captivity, accordingly, are tossed between hope and hopelessness until they face the painful truth of their situation. Again, however, we confront the fundamental tension: *although the woman might deny the truth about the destiny of the relationship, she usually develops a keen sense of what she needs to do to keep the batterer from lashing out, and when violence impends. These two mental states and the circumstances to which they refer are distinct.*

Several observers of the Stockholm syndrome speak of the way in which traumatic bonding arises from interdependency and a dialectic of fear and hope on the part of the battered woman. Dutton and Painter remark:

> During the third phase of the battering cycle, the batterer throws himself on his victim's mercy, reversing the power relationship between them dramatically. He places his fate in her hands—he will be destroyed, lost, if she doesn't rescue him by returning to the relationship. His behavior toward her, his pleas and his promises are likely to relieve her fears and make her believe that she has control, that he will change his ways, that the violence will not recur. . . . [T]he psychological consequence of the power dynamics during the battering cycle serves to create and strengthen trauma-based emotional bonds between the man and the woman which make long-lasting separation difficult or impossible to achieve.[79]

As seen in the discussion of battered women and PTSD, emotional arousal is an aspect of the special and even magical psychic states engendered by PTSD. The traumatic arousal of captivity can tighten the bonds of the relationship, making it something tormenting and special (this would constitute another appeal of "masochism" to pleasure). Herman captures this rather remarkable psychological reality:

> The same traumatic bonding may occur between a battered woman and her abuser. The repeated experience of terror and reprieve, especially within the isolated context of a love relationship, may result in a feeling of intense, almost worshipful dependence upon an all-powerful, godlike authority. The victim may live in terror of his wrath, but she may also view him as the source of strength, guidance, and life itself. The relationship may take on an extraordinary quality of specialness. Some battered women speak of entering a kind of exclusive, almost delusional world, embracing the grandiose belief system of their mates and *voluntarily* suppressing their own doubts as a proof of loyalty and submission. Similar

experiences are regularly reported by people who have been induced into totalitarian religious cults.[80]

Herman's observation suggests that some battered women are more or less *addicted* to their mates (so it is not simply a matter of lack of resources, opportunity, etc., as some advocates exclusively stress; remember the A. V. W. interview, and Bone's mama in *Bastard out of Carolina*). As Foucault has remarked, "If power were never anything but repressive, if it never did anything but to say no, do you really think one would be brought to obey it? What makes power hold good, what makes it accepted, is simply the fact that it doesn't only weigh on us as a force that says no, but that it traverses and produces things, it induces pleasure, forms knowledge, produces discourse."[81]

Interviewees express the yo-yo-like nature of their feelings about their batterers in language redolent of the dialectic under discussion. A prison inmate painted the most pertinent picture to one of my research assistants:

When I was listening to you . . . and Mr. Downs . . . talking about that love-hate [relationship], that's exactly how I felt. It was like, you love the person that's there when he's nice and everything, but you fall into that abuse, and you hate it. And I felt hopeless. He controlled me. Like I said, he seriously would snap his fingers and I would jump. That was the way it was. I was at his every command just to keep him peaceful so that there wouldn't be any more abuse or towards the kids . . .

Now that I got away from him, I can see where I was like that. But now, it's like I'm trying to break it, but . . . when I'm on the phone with him, it's really weird. I can get all fired up . . . "I'm going to tell him to do this and not be afraid," and as soon as I'm on the phone and he starts mentioning a threat of any little thing, right away I turn back into my old self and I do everything to please him. . . . It's like I get on the phone and I'm better off not even talking to him because I go right back into the old behavior.[82]

Though the evidence demonstrates that most battered women are glad to be free of the abuse, some stay within the traumatic security of such a relationship (perhaps like Vietnam veterans who perpetuate the conditions of war). John Burr, assistant district attorney in Dane County, told us that "I have had the same victim be the victim of three different men. She goes from one abusive relationship to another."[83]

The Stockholm syndrome's direct relevance only to the more extreme cases of domestic abuse is critical to legal policy concerning battered women who kill. First, it provides a powerful analytical means of distinguishing situations of necessity from non-necessity and, concomitantly, of justifiable from nonjustifiable resort to lethal force. Second, it deals with women being held hostage and under a constant threat of death. These predicaments will prove to be keys to the legal conundrum with which we struggle.

Herman's insight points us toward the last model of the battering relationship: Benjamin's theory of the bonds of love.

The Bonds of Love

Benjamin's theory of the bonds of love resembles the theories of traumatic bonding, but it goes further in two respects. First, it deals more fully with the phenomena of intersubjectivity, dependency, and the way the need for recognition (a manifestation of the will to power) is worked out in cases of personal domination. Second, the work integrates the phenomenon of bonding with critical philosophy (in particular Hegel), revisions of psychoanalysis, and critical social theory. In the end, Benjamin crafts a thorough and subtle account of the psychological manifestations of patriarchal society.

Benjamin's theory centers on the "longing for recognition" in men and women, and how this longing often leads to domination and submission in a world structured as ours has been. Domination and submission are the products of failure to achieve mutual recognition in a culture bound by sexism and family relations in which men can achieve independent existence only by separating themselves psychologically from their mothers (who are the first object of desire in their infantile lives and, consequently, the symbolization of the feminine) at the same time that they need feminine recognition to confirm that existence. Male transcendence requires not only female acquiescence but also female appreciation and reflection. As Virginia Woolf expresses it in language and imagination that anticipated de Beauvoir by some twenty years, "Women have served all these centuries as looking-glasses possessing the magic and delicious power of reflecting the figure of man at twice its natural size. Without that power probably the earth would still be swamp and jungle." [84] But as Woolf knew so well, women also desire recognition, so struggle is inevitable. Along these lines, Benjamin observes, "domination and submission result from a breakdown of the necessary tension between self-assertion and mutual recognition that allows self and other to meet as sovereign equals." [85]

The focus on recognition and intersubjectivity follows contemporary object-relations revisions of psychoanalysis (a revision pioneered partly by theorists who see the self in more relational terms than Sigmund Freud did). "The concept that unifies intersubjective theories of self development is the need for recognition. A person comes to feel that 'I am the doer who does, I am the author of my acts,' by being with another person who recognizes her acts, her feelings, her intentions, her existence, her independence. Recognition is the essential response, the constant companion of assertion." [86] Unfortunately, the ineluctable failure to achieve adequate recognition instigates power struggles and anxiety (separation), which all too often turn into aggression, for aggression compels recognition and can relieve troubling anxieties. Domination follows from the essential tension between assertion and recognition.

Benjamin turns to Hegel to illuminate the key paradox of recognition (recall the reference above to the Hegelian master-slave relationship):

> Hegel analyzed the core of this problem in his discussion of the struggle between "the independence and dependence of self-consciousness" and its culmination in the master-slave relationship. He showed how the self's wish for absolute independence clashes with the self's need for absolute recognition. In Hegel's discussion two hypothetical selves (self-consciousness and the other, who is another self-consciousness) meet. The movement between them is the movement of recognition; each exists only by existing for the other, that is, by being recognized. But for Hegel, it is simply a given that this mutuality, the tension between asserting the self and recognizing the other, *must* break out; it is fated to produce an insoluble conflict. The breakdown of this tension is what leads to domination.
>
> The need of the self for the other is paradoxical, because the self is trying to establish himself as an absolute, an independent entity, yet he must recognize the other as like himself in order to *be* recognized by him.[87]

Benjamin's understanding of the paradoxes of recognition and freedom unlocks the meaning of many battering relationships. On the one hand, batterers' needs for power and control, as we have seen, seem to embody deep and powerful needs for recognition and dependency, for everlasting devotion to counter the fear of abandonment. On the other hand, battered women might seek recognition in the forms available to the oppressed. They often love their mates, however traumatically, and attempt to salvage respect and recognition in a variety of seemingly self-destructive ways. Like good mothers, they acknowledge and serve their man's desperate need for recognition, even in the form of domination. He fears her absence (established primordially in the Oedipus metaphor and relationship), the "lack" that is key to being an object of desire (but the omnipresent possibility of absence or lack is the very condition of desire).[88] And if the model of traumatic bonding holds, she joins him in this paradox of desire, becoming acutely aware of his needs and fearing abandonment as much as he.

Benjamin's model also casts light on the deadly turn these ambivalent relationships can take: when he no longer needs her presence or positive recognition, her humanity and conscious existence are suddenly thrown in jeopardy. Recall the interview with Nora Cashen quoted above, in which Cashen portrayed the mental and ethical states of battered women as a kind of "liminal" and "extraordinary" sensitivity. Bound intensely by intersubjectivity, battered women such as Judy Norman often perceive this shift with extraordinary acuity. By the time Norman killed her sleeping husband that night in Carolina, death had already written its signature on their relationship.

In some cases, the circle of such domination ineluctably proceeds toward numbness, deadness, and even death; the tension between domination and recognition is too hard to sustain, and satisfaction seeks deeper abuse, a process that furthers the obliteration of the object of recognition. As Sartre and Kristeva have discovered, nothing is static in the life of love except deadness. "The psyche is one open system connected to another, and only under those conditions is it renewable. If it lives, your psyche is in love. If it is not in love, it is dead. 'Death lives a human life,' Hegel said." When relationships of domination reach this stage, violence could be near. Days before she stabbed him, Ronda Richardson dreamed of David Sherman in heaven, which is in line with Browne's finding that women often resort to violence because they perceive destiny crossing a fatal line.[89]

Conclusion: Implications for Policy

We can glean several points from the discussion in this and the preceding chapter, which will serve the policy analyses below. First, battering relationships differ in terms of severity. Though the facts surrounding the fatal act in each case are ultimately most important, the severity of the battering is important in the woman's subjective understanding of danger and the reasonableness of this determination. The severity is also highly relevant to "mistake of fact" defenses (perfect versus imperfect self-defense), which is one of the critical issues in such cases. If one uses deadly force based on a *mistaken* belief in the necessity of such action, one is excused if the mistake is reasonable (or if, in the Model Penal Code formulation, one has not made the mistake of fact negligently or recklessly).[90] If the mistake is unreasonable, culpability exists, though the laws in different jurisdictions vary: some make one guilty of murder, others of manslaughter, others of nothing at all.[91] Mistakes of fact must be excuses rather than justifications because the act itself is wrong based on the objective facts. But if the mistake is reasonable, wherein lies the culpability? Mistakes of fact are crucial to the issue of the legal culpability of battered women. *When all the smoke clears, it seems that BWS and related reform are basically attempts to open our eyes to the actuality and/or reasonableness of the woman's perception of danger.*

Prior severe abuse does not in itself justify resort to deadly force in the case at hand; conversely, the absence of prior severe abuse does not disqualify a woman from reacting with deadly force. But prior abuse can shape a battered woman's perception of what is impending; thus, even if she is wrong about imminent danger, her mistaken belief might be reasonable given the circumstances. *As Dutton,*

Blackman, Benjamin, and others show, each relationship takes on patterns and an inter-subjective intensity that sharpen the woman's perception of danger. This is a crucial point that will comprise the heart of my legal policy recommendations. *And BWS per se has little to do with this observation, except to the extent that it illuminates the nature of cumulative terror and the sharpness of the battered woman's perceptions. Its ultimate use is to ward off misconceptions (e.g., if she was in such danger, why did she not leave the relationship?) that can be dealt with much more efficiently by straight-forward jury instructions rather than by complicated and questionable psychological inquiry.*

Second, the concept of learned helplessness is problematic because it entails a degree of passivity that is unlikely to be present. Battered women employ forms of power that are available to the oppressed; but such strategies are weak forms of the will to power, not abandonment of the will to power. As Nietzsche, Foucault, and Benjamin teach in their different ways, there is no such thing as the abandonment of the will to power (even suicide is a manifestation of the will to power). The portrayal of the state of battered women as learned helplessness constitutes shallow psychology. Grasping this point reinforces the movement away from incapacity excuse as a legal ground for dealing with the responsibility of battered women who kill.

The interview with Nora Cashen, quoted above, reinforces the claim that battered women often develop heightened sensitivity to the various dimensions of their situation. It also challenges a simplistic notion of learned helplessness. If the bonds of brutal love deaden in some respects, they can heighten awareness in other respects. "Many battered women have liminal experiences outside the realm of ordinary experience. It's not meditative, but it's a sense of being outside of ordinary experience. . . . A lot of hyper-vigilant behavior, monitoring his behavior to know all the time what he is up to. They become experts of his cues, very externally motivated, they don't think of themselves. They monitor their own behavior to see what they can do to maintain control over the situation." [92]

Third, three conditions of battering relationships stand out as relevant to criminal defense claims:

1) The presence of rational fear for life or bodily integrity. This fear—rather than learned helplessness and other factors of BWS (low self-esteem, depression, etc.)—should be the fulcrum of legal policy, for its implications for self-defense are clear, powerful, and principled. Emphasis on fear also keeps legal policy within the parameters of liberal theories of justice instead of the questionable tenets of victim ideology.

2) The presence of captivity in terms of hostage syndrome. Individuals have a right to resort to all necessary force to extricate themselves from illegal forms of captivity. Although the situation of battered women typically differs from kidnapping or related forms of hostage captivity, severe battering accompanied by threats

of death if the woman separates herself from the batterer (Mahoney's separation thesis; the *Norman* case) are analogous. I will address the appropriateness of using kidnapping and captivity models as backup defenses to the law of self-defense.

The twin factors of fear and captivity make up the Archimedean point of legal justice in this domain. No one (including a spouse) has the right to threaten one with destruction or to hold one captive in these senses. These factors provide a rationale for justifying the use of liberatory force as the most rational way to secure freedom. Such relationships embody Hegel's portrayal of the master-and-slave relationship, which logically entails the confrontation of life and death rather than the communal dialectic and struggle of recognition that Benjamin depicts. The realm of captivity is governed by Hobbesian necessities that differ profoundly from the travails and conflicts that bedevil the normal struggles for equal respect. We will see in later chapters that we must be careful to distinguish these two realms of fear and gender conflict, and that the syndrome/victim ideology worldviews threaten to collapse these realms. But the fact that these undiscriminating philosophies fail to draw proper lines does not mean that there is not a realm of brutal victimization. Denial of this reality is as bad a form of inconsiderate judgment as the ideological aggrandizement of the realm of deadly peril. Later I will suggest that the law of self-defense be modified to take the domestic realm of deadly danger more fully into account.

3) The concept of "syndrome" is of less utility to the resolution of these issues than its advocates proclaim. The evidence in this chapter shows that psychological trauma and dysfunction do accompany battering, but (à la Szasz's notion of the paradox of "diminished capacity") battered women typically develop a heightened rationality and interpretive awareness of the batterer's actions and impending intentions. When it comes to the crucial issue of reasonably perceiving deadly danger, battered women may have broken wings, but they have the eye of the eagle. Should the law focus on the helplessness of their wings, or the sharpness of their vision? BWS attempts to balance unreason and reason, incapacity excuse and justification. This merger is confusing and, ultimately, contradictory. A and not-A cannot join to form a reasonable defense. BWS unnecessarily complicates analysis, and it seems to represent expediency more than justice.

Finally, the presentation of the often complex intersubjectivity at stake raises a very important point: *even if battered women are in some cases morally responsible for not escaping or for contributing to the perpetuation of the relationship, this does not mean that batterers are any less culpable, or that the women forfeit any of their right to defend themselves from imminent or impending harm.* As Richard Rosen notes, there is a telling difference between responsibility in this sense and legal fault.[93]

Character is irrelevant to criminal culpability, and to the right to be safe from victimization. A woman who wears scanty clothing to a bar deserves to say "no" to sexual overtures as much as a nun. A drug dealer has the right to defend himself against a dissatisfied customer who stalks him on the street. A battered woman has the right to defend herself regardless of the reasons she returned to the relationship. Defendants use BWS primarily to show why they did not leave, thereby making the jury less likely to hold their failure to leave the relationship against them, or to assume that their failure meant the violence they confronted at the fatal moment was insufficiently threatening. But to the extent that BWS dwells on the whole relationship, it can actually accentuate these associations (see below). Would we not achieve greater clarity by simply abandoning BWS, except in insanity-related defenses?

Let us now turn to part 3, in which I will explore the positive and negative aspects of BWS in detail.

PART **III** *BWS Reconsidered: Weighing Positive and Negative Consequences*

CHAPTER FIVE

Positive Aspects: BWS and the Narrative of Abuse in Law and Society

In discussing the positive contributions to knowledge and pragmatic life by BWS, we will unavoidably encounter problems which will set the stage for critiques. First, however, let us look at several matters: legal applications in formal hearings and trials, informal bargaining contexts, and other pragmatic as well as symbolic uses; as well as at the importance of creating what I will call a "narrative of abuse," since such a narrative brings the victimization perpetrated by batterers into stark relief. At the same time, however, a narrative of abuse threatens to turn into "victimization ideology" if it is accepted without critical thinking. This tension or seeming contradiction stems from the fundamental tension of this book: that victimization needs to be recognized and provided for without abandoning the standards of responsibility upon which the criminal law, the law of self-defense, and constitutional freedom depend. The difficult trick we must attempt to perform is to establish legal standards that account for the severity and dangers of abuse without forsaking the principle of responsibility. In other words, there is a difference between understanding and appreciating the enormity of victimization and endorsing a form of judgment that eschews drawing the lines that balance such understanding with the normative standards of criminal law. In the subsequent chapters we will see that BWS fails to draw the lines that make possible responsible sympathetic judgment. But justice cannot be achieved without vehicles that convey the enormity of abuse in legal contexts, as the present chapter will show. Later I will draw on the evidence of this and other chapters in order to ascertain what factors of this knowledge to maintain and build on in making policy recommendations.

Legal Hooks and the Narrative of Abuse

We were struck by the variety of ways that our various interviewees interpreted the term "BWS." Prison inmates approached the term with care; deciding that one is a battered woman is not easy because the term carries an existential meaning or label that constitutes a redefinition of the self or an acknowledgment that one is a victim. Some interviewees were reluctant to adopt this label because they believed they had not been beaten enough to justify its use, or because it did not comport with their self-images. One defined a battered woman as one "whose husband beats them all the time when they don't do what they want or they don't have sex with them enough or they just don't like anything they do. They beat the heck out of them. No, I don't consider myself a battered woman. . . . Black eyes, busted teeth— that's a battered woman."[1] Others accepted the label the way an alcoholic faces the truth of addiction; only by accepting hard truths about oneself or one's predicament can one rise above one's situation. Finally, others used the designation as a reason to feel less culpable for what they did: after all, they were battered. Other interviewees jumped back and forth between definitions or interpretations tied to usage in courts and uses appropriate to therapy, shelter work, and social/political advocacy. Evidently the designation BWS bears different meanings depending on the context, purpose(s), and institutional use of the term.

Though such lawyers as Holly Maguigan contest the point, others aver that BWS provides a legal basis for introducing considerably more evidence about the nature of the abusive relationship than was the case in the past. Of course, the discretion of trial judges is great, so much depends on their judgment. Still, several interviewees who have handled battered woman homicide cases have stressed that the use of an expert to testify about BWS compelled the judge to allow much more background evidence than they had previously seen admitted. Mueller told me that "there is no way I would have been allowed to get in all that evidence about him [the batterer]" had the judge in the *Richardson* case not allowed BWS testimony about self-defense. The reason: self-defense doctrine per se sometimes highlights only the incidents immediately surrounding the act and leading up to it. In *Richardson* the evidence might have contributed to the jury's finding the defendant guilty of second-degree reckless homicide rather than first-degree reckless homicide or first- or second-degree intentional homicide. But jurors told us that the expert testimony that followed the Walker line did not impress them; instead, they zeroed in on the extent and nature of the danger Ronda confronted at the time of the stabbing, and whether Ronda reacted appropriately to it.[2]

Two other defense lawyers have fared better. In Madison, public defender Dennis Burke secured probation for Lisa Skalaski because the psychological reports showed a very victimized woman who had no history of violence. Though the experts who prepared psychological reports differed in their approaches (see the next chapter), they agreed that Skalaski suffered severe mental problems. Burke informed us that BWS helped his client's cause in at least three respects. First, it supplied an important "legal hook" upon which to hang the defense argument. In other words, BWS serves legal pragmatism: "A defense attorney looks for all plausible theories to apply what happened to the law and to make sense of things to the jury. BWS is certainly one of those hooks." Robert Donohoo, an assistant district attorney in Milwaukee County, said the same thing about all the new syndrome defenses: "That's what they all come down to: new legal hooks for making a case." Second, Burke pointed to the legal culture in Madison, which has accepted the logic of BWS and the new knowledge about domestic abuse.[3]

Third, BWS and related knowledge served to remake the meaning of Lisa as a person. Burke said the history of her abuse uncovered by professionals made her "the quintessential victim. . . . Everyone felt pity for her." Skalaski became redefined by the victim narrative that has such currency today. But as in the case of Ronda Richardson, the narrative did not arise from her own creative powers. It was placed upon her by mental health, legal, and shelter professionals. After interviewing her, Evan Gerstmann told me, "It was clear that her story was no longer her own. It had been taken over by the system."[4] Perhaps Skalaski's amnesia about her childhood (see chapter 6) encouraged redefinition, for her victimhood took place upon a *tabula rasa*.

Dale Cobb of Charleston, South Carolina, is one of the leading battered women attorneys in the country; he was a keynote speaker at the first national conference on PTSD and the law, held in 1993 in Colorado. When I asked Cobb about what BWS meant to him, he spoke about the same legal hooks, and how BWS had to be tailored to the specific excuses and justifications in particular states. But then he talked about BWS as a signifier of a deeper understanding, an epistemic shift that amounted to a form of consciousness-raising:

> It certainly opened up my mind. In lectures I claim I'm a "recovering male chauvinist." Three times prior to my first BWS case I argued successfully with the prosecutor or judge to get charges dismissed or reduced against a woman who attacked her husband, only to find out later that two of the husbands were eventually killed by my clients, and that in the other case the husband killed the woman. The old way wasn't in the best interest of my clients. The "good old boy" system being what it is, I sent her [the woman whose husband killed her] back into the danger without thinking about the whole process. The whole system just turned its back on women in this situation.[5]

But another interviewee, Seeger of Dane County Advocates for Battered Women, expressed reservations about the empirical accuracy of BWS as a portrayal of the battering relationship, and she questioned its utility as a therapeutic formula for battered women even as she acknowledged its forensic uses:

> The Walker theory comes under a lot of fire by people in the domestic violence field. *Politically* it is not so widely accepted. But it is a *useful* tool for defense attorneys and advocates. . . . I don't like the application of mental health terms to the victims of domestic violence, as each victim's

circumstances are unique. There is always a danger of applying one theory to everybody. It is useful to categorize, but a problem, too. In our area, we seldom use words like that ["syndrome"] because we recognize the problem of pigeonholing. I am an expert witness in cases, so I will use BWS in court: but not in the context of my other work and in training people. What I use in these other areas is a theory of power and control. [So it is a conscious decision on your part to use BWS in one context, but not in others?] Absolutely. In other contexts I would love people to grasp the "political" context of my work. But they often need the authority of empirical studies. They don't understand the political context.[6]

The emphasis on consciousness and legal culture reveals a narrative function of BWS. Like all such functions, BWS draws on a larger cultural narrative that differs from the sexist culture Walker presupposes is prevalent. Though advocates of BWS often portray it as embattled, Schulhofer is right in declaring that "[t]he Walker approach has won extraordinarily rapid and widespread acceptance in the courts . . . even in cases in which the abusive spouse was killed while sleeping, or ambushed by a hired killer."[7] BWS could not have achieved the success it has enjoyed without the connection with the new worldview of victimization. In *Reconstructing Reality in the Courtroom*, W. Lance Bennett and Martha S. Feldman emphasize that "most social action is problematic. Almost any act can be associated with diverse causes, effects, and meanings."[8] Facts do not always speak for themselves unless there is social consensus about the normative meaning of the act. When social and legal norms are contested, as they certainly are in the new politics and law of victimization syndromes, what one "makes" of an erstwhile criminal act will depend on one's normative assumptions and the narrative that surrounds the act. This understanding underscores the importance of narrative in the courtroom. Bennett and Feldman state:

> Perhaps the most significant application of the storytelling perspective involves clarifying the nature of bias in the justice process. Stories are symbolic reconstructions of events and actions. People who cannot manipulate symbols within a narrative form may be at a disadvantage even when, as witnesses or defendants, they are telling the truth . . .
>
> The inadequate development of setting, character, means, or motive can, as any literature student knows, render a story's action ambiguous. In a novel or film, such ambiguity may be an aesthetic flaw. In a trial, it is grounds for reasonable doubt.[9]

This understanding does not mean that juries are free to play loose with the facts. Facts and traditional notions of the truth are crucial. But facts must be applied to legal standards and notions of proper conduct. Bennett and Feldman refer to the absence of a brainwashing defense in the Patricia Hearst trial. Although her chief attorney, the famous F. Lee Bailey, "outgladiated" the ostensibly overmatched and less dramatic prosecution, the otherwise sympathetic jury found Hearst guilty because the defense had not provided a rationale that supported the story of innocence. The defense argued that Hearst was physically coerced, but she had many opportunities to escape, so this interpretation was undercut at every turn. A defense of brainwashing would have supplied the missing bridges. "A new norm would emerge here as a basis for other categorical and empirical connections: persons who have been brainwashed should not be held accountable for their subsequent behavior. This understanding could have provided consistent connections for the defendant's numerous failures to escape her captors. . . . This example suggests in graphic terms that issues of truth or fact in our adjudication (and social judgment) processes are intimately tied to the form and content of the stories in them." [10]

Abuse narratives create a logic about the woman in relation to legal standards. As we have seen, Walker envisions herself as a storyteller. "Once battered women are allowed to speak, they will be able to tell their own stories. And to know a battered woman's story is to understand, without a doubt, why she has killed." [11] Faith McNulty's bestseller about the "burning bed" case is a literary version of what Walker and like advocates hope to attain in court. Only the heartless can read *The Burning Bed* without being captivated by the power of the narrative, which dramatizes Francine's victimization and her desire to transcend the state of immanence and bondage to which Mickey had subjected her. [12] Victimization narratives in the courtroom and elsewhere can release truth from the bondage of denial.

The results in the *Bobbitt* case reveal the potential success of the narrative and new knowledge in the presence of other salient factors. Seldom will a new narrative succeed without support from established beliefs or norms. Jurors told the press that John Bobbitt was simply not a believable witness, and that they took the legal standards of insanity seriously. In addition to these more traditional aspects of the interpretation of evidence and testimony, Lorena presented herself as a good, traditional, Catholic wife whose hopes for a decent marriage were betrayed by John's depravity. A defense attorney, Lisa Kemler, told the country that "[a]t the time when Lorena Bobbitt cut off her husband's penis, she was a battered woman in the classic sense." [13] The press quoted one law professor who declared that the defense strategy was to drape the case in a new narrative based on new public opinion.

The reason, [Professor Charles] Weisselberg believes [that the jury found Lorena not guilty by reason of insanity] . . . is the new, heightened attention to sexual and physical abuse within families. Lorena Bobbitt claimed that before slicing her husband's penis, she remembered all the times he physically abused her, and "all the put-downs and insults he told me." . . . The jury knew that in a high-profile case its verdict would be scrutinized. Having accepted her account . . . the jury seems to have simply chosen the most convenient legal avenue of acquittal, the insanity defense. By creating an atmosphere of support in the press and in the courthouse, the defense let the jury know that a not-guilty verdict would be acceptable.

This strategy harkens back to the Jennifer Patri case in Wisconsin, in which defense attorney Alan Eisenberg engineered favorable publicity in the first trial to actually use BWS.[14]

Of course, this strategy also threatens to spill over into victim ideology, since Lorena's narrative of victimization camouflaged standards concerning her responsibilities for her own actions outside the context of self-defensive necessity. In the absence of imminent harm, her act appears to have been motivated by revenge and vigilante justice. And by painting herself as the perfect, pure victim who finally snapped, Bobbitt buttressed a stereotype of victimhood which could create problems for battered women defendants who do not conform to the stereotype. Syndrome defenses indebted to such profiles play with a double-edged sword.

Rewriting the narrative also furnishes an opportunity to shift the attribution of responsibility, which is influenced by more than simply "discovering" causation. David G. Myers observes in *Social Psychology*, "We find causes where we look for them."[15] BWS's focus on the nature of the abuse creates an opportunity to construct a victimization narrative that shifts responsibility for the woman's crime to the batterer. In his closing argument to the jury in the *Richardson* case, Mueller labeled the deceased "that diabolical man."[16] Some commentators with long experience in criminal law contend that this strategy is a psycho-scientific version of the classical "son of a bitch" defense.[17] Stephen Hurley, a prominent Madison lawyer whom we interviewed, said,

> I'm also going to raise it [BWS] because of the sympathy of the syndrome effect. I'm hoping that at the end of the case, if we try it, that the jury is ready to jump out of the box and strangle the husband. Look, if BWS didn't arouse sympathy, there wouldn't be so many shows about it on the TV movie of the week. It sells.
>
> [So you use BWS to get the jury's sympathy?] You're damned right![18]

Attribution theorists maintain that we adopt different perspectives depending on whether we are observing or acting. When we observe others, we tend to attribute control to them because the actors are at the center of our field of perception;

when we act, however, we do not perceive ourselves but rather the environment around us. (The latter attribution perhaps serves self-interest in the Sartrean sense that we illegitimately deny our own responsibility, but it also stems from our inability to see our faces except in the mirror or other reflections.)[19] Time is another factor, because the influence of the situation diminishes in our recollections as time marches on. The particular objects that we observe also influence attribution. Myers describes an interesting example: "In another experiment, people viewed a videotape of a suspect confessing during an interview by a police detective. If they viewed the confession through a camera focused on the suspect, they perceived the confession as genuine. If they viewed it through a camera focused on the detective, they perceived it as more coerced."[20]

Criminal law concepts of excuse and responsibility present many opportunities for such discretionary balancing. One can construe the criminal act and the defendant in terms of narrow or broad time frames, personality, and intention. For example, in self-defense cases, do we simply look at what triggered the criminal act, or at the broader relationship between the victim and the defendant? BWS beckons us to "open up" or to "broaden" the meaning of the criminal acts of battered women. Set against a history of abuse, such women appear less blameworthy, especially if the ultimate victim of their actions is the main perpetrator of the abuse they suffered. The application of concepts such as duress, provocation, and self-defense will vary depending upon how broadly or narrowly we construe the defendant, the victim, the relationship, and related factors.[21]

Studies have shown that people appear more willing to excuse or justify erstwhile criminal behavior when another source is available that enables them to attribute the blame to someone other than the direct perpetrator. Research has shown that to vindicate the deep desire to see the world as just (the "just world" hypothesis based on the notion that someone or some thing should be blamed) people need to be able to attribute responsibility for harm. The more diffuse and less identifiable or discrete the environmental factor, the more blame will reside with the actor. Conversely, the more identifiable and discrete the environmental factor or the stressor, the more willing people will be to shift blame away from the actor. As we have seen, juries might divine a difference between batterers (who are readily identifiable) as stressors and such diffuse things as war or PMS.[22]

Attributing blame in self-defense cases is also influenced by background social factors. In his thoughtful book on the Bernard Goetz case, George Fletcher explains that there are four competing underlying paradigms of self-defense law, and that social conditions affect the respective weight each model will carry in a particular case. Individualist models focus on autonomy and the rights of the target of aggression, downplaying the need for proportionality in the resort to lethal force; communitarian models stress proportionality and imminence of the danger because of the target's obligation to respect the rights of the aggressor. Other models stress the instinct of self-preservation that takes over in the face of danger (*se defendendo*), thereby diminishing the importance of imminence and proportionality:

> The requirements of imminence, necessity, and proportionality, expressed in different terms in different languages, are found in virtually every legal system in the world. Yet these basic structural elements account for only the surface language of the law. Beneath the surface there surge conflicting moral and ideological forces that drive the interpretation of the law in particular directions. We may all be united in the terms in which we discuss self-defense, but we are divided in our loyalties to unarticulated theories that account for our willingness now to stretch the law broadly, now to interpret it narrowly. These deeper forces shaping our interpretation reflect the confrontation between passion and reason in the law.[23]

Although we can credit BWS with providing a potentially more constructive narrative about the meaning and culpability attached to abuse, we should not rush to judgment about the extent of its corrective necessity. We will see in the next chapter that the few empirical studies conducted on actual juror attitudes and knowledge do not support the belief that jury myths are prevalent, at least not since the first such study was conducted in 1987. In addition, opening up the relationship for the purposes of a victimization narrative can backfire, as in Catharine MacKinnon's remark: "[I]f one can expand time back to defend a woman who kills in self-defense, to understand the contextual determinants of her immediate response to a threat, symmetry would urge the equitability of expanding time back for the prosecution also"—such as the woman's failure to leave the relationship.[24] And when we address the larger cultural implication of the syndrome, which I have discussed at length, negative consequences fly out of Pandora's box.

Helping to Capture a Special Reality and Dispelling Myths

Another important aspect of the knowledge field that embeds BWS is the way the field assists us in understanding the nature of the battering relationship, in particular the seemingly paradoxical balance of fear, emotional and cognitive strain, and heightened rationality that constitutes the "special reality" of battering. On the one hand, this blend of factors reflects an aspect of reality; on the other hand, it engenders a murky state of affairs that makes BWS subject to manipulation.

BWS might reflect the paradox of the battering relationship that we examined earlier. The man often feels love and hate; the woman often feels love, hate, and terror. Each partner harbors his or her own mixture of reason and unreason. From this perspective, the logical paradox of excuse and justification perhaps reflects the deeper paradox in the souls of the tragic lovers.

Most importantly, testimony about BWS or related information about battering can help jurors, to some extent, to understand the special knowledge or "expertise" that a battered woman possesses about her batterer. We saw earlier that the battering relationship often propagates intense emotional bonding, and that the battered woman typically develops an uncanny ability to "read" her mate, to be attentive to cues of his imminent behavior (this suggests that we might need to expand our understanding of what evidence constitutes imminent danger in self-defense cases). Thus, it makes sense to think of the various effects of battering as elements of a pattern. The battered woman's fathoming of actions and the meanings of such things as gestures stems as much from her sometimes "inarticulate" understanding of this pattern or web as from articulated understanding. As Leo Katz remarks in a comment on Michael Polanyi's notion of "tacit knowledge,"

> Much of what we know we cannot say. For instance, we can pick a familiar face out of a crowd but could not say how we recognized it. We can ride a bicycle but could not explain the intuitive knowledge of physics that goes into it. Often judges know what the right decision in a case is but could not explain it. (The law takes account of that by giving more precedential weight to the facts and the outcome of a case than to the reasoning that connects them.) The inarticulable nature of much of our knowledge—the philosopher Michael Polanyi dubbed it "tacit knowledge"—severely limits our ability to provide for the future with explicit rules.[25]

Along these lines, BWS (or knowledge related to it) can be useful in countering myths or stereotypes about battered women—viewpoints or assumptions that compromise the individuation of justice (again, the question is whether the law can accomplish this end by other methods which lack the drawbacks I will disclose as we proceed). Four rulings highlight this propitious influence. In *State v. Kelly* the New Jersey Supreme Court ruled that the trial court erred in refusing to admit BWS testimony. The prosecution had downplayed the severity of the beatings and argued that Kelly would have left had her husband been as abusive as she alleged. *Kelly* concluded that the effects of being battered lie beyond the normal experience of most jurors, so expert testimony is necessary to counter the myths propagated by the prosecutor:

> [O]ne of the common myths, apparently believed by most people, is that battered wives are free to leave. To some, this misconception is followed by the observation that the battered wife is masochistic, proven by her refusal to leave despite the severe beatings; to others, the fact that the battered wife stays on unquestionably suggests that the "beatings" could not have been too bad for if they had been she certainly would have left.[26]

And in 1985, in *People v. Torres,* the New York Court of Appeals concluded that BWS was relevant evidence in a self-defense case in which the defendant shot her husband as he sat in a chair. Though her husband was unarmed, he had threatened her with a gun, and told her he intended to kill her just moments before the fatal shooting. The court's comments reflect the central logic of BWS in self-defense cases:

> It was the theory of the defense that the defendant was a battered woman; that is, a victim of prolonged physical and psychological maltreatment *who, as a result of her long-term familiarity with the deceased's history of violence, was convinced at the time of the shooting that she was in serious danger.*[27]

Torres was important because the facts did not exactly fit a classic self-defense situation. The court admitted BWS to show that a meaningful threat existed and because of the court's recognition of the special plights and perceptive abilities of battered women.[28] In *People v. Aris* (a case we will return to later), the California Court of Appeals discussed several uses of BWS (including learned helplessness). The court remarked that Walker is "a nationally recognized authority on battered women and is largely responsible for the development of BWS."[29] Among the symptoms of BWS, the court related, "One is greater sensitivity to danger."[30]

Finally, in *Commonwealth v. Stonehouse,* the Supreme Court of Pennsylvania ruled that defense counsel was incompetent for failing to request a jury instruction on the cumulative effect of abuse and for failing to present expert evidence on BWS. Carol Stonehouse was convicted of third-degree murder. The facts in the case presented a classic situation of violence, terror, harassment, stalking, threats, and lack of police support of the woman (like the defendant, the abuser was a police officer, and police demurred from getting involved). The deceased appears to have fit one of the more pathological profiles discussed above. The appellant attempted to get police support, including investigations by Internal Affairs and filing harassment charges, but nothing worked (they said it was "just a domestic matter"). According to the Supreme Court, "The events culminating in Welsh's death are so bizarre that one would be tempted to dismiss them as the stuff of pulp fiction were it not for the corroboration of disinterested witnesses and for the fact that the literature on the 'battered woman syndrome' is replete with similar cases." (The court then cited Walker's 1979 work, *The Battered Woman.*)[31]

The night of the incident Welsh became more menacing than usual, and threatened Stonehouse with a gun. She described him as "wild-eyed. . . . He was crazy. He didn't even know who I was in his eyes." He pointed a .357 Magnum at her. She "begged him not to kill her." During a fight in her bedroom, she was sure she would die. Then Welsh suddenly disappeared. "Appellant knew Welsh would return because he always returned, so she stepped out onto the back porch to look for him, not wanting to be caught with her guard down. . . . As she leaned over the railing, appellant saw Welsh on the ground below aiming his gun at her . . . Believing that she heard a shot, appellant fired her gun twice." [32]

Amazingly, the prosecutor in his closing argument to the jury, and the Superior Court on appeal, concluded that the defendant was not an innocent victim because she could have left the relationship! The Superior Court found Stonehouse's self-defense claim unreasonable because of "[t]he continued relationship between appellant and the victim." [33] The Pennsylvania Supreme Court correctly found this state of affairs unjust, and concluded that counsel was incompetent for not introducing BWS and asking for an instruction on cumulative abuse and terror. The court referred to widely cited work on battered women, devoting special attention to Walker's work. It underscored the need to counter the myths upon which the prosecution relied: "Had trial counsel introduced expert testimony about the battered woman syndrome, the actions taken by appellant on the morning of March 17, 1983, would have been weighed by the jury in light of how the reasonably prudent *battered woman* would have perceived and reacted to Welsh's behavior." [34]

Thus, *Stonehouse* and the other cases cited above show how the field of knowledge out of which BWS comes can be crucial to the achievement of justice. The legal system that Carol Stonehouse confronted had to be shaken out of its prejudice and complacency, and jurors had to fathom that Stonehouse perceived danger in a reasonable fashion. Nonetheless, a more probing look at *Stonehouse* does not lead to an unqualified endorsement of BWS as the vehicle to accomplish this end.

First, the court contradicted the excellent point about Carol Stonehouse's greater perception of danger by stating that BWS is a mental dysfunction. It quoted from *State v. Hundley*, a major case from Kansas: "Battered women are terror-stricken people whose mental state is distorted and bears a marked resemblance to that of a hostage or prisoner of war." [35] This understanding turns BWS into a medical condition that undermines the justice of Stonehouse's act of self-defense based on the acuity of her perceptions of Welsh's intentions. As we will see in the following chapter, the concept of learned helplessness has the content or connotation of a medical term or a clinical condition. It is also often factually problematic. *Indeed, the facts abundantly show that Carol Stonehouse embodied the opposite of the profile of learned helplessness:* she sought legal help several times, had attempted many times to escape his clutches, had completed her training as a police cadet, and had engaged in physical confrontations with the deceased. Just how useful to the defense and the truth would testimony about learned helplessness be in her new trial?

The Supreme Court of Kentucky comes to a better position in *Commonwealth v. Craig*, where it eschews medicalizing the concept of syndrome in favor of relying on the common Webster's notion. It defines the word "syndrome" as "a characteristic pattern of behavior . . . a set of characteristics regarded as identifying a certain type." [36] Though the Webster's definition still downplays the individuality of cases, it is preferable to the medicalization of the problem. Indeed, to the extent that it emphasized Stonehouse's growing fears and desperation, this notion of "syndrome" is appropriate. But again, the keys are what she accurately confronted that fateful night and the reasonableness of her perceptions.

It is also instructive to note that the other linchpin of BWS—the cycle theory—was absolutely irrelevant to the case. Nowhere in *Stonehouse*'s extensive narrative of the facts of the relationship do we find anything resembling a cycle of abuse. And if such evidence surfaced at trial, it would still be irrelevant to the type of danger that Stonehouse confronted. Once the abuse started, it just got worse. At no time was Stonehouse fooled by her tormentor's contrition. Yet the court never addressed this and related lacks of fit between the facts of the case and the syndrome that it endorsed.

Second, the *Stonehouse* court showed how knowledge of such abuse can be assimilated to the law of self-defense without having to rely on the full panoply of BWS symptoms, especially learned helplessness. In ruling that the counsel was incompetent for not asking for an instruction on cumulative abuse, the court cited and quoted from *Commonwealth v. Watson* (1981). Whereas *Watson* shows the necessity of testimony and evidence concerning past abuse, it also shows how present self-defense doctrine can achieve justice when properly applied along with evidence of the abuse the woman suffered. Watson shot and killed her common-law husband as he was choking her during an attack he initiated. The prosecution argued, and the trial court agreed, that Watson's belief in imminent deadly harm was contradicted by the facts that she had stayed with him and survived beatings. In other words, the prosecution deployed the most pervasive myth Walker designed BWS to counter. The Supreme Court of Pennsylvania in *Watson* mentioned "battered woman" briefly, but the decision rested entirely on traditional self-defense law:

> *A woman whose husband has repeatedly subjected her to physical abuse does not, by choosing to maintain her family relationship with that husband and their children, consent to or assume the risk of further abuse. . . .* In a case such as this, where there has been physical abuse over a long period of time, the circumstances which assist the court in determining the reasonableness of a defendant's fear of death or serious injury at the time of a killing include the defendant's familiarity with the victim's behavior in the past.[37]

People v. Yokum, a 1956 California case, also shows how traditional self-defense doctrine can serve justice. In that case the court declared that the evidence of domestic violence was admissible in a battered woman's homicide case. *Yokum* is but one of several such cases that reached this conclusion before the advent of BWS.[38]

Equity and Individualized Justice

The above discussion strongly suggests that BWS is, among other things, a tool by which legal authorities, including juries, can bend or tailor stringent legal rules to achieve justice in individual cases. Under proper circumstances, BWS can provide a means for "individuating responsibility."

One means of achieving just discretion, of course, is jury nullification (i.e., cases in which the jury refuses to convict the defendant even though the evidence meets the legal standard of guilt) or "liberation" from the stringent standards of law.[39] Another means is the creation of what Lon Fuller calls a "legal fiction." A legal fiction is a concept that is not really empirically verifiable but corresponds in some sense with what we think the case to be (or should be). It facilitates legal judgment by providing assumptions upon which reasoning can build. Presumptions of innocence, burdens of proof, the concept of duty of care, and such concepts as the reasonable man or woman are examples of legal fictions in action.

> Everyone who has dealt with legal problems must, at one time or another, have had the experience of feeling that a certain doctrine of the law was expressed in terms of fiction, and yet have found himself, to his dismay, unable to restate the doctrine without resort to fiction. At such moments one is apt to succumb to the feeling that "a fiction that we needs must feign is somehow or another very like the simple truth."
>
> A fiction is frequently a metaphorical way of expressing a truth. The truth of any given statement is only a question of its adequacy. No statement is an entirely adequate expression of reality, but we reserve the label "false" for those statements involving an inadequacy that is outstanding or unusual. The truth of a statement is, then, a question of degree.[40]

Although BWS is not exactly a legal fiction in the sense Fuller delineates, it does appear to be a forensic construct of quasi-empirical validity that enables juries to reinterpret factual situations and to bend the letter of the law without consciously forsaking it.

In *People v. Aris*, the California Court of Appeals for the Fourth District made a now classic statement about why the criminal law should not abandon the imminence standard for self-defense. The defendant killed her husband in his sleep after ten years of severe abuse that did include the cycle. The trial court refused to allow expert testimony on BWS, which was meant to show the defendant actually believed she was in imminent danger, because as a matter of law she was not in such danger at that point in time. It also refused to allow testimony about how the defendant's BWS influenced her perceptions. The Court of Appeals ruled that the trial court properly refused the testimony on the first ground, but that the testimony should have been admitted on the second ground. This latter failure was harmless error, however. The key to the higher court's decision lay in the court's view of the significance of the imminence standard, which the court took to mean that the defendant had to perceive danger "at the moment." It quoted Thomas More from *A Man for All Seasons* on the need to extend the rule of law even to the Devil ("And when the last law was down, and the Devil turned round on you—where would you hide, Roper, the laws all being flat?"), and averred:

> This definition of imminence reflects the great value our society places on human life. The criminal law would not sentence to death a person such as the victim in this case for a murder he merely threatened to commit, even if he had committed threatened murders many times in the past. . . . [I]t follows that the criminal law will not even partly excuse a potential victim's slaying of his attacker unless more than merely threats and a history of past assaults is involved.[41]

This standard is exacting, especially if the woman confronts a virtual captive situation akin to kidnapping. In such a case, BWS furnishes a narrative that can allow for equitable adjustment. As Aristotle taught, no laws can perfectly predict the occasions for their application, so equitable adjustment is needed to balance the letter of the law with the subtlety of reality.[42] By bringing to bear its mixed message of incapacity excuse and justification and revealing the nature of cumulative terror, BWS in its best moments adjusts the standards of self-defense to the shaded nature of the battering situation.

Three of our interviewees involved in cases of domestic violence and sex crimes tellingly articulated the tension between the standards of law and the state of mind and culpability of individuals. Detective Dennis Reilly declared that in some cases a batterer gets his "just deserts" when he is killed (he was referring to the Madison axe murder discussed below). "I've seen what happens to battered children and women. Batterers often go for the head, can cause head injuries. If you just keep beating on a dog, it will turn to bite you. Self-defense is a basic human instinct. Battered women have children and have to protect them. A mitigating circumstance is when the kid gets knocked out, and the wife goes bonkers and kills." But when we pointed out that under this logic batterers "deserved" to get killed, Reilly interjected, "O.K. But the law is different. The excuse and the reason for the act are different. I gave you my opinion for the reason. But the law is the law. In my opinion, I'd vote for the woman. But legally, she took a life, and should be punished for it."[43] When pushed, Reilly refused to see the issue in simplistic or unidimensional terms.

John Burr, a first assistant in the Felony Unit of Dane County, also voiced this tension, though he was more emphatic about recognizing the gray area of culpability. Like others we interviewed, he stressed repeatedly that "everything depends on the facts of the case." But battered women are often less blameworthy:

> [Is a battered woman less blameworthy than someone else who commits the crime in other circumstances?] Oh, sure. If I murder my spouse because he's abused me, that's a lot different from walking into a liquor store with a gun and killing. They are both murderers but are entirely different situations. But few homicides are really "justified." There are usually other options or opportunities for choice, unless it is true self-defense. Hindsight is always 20/20, but you've got a choice. Whether the person can rationally sort it out is another matter. [Is her perspective the key, or that of a normal reasonable person?] I don't think you can limit it to any one fact [contra Walker!].[44]

Assistant District Attorney Linda Dawson, like Burr and Hurley, kept emphasizing the importance of the totality of circumstances in each case. Her comments illustrate the ambiguity of judgment, as well as the way in which "truth" is often shaded by one's role or institutional obligations. It is also important to note that prosecutors deal with all sorts of violent crimes, so their perspective is broader than those who focus on particular issues such as those posed by battered women. Asked about the case of a severely abused woman who cut off her sleeping husband's head with an axe (see below), Dawson weighed her words carefully:

> From a prosecutor's perspective, we have to sort out whether this person's actions were justified. If we say "unjustified," then we will attack this label [BWS] or pattern, or that even given a history of battering, this action went too far [contra Walker]. So we are rather caught in a bind. We have to understand what caused her to do what she did, but we are not going to just blindly accept what she says. . . . There is a point where we say, "No, it doesn't fit." So we are sort of caught, having to see both sides.
>
> We are primarily concerned with the objective facts of the case rather than the woman's subjective state. What you look at is whether the conduct and facts make sense, the conduct before, during, and after, the facts surrounding the offense.[45]

In the end, my use of Fuller's notion of "legal fiction" and the views expressed by interviewees resemble what Herbert Wechsler and Jerome Michael construe as a "social utility" theory of self-defense. Under this view, because we consider the result just and good for society in the long run, killing is sometimes permissible when the situation does not meet the strict requirements of self-defense doctrine. Such situations arise when deadly force is "a necessary means to the prevention of physical and psychic injuries that usually prove to be permanent and seriously impair the human capacities of those who suffer them. . . . There remains, of course, the difficult problem of determining what physical and psychic injuries so gravely impair the capacity to function that the value of life itself is seriously impaired."[46] But such exceptions (or partial exceptions) to the prohibition of murder cannot be written into the law for normative and practical reasons. It is clear that some advocates of battered women believe that certain batterers cross this line into the realm of deserving death regardless of imminence.[47] Problems beset this position which I will discuss in later chapters. But it merits mention because considerations of substantive justice should influence the application of law, even if equal protection of the law dissolves when such considerations become paramount.[48]

Finally, for better or worse, experts present BWS as a psychological truth that bears the power of science. This trapping enhances the effect of the "legal fiction." Believing in the power of science, we can feel better about making the difficult moral judgment in the case at hand. In this respect, BWS hitches its wagon to the ongoing medicalization of social, personal, and moral problems in the West. This process furthers the extension of the therapeutic ethic's reformulation of the self and moral order.[49]

Perhaps the ambiguity of the victimization syndrome (as a blend of psychological science, social construction, disorder, and heightened reason) reflects the ambiguity we feel about self-defense in nontraditional contexts. Although the special situations and claims of battered women must be respected, many of us remain reluctant to abandon norms of self-defense law because such abandonment opens the door to vengeance rather than justice. And while we fear extending such license to many other cases, limiting it to battered women discriminates against other individuals similarly situated. We find ourselves between a rock and a hard place. One way out of the dilemma or paradox is to develop a psychiatric or scientific concept that allows us to balance our concerns behind the comfort or reassurance of a scientific label. To borrow from Nietzsche, such a label gives us comfort in the face of painful or uncomfortable truths.

Equity as Necessity

A similar functional use of BWS points toward another traditional defense that intentionally incorporates the notion of fairness or equity: necessity. Though necessity is not the same thing as the syndrome, the equitable adjustment that BWS might facilitate is akin to the adjustment behind the doctrine of necessity. *Indeed, cases like Hughes (the burning bed case) might indeed be necessity cases in disguise*, for, like BWS, the necessity defense opens the door to considering self-protective acts outside the comparatively narrow confines of confrontational violence. (*Bobbitt* is different because the facts do not support the conclusion that Lorena was trapped like Francine Hughes was. The lack of such evidence suggests that Lorena acted out of vengeance rather than necessity.) Indeed, Richard Rosen and Stephen Schulhofer have recently argued that battered woman self-defense cases not involving confrontational defense should be premised on necessity rather than on the stricter standards of self-defense.[50] But an important difference stands out: necessity defenses do not entertain the logic of incapacity upon which BWS depends.

Necessity as Justification

Necessity is a broader defense that forms the backbone of self-defense and duress. In the past, courts limited it to pressure brought about by nature, as opposed to duress, which involves personal pressure. Today, many codes provide a necessity justification that encapsulates both forms of pressure under the concept of the "choice of lesser evils," which constitutes a justification. But there are not many reported cases in this area for at least two reasons. First, courts often find "implied exceptions" in statutes, making an independent necessity defense unnecessary.[51] Second, such cases do not arise all that often. The law presumes necessity cases to be exceptional by their very nature.

Two competing theories underlie the necessity doctrine as justification: a theory that combines utilitarian and positivistic notions of law and legal obligation, and a theory derived from notions of higher right or justice. The utilitarian theory acknowledges that citizens must obey the law, but stresses that until legislators become omniscient, situations will always arise in which the law does not cover a difficult choice confronted by the defendant. When such trying situations arise, the citizen may break the law if such an act would be more beneficial than would obeying the letter of the law. For example, we would approve of breaking into a bank on a Sunday to obtain a fire extinguisher to put out a fire in a car parked nearby, for the social good is promoted by the erstwhile illegal action. Among other things, the necessity defense allows citizens to "legislate" by their actions in the inevitable interstices of the law or conflicts between laws.

Under the sway of the Model Penal Code, the American approach is largely utilitarian; necessity justifies otherwise illegal conduct if "the harm or evil sought to be avoided is greater than that sought to be prevented by the law defining the offense charged."[52] But most jurisdictions have limited the defense. Courts have disallowed necessity defenses in the following situations: economic necessity due to unemployment; most prison escape cases (except when a fire is raging); and claims that the evil effects of broader social policy such as the Vietnam War created a necessity to oppose the war effort violently.[53] Cases that go the other way have included a ship master violating an embargo law forbidding entry into a port because of a severe storm; sailors refusing to obey a captain's orders that jeopardized the safety of the crew; an ambulance driver violating speed limits on the way to the hospital; and a prisoner escaping from prison because of a fire.[54]

In general, necessity defenses must meet several requirements.[55] First, one must have acted with the intent of avoiding the greater harm. That is, the act under necessity may not be simply a pretext for what would otherwise constitute an illegal act. Some courts require actual necessity, not simply that the actor harbor a belief in necessity (the logic of justification). Second, the harm avoided must outweigh the harm done. Some jurisdictions require that the harm prevented "clearly outweigh" the harm caused. A third requirement involves imminence of the harm and less drastic courses of action. The availability of a third alternative that does not violate the law or is less harmful eliminates the necessity. Fletcher remarks, " *The significance of limiting the privilege of necessity to cases of imminent risk is that the individual cannot pick the time, the place, or the victim of his judgment about what the law requires him to do.* " [56]

The "higher justice" approach is used more in continental Europe but it is not completely alien to the Anglo-American tradition. Fletcher says it arises "by way of judicial recognition of transcendental norms in the legal system. . . . Like other Continental European legal systems, German law recognizes the distinction between enacted laws (*Gesetz*) and a notion of transcendent, unenacted law (*Recht*). The former laws are binding by virtue of formal criteria; the latter by virtue of inherent rightness." [57] In 1975 the West German legislature adopted the lesser evils approach. The code requires that the harm committed be "essentially" or "substantially" less than the harm prevented, and that the "act be an appropriate means" to avoid the risk. [58]

Necessity as Excuse

Like self-defense and duress, the concept of necessity can also be treated as an excuse. For example, in cases in which one must choose quickly between one's own life and that of another, the principle of *se defendendo* (defensive force when one's back is against the wall) may operate, as the pressure of self-preservation overwhelms rational calculation and the sense of right. Kant claimed that although such an act could never be justified, the overwhelming pressure involved would make it unjust to punish the actor. In 1926 the German Supreme Court upheld an acquittal of a battered child who killed his father on the grounds of family necessity, even though the act did not formally constitute self-defense. [59] Note that the excuse side of necessity concerns a normal person's response to external pressure, not the type of incapacity associated with insanity or diminished capacity. This form of excuse takes account of the situation, not mental disorder or syndrome.

The famous 1884 case *Regina v. Dudley and Stephens* furnishes a classic example of a necessity defense. The defendants were found guilty and sentenced to death for murdering and eating a seventeen-year-old boy on board a lifeboat after some twenty desperate days at sea. Lord Chief Justice Coleridge extolled the duty of sacrificing one's life under the circumstances and told of the practical unworkability of the necessity doctrine in such cases. "Who is to be the judge of this sort of necessity? By what measure is the comparative value of lives to be measured? Is it to be strength, intellect, or what?" But authorities had already arranged pardons, and at the sentencing the judges did not even don the customary black hoods. Six months later the defendants were freed.[60] The disposition of the defendants exemplifies the conundrums necessity cases can engender.

The criminal law cannot make the necessity defense available to every bidder without sacrificing standards of care and responsibility upon which ordered liberty rests, however. This is especially true when it comes to killing. Katz expresses the tensions well:

> Even if inclined to acquit [in cases of murder and necessity], one must feel eerie qualms about doing so, a gnawing unease . . .
>
> We may have to deny ourselves liberal use of the necessity defense, the way Odysseus denied himself the power of command when passing by the Sirens. (Because he knew that sailors were apt to be seduced by the song of the sirens so that their ship crashed into the cliff, he ordered his crew to stop their ears with wax. But because he wanted to hear the song, he had himself tied to a mast, and told the crew to ignore his orders until they had passed the cliff.) . . .
>
> Having recognized the necessity defense in principle, we run into several snags as we try to apply it to some special circumstances.[61]

Perhaps this concern lurks behind the absence of necessity defenses in cases of battered women who use deadly force. Nonetheless, Rosen (and Schulhofer) recommends that courts should consider offering battered women necessity defenses when they kill in nonconfrontational situations. Rosen argues that "[i]n self-defense, the concept of imminence has no significance independent of the notion of necessity."[62] The law requires that the harm be imminent because it assumes that there is no necessity without imminence. There can be times when killing might be necessary to prevent a nonimminent harm, however. Rosen presents the example of kidnapping in which the kidnapper tells his hostage he will kill him, but not yet. Clearly, if the hostage seizes an opportunity to kill the kidnapper and escape, he may do so even in the absence of imminent harm. Most jurisdictions allow the use of lethal force to prevent a kidnapping from happening at all. Along these lines, Rosen advocates modifying the law of self-defense by giving judges the discretion to bypass the imminence standard in favor of the standard of necessity. The jury would have to decide whether the defendant's use of lethal force was necessary to avoid serious bodily harm, regardless of the imminence of the danger. We will deal with Rosen and Schulhofer's arguments in the concluding policy chapter.

Even if formal resort to a necessity test proves problematic for reasons we will address in that last chapter, juries evidently sometimes take such logic into consideration in reaching verdicts. The *Bobbitt* and *Hughes* juries found the defendants not guilty by reason of temporary insanity, but, as stated above in the press report of Weisselberg's opinions, "Having accepted [Bobbitt's] account . . . the jury seems to have simply chosen the most convenient legal avenue of acquittal, the insanity defense."[63] BWS played a role in this decision. But so would evidence of abuse that did not dwell on syndrome logic. The key to justice lies in presenting sufficient evidence to the jury of the dangers, fears, and difficult choices the defendant had to make (the narrative of victimization), enabling the jury to apply the law in an equitable fashion without prejudice and ignorance. *Understanding the necessity of the situation is essential to justice, even if resort to formal necessity defenses is problematic.* In the concluding chapter we will attempt to incorporate the logic of necessity in a manner that remains within more established and controllable defenses.

Other Contexts

BWS and related knowledge have factored in other contexts, including sentencing, pre-trial dispositions, and even pardons and clemencies. Indeed, BWS is now the term of art for the legal system's treatment of battered women. Let us look at other important contexts.

Informal Justice

Lawyers and defendants have also used BWS and the understanding attached to it as tools for settling cases out of court. While interviewing some sources in Madison, Milwaukee, and via telephone we discovered several examples of the uses of BWS in the disposition of informal justice.[64] Beverly Brickford, a family violence specialist in the district attorney's office in Dane County, told us that in her jurisdiction "the biggest difference between abusers and abuse victims fighting back is the end disposition of the case. Most women in battering situations get referred to treatment by Advocates for Battered Women. So those cases still get charged. If she's at a point of escalating the violence, at that point she needs to be held accountable for that particular encounter, and at the same time she needs to figure out other ways to be safe."[65]

Dale Cobb said he used BWS, and the retinue of experts and arguments that come with it, in a variety of settings outside the trial, especially in plea bargaining and grand jury proceedings. Cobb portrayed his growing awareness of the importance of pre-trial disposition of such cases:

> I've used BWS with grand juries, in pre-trial motions, plea bargaining, etc. Once I even got double indemnity on an insurance policy for the woman who killed her husband.
>
> Now they aren't even making these cases against my clients. In one case they offered a plea of voluntary murder with work release. My client

wouldn't bite, though I told her she should. So it went to trial. The judge was missing his daughter's wedding party, so he said to me he should have dismissed the case! Even the prosecutor told me he was sorry he had to try the case. This made me realize that I needed to work more at the pre-trial level. It sensitized me to the issue and how to use BWS. It is easier to do pre-trial stuff now . . .

One case I had didn't fit the profile [because the woman fought back and was independent: see chapter 6]. I worked out a plea of "no contest." [66]

In 1984, Dane County District Attorney James Doyle (who became state attorney general in 1991) confronted a case of a seriously battered woman who essentially decapitated her sleeping husband with an axe. The case inaugurated the new conceptual paradigm in Madison by being the first instance in which the concept of BWS was used in a case of a woman who committed an illegal act. It was instructive to get officials' perspectives on the incident a decade later. According to interviewees familiar with the case, Doyle agonized over the case because of the seriousness of the act and the seriousness of the abuse. He was reluctant to prosecute because he felt that she was not blameworthy, but he knew the case would generate controversy. Like Cobb, he decided to take the case to the coroner's inquest because in this forum he maintained more control. The inquest jury decided not to find the woman the legal cause of death, ending the matter from a prosecutorial perspective.

Although some interviewees accused Doyle of seeking an easy way out, others appreciated his handling of the case because of the difficulty of the question of justice. Dawson said she applauded the disposition as a law student because she shared the burgeoning feminist consciousness in the University of Wisconsin Law School, but she confided that she has grown more uncomfortable with the case now that she has taken on more of a prosecutor's perspective.[67] Yet one police officer we interviewed said the man "got what he deserved." [68]

I will mention three other cases in Madison because they illustrate the quality and range of potential "bendings" of the law in informal situations. One case involved a prostitute who poured burning grease over her husband pimp in the early 1980s, leaving sixty to seventy burns all over his body. (A narcissistic wound compounded the physical harm—he was reportedly obsessive about his masculine body image.) He beat her terribly all the time, and the police begged her to leave him. One night, while drunk, he called her from a bar and told her he was "going to kill her." This act pushed her over the line. She put a large kettle of grease on the stove. Hours later, he arrived home, went to bed, and passed out. Meanwhile, she gathered her possessions and money, and arranged a pile of junk to impede his path to the door. She then poured the grease over him and ran to the shelter, eventually escaping to Minnesota. The police knew about everything that happened but did nothing for twelve hours so she could make her escape.[69]

When we interviewed Stephen Hurley, he had just finished work on one battered woman case and had one pending. Hurley's descriptions of the cases reveal the way in which lawyers will tailor BWS to the facts of the case, as well as the way in which knowledge about battering has permeated the system in this admittedly "progressive" town. I will discuss the case in which Hurley secured a pre-trial diversion of a woman accused of embezzling a significant amount of money from a bank over several years. She had been subjected to twelve years of physical, sexual, and psychological abuse. Hurley called it the worst case of abuse he has witnessed. I quote Hurley's fascinating account at length:

> I think about my audience. In this case I knew my audience would be receptive to BWS. My audience was the U.S. Attorney's office and the parole and probation service. This was the first case in twenty years that I was able to get a pre-trial diversion in federal court . . .
>
> Her husband had a construction business and forced her to maintain his books. He forced her to pay all household expenses out of her salary, and her salary was not capable of doing this. He did not report to her all of his income. He held her responsible for sufficient funds through beatings, beratings, etc., so after a while she started embezzling funds.
>
> The U.S. attorney had the goods on her right away. So I went right to them and said, "Look, this is one of the two worst cases of abuse I've worked with." I didn't get a knee-jerk negative reaction like "they are all like this." He referred me to an FBI agent in charge of the investigation. When I talked to the agent the first time, he was extraordinarily kind. And I found out that my client's husband had been actively trying to do her in with the FBI because this time she was actively trying to get a divorce and trying to get her children away. The FBI agent detested her husband, so I let him know the facts, and he detested him even more after that. He began to say things to the U.S. attorney about the plight of this woman. I went back for further discussions with the U.S. attorney about disposition, and said that given the divorce proceedings, if she went away to prison, she'd lose the children to this man.
>
> I could tell the U.S. attorney was troubled, so we decided to work together to manipulate the federal guidelines in a legal way to try to get probation. So then I talked to the probation officer who would have to recommend probation to the judge. He volunteered the information that his sister had been married to such a man. So I really laid it on and made him privy to all these facts. . . . As a result of that meeting, he went

to the U.S. attorney and said "I don't want to risk prison, let's go for probation." [70]

A final case in the Madison area involved John Burr, who has worked in this area of law for more than twenty years. A battered woman was charged with first-degree reckless endangerment after she shot a police officer in the chest through a locked door. She fired two shots, thinking he was her estranged boyfriend. She had been drinking and had a serious drinking problem. Burr showed a sensitivity to the various factors that go into the consideration of justice:

> I had no doubt that she had been abused, but I thought the extent and severity and frequency were less than she said. She had little or no prior convictions, was employed, but had a severe alcohol problem. She was in treatment at the time. The battering made a difference in the sense that it would have been a harsher punishment had she known the police were there. It was one factor among others. There was a chance you'd never see her in the system again. I also talked to the officer who almost got his head blown off. We decided that probation and county jail was the appropriate response, plus treatment. Her victimization was taken into account. But the door was locked, he [the boyfriend] didn't have a key, the officer didn't come through the window, she hadn't sought help, and she had been drinking. All these things worked against her. [71]

Some of these cases involve police officers who are knowledgeable of the nature of domestic abuse and BWS. Many writers criticize police for failing to protect battered women from abuse. This criticism has merit. But as knowledge of domestic violence spreads, police attitudes are changing. One of our police interviewees, for example, stressed that the mandatory arrest law in Wisconsin has contributed to his effectiveness in protecting women, and that the law can help battered women in the strategic games they are forced to play with their victimizers. "A lot of times he can accept the fact that she has called the police for her protection. Even though he is beating her, he often doesn't blame her for calling the police because he recognizes her fears. Then I arrive and I have to arrest him because the law makes me. He can blame me or the law rather than her. So I get him out of there, and she's safe for a while." [72] Of course, Madison is not typical of many communities; we constantly heard allegations that "counties up north" and elsewhere have yet to incorporate the new understanding. Still, such knowledge is spreading. In the *Richardson* case, police officers from a small northern Illinois community where the deceased once lived made this statement to defense investigators from Kenosha when informed of the killing: "We're surprised he didn't kill her first. She did everybody a favor." [73]

The reader should not take the examples of this section to mean that police and society in general have accepted the tenets of the new knowledge concerning domestic violence. The examples are meant only to show how the new knowledge of domestic violence can shape the informal practices of the law. In many jurisdictions the voices of battered women have gone unheeded or unheard (though studies on potential jurors' attitudes suggest that this state of affairs is changing, as I will show in the next chapter). Society must be vigilant in facing up to its obligations to protect battered women.

Sentencing

A smattering of cases at the federal level shows how taking BWS or related knowledge into consideration can help courts to achieve more equity. Several courts have recently considered or required BWS as a basis for a "downward departure" (sentence reduction) in sentencing under the new, relatively rigid sentencing guidelines. The most prominent area concerns duress claims. Duress is difficult to prove at trial. In several cases, courts have recently begun to construe BWS as a form of duress. "The battered woman defense is a species of the defense of duress. . . . We recognize that the unique nature of battered woman syndrome justifies a somewhat different approach to the way we have historically applied these principles," the Ninth Circuit Court of Appeals declared in 1992.[74] As early as 1988, a federal court, in an unpublished opinion, asked for more specific proffers on duress and on the question of whether a battered woman's will had been overborne because "[j]uries are always instructed (properly) that every defendant and every charge must be considered separately, based on the evidence relevant to that defendant and that charge."[75]

Sentencing is perhaps the most illustrative area in which the formal standards of law are mixed with discretionary justice. This is most important because the new Federal Sentencing Guidelines restrict judges' discretion in substantial ways. In *U.S. v. Johnson* (1992) the U.S. Court of Appeals for the Ninth Circuit authorized a downward departure from federal sentencing guidelines for drug dealing. Several women were convicted for serving as low-level operatives in a large drug ring. The defendants claimed they complied with the drug dealers because of duress. Among other inhuman acts, the dealers put a gun in the mouth of one woman and threatened her daughter's life. Despite such acts, the jury refused to believe her defense. Dealers repeatedly threatened another woman defendant and her husband, and forced him to watch as they almost killed another man; the jury acquitted this woman of three counts of distribution but convicted her of conspiracy. Though it conceded that a third woman had been "psychologically dominated," the court found that she had failed to establish a *prima facie* case of duress because she could have escaped the man's control.[76]

In holding that some of the appellants were entitled to lesser sentences because of the pressures to which they were subjected, the court pointed to BWS and acknowledged that cumulative domination and fear have a bearing on responsibility, even if such fear falls short of the specific standards of duress in the criminal law. The court stated that although the criminal law normally does not take special subjective vulnerabilities (including those related to gender) into consideration, "there are sets of circumstances in which gender is also a factor to be considered. Moreover, a purely subjective element that cannot be taken into account in determining criminal liability may be taken into account in sentencing."[77] The court discussed BWS and the Walker model:

> Battered woman syndrome is a set of psychological and behavioral reactions exhibited by victims of severe, long-term, domestic physical and emotional abuse. L. Walker, *The Battered Woman Syndrome* (1984). Battered woman syndrome is not a mental disease or defect; rather, battered woman syndrome is a post-traumatic distress disorder. Its psychological effects are often similar to the effects of imprisonment on kidnap victims and prisoners of war. Once battered women believe themselves to be helpless victims of abusive men, they behave like hostages and link themselves to their captors out of fear that it is the only way to survive. . . . Repeated beatings diminish the battered woman's motivation to respond and instill in her a negative belief about the effectiveness of her actions.[78]

Finally, the court linked this understanding of the BWS model to the Model Penal Code's expanded notion of ongoing duress, then ordered resentencing in some of the cases.

> This substantial expansion of the defense may go too far if not linked to gross and identifiable classes of circumstances. Battered women are in circumstances forming such a class. Our own law recognizes that for a substantial period of time a brutal man may subject women to severe psychological stress such that they "failed to escape or cry out for help when in a public place because they lacked sufficient ego strength, self-confidence and willpower when they were in the threatening shadow of [the man's] complete domination over them."[79]

In *U.S. v. Gaviria*, the U.S. District Court for the Eastern District of New York built on *Johnson* in ruling that a downward departure to the statutory minimum of sixty months imprisonment (from a normal range of seventy to eighty-seven months) was justified in the case of a defendant convicted of knowingly and intentionally possessing cocaine with intent to distribute. Justice required a lighter sentence because of Gaviria's "subservience" to her husband, who was primarily responsible for the crime. Gaviria was "a sad and lonely woman with little sense of her worth and with a potential for further victimization."[80] According to the appeals court, "only the extraordinary case will meet this demanding test [duress]. It does not recognize the effects of subtle, ongoing forms of physical and psychological abuse."[81] The court held that the failure of the sentencing guidelines to account for "these endemic sociological and psychological realities" conflicted with the congressional mandate "to provide for just punishment for the offense."[82]

Ineffective Counsel and Cases Other than Self-Defense

Effectiveness of counsel is crucial to any defense. In 1984 the Supreme Court promulgated a two-prong test that sets a constitutional minimum: 1) if the counsel's performance was deficient, in that he or she made errors so serious that the defendant was denied "counsel" in a meaningful sense; 2) that this deficiency prejudiced the defense so as to deprive the defendant of a fair trial.[83] Failing to raise an accepted, prevalent defense is one ground for finding counsel ineffective. Consequently, as BWS gains in recognition, failure to raise the syndrome as an issue opens the door to ineffectiveness.

We have already seen how the *Stonehouse* court found counsel incompetent for not asking for an instruction on cumulative terror and for not using testimony on BWS. In 1992, a California court of appeals came to the same conclusion. A jury found Valoree Jean Day guilty of manslaughter in a situation that bore aspects of pure self-defense. The deceased, Steve Brown, threatened to kill Day and chased her around the house and into a bathroom. "Hot and hyperventilating," Day grabbed a knife for her protection. Brown then pounded in the door and came at her with a knife. In the ensuing scuffle, she fatally stabbed him.

Citing *People v. Aris,* the appeals court ruled that although BWS was not relevant to the objective reasonableness of the defendant's belief in danger, it was highly relevant to rehabilitating the witness in the wake of prosecutorial reliance upon stereotypes and misbegotten "common sense" about how a battered woman would normally act (the court drew on *People v. Bledsoe,* the rape-trauma syndrome case discussed in chapter 2). Among other things, the prosecutor presented evidence that Brown and the defendant were engaged in "mutual combat" and that she could have left him. "Because trial counsel was not aware of the battered woman syndrome, he presented no evidence to 'disabuse [the] jurors of commonly held misconceptions about [battered women].' . . . The expert evidence would counter any 'common sense' conclusions by the jury that if the beatings were really that bad the woman would have left her husband much earlier. Popular misconceptions about battered women would be put to rest."[84]

Later that year, the California Court of Appeals for the Second District applied *Day*'s ruling on ineffective counsel to a duress defense in a robbery case. The court's probing discussion of the role of BWS and myths amounted to a tribute to Walker. Its treatment of the role of BWS, however, differed from *Day* in making BWS relevant to the question of reasonableness. The court then concluded that "[i]f BWS testimony is relevant to credibility when a woman kills her batterer, it is *a fortiori* relevant to her credibility when she participates in robberies at her batterer's insistence . . ."[85]

Some courts have been less accommodating to BWS when it comes to crimes other than self-defense. In *Neeley v. State,* the Court of Criminal Appeals of Alabama ruled that counsel was not ineffective for failure to raise a BWS defense for a defendant who helped her husband kidnap and murder a thirteen-year-old girl. "[I]n the overwhelming majority of cases dealing with the battered woman syndrome, the abused woman turns her wrath on the abuser. In fact, one of the experts testified that she was not aware of a situation where the syndrome had led to the torture and murder of an innocent, uninvolved third party."[86] In some other cases not involving effectiveness of counsel, courts have recently ruled that lower courts properly excluded BWS testimony because BWS does not apply outside the context of self-defense.[87] Finally, the U.S. Ninth Circuit Court of Appeals ruled in 1992 that BWS was not admissible to a duress defense given the facts of the case, but that expert testimony was admissible in terms of a diminished-capacity and mental-state defense.[88]

Custody and Parental Rights Cases: The Problem of Indivisible Responsibility

Though child custody cases do not involve criminal law, they do illustrate a most propitious use of the new knowledge concerning domestic abuse. Unfortunately, they also highlight BWS's major flaw, which is its emphasis on battered women's lack of reason. A trend appears to be emerging in the case law and legislation: being battered cannot be held against mothers when it comes to termination of parental rights or custody decisions, but it can be held against the batterer. Yet a major intervening factor can trump the first stipulation: if the mother failed to protect the child or children from abuse. Of course, the interests of children predominate in such cases. The issue of custody in cases in which children have been abused is related to criminal culpability for omissions (i.e., failure to perform legally specified duties, including failure to protect children), which I will touch on later.

Elizabeth Schneider and others have alleged that battered women are discriminated against in custody cases. Battered mothers suffer because they are viewed as incapable of the agency needed in parenting.[89] But such allegations might hold less validity today than several years ago, as the cases and legislation to be discussed suggest. At least significant enactments and cases have declared that being battered per se does not constitute unfitness for parenting.

Because of the new knowledge concerning domestic violence, we now know that battered women should not be blamed for their abuse, and that batterers are dangerous and often unlikely to change. Consequently, if joint custody is given after divorce, the battered woman and the children might be endangered once again.[90] Thus, awareness of the nature of domestic violence creates presumptions for the disposition of custody cases.

For example, several states have enacted statutory provisions in recent years that require courts to favor nonviolent parents in custody hearings. Texas passed such a statute in 1987. In addition, in 1990 Congress unanimously passed Concurrent Resolution 172, which recommended that "for purposes of determining child custody, credible evidence of physical abuse by one's spouse should create a statutory presumption that it is detrimental to the child to be placed in the custody of the abusive spouse." Also in 1990, the National Council of Juvenile and Family Court Judges adopted official recommendations on improving court practices concerning family violence, which included a stipulation that "violent conduct should be weighed and considered in making custody and visitation orders." [91]

The rise of the children's rights movement and laws designed to protect children from abuse rekindled concern about parents' rights to custody. Indeed, cases of battered women who fail or are unable to protect their children from abuse can easily result in a collision between the rights and needs of mothers and children. In 1982 the U.S. Supreme Court tackled the custody issue in *Santosky v. Kramer* by acknowledging the "fundamental liberty interest" of natural parents to custody of their children, which "does not evaporate simply because they have not been model parents or have lost temporary custody of their child to the State." [92] Accordingly, the state may terminate parental rights only if the evidence demonstrates their unfitness by clear and convincing evidence.

At the same time, the state is the ultimate protector of children under the doctrine of *parens patriae. Parens patriae* is normally promoted by maintaining the family unit. But when child abuse threatens the safety of the child to a significant extent, *parens patriae* dictates temporary or permanent removal of the child from the parent's custody. Difficult questions arise when a battered woman proves unable to protect her children from abuse.

Lewelling v. Lewelling, decided in 1990, provides a classic example of constructive use of knowledge about domestic violence. In this case, the Texas Supreme Court relied on such legislation in granting custody to Brenda, the abused mother of Jesse, overruling the lower courts that had granted custody to the husband's parents because of several facts: the mother was still prone to seeing her abusive husband; she was unemployed; she was living in a small house with her own mother; and she had spent time in the state mental hospital. The court of appeals had even found that Billy's abuse of Brenda constituted harm per se to Jesse. The Texas Supreme Court held that the hospitalization and the living arrangement did not show bad mothering (indeed, freeing herself and moving in with supportive family should be seen as highly praiseworthy, even heroic acts). In awarding custody to Brenda, the court exhibited commendable use of knowledge about domestic abuse:

The court of appeals seems to place great weight on the evidence relating to the alleged physical abuse of Brenda, without any evidence that such abuse would significantly impair Jesse's physical health or emotional development. A parent should not be denied custody of a child based on the fact that he or she has been battered. We hold that evidence a parent is a victim of spousal abuse, by itself, is no evidence that awarding custody to that parent would significantly impair the child. Any other result is contrary to the public policy of our state.[93]

Lewelling is an exemplary model of the best understanding and use of knowledge concerning domestic abuse. It places blame for the battering where it belongs: in the lap of the batterer. And it strives for fairness and justice in the context of domestic abuse by cutting through prejudice and stereotypes. But it should be noted that *the Texas Supreme Court could achieve justice only by prying its understanding of domestic abuse away from the profile-syndromic logic that the court of appeals employed somewhat disingenuously.* The court of appeals feared that Brenda's symptoms of BWS would endanger Jesse because Brenda would be more likely than a woman not suffering from BWS to return to her abuser. Unfortunately, this is an entirely valid interpretation of the profile logic of BWS, even though Walker has contended (without supportive evidence) that most abused women develop independence and responsibility once they free themselves.[94] BWS invites trouble in predicting that women will somehow be cured of their passivity upon leaving the relationship. But the assumption of recovery is scientifically baseless. In other forms of PTSD, such as Vietnam veteran's syndrome, the debilitating effects linger long after the exposure to trauma (see above). The dogs upon which Walker generated the theory of learned helplessness did not regain their capacity to act freely.

This problem is not limited to custody cases. For example, many major insurance companies have begun to deny health and other insurance benefits to victims of domestic violence (including children) on the grounds that being a battered person is a "pre-existing condition" of a psychiatric nature. Cases of discrimination have been documented in Pennsylvania, Delaware, Washington, Iowa, and Minnesota. In Wisconsin, State Senator Brian Burke and Representative Sheldon Wasserman have introduced bills to prohibit such denials of coverage.[95] And at the national level, Democratic Senator Paul Wellstone of Minnesota has introduced legislation in 1995 to remedy this problem (the "Victims of Abuse Access to Health Insurance Act"). According to Wellstone, "Insurance company policies that deny coverage to victims only serve to perpetuate the myth that the victims are somehow responsible for their abuse."[96] He is correct. Unfortunately, BWS contributes to sustaining such myths by treating learned helplessness as a syndrome and mental disorder. On the same day that Senator Wellstone introduced his bill, National Public Radio reported that the insurance companies opposed the bill because they "want to reserve the right to consider any current and past *mental* and physical conditions."[97] So long as battered women are depicted as mentally defective, they will be seen as insurance risks and as unable to carry responsibilities.

In *Lewelling*, the Texas Supreme Court was right to require more specific evidence of failure to protect the child. Otherwise, the status of "being battered" would be grounds for losing the right to have custody over one's children. As the U.S. Supreme Court ruled in *Robinson v. California*, culpability for a status is presumptively unconstitutional.[98] Though *Robinson* dealt with criminal liability rather than custody, its concerns seem relevant to custody decisions. As the Texas Supreme Court stated in *Lewelling*, only concrete acts or omissions should provide a basis for the loss of a fundamental right. *But such logic requires that courts downplay the syndromic and "helplessness" notions that lurk within the logic of BWS. As Schneider and others have fathomed, BWS puts undue focus on the battered woman and turns her situation into a kind of label and status.* Thus, *Lewelling* challenges important aspects of BWS at the same time it vindicates the syndrome's goals.

This tension points to a key factor in the case: "[T]here was no evidence to indicate that the child had been physically abused."[99] If such abuse had been inflicted, the question of culpability and custody would be problematized. *In re Interest of C.P.* provides a telling counterexample to *Lewelling*. It is hard to keep track of all the characters in this case of shocking "family" dysfunction, but try we must. M.A., the juvenile mother of C.P., contested the termination of her parental rights over C.P. The natural father, T.P., was a psychopathic, violent person who severely abused everyone in his path. M.A. left him several times, only to return. Finally she left for good, and police beseeched her to take legal action against him. She eventually married someone else but, incredibly, returned C.P. to the clutches of T.P. Though she knew of T.P.'s demonic capabilities, M.A. checked up on C.P. only once from 1987 through 1988. In May 1988, C.B., another child living with T.P., died in the hospital of injuries T.P. inflicted.[100] Concerned police advanced on T.P.'s home to check on the condition of the other children living there, and found the place appallingly filthy. There they discovered C.P. in a state of unspeakable abuse.

M.A. eventually lost custody of C.P. She appealed on the grounds that the state had failed to show her unfitness by clear and convincing evidence. The Nebraska Supreme Court disagreed. The presumptive natural right of a parent to maintain custody of a child is overcome because "[d]ue to M.A.'s neglect, her child was placed in an intolerable situation where she witnessed long-term abuse which resulted in the death of an 18-month-old infant."[101] The court refused to let M.A.'s fear of T.P. excuse her neglect. "Even if we accept this qualified expression of fear, a mother's fright does not, by itself, excuse her failure to extricate children from a dangerous environment."[102]

Unlike the Texas Supreme Court in *Lewelling,* the Nebraska Supreme Court in *C.P.* considered BWS testimony irrelevant, since it upheld the lower court's refusal to admit testimony that M.A. suffered from BWS. But the court did find it relevant that M.A. had failed to carry through on her commitment "to obtain treatment for the battered woman syndrome she suffered," finding that "there is no evidence that she had obtained treatment for her malady by the time of the termination hearing."[103] Thus, given the clear failure to protect C.P., the court construed BWS as the lower court did in *Lewelling:* a "malady" that constituted continuing danger to the child.

Although this interpretation poses the same problems I discussed in relation to *Lewelling,* three differences are important. First, unlike Brenda Lewelling, M.A. had committed acts of omission that could be criminally culpable in themselves (Brenda, after all, took Jesse out of the environment and into a safe one). Second, *C.P.* reveals a further institutional use of BWS as a "malady": resort to treatment for BWS is a sign of good will and a desire to gain the ability to be a responsible parent. Third, though one could argue that BWS is being used in this case against the mother, one could reasonably maintain that *given the demonstration of culpable omission* (such evidence was not persuasive in *Lewelling*), the presence of BWS does suggest lack of responsibility, and since the key interest lies in protecting the child, justice was served. Thus, given the exceptional facts of the case, BWS justifiably worked against M.A.'s claims. Absent such unusual facts, however, the presumptions of *Lewelling* should prevail.

Knowledge of the nature of domestic abuse, women's rights, and BWS have led to other changes. The *C.P.* case brought up the issue of M.A.'s failure to improve her mental state and responsibility. But we have seen that the battering relationship begets a "separate reality" for many women, and that we should not expect battered women to make the movement from the one reality to the other without difficulty. Accordingly, it would be unfair to extend the *C.P.* court's approach to all cases. Courts must engage in a principled balancing of the rights of the parents, the children, and the state in its role as *parens patriae.* Several states have responded to this problem in recent years by passing custody laws that mandate "improvement periods" in which parents lose custody only temporarily, pending improvement in their ability to parent. A 1988 case highlights the benefits this approach can achieve. In *In Interest of Betty J.W.,* the West Virginia trial court had twice denied Mary W. custody of her children, whom her husband had sexually abused, because it "found the alleged history of abuse by her husband, J.B.W., to be a compelling circumstance justifying the denial of an improvement period." The court conjectured that returning the children to Mary W. "would put these children at great risk again" because she continued to see him.[104] The Supreme Court of Appeals of West Virginia reversed, stressing several points. First, the court must authorize an improvement period unless "compelling circumstances" merit denial. In the trial court's eyes, the history of child abuse by the father constituted compelling circumstances. But the Court of Appeals pointed out that Mary W. had no actual knowledge of the abuse, and that her slight delay in reporting once she discovered it "could well have been caused by her own fear of her husband." [105] This conclusion entailed acknowledging the fear triggered by abuse and placing oneself in the shoes of the battered woman. Note that compassion is not absolute or overdetermined because the welfare of the children and the mother's responsibility to protect them is not forgotten: had Mary W. known of the abuse longer, or refused to report it at all once she found out, this decision could have gone the other way. *Yet the court's balanced position represents appreciation of a battered woman's plight without sacrificing standards of responsibility.*

Second, echoing *Lewelling,* the Supreme Court of Appeals refused to let the trial court's interpretation of BWS sway its opinion. *The trial court construed the "cycle theory" of BWS to mean that Mary W. would be unable to separate her husband's interests from her children's interests.* The Supreme Court of Appeals ruled that an improvement period without custody would provide Mary W. with a chance "to overcome this perceived problem." [106]

The requirement of an improvement period seems to balance the interests of the battered woman, the child, and the state. Because children have suffered abuse, the state is necessarily concerned about the mother's ability to protect them and provide for them. But the approach in *Betty J.W.* appears to favor the mother. In certain respects, BWS has contributed to this trend and the other trends mentioned above, for BWS has been the major legal vehicle for growing awareness. A key example of this effect is the 1993 case *Knock v. Knock.* The Supreme Court of Connecticut upheld the marriage dissolution order of the trial court, which awarded primary custody to the battered mother, Lynn Knock. The trial court had admitted classic BWS testimony by an expert and relied on this and other evidence in making its decision. The state supreme court cited Walker's *The Battered Woman* and declared "the presence of battering in the household has, at a minimum, some effect on the parenting skills of both spouses and the child's response to the parents even after their separation. . . . We therefore conclude that testimony concerning battered woman's syndrome was relevant to the best interest of the child in determining custody." [107]

But *Betty J.W.* and *Lewelling* also show *how BWS can backfire in custody cases by portraying battered women as too helpless and prone to cyclical behavior to take the initiatives necessary to protect their children. Although the facts might support such assessment in particular cases, BWS creates a problem because it assumes that such inadequacy is typical. Although the attribution of responsibility is often contextual (see below), responsibility is also often indivisible: a doctrine used to show nonresponsibility in one context will naturally be used to show nonresponsibility in another.* For example, MacKinnon's arguments that pornography directly "causes" harm and criminal acts against women implies that pornography diminishes the responsibility of those who actually commit the crimes. Ted Bundy, the famous mass murderer of women, used this logic to attempt to deflect blame from himself for his sex crimes. Recently a "pornography made me do it" defense has been raised in a state murder case.[108] Edward Donnerstein, upon whom MacKinnon relied as an expert to justify her antipornography ordinances, testified on behalf of the defense.[109] *Is it coincidental that in reversing the direction of the presumption of parental responsibility in* Lewelling *and* Betty J.W. *the highest courts of Texas and West Virginia completely ignored BWS?* Thus, although I have discussed these custody cases as examples of useful effects of BWS, we must be guarded in concluding that its uses in such cases amounts to an unalloyed good. In a democratic order that depends upon commitment to the norm of personal responsibility (see below), any doctrine premised on presumptions of nonresponsibilty can boomerang against its would-be beneficiaries. Accordingly, this flaw is ultimately insurmountable.

Battered women's objective psychological status might be the same in these as in the other cases, but society assigns an affirmative obligation to act to protect your child. Such cases pertain to what Marion Smiley calls "role responsibility" in her book on moral responsibility.[110] Along these lines, in 1993 the Illinois Supreme Court upheld two murder convictions in cases in which the women did not strike the fatal blows that killed the children (in one case, the mother was not even present). Other state courts have upheld similar convictions when the mother or father never disciplined or struck the child. The Illinois Supreme Court remarked, "The evidence presented against both defendants is sufficient to provide the inference that they both either knew *or should have known* the serious nature of the injuries. The defendants entirely ignored the dangers posed by these two men, and in doing so aided them in the murders."[111]

As of 1992, thirty-five of the forty-eight states that criminalized child abuse included omissions as well as commissions in their definitions of child abuse. A few states do provide statutory defenses for battered women accused of child abuse if they can show that they feared that intervention would endanger her or her child;[112] Minnesota prohibits "knowingly permitting the continuing physical or sexual abuse of a child," but holds "[i]t is a defense . . . that at the time of the neglect there was a reasonable apprehension in the mind of the defendant that acting to stop or prevent the neglect would result in substantial bodily harm to the defendant or the child in retaliation." But the author of a leading article on this issue maintains that courts are reluctant to be generous with this defense.[113] One reason is that such defenses clash with the rise of children's rights chronicled earlier in this work. Also, many states do not provide such defenses, and Schneider recently reported that the trend is toward greater prosecution in this area.[114] The case law is somewhat limited (partly because courts often do not mention the abuse in these cases despite its presence), but the reported cases reveal a wide range of contexts in which battered women fail to protect their children. In some cases, the battering and fear seem very relevant to omissions, in other cases less so because of other factors like indifference or sheer incompetence on the part of the mother (demonstrated to have been present despite the abuse).[115] We should note that the case law also includes convictions of husbands who failed to protect their children from deadly treatment by their wives.[116]

The criminal law dealing with culpability for carrying out illegal acts under orders from higher authority (Watergate, My Lai, etc.) raises similar points about the normativeness of the attribution of responsibility.[117] As Smiley and others have shown, the notion of "causation" in law often depends on value judgments about who should be responsible for certain outcomes. In *State v. Willaquette*, the issue was whether the state could convict Terri Willaquette of being a direct principal in child abuse because she left her abusive husband alone with the children (a seven-year-old boy and an eight-year-old girl) knowing that he had repeatedly abused his children sexually and physically. Terri argued in her defense that the statute allowed such a conviction only for those who themselves directly abused children, as her husband had. In ruling that she had so subjected them, the Wisconsin Supreme Court said,

> The ordinary and accepted meaning of "subjects" does not limit the application of [the statute] only to persons who actively participate in abusing children. The common meaning of "subjects" . . . covers situations in which a person with a duty toward a child exposes the child to a foreseeable risk of abuse.
>
> Causation in this context means that a person's conduct is a substantial factor in exposing the child to risk, and there may be more than one substantial causative factor in any given case . . .
>
> The concept of causation, however, is not solely a question of mechanical connection between events, but also a question of policy. A particular legal cause must be one of which the law will take cognizance.[118]

Similarly, courts consider BWS more relevant when the woman attacks her abuser, but less relevant when she lashes out at an innocent party, as in the *Neeley* case above.[119] What if Lorena Bobbitt had gone to a bar, picked up a one-night stander, and severed his penis?

Conclusion

Narratives of abuse that highlight the nature of domestic violence contribute to justice so long as they do not submerge standards of responsibility. *Accordingly, testimony about the fears, the cumulative terror, and the acuity of battered women's perceptions are crucial to justice. So are knowledge and normative presumptions that counter empirically inaccurate and/or prejudiced understandings. Juries must appreciate the fact that women are not to blame for their abuse, especially in a legal sense. In other words, the law should make every reasonable effort to allow such victims to "tell their story" to the jury.*

But the discussion of the custody cases with which this chapter concludes discloses the dangers that lurk in the logic of the syndrome approach to the problem. Indeed, abandonment of BWS's cycle and learned helplessness theories was necessary to do justice for battered women in these cases, just as such a move might be needed when it comes to insurance companies' provisions of health insurance for battered women. And the discussion of the omission cases showed how doing justice can be more complex than BWS's sometimes simplistic narrative acknowledges. A way has to be found to preserve valid knowledge without succumbing to the pitfalls of the syndrome. We should rely on testimony that emphasizes the nature and effects of victimization without dwelling on the theories of learned helplessness and (to a lesser extent) the cycle of violence. Reliance on the psychological speculations behind these theories (along with the baggage that accompanies the term "syndrome" today) unnecessarily obfuscates understanding of the meaning of the abuse and the necessities the victim of abuse confronts. The answer to the problem of justice lies in directly factoring relevant knowledge into the framework of established defenses like self-defense, duress, and the right to use force to free oneself from captivity.

CHAPTER SIX

Legal Critiques of Battered Woman Syndrome

> The process of learned helplessness results in a state with deficits in three specific areas: in the area where battered women think, in how they feel, and in the way they behave.—LENORE WALKER, *Terrifying Love*

> What I don't like about BWS [battered woman syndrome] is that it is tied to "learned helplessness." I disagree *totally* with this whole theory. Rather than being helpless, battered women adopt survival skills. We get women in our shelters with unbelievable survival skills, who do unreal things. . . . To call this "helplessness" is pure crap. It is learning to survive in a terrorist environment. They make whatever psychic changes that are necessary. They are intense survivors.—PATTI SEEGER, Dane County Advocates for Battered Women

We saw in the previous chapter that BWS and the knowledge field surrounding it can help to achieve justice for battered women by providing a perspective on the nature and meaning of abuse that highlights the dangers and necessities that plague the victims of domestic violence. Such knowledge can contribute to the equitable adjustments that make up justice and no legal policy concerning battered women can forsake these insights. But we also observed that the narrative of abuse can lead to three problems: it can slide into victim ideology if it is not controlled by the standards of responsibility upon which the criminal law rests; it can encourage stereotypes of the "right kind of victim" that undermine justice for women who do not fit the stereotype; and it can compromise the rights of battered women in other contexts where the norm of personal responsibility properly holds sway. These are substantial problems which beckon us to look more closely at the problems associated with BWS. I will argue that the solution to the conundrum lies in prying the narrative of abuse away from the logic of the syndrome. In other words, we should abandon BWS when it comes to self-defense or related claims.

In this chapter I will explore several specific problems associated with BWS that add to the case against its use in self-defense trials. In the following chapter I will discuss the problems BWS and syndromes in general pose for the political theory of citizenship.

The Key Assumption about Nonconfrontational Cases

Many advocates of battered women assume that the traditional law of self-defense is male-oriented, rendering it unresponsive to battered women. Cathryn J. Rosen asserts, "Most battered woman's defense cases involve situations in which the defendant was not, in fact, in imminent danger of death or serious bodily harm at her victim's hands."[1] But until 1991 no one had actually empirically tested the veracity of this contention. Then Holly Maguigan conducted such a study by scrutinizing all reported cases involving appeals by women convicted despite self-defense claims. Maguigan comments, "Much current legal scholarship is premised on, or accepts uncritically, the assumption that the majority of battered women defendants kill in nonconfrontational situations that would not raise a traditionally defined self-defense claim, that sleeping-man and lull-in-the-violence cases are the norm. In most of this scholarship, this 'fact' is asserted without any empirical support or is based on unsystematic review of cases."[2]

Of the 223 cases (generating 270 opinions) that met her criteria, Maguigan found that 75 percent involved confrontations; of the 20 percent that dealt with nonconfrontation, 4 percent were contract cases, 8 percent were sleeping man cases, and 8 percent had the woman as the aggressor during a lull in the violence. In 5 percent of the cases the appellate court did not discuss the facts, making determination of the context impossible.[3]

Some reservations concerning Maguigan's findings are in order. Though no one knows for sure, it is possible that battered women who kill in nonconfrontational cases are the most prone to accept plea bargains, which are seldom subject to appeal. (The strict standard of imminence in the law makes going to trial risky business.)[4] If so, Maguigan's sample would be biased in favor of her premise. But the prosecution has more incentive to accept pleas (or simply not charge at all) in confrontation cases, creating a potential counterbias in the data. Maguigan's conclusion suggests that self-defense law is not so stubborn an obstacle to justice as the new conventional wisdom asseverates. (See also the discussion of *Commonwealth v. Watson* in the previous chapter.)

Evidence from earlier times also suggests that self-defense law can achieve justice for battered women without employing syndrome logic. It is true that the common law tradition subordinated the wife to the husband, allowing a significant degree of physical abuse by the husband. Blackstone held that a man owned his wife, and he considered husband-killing a form of treason.[5] Still, it is interesting to note that Ann Jones, the author of *Women Who Kill*, a book on the history of homicides committed by women which became a classic in the field, shows that most women who killed their mates *were not prosecuted* very much until sometime in the twentieth century, and that the few who were prosecuted were often not convicted, even though many such cases often did not involve plausible claims of self-defense. Poison was the weapon of preference in the nineteenth century. Only with the ascension of women's liberation did prosecutions commence.[6]

Jones ironically attributes the *lack* of prosecution to patriarchal prejudices: men and juries (veritable synonymous terms in the nineteenth century) were afraid to admit that women could be so dissatisfied with family life as to resort to criminal action against their mates. The lack of prosecution disguised acts of denial. Nor did men take women's capacity for responsibility seriously.

Along similar lines, Cynthia Gillespie finds only three reported appellate self-defense cases involving women defendants from the founding of the American colonies to the beginning of the twentieth century, and these occurred only after the 1890s. The earliest case Gillespie locates of a woman who killed her abuser was *Williams v. State* in 1902.[7] Though Jones's work is cited often, few writers confront the implications of her analysis: that the traditional law did not persecute (or prosecute) women who kill.[8] To be sure, Jones's analysis of the law of recent decades chronicles the rise of such cases, and prisons are full of women who acted in self-defense. Many men languish in prison for the same reason (see below).

Even with BWS, defense attorneys often agonize over the decision to plead self-defense or mental excuse. This was the very first question the *Richardson* defense team had to address. Had the facts more clearly indicated self-defense, the team would have been strongly inclined to abandon BWS entirely. Although the team ultimately did plead self-defense, it deployed BWS because the facts were murky. But later the defense attorney confided to me that BWS might not have been very helpful.[9]

Incapacity Excuses, Public Opinion, and Validity

As seen above, BWS and other victimization syndromes are presently "hot" defenses, whether presented as excuses or as justifications. But a perusal of the history of the criminal law discloses that incapacity excuses wax and wane in their acceptability. Already articles have appeared in the wake of the *Bobbitt* and first *Menendez* verdicts which accuse victimization defenses of going too far.[10] Just a few weeks after *Bobbitt*, the March 9, 1994, episode of *Law and Order* on NBC-TV played to this sentiment in depicting an allegedly battered woman (there was no evidence for battering except the defense attorney's insistence) who severed her husband from his penis for being unfaithful. In the ambulance on the way to the hospital the unfortunate adulterer died of cardiac arrest. The woman defense attorney at the scene contended that the defendant's BWS compelled her to act with an "irresistible impulse," asserting the claim in an unmistakably formulaic and dogmatic fashion that left little doubt about the producers' intentions. At the arrest, one of the show's leading detectives teased his partner after the attorney's first foray: "Come on, Frank, but you know that every homicide now has political and social implications."

At the arraignment, the defense attorney entered a plea of not guilty to manslaughter, only to be interrupted by the defendant: "That's not right! I did it! I did a terrible thing! I killed my Bruno!" To the attorney's dismay, the judge accepted this guilty plea. Finally, back at police headquarters, the attorney and a policewoman got into a debate about the meaning of the crime. After the officer pointed out that the defendant pled guilty, after all, the attorney countered that feeling guilty was part of BWS after years of abuse. "The world will see that *she's* the victim." Unconvinced, the recalcitrant officer responded that the defendant felt guilty for a more obvious reason: she had just committed a great crime in killing her husband. Although the show recognized the reality of domestic abuse and the deep wounds caused by battering, it clearly conveyed the message that BWS is not immune to disingenuous uses.[11]

Other incapacity excuse–oriented defenses have declined in acceptance over the last twenty years, including the insanity defense (especially after *Hinckley*), diminished capacity, and extreme emotional disturbance as an expanded manslaughter defense.[12] Over time, society often loses patience with such excuses, especially if they generate the perception that someone is "getting away with murder." This sentiment could stem from several factors. First, in the longer run people endorse the view that citizenship and justice require the capacity to be responsible for the consequences of one's actions. Second, incapacity excuses ultimately rely on vague constructions of the psyche that are shifting and uncertain, whereas justification and necessity-based excuses are anchored to factual contexts that remain relatively more constant. Defenses resting on common sense and demonstrable facts might have more staying power than speculations based on psychological categories, even in ages susceptible to politically correct emotionalism like ours. If so, the association of BWS with the logic of incapacity excuse could undermine its credibility, especially if the ideology of victimization loses force in society.[13] Third, as we saw in chapter 5, the concept of nonresponsibility is inelastic, and can boomerang in several ways against victims we want to protect. Findings of incapacity in criminal law can translate into incapacity in child custody cases, just as arguments about how pornography "causes" sex crimes as much as the decisions of perpetrators have begun to be deployed by defendants accused of violent sex crimes (the "pornography defense").[14] Unfortunate things start happening when we play games with the presumption of personal capacity for responsibility like so many sorcerers' apprentices.

The recent successes of BWS could also work against it in these regards. We saw earlier that one reason for the failure of PMS to establish a beachhead in criminal defense is simply that so many women are prone to it. In addition to the obvious problem PMS poses for the social image of women as equal citizens, we are loathe to accept PMS as exculpatory in the social practice of blaming because doubts linger about our capacity to delineate consistently its effect on responsibility. If one side of the coin says no one is responsible, the other side says everyone is responsible. Herein lies one of the dangers lurking in the expansion of the concept of "battering" we discussed above, and in the claims or intimations by such writers as Herman and Miller that victimization abuse is the norm rather than the exception in society.[15] Once we perceive child abuse and domestic violence as typical rather than exceptional, we ironically undermine their power as syndrome defenses.

Similarly, psychiatric classification and diagnosis—the domains of incapacity excuses—are hardly infallible. We saw in chapter 2 how political pressure has impinged on psychiatric classification, in particular in the declassifications of homosexuality and masochism, and in the classification of PTSD.[16] Diagnostic classification is an inexact art by nature. Professionals have advanced in the effort to establish more "reliability" for diagnoses, especially with the revolutionary passage of DSM-III.[17] But DSM-III and its offspring (which officially recognized PTSD for the first time) have not taken over without serious philosophical and professional debate; DSM-III represented the ascendancy of a new psychiatric nosology and framework as much as the recognition of an independent truth. Throughout the twentieth century, the establishment of all major codifications or classificatory schemes has been driven by administrative and governmental needs as much as by the needs of practitioners. Earlier in the twentieth century a somatic nosology reigned, to be supplanted by a psychodynamic, psychoanalytical paradigm after World War II. This paradigm gave shape to DSM-I and II. Psychoanalysis had "caught on" in America more than any other model in the intellectual culture.[18]

But the years after DSM-II led to a crisis of validity and legitimacy for psychiatry. As psychiatry and psychology grew as professions, diagnosis became increasingly uncertain and contested, and the perception rose that psychiatry effectuated "cures" no better than any other kind of counseling.[19] "The continuing public embarrassment for the APA as it tried to decide what was a mental disorder—amidst the political clamoring of various factions—gave the appearance that scientific psychiatry was an oxymoron."[20] Anguish over this crisis actuated the attempt to reformulate psychiatric diagnosis in DSM-III, which would enshrine reliability of diagnosis as the psychiatric mission.

But as Kirk and Kutchens disclose, DSM-III achieved higher reliability at the expense of not dealing with the underlying causes and etiology of disorders.[21] "Reliability" has to do with the extent of agreement among practitioners concerning the nature or diagnosis of the disorder; "validity" pertains to the accuracy of the diagnosis, independent of the agreement. In the eyes of its critics, this shift amounted to an abandonment of psychiatry's soul in favor of the classifiers and an implicit behaviorist logic (the rebirth of Emil Kraeplin, the great classifier of the nineteenth century). A vigorous debate along these lines erupted at the 135th annual meeting of the American Psychiatric Association in Toronto in 1982. It seems that the choice lies between profundity at the price of ambiguity and relative precision at the price of shallowness. One critic, George Vaillant, denounced DSM-III:

> In its reductionism and its laundry lists, DSM-III becomes needlessly complex and trendy. Its categories are too numerous and its avoidance of old-fashioned general terms such as "neurosis" and "psychosis" only makes things worse . . .
>
> The historian Walter Kaufman suggested that Freud created a "poetic science." Poets and novelists have always been able to take etiology into account, even when they were not sure. How? They paid attention to dynamics. Perhaps in parasitology, in orthopedics, and in computer technology one can escape from humanism, but not in psychiatry. Like it or not, psychiatry *is* dynamic. It has more in common with the inevitable ambiguity of great drama than with DSM-III's quest for algorithms compatible with the cold binary logic of computer science.[22]

Depth psychology is as much art as science, traveling the same path as literature, philosophy, political theory, and art on the journey to understanding. But Vaillant concedes that depth psychology is "ambiguous." Stephen Morse's claim in 1978 still rings true: "[T]here is no scientifically agreed on definition of mental disorder."[23] DSM-III, DSM-IIIR, and DSM-IV attempt to create such definitions, but only at the price of creating disorders for all sorts of things previously viewed as part of the struggle of living, and by emphasizing reliability (agreement among diagnosticians) rather than "validity," which refers to the underlying nature and etiology of the disorder (consensus only signifies agreement; it does not constitute truth).[24] Perhaps the emphasis on agreement (convention) over independent truth makes the recent DSM approach consistent with postmodern theory, which eschews the ontological status of a reality independent of social construction and language (this possibility is worthy of investigation). But the fact that knowing "something" completely is beyond human reach does not mean that that "something" does not exist. We need to avoid the category mistake of conflating epistemology (how can we know something?) and ontology (what is something?).[25]

And even with the ascendance of the DSM approach, several theories of personality compete for adherence: classic and variations of psychoanalytic theory; object-relations theory; psychoanalytic ego theory; self psychology; humanistic theories; factor analytic theories; field theories; systems-information theories (cognitive); phenomenological theories; and learning theories (of which Walker is a proponent).[26] Each designates a different etiology of disorder, a different treatment, and a different relationship between the disorder and individual responsibility. Finally, some studies have shown that experts have been fooled by "malingering," or the faking of a disorder or craziness in order to gain the benefit of the designation.[27] In the criminal setting, the incentive to malinger reaches its peak.

In addition to the plurality of theories and assumptions contending for diagnostic and etiological authority, a crucial question remains to be asked of all psychological theories, including BWS: even assuming a "disorder" like PTSD (of which BWS is, essentially, a subspecies), just what is the relationship between this disorder and human behavior, including criminal conduct? No one knows. Given the nondiscriminating way that Walker applies BWS (see below), she implies that BWS "causes" conduct. In a 1991 case, *Commonwealth v. Grimshaw*, the Appeals Court of Massachusetts stated that the defense was "that she was driven to violent retaliation in self-defense by a psychological phenomenon described as battered woman's syndrome, a subcategory of post-traumatic-stress disorder."[28] This depiction portrays BWS, rather than the situation at hand or the choice of the woman, as the cause of the retaliation. But there is no evidence that shows that disorders or "craziness" cause criminal conduct.

Morse points out that there are four kinds of causes: necessary and sufficient (a factor that by itself invariably produces the result that no other factors can produce); necessary (a factor that must always be present but with others); sufficient (a factor that will always cause the result but need not be present for the result to occur); and predisposing (a factor that is neither invariably necessary to produce the effect nor able to produce the effect by itself).[29] "Nearly all causes identified in the medical and behavioral sciences are of the predisposing variety. There are almost no known necessary, or necessary and sufficient causes. . . . Who is to be considered responsible, for both positively and negatively valued behavior, does not depend on proof of some degree of biochemical or other causation. It depends on social evaluation of how predisposing the causes are."[30] Following Kant, Lacan ventures further, claiming that a gap inheres in the concept of cause because it is ultimately mysterious and "unanalyzable—impossible to understand by reason."[31] Many factors in life predispose one toward crime, including genetics, constitutional factors such as age, gender, intelligence, and personality (to varying extents), environment, poverty, and addiction. No evidence confirms that psychological disorder predisposes one to crime more than these other factors.

In the end, theories of personality provide explanations or, more realistically, interpretations of behavior, rather than demonstrations of anything more than predisposing causation. "Dynamic theory can be understood as offering an interpretive rather than a mechanistic account of behavior. Freud treated behavior as a language that needed to be interpreted, and he attempted to provide both the grammar and the dictionary."[32] Those who maintain that psychoanalytic or even behavioral (BWS) tenets flush out the "causes" of behavior ignore the crucial distinction between motive and act. Motives arise from a variety of discernible as well as mysterious sources. In cases of children who kill their parents, the motive might be clear: abuse could have *"caused" the motive*, even in a necessary and sufficient sense. But motive only predisposes one toward the act: *the act itself* (except in special circumstances) follows a choice. Recall the *Thrasher* case discussed at the beginning of chapter 2: Jeffrey Thrasher killed to avenge years of abuse. *It is undeniably clear that our choices to act are relatively freer than our motives, unless we are nothing but automatons.*[33]

Of course, oftentimes we shape our actions to express our motives. Self-expression is furthered by the creation of a personal narrative that weaves motives and actions together, making one's life a kind of art form. At the most disturbing end of this pole is the serial killer, whose style of murdering usually personifies a twisted and evil personal statement or narrative. For the serial killer such as Ted Bundy, murder is a personal art, a deformed creativity laced with deeper personal pathologies. Or for Dostoievski's Raskolnikov, it is a manifestation of a deep inner struggle driven by powerful forces replete with pathology, grandeur, weakness, self-distinction, religious spirit, and philosophical posture.[34] So phenomenologically speaking, motive and act are not neatly severable. But who would gainsay that this mixture of obsessive motive and criminal act should not exonerate Bundy? Indeed, such an "artistic" blending of motive and act bespeaks a deeper kind of responsibility for one's actions.

In conclusion, incapacity excuses are problematic *grounds* for promoting the defense of battered women who kill. In the concluding chapter we will see that *situational excuse* is still relevant but psychological forms of excuse should be limited.

Walker, BWS, and the Problem of Advocacy Science

In this section I will address a number of problems that accompany BWS as a form of advocacy. Morse, Szasz, and others have dealt more generally with the problem of psychiatric testimony as advocacy science. In a key critical article on BWS published in 1986, David L. Faigman broached the issue of scientific advocacy under discussion. Faigman describes Walker's testimony in one case which in his estimation "illustrates the troubling implications of this line of thinking and demonstrates Walker's willingness to offer her testimony on battered woman syndrome even in extremely implausible cases."[35] Dispute over the relationship between "neutral" science and advocacy has spawned a major debate between feminists and others in the heated field of domestic violence.[36] As Polanyi and other students of science aver, value choices and normative interest have more to do with scientific research than the pure model of neutrality and the fact/value distinction acknowledge.[37] But Polanyi's insight should either encourage us to strengthen our guard against those who cloak normative arguments in the garb of scientific discourse, or encourage theorists to be more honest and "up front" about their own values when they make empirical and related claims.

This problem of advocacy science is exemplified by Walker's proposed testimony in *Buhrle v. State*. In this case the defendant had suffered through an eighteen-year marriage involving numerous instances of sometimes mutual physical abuse. In September of 1979, *her husband* initiated divorce proceedings and sought a restraining order *against her*. The next day, the warring couple got into an argument during which Ms. Buhrle threatened her husband with a shovel, and he retaliated by beating her with a pair of work boots. The following day Mr. Buhrle moved out of the family home to a motel.

One week later, Ms. Buhrle showed up at her husband's motel room with a rifle and a pair of rubber gloves on her hands. She stood outside her husband's room and argued with him over money and the divorce. Throughout the encounter, he kept the night chain on the door secured fast. After about forty-five minutes of argument, Ms. Buhrle let loose and shot her husband dead. Then she hid the rifle, took his wallet, and "began shouting that someone had shot her husband." [38]

Ms. Buhrle's defense lawyers engaged the services of Lenore Walker, and submitted an offer of proof indicating that Walker would testify that: 1) Ms. Buhrle was a battered woman and that a battered woman's behavior differs from that of other women; 2) Ms. Buhrle "was in a state of learned helplessness resulting in loss of free will"; 3) "[b]ecause of learned helplessness, Ms. Buhrle's ability to walk away from a situation or escape was impaired"; 4) Ms. Buhrle perceived herself to be acting in self-defense. [39]

Far from being trapped or helpless, however, Ms. Buhrle drove to her escaping husband's hotel, armed with a gun, wearing rubber gloves to conceal her fingerprints. She shot him while he hid from her behind a locked door. A strange form of learned helplessness, this! To be sure, Ms. Buhrle's subjection to battery probably did make her act "differently" than she would have acted had she not suffered such victimization; but just as surely this potential fact is not very relevant to her culpability unless we deem the status of being battered to be a defense in itself and a sufficient explanation for whatever actions she takes. If defenses of battered women pivot around the notion of being trapped (as they should), then Ms. Buhrle does not qualify, since it was her husband who was trying to escape *her*. The court correctly refused to let Walker testify.

Other evidence from Walker's writings piques one's concern. For example, Walker begins *Terrifying Love* by defining a battered woman as someone who is "repeatedly subjected to any forceful physical or psychological behavior by a man in order to coerce her to do something he wants her to do without any concern for her rights." [40] But later Walker shows her willingness to expand this definition so far that it becomes a snake devouring its own tail. She describes one woman's situation by declaring, "[I]t is also clear from the rest of her story *that Paul had been battering her by ignoring her and by working late,* in order to move up the corporate ladder, for the entire five years of their marriage."[41] Normally, a husband's absence constitutes the opposite of the captivity that is an essential aspect of the battering relationship and that is a crucial factor in the need to resort to self-defense! In her discussion of one case, Walker even speculates that battering caused cancer in a victim: "Unfortunately, Roberta died from cancer a few years later. Perhaps the delicate, healthy balance of mind and body gave way under the severe stress of repeated abuse."[42]

BWS experts have depicted defendants as women without wills. Another Walker case, *U.S. v. Gordon,* illustrates the problems associated with undue use of the psychology of victimization. Walker testified in court that the woman defendant in a contract murder case lacked enough agency and will to waive her *Miranda* rights voluntarily in custodial interrogation because of the presence of men. But the facts in the case disclosed meticulous efforts on the part of the military police to honor her rights, including putting a woman in the room with her during her questioning. In a motion hearing on the validity of her confession, Federal District Court Judge Stagg criticized Walker's portrayal:

> From a purely philosophical point of view, the theory of the defense (stripped of any attempt to put it in the terminology of our legal system) is that, when it comes to responding to males in certain situations, *Karen Gordon was a woman without a will.* With no will, ipso facto, she cannot make a voluntary statement.
>
> In a college ethics course or a law school jurisprudence class, this theory would be provocative material for discussion, papers, and exams. However, when this issue is translated to the sphere of legal, rather than philosophical resolution, the result is clear. It is not psychology which establishes the norm for determining whether someone has a will—it is society which enforces its collective judgment through its legal system.[43]

In addition to the harm such portrayals of incapacity commit on women in general, Judge Stagg's comments show how the capacities for responsibility and willing constitute an important aspect of equal citizenship under the law. And presumptions pertaining to these capacities mean that some battered women *are* responsible for their acts. Promoting images of women without wills is hardly conducive to equal citizenship, let alone to a commitment to the subtleties of reality. As Elizabeth Schneider, one of the most thoughtful and distinguished legal scholars in the field of defending battered women (Schneider was counsel in the famous *Wanrow* case, for example), remarks, "[T]o the degree that the explanation is perceived to focus on her suffering from a 'syndrome,' a term which suggests a lack of control and passivity, the testimony seems to be inconsistent with the notion of reasonableness, and the substance of the testimony appears to focus on incapacity."[44] Schneider also fears that the emphasis on syndrome echoes stereotypical notions of women as less capable of rationality and judgment.

Indeed, nowhere in any of her work (in court or in her writings) has Walker provided a single example of a battered woman who is responsible for her actions in any way, and nowhere does she provide concrete examples of battered women who do not have the syndrome (only statistical examples, in *The Battered Woman Syndrome*).

Another of her discussions is about "Pattie's Story," a case that is similar to the *Buhrle* case. Pattie was a battered woman. One evening after a day of abuse (Walker does not say how much abuse) and emotional betrayal, Pattie trailed her husband and his lover to a motel room. Along the way she obtained bullets for the gun in the car. She knocked on the room door and threatened the woman. She wanted only to scare them, Walker claims. "It was a game they had played before." (One cannot help wondering if Walker would describe the encounter as a "game" if the roles were reversed and the husband was charged with killing Pattie.) After she ordered her husband to "get rid of the bitch," he jumped at her and the gun went off, killing him. Naturally, one can read a variety of motives into this act and raise many questions concerning Pattie's culpability in criminal law (many men and women languish in prison for similar acts under similar circumstances). But Walker steadfastly refuses to wrestle with these difficult issues, preferring a logic that inexorably turns "having been battered" into a universal exculpatory logic that conflates incapacity excuse and justification:

> Pattie had, indeed, been angry with Tom. But from the history she gave me, and from my own clinical impressions, I had no doubt that she'd been a battered woman in that relationship. It wasn't anger that had motivated her to pull the trigger, but pain, fear, and a terrible sense of grief. (I wasn't at all sure that the facts of the homicide, or even of her current psychological condition, supported an insanity defense more than a plea of self-defense, although her recent history documented her impaired state of mind.)[45]

The defense eventually had to rely on an insanity plea because the facts were too inhospitable to a self-defense plea. But the jurors found Pattie guilty because "they reacted like the lay people they were, armed only with their own common sense, lacking the knowledge of trained professionals. They found Pattie sane."[46] In this remark, Walker casts derision on all jurors who refuse to accept insanity pleas, and she implicitly links the mental state of all battered women to insanity, for Pattie appears to be in a less desperate situation than most battered women who kill. Walker's derision is due to the jurors' rejection of the *insanity* defense, not their understanding of self-defense.

The advocates of battered women maintain that BWS is not a defense in itself. Walker's treatment of it in nonconfrontational contexts suggests otherwise. This means that Walker envisions BWS as a necessary or sufficient cause of conduct. But the presence of mental disorder (or what Walker calls a "mental health defense" in her commentary on one case) tells us little about the moral or criminal responsibility of those who suffer from a disorder.[47] Most people with disorders (whom Morse calls "crazy people" for reasons of exegesis) do not commit criminal acts, and the same fact applies to battered women. A gap exists between mental states and the *actus reus*.

> There is little persuasive scientific evidence that crazy people should be treated differently from noncrazy people. Crazy people have a great deal of control over their behavior and their future behavior is not more predictable than that of normals. Craziness is only a predisposing cause of other legally relevant behavior. If the law is unwilling to consider the relevance of other predisposing causes, such as poverty, to legal questions such as dangerousness and criminal responsibility, it is difficult to maintain a compelling argument that craziness is different and therefore should be relevant.[48]

John Burr made a similar observation about BWS, though this time focusing on whether BWS is a disorder: "A woman may suffer so much that it is material to her capacity. But I know of no psychiatrists who have said that the suffering is itself a mental disease."[49]

If craziness means noncontrol, then even those who do not break the law pose sufficient danger to justify relinquishing their rights accruing to citizenship. This understanding underlies Szasz's and Foucault's libertarian critiques of psychiatry. In an era characterized by a vast stretching of the concept of disorder beyond its previous moorings, the presumption of noncontrol rhetorically justifies paternalistic expansion by the state and those acting in its name. Along similar lines, if battered women are "disordered" or "crazy," and society believes that being "crazy" makes one unable to control one's behavior, then being battered becomes a ground for losing rights that rest upon the capacity for acting responsibly. This is precisely the logic under which battered women lose custody of their children, as we saw in the previous chapter. And it is a logic that has little to recommend itself.

In a similar vein, Walker has not distinguished confrontation from nonconfrontation in her consideration of the effects of battering. *The theory of cumulative terror is important and valid for reasons I will articulate,* but in the hands of the expert with whose name it is synonymous, it threatens to become a license to kill the batterer at any time, for the simple reason that it is not mediated by any theory concerning the imminence or time horizon of the deadly danger. If cumulative terror per se justifies resort to deadly force, then it does not matter when a battered woman kills her husband: while he is asleep, alone in a distant city, or just before he attacks. This problem is especially acute given Walker's elastic handling of the concept of "battering," pointed out above. If a battered woman is justified in attacking her sleeping husband, may he not defend himself against the attack? (Both parties cannot claim justification!) Nor does it matter how she kills him, by herself, or by contracting with a third party to do it. Nor has Walker distinguished degrees of battering or responsibility in different contexts, such as the obligation to protect one's children from a batterer, in comparison to protecting one's self or torturing a third party. Independent of normative legal considerations, to what extent, if any, does the syndrome vary based on the type of potential criminal action the woman confronts? Since the syndrome is based on the intersubjective relationship between the batterer and the battered, what meaning does the syndrome bear in cases of duress or omission? Walker exhibits no awareness of these important tensions or distinctions.

In addition, Walker has developed a logic of knowledge that dissolves the line between objectivity and subjectivity. In *Terrifying Love*, she proclaims her mission to give voice to battered women and argues that BWS and the special insights of feminism can adjust the inequities that plague the doctrine of self-defense. Yet the logic she uses to support this contention indulges in stereotype and platitude:

> Women tend to see events as occurring in patterns rather than in discrete individual increments or incidents. What a court calls factual information is well understood by most women only when it is supported by context and background. Women tend to see a man's facial features and the clothes he is wearing, as well as hear his words. Their interpretation of the emotions expressed by his nonverbal body language provide as much information as does his verbal behavior. Women also use their prior knowledge or history of a situation in order to understand them. "What happened" in a particular situation often blends, in a woman's mind, with her own analysis of the process.
>
> Given women's need to be involved in relationships with others, *opinions count as much as facts to them.* Such distinction does seem to be typical of male thinking, however. In the male model, events are seen as factual entities, taken separately from the context in which they occurred; intellectual understanding is separate, too, from process analysis. Patterns may be perceived, but usually they are not interwoven in the male mind with discrete individual incidents. Men, therefore, can more easily tell their stories using male rules of the legal system.[50]

Walker is on the mark in this statement when she stresses the importance of the battered woman's tacit knowledge of the true nature of the batterer's behavior. But two problems beset her logic in the above remarks. First, the traditional law of self-defense can be more accommodating to context than Walker and her colleagues admit. We saw in the last chapter that some attorneys in such cases claim that BWS allows more evidence to come into the case. But Maguigan contests this claim in her meticulous article. "Like the assumption that most cases are nonconfrontational, this assumption is drawn from a limited review of appellate opinions. . . . [T]he criminal law does not generally assume the one-time and time-bounded encounter that many scholars believe is the foundation of its male-identified definitions. Rather, the law's definitions have developed to reflect the reality that the most common homicide case is one in which the parties have a history with each other." [51] Indeed, the evidence law of every state now allows evidence of the history of abuse between the parties to be introduced. [52]

In addition, Walker's logic elevates advocacy over truth in a telling way. Let me reconstruct the implications of her argument. It distills into the following propositions: a) "facts" are no more important than "opinions," to use her own words in the quotation above; b) men have faulty logic, at least when it comes to thinking about the dynamics of violence in relationships; c) the legal system is male-oriented; d) women think differently from men (at least if they are true to their real voices); e) since men's truths are already entrenched in the system, fairness requires pushing the other gender line. The logic of her argument justifies simply taking the other side.

Walker's logic is indebted to Carol Gilligan's famous analysis in *In a Different Voice*. Gilligan presents evidence that women practice a form of moral reasoning that is more subtle, nuanced, and contextual than the deductive, abstract, universalist form of reasoning practiced by men. She developed her theory in order to explain why women have not scored as high on Laurence Kohlberg's famous scales of moral reasoning as men. Kohlberg's scales attempt to measure the ability to engage in abstract moral reasoning, yet Gilligan purported to show that women are prone to think more in terms of relationships and ambiguities than of rules and abstractions. In a study of responses to questions dealing with abortion, moral and political choices, and rights and responsibilities, Gilligan's respondents passed through three distinct stages of moral reasoning revolving around the concept of "care" for others. [53]

Gilligan's theory is interesting and suggestive, but it raises as many questions as it answers, as several commentators have pointed out. [54] In addition to certain methodological problems (not controlling for such factors as degree of education, social-economic class, etc.; not following her subjects through the sequence of moral reasoning she claims exists), a review of the broader literature on moral reasoning confirms the conclusion that men and women reason alike; but Gilligan does not address this discrepancy. [55] In the few studies that do show sex differences, "[I]t appears that education, not gender, accounts for women's seeming lesser maturity. . . . [T]hinking about moral issues is closely linked to, although not identical with, general cognitive development, and we know that the sexes do not differ at the average rate at which they climb the ladder of cognitive growth."[56] Carol Stack has shown, for example, that "under conditions of economic deprivation there is a convergence between women and men in their construction of themselves in relationship to others, and that these conditions produce a convergence also in women's and men's vocabularies of rights, morality and the social good."[57] Despite these and other powerful critiques of Gilligan's thesis of "different voice," her work has achieved a large academic following because it is intuitively satisfying to the powerful intellectual and political forces in favor of "difference" and the psychology and politics of identity.[58]

Cycle Theory

The cycle theory is particularly important in its illumination of the nature of cumulative fear and the intersubjective dynamics (mutual needs) of the partners in a battering relationship. Nora Cashen, a former battered woman who works with battered women, told us:

> The cycle theory is very interesting. I talk to a lot of women who are letting go of the cycle theory, but I see a lot of value to it. I hear it's like using stick figures to describe someone's life. But there can be truth in stick figures. I was in an abusive relationship myself, though not as long as many. I worked during it. But I kept mining the relationship for pieces of emotional truth. While many would say the cycle theory wouldn't apply to me, there are many ways in which it does—the honeymoon phase, etc.[59]

But the cycle theory nonetheless raises some key questions that we should address. First, as Faigman and others have pointed out, Walker's method of deriving the theory is suspect.[60] To begin, Walker and her associates did not employ a control group of nonbattered women in their 1984 study. They based their research on four hundred "self-identified" battered women who responded to advertisements in a six-state area. In addition, they asked leading questions of their respondents, such as "Would you call it . . . ?", which are much more likely to steer respondents toward a certain conclusion than less leading questions.[61] If battered women tend to want to please others, as Walker and others maintain, asking such questions is particularly questionable. Also, the researchers derived the cycle theory not from what interviewees actually told them but from their own interpretations of what was said. The results are beset by the problem of "experimenter expectancies."[62]

The point of this critique is not to discredit the claim that battered women suffer serious abuse. The evidence that they do is incontrovertible. The problem is more specific: asking leading questions can skew one's interpretation of the meaning of abuse in relation to the standards of self-defense. Everything depends on the facts, so intellectual circumspection is of the essence.

Asking leading questions in the context of a new social paradigm concerning psychology and the nature of crime is hardly new. In *The Discovery of the Asylum: Social Order and Disorder in the New Republic*, David J. Rothman chronicles the way in which new criminologists of the Jacksonian period interviewed prisoners to "discover" the causes and meaning of crime. Dedicated to social environmentalist explanations of criminality and the tenets of Jacksonianism and the Enlightenment, these researchers were disinclined to construe crime in terms of the traditional emphasis on original sin. Attributing crime to family decline and disorder, and alcohol, they discovered what the new paradigm told them was there:

> Sympathetic questioners, letting the criminal know that they thought that much of the blame for his fate rested with his parents, would soon hear him recount his father's drinking habits and the attraction of the tavern around the corner. These sketches reflected the ideas of the questioner, not some objective truth about the criminal. The doctrine was clear: parents who sent their children into the society without a rigorous training in discipline and obedience would find them in the prison.[63]

E. L. Quarantelli makes a similar discovery in his investigation of the ways in which professionals propound conflicting psychological interpretations of the aftereffects of such community disasters as hurricanes and mud slides. Mental health professionals frequently find what their paradigms tell them they should find, and these paradigms are seldom congruent with the mental states and needs of the victims.[64] This state of affairs has led sardonic observers to point out that victims of disasters confront two traumatic events: the cataclysm itself and the subsequent intervention of the professional helpers!

The psychiatric reports in the Lisa Skalaski case in Madison, Wisconsin, present a contemporary replay of this process of discovery. John P. Jendusa, M.S.S.W., prepared one of the evaluations after conducting numerous tests. Jendusa applied the tools available to the new narrative of victimization, which embraces the concepts of repressed memory and multiple personality due to this repression. In addition to administering several tests for dissociation, incest, and family violence, Jendusa recommended that the psychiatrists superintend the ubiquitous sodium amytal interview, the controversial method to "recover" repressed memory. Jendusa confidently blamed the gap in memory on incest and related victimization. Skalaski had "an almost total loss of childhood memory."[65]

Another report, filed by Dr. Patricia A. Jens, of the Dodge County Department of Human Resources, expressed skepticism. Though Jens concurred with the assessments of PTSD, depression, and extreme self-blame, the entire tone of her report differs from that of Jendusa. Striking a tone of skepticism, Jens proceeded to question Jendusa's findings. Jens's challenge is perhaps a manifestation of the normal professional competition that arises with different training and competing paradigms of analysis.[66] And in the conflict over recovered memory, those with greater credentials do tend to be more skeptical than those with lesser credentials, since knowledge slows down the rush to conclusions. Jens's report casts a jaundiced eye on the validity of the narrative and diagnosis that Jendusa painted with such an eager brush:

> It is unclear to me how he jumps from a scale which is designed to be used with adolescents talking about relationships, to the presence of a Dissociative Disorder in an adult female . . .
>
> He states that he feels that the subject has "an almost total loss of childhood memory." He concludes with Lisa Skalaski's recall of abuse she suffered at the hands of her sister-in-law between the ages of 3 and 6. (This conflicts with "an almost total loss of childhood memory".) . . .
>
> He does not talk about validity studies for any of these instruments used. . . . He does not describe any training he has had which enables him to be an expert at using these instruments, [but] he states that "Lisa is a seriously troubled woman who requires professional mental health attention and long-term individual psychotherapy."[67]

More important than the problem of suggestion and steering that these examples spotlight, Walker's cycle theory fails to place the three phases of the cycle within any meaningful time frame.[68] Given the standards that must govern any self-defense law, this shortcoming is vexatious. For example, what if, for some reason, a batterer erupts into a rage during the period of "contrition," when by Walker's very logic the woman's guard is down? How does the doctrine of "cumulative terror" affect her judgment in this case? Further, as Faigman wonders, it is possible that a period of "normality" occurs between loving contrition and the renewed buildup phase. If so, what is the status of the syndrome in this state? And what about tension-building phases that do not lead to battering?[69] Are we to believe that tension building always results in a battering incident?

Even if there is a cycle, the theory does not, in itself, provide the jury with insights into the nature of the harm at the time of the self-defensive act—a problem that arises whether one applies the imminence test or any broader test. Cycle theory does not distinguish apprehensions of deadly harm from other types of fears. Walker and other BWS experts have not presented a single instance in which a battered woman overreacted or acted too precipitously, and the theory of BWS does not help in making this determination. Nor does BWS help juries decide whether the battered woman acted with proportionate force, which is often the most important question in the case (jurors in the *Richardson* case told us that this proved to be a crucial issue for them, and that the BWS testimony did not help them in this regard).[70]

In addition, Walker's findings do not necessarily confirm that a complete cycle characterizes most battering relationships. In her 1984 study, she found that 65 percent of respondents experienced the tension-building phase, and 58 percent endured the loving contrition stage. She does not provide evidence of what percentage suffer through *both* stages, however. Given Walker's actual findings, it is reasonable to assume that 38 percent experience the full cycle (65 percent $\times$ 58 percent).[71] But the logic of the cycle requires that all stages be experienced. One thoughtful interviewee told us that her battering father never expressed remorse and that the abuse was constant. Another interviewee told us that her father was like Jekyll and Hyde; after beatings, he would be incredibly warm and charming. Still, no cycle characterized his swings, since he could erupt "out of the blue."[72]

Learned Helplessness: Empirical Problems

Agency versus Passivity

For Seligman's unfortunate dogs, the state of learned helplessness proved to be a condition of no return; Seligman found it exceedingly difficult to retrain them to exercise a measure of control.[73] Accordingly, how can learned helplessness explain the battered woman's finally striking out against her tormentor?[74] Beholden to behaviorism, BWS appears to assume that the conditioning of victimization explains every act, including the fateful decision to kill or protect oneself. But a qualitative gap exists between the state of victimization and the act of self-defense; the latter involves a choice related to a number of factors, none of which is consistent with the model of learned helplessness. Remember Walker's surprise at finding that her battered women respondents actually felt more "locus of control" and "self-esteem" than others, reported in *The Battered Woman Syndrome*. These findings, as well as the reports of people who have worked with battered women and the findings of researchers into "survivor" behavior, suggest that battered women are not "helpless" when they engage in self-protective and other actions. Recognizing this has a profound effect on thinking about the appropriate legal response. Battered women are certainly often desperate. But learned helplessness is not about desperation, it is about helplessness.

Learned helplessness reduces battered women to the status of dogs. It denies the very integrity and potential agency that the women wish to attain. When BWS strips battered women of any potential responsibility, it strips them of potential dignity. To be sure, Walker's treatment of learned helplessness is not so reductionist as to eliminate volition (though we have seen that her depictions in court often boil down to this portrayal). In *The Battered Woman Syndrome*, Walker still analogizes (indeed, equates) battered women's responses to violence to the behavior of dogs, but she interposes the notion of "survival or coping skills," which entails using "passivity as their way to stay alive. The analogy [to animals] is in the failure for both the dogs and the battered woman to develop adequate escape skills. Failure to develop such adequate problem-solving skills can be seen in Seligman's (1975) later human subjects caused by experimentally-produced learned helplessness."[75] Later, in *Terrifying Love*, she goes further, saying that "a closer look revealed that these dogs were not really passive. They had developed coping skills that minimized the pain."[76]

But three problems persist with this logic. First, Walker seems to go back and forth between concluding that learned helplessness entails passivity and that it does not, revealing that the question of passivity is controversial and open to interpretation. Second, Walker consistently endorses the analogy between human behavior and dogs. This analogy is extremely problematic. Even though the most heinous batterers attempt to reduce their mates to the status of dogs, many battered women manage to maintain (often heroically) much more dignity, cognitive choice, and survival skills than Seligman's dogs. The reasons that many stay in the relationship are suggestive. To the extent that they stay because of fear, the analogy to dogs is tighter because fear reduces us to a primal state centered in the limbic system. But we have seen earlier that battered women will stay for other reasons, such as love, guilt, traumatic bonding, the normative belief in the need to keep the family together, and the desire to achieve the traditional American Dream of the family. To the extent that these cognitive beliefs and needs affect the decision to stay or to not develop escape skills, fear is mediated by moral beliefs that dogs do not possess.

Third, although Walker's treatment of helplessness in these passages is somewhat subtle, the image that the concept of learned helplessness conveys in court and in the popular imagination is one of passivity and lack of agency. Interviewees in the shelter movement and related positions in Wisconsin scorned learned helplessness for this reason. *We did not find a single interviewee involved in the movement who accepted the theory without serious reservations,* though several prison interviewees and other interviewees portrayed themselves or their mothers as "largely helpless." One said of her mother, "I think she sorta felt trapped. Um, she thought that that was her life and she had nowhere else to turn to, nowhere else to go. . . . She had plenty of, she had six years to leave the marriage. She never did."[77] Tensions between activists on the line in the shelters and the "professionals" who advocate sociological or psychological approaches to the problem of domestic violence have split the movement from its inception in the early 1970s; the dispute over learned helplessness is the latest incarnation of this tension.[78] Patti Seeger, spokeswoman for the nationally recognized Dane County Advocates for Battered Women, located in Madison, Wisconsin, denounced the theory in an interview:

What I don't like about BWS [battered woman syndrome] is that it is tied to "learned helplessness." I disagree *totally* with this whole theory. Rather than being helpless, battered women adopt survival skills. We get women in our shelters with unbelievable survival skills, who do unreal things. . . . To call this "helplessness" is pure crap. It is learning to survive in a terrorist environment. They make whatever psychic changes that are necessary. They are intense survivors.[79]

Two other advocates who are widely cited in the press and in legal circles as leaders of the battered woman movement in Dane County offered similar viewpoints. Cashen, a former battered woman who has provided expert testimony in court, redefined BWS in her mind to mean a set of symptoms such as depression and PTSD, combined with a pattern of hypervigilant behavior that is the antithesis of learned helplessness. Cashen also questioned construing battered women's mentality as a form of diminished capacity. Like Szasz, who points out that diminished capacity is often really a form of hypercapacity, Cashen portrayed battered women as having extraordinary rationality and capacity in their own circumscribed environments. Her portrayal is also consistent with Browne's concept of a "continuum of tolerance":

BWS means a variety of things. But I'll tell you up front that I have some difficulties with Walker's learned helplessness model. But BWS is a set of behaviors or attitudes that are learned over time to deal with the problems. . . . A lot of hypervigilant behavior, monitoring his behavior to know all the time what he is up to. They become experts of his cues, very externally motivated, they don't think of themselves. They monitor their own behavior to see what they can do to maintain control over the situation . . .

I wouldn't phrase it as diminished capacity. It is someone whose survival has been so focused on maintaining peace, their energy is so channeled, they lose their ability to have perspective. It's like anything else— a job with long hours, you lose your social skills. So there is diminished capacity in this sense . . .

I don't like the phrase "learned helplessness." I have seen women in extremely abusive relationships who still scheme after 50 years! They are still active problem solvers, which, by definition, is not learned helplessness. They have made a conscious decision that certain avenues we would use are not useful. For example, calling the police. It only takes once: she pays for it, learns it doesn't work. But this isn't the same thing as learned helplessness.[80]

Kathleen Kreneck, policy coordinator of the Wisconsin Coalition against Domestic Violence, made similar remarks:

> I don't believe in BWS theory, both philosophically and practically. Lenore falls short in saying women perceive it. Battered women are keenly aware, and do not lose sight of reality. . . . Research shows on average that women reach out five times before attempting it [violence]. And I think batterers are all-knowing, for they are consumed with having control. I never would have believed there are men who would put sugar in the gas tank at shelters, show up at work seventeen times to get her fired. BWS's assumption of irrationality is wrong. I've talked to hundreds of battered women and read accounts of hundreds more: they are acutely aware. Those who kill do so because they know if they don't they will die. [BWS has penetrated the legal system so much] because we are a victim-oriented society. It is easier to deal with this than real social change. It is a therapeutic concept, Walker is a therapist. We easily blame victims, we find fault in them. Domestic violence is political, an oppression of women, an expression of sexism.[81]

These critical viewpoints suggest that the courts and the shelter movement have moved in different directions in the matter of learned helplessness. *Although the courts rely on the model of science provided by Walker, the shelter movement and related advocates use a more situational logic.*

It is ironic and telling that the theory of learned helplessness is derived from the behavior of dogs, for that is precisely the status that battered women wish to transcend. Recall the scene that triggered Francine Hughes's fateful act, in which Mickey forced her to eat on the floor like a dog, or the interviewee whose husband treated her "like a trained dog," or the woman whose husband would make her bark like a dog. One could say this point is disingenuous because battered women often *are* treated like dogs; but BWS is based on findings of the behavior of dogs, which implies that women and dogs behave the same way under similar circumstances. In de Beauvoir's terms, BWS wraps battered women in the very immanence that modern feminism has devoted itself to defeating.

The Problem of Human Motivation

The previous discussion points to another issue: BWS's scientific gloss simplifies the complex questions of motivation and intent in certain cases. The cases reveal a multitude of motivations and intentions, even though fear predominates, as such writers as Browne and Mahoney stress. Browne shows how women who kill have often been subjected to more violent and sometimes psychopathic mates than women who do not kill.[82] But the case law, interviews, and the literature disclose other reasons for "crossing the line" that can arise in certain cases.

One reason for "crossing the line" is related to helplessness, but mainly in the sense that it represents a deeply rooted desire *to prevent* oneself from falling into helplessness. This threshold can materialize because of the intensifying spiral of abuse (Browne) or because of emancipatory changes in the consciousness of the battered woman (the case of Francine Hughes). In some cases the triggering device is the opposite of helplessness and self-defense: change in the woman's attitude or the discovery of upsetting news (e.g., the batterer obtaining a new lover or wanting a divorce, as in the *Skalaski* and *Buhrle* cases) seems to actuate violence.[83] The BWS model cannot account for these real cases. Indeed, even Walker admits that her clients sometimes kill for reasons other than self-defense: "Rich or poor, the women described in this book are a small minority: a minority that did not sit and wait to die. Instead, in a moment of self-defense (or, in some cases, *self-realization*), they finally took matters into their own hands and kill their abusers."[84]

Sometimes Walker drastically simplifies the motives of her clients and other battered women who kill. Murder-for-hire cases provide prime examples of this tendency.[85] In such cases women generally take the initiative, exercising a premeditation that confounds the theory of learned helplessness. To be sure, the level of a particular woman's involvement is not always clear, and it can vary in different cases. One prison inmate told us that though she initiated an agreement with a friend to kill her husband after he threatened to make her have sex with dogs for pornographic purposes, her accomplice would not let her abandon her scheme. He threatened to kill her and her daughter if she reneged.[86] But there is no reason to think that such cases comprise the norm. In a Lexis search we found seventy-nine state appellate decisions from 1981 through mid-1992 that dealt with women killing their alleged abusers and the use of BWS.[87] Only six of these cases involved women who hired someone to kill their abusers, and in only one of these did the court's recitation of the facts indicate a third party's taking the major initiative by acting as a "rescuer."[88] In *Terrifying Love,* however, Walker assumes that battered women who contract out do not deviate in any way from her model of BWS and responsibility:

> Rarely, though, are these cases anything like the typical "murder for hire" cases one hears about in the media. Money rarely changes hands. More often, the actual perpetrator has heard nauseating tales of the batterer's violence and has decided to take the law into his own hands. Sometimes, too, the perpetrator does not intend to actually kill the batterer; he wants, most of all, to protect the battered woman (and, in some cases, her children) from further harm.[89]

The case law out of the states belies this assessment, as a host of motives present themselves, including self-realization, profit, jealousy, and anger over discovering sexual abuse of children. A look at "contract" cases reveals how motives can be more complex than the BWS model assumes. Battered women are as human as the rest of us. In *People v. Yaklich*, the defendant hired two men to shoot her husband and paid them $4,200. The courts ruled that no self-defense instruction was merited because of the utter lack of imminence.[90] in *People v. Jackson*, the mercenary motives of the wife stood out. The defendant and two male co-defendants killed her husband for insurance money. Jackson and the men had made previous attempts on her husband's life, and she had even cajoled him into purchasing more life insurance before his death. She was not living with him at the time (so she was not "trapped"), and the men had to lure him to their farmhouse. The court declined to allow BWS testimony because the facts did not support self-defense as a matter of law.[91] In *State v. Daniels*, the defendant and her son made the murder of her husband look like a burglary in her husband's hotel room. Again, the court refused to allow BWS testimony, this time because of Montana's strict rules of evidence.[92] Finally, in *State v. Leaphart*, the defendant hired two men to kill her husband, partly because her religious beliefs frowned on divorce (her religion presumably looked more favorably upon homicide). Her husband had been very violent, unfaithful, and addicted to drugs. Leaphart had talked to others about killing him for the previous five months. After the murder, she confided to her secretary that she had witnessed the actual killing scene. Her request for a self-defense instruction was thwarted by the clear absence of imminence.[93]

Walker discusses *Yaklich* in *Terrifying Love*, alleging that "all Donna [Yaklich] ever gave them [the assassins] was ten dollars, here and there, for gas money,"[94] but the defendant admitted paying them $4,200.[95] Walker also argues that cumulative terror stretches the coverage of imminence to the entire relationship, an argument with troubling implications, as my research assistant, Ann S. Jacobs, observed:

> [T]his conclusion fails to look at the law. Hiring an assassin takes time. It would be hard to argue that during that entire time, the defendant was in imminent danger. Surprisingly, that appears to be exactly what Walker argues. She states that "[g]iven the escalating nature of battering behavior, 'imminency' refers to a reasonable perception that, as the abuse starts again, it will cause serious bodily harm or death." If that is indeed the argument, then BWS becomes nothing more than *carte blanche* to kill an abusive husband. If one is always in imminent danger at the hands of an abusive spouse, then one may always use self-defense, regardless of the husband's actions at that particular time. In an ordered society, this is not the type of situation that should be condoned . . .
>
> [T]hese cases stretch 'imminency' to its breaking point. . . . This is not the law. Nor should the law be changed to reflect this. Self-defense is a last resort.[96]

The cases furnish other motives. Finding out about child sexual abuse naturally triggers anger and shock, which can turn into retributive motives or verbal confrontations that escalate into violence and self-defense, accidental death, heat-of-passion manslaughter, or intentional homicide.[97] In the *Skalaski* case, finding out about her husband's possible adultery and/or plans to leave the relationship sparked retaliation. Sometimes such cases involve on-again, off-again relationships that do not conform to the key premise that all battered women are trapped, necessitating resort to violence.[98] In *State v. Pascal,* the defendant killed her boyfriend when he threatened to leave her and her child. She used BWS as a defense, and the jury found her guilty of manslaughter. The court then relied on BWS to reduce the sentence to ninety days in jail and one year of community service! Jacobs perceptively remarks that in this and similar cases, "There was no danger of any kind of imminent harm to these individuals. Somehow it is assumed that suffering from BWS necessarily eradicates any other motive for the actions taken by the battered women. As these cases indicate, sometimes other motives are much stronger than any self-defense claim."[99]

Along these same lines, though the case law with battered women defenders overwhelmingly provides evidence of abuse, there are some instances which are less straightforward. Defendants can "malinger" or feign the defense; or, more likely, they might exaggerate the abuse.[100] Even acknowledging the enormity of abuse and its gendered nature does not excuse us from scrupulous attention to the facts of each case. Indeed, the very origin of BWS as a defense in a trial, and how this trial was perceived by activists, show why we must be careful in our generalizations about the meaning of abuse in the context of criminal cases.

The Jennifer Patri case in Waupaca, Wisconsin, in 1979 featured the first legal presentation of "battered woman's syndrome" at trial, pioneered by attorney Alan Eisenberg to get Patri convicted for manslaughter rather than murder in one trial, and found not guilty by reason of insanity in a separate trial for arson that took place in another jurisdiction. Patri had shot her husband with a rifle, buried him in the basement of their farmhouse, and set the place afire. The case gained national and statewide attention.[101] But the case has been somewhat forgotten because its chronicler ended up telling the wrong story.

After a year or so of working on his book about the case, Steven Englund, a former Waupaca resident and accomplished historian at UCLA, came to the reluctant conclusion that Patri was simply not a battered woman. Robert Patri had more reason to be afraid of Jennifer than she did of him. Jennifer was enraged that Robert had found happiness with another woman, and that he was going to leave her. It was Jennifer who possessed the traditional patriarchal views concerning family and property. Englund found no evidence indicating Robert abused his wife. Jennifer did not embark on a narrative of abuse until Eisenberg took over the defense and suggested that Robert was an abuser and that he might have been carrying a butcher knife before the fatal act.[102]

Englund's book is by far the most thorough case study of a battered woman defense case, yet it is virtually never cited in the literature, and those who do cite the case simply assume that Patri was a battered woman. Cynthia Gillespie, whose book on battered women and self-defense is widely cited, talks about "Jennifer Patri, a Waupaca, Wisconsin, housewife who shot her brutal estranged husband when he threatened her with a butcher knife." Ann Jones makes an identical remark in her classic *Women Who Kill* and indicts the press for not being one-sided enough in the case. Englund's book was published six years before Gillespie's, yet she does not mention it.[103]

The recent false alarm concerning the upsurge of domestic battering that accompanies the Super Bowl provides another example of ideology or belief prevailing over fact. Activists across the country, including the feminist wing of Fairness and Accuracy in Reporting, claimed that Super Sunday was the most violent day of the year for women. BWS's creator, Lenore Walker, showed up to substantiate this claim in an appearance on "Good Morning America." Groups disseminated the message, "Don't remain alone with him during the game." But Ken Ringle of the *Washington Post* actually contacted the sources upon whose work these contentions were based (including shelters), and each source categorically denied that his or her work showed this to be the case. Katherine Dunn summarizes: "The entire campaign was a lie. One authority on battered women told Ringle, 'I hate this. I've devoted fourteen years of my life to bring to the public's attention the very serious problem of battered women. And when people make crazy statements like this, the credibility of the whole cause can go right out the window.'"[104]

In the end, instances such as the *Patri* case and the Super Bowl hoax obviously do not discredit legal defenses of battered women who commit crimes; evidence compels us to take battered women's claims seriously. But we should approach such cases with an open mind that is free of prejudicial preconceptions arising from any source. Being battered can present incredibly difficult and oppressive circumstances, but its relevance to criminal defenses depends upon an honest assessment of the facts.

In *Battered Women Who Kill: Psychological Self-Defense as Legal Justification*, Charles Ewing introduces another motive akin to Walker's notion of "self-realization": the concept of "psychological self-defense." Building on the theory of learned helplessness, studies of the psychology of victimization, and the psychology of "self" pioneered by such psychiatrists as R. D. Laing and Heinz Kohut, Ewing theorizes that the ultimate battlefield in abusive relationships is the coherent self. Battered women confront the danger of psychological death:

> [T]he law of self-defense equates "self" with only the corporeal aspects of human existence—physical life and bodily integrity. This simple equa-

tion has proven convenient and, in many respects, functional for legal standards, which reflect the law's need for reasonable certainty and society's generally preeminent concern for the preservation of physical life. Yet this equation . . . denies what psychologists, philosophers, theologians, and people in general have long realized: namely, that there is more to "self" than mere physical being or bodily integrity.

As commonly understood outside the law, "self" encompasses not only the physical aspects of being but also those psychological functions, attributes, processes, and dimensions of experience that give meaning and value to physical existence. [Battered women kill] to prevent their batterers from seriously damaging, if not destroying, psychological aspects of the self which give meaning and value to their lives. In short, they kill in *psychological self-defense.*[105]

Ewing's thesis is empirically insightful, for in relationships, as we have seen, the partners struggle for freedom and intersubjective recognition.[106] Francine Hughes burned Mickey not only because he threatened her. Her act appeared intimately bound with her desire to make something of herself through education. The raising of her consciousness toward self-determination (her education would make her words and thoughts her own) might have heightened her awareness of her bondage and given her a new perspective on her condition.[107] When Mickey fathomed the meaning of Francine's books, he destroyed them and began to treat her like a dog.

The case symbolizes the themes of power, control, and self-determination at the heart of the battered woman issue. On the one hand, Francine was trapped in many important respects: every time she left, he hunted her down and threatened to kill her. On the other hand, an honest appraisal of Francine's motivations reveals a desperate movement toward freedom rather than pure self-defense or learned helplessness. Jack Katz portrays Francine's act as an act of transcendence:

The version of the Good she was defending was not simply the right to physical self-defense. It was also a version of the American dream that is widely accepted among people of all political persuasions: to better yourself through education and to escape the welfare rolls by applying yourself to serve business.

When Francine Hughes set her sleeping husband on fire, she was reacting to his destruction of her school materials and to his prohibition of her return to school, in essence daring her to defy him and to escape degradation.[108]

Despite Ewing's insight, the theory of psychological self-defense falls short as a criminal defense. For starters, the concept is contumaciously broad. It is simply too vague or all-encompassing to serve as a valid legal defense. Most people would not consider psychological pressure alone a justifiable basis for the use of deadly force. Psychological pressure is relevant to self-defense claims only if it signifies, or is backed up by, fear of physical harm or captivity. Like Walker's cycle theory, the doctrine provides absolutely no criterion for assessing when the harm is imminent or impending, or for how much force would be allowed. Once one felt endangered with psychological "death," one could presumably kill at any time, for psychological danger as Ewing portrays it is omnipresent. All contract murders and killing while the victim is sleeping appear to qualify for justification status under the sway of this theory. And just what type of force would be proportionate? Would it be legitimate to knock someone out with a pipe if he threatened to make you "quasi-psychologically dead?" At what level of psychological harm would it be justified to resort to deadly force? Such thorny questions know no empirical answer.[109]

Furthermore, Ewing's doctrine would yield unintended consequences, for a similar logic could pertain to many cases involving "overbearing personalities." Recall the women at the University of Washington who claimed that heated criticism of their teaching methods wrought a psychological trauma akin to "rape-trauma syndrome." In our time, psychological death looms like Damocles' sword over many nondiscriminating heads. For example, we witness the use of the Holocaust as a metaphor for many forms of victimization, as in a major art display at Chicago's Spertus Museum in April 1994 by Judy Chicago, which links the Nazis' brutality to the sexism, meat eating, and nuclear weapons of the West.[110] In a later article, Ewing compared battered women to concentration camp survivors.[111] In our age of great sensitivity to all manners of psychological pressure and trauma, a defense of psychological self-defense could be tantamount to a license to kill. It is better to leave the notion of psychological self-defense to jury discretion and nullification.[112]

Finally, what about women who feel threatened but do not suffer psychological extinction? If Ewing's theory won adherence in the courts, it would undoubtedly create a narrative based on features of psychological self-defense. And narratives can be like zero-sum games: one prevails as others fail. By taking the focus from the objective circumstances surrounding the self-defensive act and placing it in the realm of the psychological and the subjective, the doctrines of learned helplessness and psychological self-defense might make it more difficult for physically and psychologically autonomous women to win acquittal in cases of actual danger.

A brief look at the expert's testimony and report in the *Richardson* case yields a concrete example of the problem of formulaic reduction that plagues such BWS-related theories as Walker's and Ewing's theory of psychological self-defense. In the *Richardson* case, defense counsel Mueller obtained the services of Marilyn Hutchinson, a clinical psychologist from Kansas City.[113] Hutchinson testified at the trial in Kenosha, Wisconsin, in 1993, and prepared a psychological evaluation.

Hutchinson spoke with poise and presented BWS in a simple, straightforward way that was accessible to the jury, following the by now classic BWS line. She stressed the importance of learned helplessness, and then the trial broke for lunch. During this time an observer who was also involved with the defense slipped Mueller a note that read, "Given the testimony about helplessness, the jury will wonder why or how Ronda found the will to stab David. They *will* wonder about this." Upon returning from lunch, Mueller asked a few more questions and then wrapped up the direct examination by asking this question:

Q. One final point, [d]octor. You discussed learned helplessness, a situation when a dog, a rat just lays down and lets it happen. How can it be, how can it be that a battered woman, who is suffering in part from learned helplessness, can kill her abuser?

A. Well, fortunately, we have some psychological and cognitive gifts that rats and dogs don't have and that we can, even in a state of learned helplessness, come to some kind of realization or some kind of awareness that this is, this is the time, "I really am in danger this time, I am going to get killed or I am about to be so severely damaged that this surpasses what has gone on before," and in those kind of instances I believe that the human does have the capacity to be different than dogs and rats and, and strive in some kind of way to protect themselves and save their life [sic].[114]

Hutchinson made a valiant effort. But she could not reconcile the logic of learned helplessness, which she had presented so strongly, and this last-ditch effort to retrieve agency from the jaws of the incapacity to act. It is difficult to reconcile these discourses or logics in the absence of a more thorough analysis. The evidence in the case simply did not support the thesis that Ronda was "helpless." In the end, her defense might have fared better without BWS testimony.

One striking point in the evaluation was Hutchinson's finding that Ronda had trouble generalizing and thinking in patterns. The reader should place the following quotation in his or her mind next to Walker's comments above about how women think in "patterns" and in contexts, unlike men, and how this epistemological difference is central to BWS:

There seem to be two areas in which Ms. Richardson did poorly: subtests that measured school knowledge (information and arithmetic) and subtests that required the understanding of a "whole" and then placing the parts into that whole. This inability to see the whole and then manipulate it seemed to be part of her difficulty in the picture completion. . . . It appears this [the way Ronda handled the block designs] also supports the hypothesis of understanding a perceptual field only in fragments—failing to understand the gestalt.[115]

But this finding—central to Hutchinson's evaluation—contravenes her claim in court that Richardson fit the Walker profile!

It is also instructive to note Hutchinson's understanding of why Ronda found herself between a rock and a hard place:

> She indicates it never occurred to her to stop seeing Mr. Miller. It is quite likely that her own issues about never having a father significantly clouded her judgment about the rationality of having Mr. Miller in her life "for the sake of her son." Also, her own emotional dependency, and probably her chemical dependency, kept her tied to Mr. Miller. Lastly, her judgment is faulty. A single positive act or interchange could be used to transform her ideas of the relationship and its possibilities: one piece of data could be used to define the whole.
>
> Overall, she was in a desperate emotional and financial situation. She literally was without the resources to extricate herself from a terrible situation. It is likely that the slow realization that she and Mr. Miller were not being successful at this attempt at cohabitation would have been very traumatizing to her. It seems unlikely she had not overtly communicated to Mr. Miller her intent to leave him. This combination of loss for both of them could easily have escalated a volatile situation into lethality.[116]

Hutchinson's conclusion shows not only learned helplessness but a kind of helplessness conjoined with a broader desperation (not just over David's violence, but over the fate of the relationship!) and some (often circumstantial) incapacities. In the real world of differently constituted people, helplessness is often mediated by other opportunities or lack of opportunities, and different capacities and incapacities.

A related problem with learned helplessness is that women who do not fit the mold might be denied the right to defend themselves because learned helplessness creates a kind of character expectation, which serves more passive women at the expense of women who do not exhibit the qualities of victimhood.

Sharon Angella Allard tackles this problem, postulating that BWS and learned helplessness have racially discriminatory consequences because stereotypical attitudes presume that black women have more experience with weapons and fighting than white women. Allard charges that BWS appeals to these stereotypes, thereby disqualifying women who do not conform to this notion. BWS plays on a narrative of the "good fairy princess" (Bobbitt) who is betrayed:

> While battered woman syndrome furthers the interest of some battered women, *the theory incorporates stereotypes of limited applicability concerning how a woman would and, indeed, should react to battering.* To successfully

defend herself, a battered woman needs to convince a jury that she is a "normal" woman—weak, passive, and fearful. *If the battered woman deviates from these characteristics, the jury may not associate her situation with that of the stereotypical battered woman.* . . . Race certainly plays a role in the cultural distinction between "good" and "bad" woman. The passive, gentle white woman is automatically more like the "good" fairy princess stereotype than a [b]lack woman, who as the "other" may be seen as the "bad" witch . . .

This dichotomy necessarily implies there is an "other" who can be pointed to as lacking in the characteristics of "true womanhood" . . .

Battered woman syndrome explains the behavior of battered women within fairly strict categories, i.e., that a woman is fearful, weak, and submissive. *Yet, the theory provides no means for assessing the reasonableness of the woman's act of killing unless she is given the "excuse" of learned helplessness.* "Excuse connotes personal weakness and implies that the defendant could not be expected to function as would a 'normal' person." [117]

Schneider shares this concern. In her analysis of *State v. Kelly*, Schneider registers fear that the New Jersey Supreme Court's focus on the use of expert testimony to explain why Kelly did not leave reflects gender bias in the law. "One possible explanation is that the court finds it easier to focus on those aspects of the testimony which characterize the woman as passive and helpless (i.e., her incapacity to leave) rather than active and violent but reasonable. This highlights the dilemma of battered woman syndrome: explanation of the battered woman's actions from a solely victimized perspective cannot fully explain why she believed it was necessary to act." [118] One could add that it leads to the "labeling" of battered women as less than rational, thereby reinforcing their exclusion from equal citizenship. [119]

Emrolyn Kae Whitetail's conviction for second-degree murder presents an example. Whitetail, a Native American, killed her long-time boyfriend by stabbing him in the back during a fight; she apparently removed the knife and stabbed him again. She claimed that he had beaten her, or was about to beat her. The jury did not accept her claim of self-defense based on BWS. The Eighth Circuit Court of Appeals affirmed the conviction, but remanded the case on the grounds that BWS could be considered in the sentencing decision (the District Court felt that it could not consider it in sentencing because the jury rejected self-defense). At trial the prosecution harped on Whitetail's penchant for fighting with others, producing evidence that she had threatened her boyfriend with a knife a month before the fatal fray. During cross-examination, Whitetail admitted that she liked to fight. One of Whitetail's expert witnesses "testified on cross-examination that a woman who was the aggressor in fights with her husband would not qualify as a battered woman." [120] Although any defendant's past behavior and penchants for aggression are indeed relevant to his or her self-defense claim, *Whitetail* displays how BWS can work against women whose characters and lifestyles do not fit the passive-victim image. Carol Stonehouse, trained as a police officer, furnishes another example. Such misfits can lead to a miscarriage of justice if a nonpassive woman actually is confronted with imminent danger that she has not triggered as the original aggressor. Lorena Bobbitt's defense succeeded perhaps because the defense worked diligently to portray her as a passive, good, old-fashioned Catholic wife.

For whatever reason, a racial dichotomy did prevail in our prison interviews. Three of our four black interviewees did not eschew exercising force or defensive action. One even wore her aggressiveness proudly and confessed to being tough on "weak men." Another interviewee was battered but hit back, often inflicting wounds and bruises in a version of "mutual combat."[121] Yet these characteristics should be utterly irrelevant to their right to defend themselves.

This point raises a final problem with BWS and learned helplessness: although BWS "opens the evidentiary door" to the whole relationship (as well as the "son of a bitch" defense discussed in the previous chapter), such opening can turn on the woman for two reasons. First, the more one looks at the whole relationship, the more one might ask why she did not leave, if such opportunities were reasonably present and not countered by meaningful threats based on separation danger. We have seen that battered women can indeed be effectively trapped (though self-defense is not limited to cases in which women are trapped). But it is rare for a woman to be as trapped as the dogs in Seligman's experiments, for choices and opportunities to leave will normally be present except in the more extreme cases. For all too many battered women this set of choices is extremely difficult; but extreme difficulty is not the same thing as impossibility. In comparison, until the condition of learned helplessness set in, Seligman's dogs were given *no opportunity* to leave. Consequently, Seligman's experiments—the intellectual foundation of the theory of BWS—are analogous only to battered women in absolutely captive situations. If such cases are not typical of battered women, then it does a typical defendant no service to present Seligman's findings, for a jury might conclude that some meaningful or potential opportunity to leave renders a self-defense claim illegitimate. Whereas the jury would be correct in concluding that the defendant was not learnedly helpless according to the theory, *the defense's efforts to meld the self-defense case to the syndrome and helplessness encourages the jury to make a specious judgment: that the defendant was not entitled to self-defense because she had choices that Seligman's animals did not.*

Second, a battered woman's behavior over time could make her appear less morally creditable, especially to the extent that such behavior provides evidence of motives other than self-defense, such as revenge. Allard registers concern about this type of moral judgment above. And in the *Richardson* case, the jurors told us that they had negative feelings about Ronda as well as the deceased.[122] MacKinnon pinpoints the problem in a discussion of Ann Jones's *Women Who Kill* and the *Wanrow* decision:

[I]f deducing a symmetrical standard from *Wanrow* is difficult, making it symmetrical, in the context of her analysis of gender, is disturbing. For example, if one can expand time back to defend a woman who kills in self-defense, to understand the contextual determinants of her immediate response to a threat, symmetry would urge the equitability of expanding time back for the prosecution also, to ask why she did not leave after each prior threatening occasion. This result is reinforced by any emphasis on the woman's voluntariness, her self-acting. If she was capable of self-acting at the moment of her self-defense, it is difficult to explain away the inference that she was equally self-acting in choosing to remain in the situation over a period of time, a situation which is often like the one in which she finally killed.[123]

From this perspective, the law of self-defense suddenly looks less tainted with extraneous moral judgment.

BWS as a Dispeller of Myths: Myth Meets Counter-Myth

We saw in the previous chapter that BWS is intended to counter certain myths about jury behavior. Indeed, we also saw above (e.g., the *Stonehouse* case) that some prosecutors have told the jury that the defendant's failure to leave the relationship meant that the violence was not serious. We know that this assertion is often fraudulent. Nonetheless, the assumption that juries are ridden with myths calls for scrutiny. Mira Mihajlovich and others have challenged it by revealing that Walker has not demonstrated juror bias, but rather "she has based her findings on her own intuition."[124] Mihajlovich then quotes Acker and Toch, whose words merit repeating:

This estimate of public opinion is one that requires documentation. . . . Walker's roster [of myths] is in actuality a *literary device* designed *to contrast her own inferences* to a set of contrasting *assumptions which she rejects.* . . . [Walker], however, neither has expertise nor claims expertise in public opinion assessment, which is the only basis for her to assert that the "myth" with which she disagrees, and which the court [in *State v. Kelly*] . . . *assumes to be prevalent,* are widely endorsed.[125]

This claim has spawned only a handful of studies. Ewing and Moss Aubrey published the first study in 1987. They gave a hypothetical scenario of a battering incident to 216 people in the general public and asked them eight questions about the relationship that encapsulated what the researchers believe are typical myths.

Roughly two-fifths of the respondents believed the myths that a battered woman is partly responsible for her beating, that she is masochistic, and that she is emotionally disturbed if she remains in the relationship. Also, nearly two-thirds endorsed the myth that a battered woman could simply leave (56 percent of the men, 71 percent of the women!). The authors conclude that these results provide support for the use of expert testimony as "beyond the ken" of the average juror.[126]

Unfortunately, this study is flawed in important respects. In particular, as Mary Dodge and Edith Greene point out, "subjects responded to only one hypothetical scenario of domestic abuse, so it in unclear to what extent these data generalize to other situations."[127] Since "God is in the details" when it comes to self-defense cases, the lack of grounds upon which to generalize presents a real problem. Equally important, the scenario is not typical of the battering relationship that we examined above.

The scenario depicts a single battering incident that arises after nine years of marriage in the context of the husband's prolonged unemployment and the wife's rise to a managerial position in her new job (she had been a housewife for eight years until his steel plant laid him off for good). After she returned home from a party celebrating her promotion, he accused her of cheating "and threw her to the floor. She lay there stunned and ashamed. Robert became tearful and apologetic and swore that he would never hurt Francine again. Francine forgave Robert."[128] The responses Ewing and Aubrey received are indeed disturbing; nonetheless, it is disingenuous for them to derive broad conclusions about myths from responses based on this scenario. They depicted a relationship with only a relatively minor (though explosive) incident after nine years; the scenario presented no evidence or suggestion of a cycle, no evidence or suggestion of threats or intimidation surrounding separation, no endangerment of life, and no evidence of deeper pathology or rage on the part of the husband other than his growing sense of inadequacy over his unemployment. We saw above that many battering relationships involve isolated instances of "circumstantial specific" violence, whereas others are more pathological or systematically violent.

Given the scenario presented, it is not surprising that many respondents did not agree with what the experts believe. After all, how "mythical" is it to respond that Francine could leave Robert or that Robert would remain contrite? Another flaw in this study, Greene, Alan Raitz, and Heidi Lindblad point out, is that the questionnaire should have provided a scale of degree of agreement/disagreement with each proposition.[129]

Greene and co-authors have conducted two further studies that are more credible. In a study published in 1989, Greene, Raitz, and Lindblad made methodological improvements on the Ewing and Aubrey study, and found some, but less extensive, magnitudes of beliefs in myths than Ewing and Aubrey found.[130]

Dodge and Greene conducted a follow-up study published in 1991 that compared juror beliefs and knowledge to the understandings of researchers in domestic violence. The researchers drew conclusions from a group of forty-five experts in the field of spousal abuse, and compared these conclusions to the knowledge of 141 residents of El Paso County in Colorado Springs, Colorado, who had been called for jury duty. Dodge and Greene used this comparison because it is essential to the major standard of evidence for admission of expert testimony, the *Dyas* test (see chapter 2), which requires expert testimony to be "beyond the ken" of jurors.[131]

Their "Battered Woman Questionnaire" consisted of eighteen statements about typical issues, attitudes, and myths concerning domestic violence, of which the experts agreed with fourteen, usually with a very high level of consensus (80–90 percent). Dodge and Greene conclude that these results showed a high level *of validity and reliability* in the scientific expert community on these issues. The authors took consensus (reliability) to exist when 80 percent of the experts agreed or disagreed on an item. The four items with less consensus were: battered women are helpless to stop the beatings (64 percent agreed); a battered woman might provoke violence to get it over with (36 percent agreed); middle-class women are less likely to be beaten (56 percent disagreed); a battered woman can rarely predict the violence (30 percent disagreed).

The authors used a multivariate analysis of variance to compare jurors' responses to the experts', and found "significant differences on 11 of the 14 items on which experts expressed consensus." The three items over which no significant differences prevailed were: once violence is used it is always a potential threat (both agreed); most battered women deserve to be beaten (both disagreed); many battered women are crazy (both disagreed). On the other variables the strength of the agreement or disagreement varied. Dodge and Greene use these findings to support their claims that expert testimony about the areas of difference is advisable.

Dodge and Greene hedge their conclusions in important respects, however, and other potential problems exist in their study. First, as the authors themselves show and admit, although differences exist *in the comparative extent* of juror versus expert agreement or disagreement on eleven items, the compilation of the responses found substantial juror consensus on most of the items, and this consensus was in the same direction as the experts'. It just did not cross the 80 percent threshold that Dodge and Greene posited to demonstrate reliability. For example, most jurors agreed pretty strongly (though not beyond the threshold point) that a battered woman might believe her husband could kill her, that she might feel dependent, that she might be persuaded to stay by his contrition, that she shows signs of anxiety and depression, and that she might blame herself. The jurors agreed more than disagreed that she might believe that deadly force is the only way out; indeed, the greatest difference between the experts and the jurors was over this item. But the jurors still agreed more than disagreed with this item.[132]

This item raises a legal and normative point that transcends a purely factual or behavioral understanding: more than experts, jurors might believe that it is not enough that a woman conclude that she might need deadly force. If respondents think that self-defense is to be avoided short of sheer necessity, they might be reluctant to conclude that she believes deadly force is the only way out. Juries and the public often have stronger normative views about responsibility than psychological experts. Stephen Hurley, the lawyer highlighted in the previous chapter who skillfully uses BWS in trial, expressed this normative position as forcefully as anyone. Outside the forensic context, Hurley personally believes strongly that one is never justified in using deadly force unless one confronts strictly imminent danger.[133]

This possibility raises another vital point: for some of these items, it is very difficult to separate fact from normative value. If a respondent believes that a woman should make great efforts to leave before killing her husband (a normative view as much as an empirical one), this view would no doubt influence the response about the ease with which someone could leave. Jurors might be more prone to balance the different sides of the self-defense equation than the experts, whose primary professional focus is the plight of the battered woman per se.

A related problem is the way that Dodge and Greene conflate the issue of validity with the question of reliability. They use the experts to get at *Dyas*'s second prong, which requires, in their own words, reliability as well as validity. But all they test for is agreement among the experts, which constitutes reliability. They do not discuss underlying validity, which entails the substantive truth of the experts' claims. I have suggested that truth in this area is value-laden as much as empirically based. All Dodge and Greene show is that most experts agree on the items concerning domestic violence. But we saw above that the truth of the battering relationship is often very subtle, complex, and individualistic. Trends and generalizations exist, yet individual factors always mediate them.[134]

In the end, Dodge and Greene acknowledge that although their study shows more consensus (reliability) among experts than jurors, jurors clearly agree on the whole with the experts:

> Although results of the present study generally support the idea that relative to researchers, jurors have limited knowledge regarding battered women, *they also show that most jurors do not endorse myths or hold traditional stereotypic views associated with battered women.* For example, fewer than 10% of the jurors agreed that battered women are masochistic, deserve to be beaten, are crazy or emotionally disturbed. Less than 20% supported the myths that battered women would find it easy to leave without fear of further abuse, and that battering incidents are likely to involve lower class women. Less than 30% believed battered women could simply leave their abusers if they really wanted. *Apparently the be-*

liefs of jurors are not grounded on these so-called "myths" as suggested by courts, commentators, and researchers . . .

The present study evaluated the knowledge of actual jurors awaiting jury selection. *In addition, approximately three years separated the studies and the public's awareness of domestic violence has increased considerably in that time.*[135]

Although much of the literature still bemoans the prevalence of myths or misunderstandings about battered women and other victims of domestic abuse, such concern might well be overstated, at least to some extent. If Dodge and Greene are right, the gap between experts and potential jurors may be closing; the *Bobbitt* and *Menendez* cases certainly support this estimation.[136]

Walker and others also ignore additional possible explanations (or contributing explanations) for jury prejudice. Pointing toward one, defense lawyers claim that juries are loath to accept the legal burden of proof in cases involving excuses and self-defense. Mueller, the defense counsel for Richardson, asserted that the burden of proof in any self-defense case lies with the defense, regardless of what the law or jury instruction says.[137] This remark suggests that some defenses are problematic for reasons that transcend sexism and ignorance about domestic violence. In a related vein, Stephen Hurley, the leading defense attorney in Madison, claimed that cases involving intentional killing will always bear a more difficult burden of persuading the jury than other cases. He enjoined us to avoid abstracting BWS from the nature of the allegedly criminal act: "It [BWS] sells—but it sells in context. It is one thing to raise the issue in the context of a wife signing a tax return, and it's quite another thing to raise it in the context of 'this is why I killed my husband in cold blood.' You get some sympathy in the latter case, but it's a much, much harder sell."[138]

And we should not forget a crucial fact: self-defense cases are hard sells for men as well. Stephen Schulhofer points out that criminal law is premised on three "organizing assumptions" or principles: 1) *criminal law is judgmental,* meaning that it believes in punishment, not forgiveness, in most cases; 2) *criminal law is demanding:* "Criminal law prohibitions are not addressed solely, or even primarily, to people who can easily comply. . . . Homicide prosecutions often concern those who have acted under the most substantial external or internal pressures. . . . [This point] is deeply embedded in the structure of existing (traditional) criminal law doctrine"; 3) *criminal law is "pacifist":* that is, it "rejects violence as a favored or presumptive solution to problems between or among individuals."[139]

State v. Shroeder, discussed by Schulhofer, highlights the demanding nature of the law as applied to men. Shroeder shared a prison cell with a much larger inmate, who informed Shroeder that upon awakening in the morning, he was going to rape him. Were Shroeder to inform the guards, he would have exposed himself to greater danger later. During the night, Shroeder stabbed and killed his cellmate in a preemptive attack. The trial court refused to even instruct the jury on self-defense because of the lack of imminence! Though the court might have erred in interpreting the law, "[n]onetheless, the case reflects the law's heavy presumption against resort to deadly force. Criminal law requires sacrifice of property, honor, and pride as well as acceptance of non-serious personal injury before it will tolerate the sacrifice of human life."[140]

The Collapsing of Incapacity Excuse and Justification

We have seen that BWS walks the line between excuse and justification, reason and unreason. Although this does in certain respects reflect the coexistence of trauma and insight that characterizes a battered woman's mental state, it raises a host of problems that we must confront.

We have seen that justification "speaks to the rightness of the act; an excuse to whether the actor is accountable for a concededly wicked act."[141] Although the distinction between justification and excuse is extremely important in criminal law, we must acknowledge that many defenses blend the logics of each, and that the distinction is not sharp. "All justifications have elements of excuse, and all elements of excuse have elements of justification. With only a little verbal legerdemain, you can turn any justification into an excuse (and vice versa)."[142]

Construing self-defense as a justification assigns greater value to the life of the defender than the aggressor. Excuse avoids the problems attendant to this determination by focusing simply "on the pressure the defendant faced when she acted."[143] Yet another way around this potential problem is to interpret the justification not in terms of the blameworthiness of the aggressor, but in terms of the Hobbesian right of the defender to deploy necessary force to protect herself.[144] Another is to work out a principled balance between justification and excuse. As Gerstmann and I will show in the concluding chapter, the law of self-defense does give greater leeway to the actual targets of violence than to third-party intervenors who act on the target's behalf because of the weighing of equities entailed.[145]

Still, justification is demanding, requiring conformity to objective standards of reason. Leo Katz points out that it constitutes conduct of which we "approve." As for excused conduct, we do not approve of it, but "sympathize" with it.[146]

Learned helplessness ineluctably suggests incapacity excuse (dysfunction) rather than justification (reason) or excuse due to duress-like pressure.[147] Mihajlovich underscores the contradictions that inhere in BWS's conflation of excuse and justification, and connects this tension to "the inherent inconsistency of establishing reasonableness by describing the battered woman's unhealthy mental state." In short, "Those who propose a battered woman self-defense theory emphasize the debilitating effect of abuse on the battered woman's mental state. But this debilitating effect indicates the possibility of diminished ability to make a rational decision.

This possibility should not be ignored in the judgment of whether the killing is a justified act committed by a mentally competent woman."[148] The most revealing indication of BWS's link to incapacity defenses is its link to post-traumatic stress disorder. The American Psychiatric Association has not made BWS an official disorder, but it did make BWS a "subcategory" of PTSD in the 1980 DSM-III. In the 1987 DSM-IIIR, it is not a subcategory. In 1994, as seen, DSM-IV established a new disorder called "acute stress disorder" that incorporates the logic of the new psychology of violent victimization.[149] Walker and numerous other commentators, including courts, treat BWS as a psychological disorder. In *People v. Aris*, for example, the California Court of Appeals discussed this issue in a logic that displayed the chameleon-like quality of BWS:

> Dr. Walker testified that BWS is not a mental illness and is not listed in the third edition of the Diagnostic and Statistical Manual of Mental Disorders (DSM-III), a comprehensive and authoritative diagnostic classification system of psychological disorders, to avoid stigmatizing abuse victims as having a mental illness. She testified that, nevertheless, BWS is a proper diagnosis and is recognized as a type of post-traumatic stress disorder, which is listed and defined in the DSM-III and which happens to anyone exposed to the degree and kind of trauma, such as a natural disaster or combat, that would be expected to cause psychological problems.[150]

The problem is that PTSD-related defenses in other cases invariably buttress mental incapacity defenses. Vietnam veteran cases, for example, show PTSD's relationship to unreason, not reason. The vet hears the fan in the roof of the factory and flashes back to a helicopter in Vietnam; or the vet is fired and suddenly his boss is transformed into the Viet Cong. One is left with the impression that blending of reason and unreason in BWS provides an opportunity for defendants and their attorneys to play with two hands of cards. If the situation is akin to self-defense, the defense attempts to stress the reason component of BWS; if the situation is nonconfrontational, the defense emphasizes the unreason prong, or, as in *Bobbitt*, both at the same time. A case that highlights this double hand of cards is *State v. Poling*, in which the defendant killed her sleeping husband because of jealousy. The Ohio Appeals Court had a hard time figuring out what the defense was because the defense, "without designating it as such, essentially argued diminished capacity."[151]

A simple exercise demonstrates why BWS ultimately signifies incapacity or diminished capacity, at least in cases involving nonconfrontational facts. This exercise also brings the distinction between excuse and justification into clear relief.[152] Simply consider what rights a third party possesses in committing violent acts on behalf of an endangered person. Under the law, if a person under attack may justifiably use deadly force against the aggressor, then an outside third party who *is not* personally endangered may intervene on behalf of the person who *is* in imminent danger. The reason is simple: *the act is just, so it does not matter who commits it.* Thus, it is clear that a neighbor who overhears a domestic battle may intervene and kill a batterer if the batterer is about to kill his own spouse.

But what if the case resembles cases in which the batterer is asleep, or a contract-type case like that of one of our prison interviewees?[153] If the woman is justified in using deadly force in such cases, then contractors, neighbors, and other third parties would be justified in killing the batterer at any time. But if a third party would not be justified in killing in such cases, which seems a potentially reasonable conclusion (depending on the facts), justification must disappear for the battered woman as well—unless justification means something other than the validity of the act. *When we adopt the view of the third person, we flush out the importance of the imminence requirement or something akin to it, like necessity: only compellingly clear circumstances can justify violent intervention.* However, we will see in greater detail in the last chapter that self-defense law appropriately gives more leeway (especially concerning the requirement of proportionality) to the actual target of violence than to third parties because of the situational pressures the actual target experiences. But this important adjustment does not change the fundamental point that the rights of third parties and the actual targets of danger are cut from the same cloth.

Along similar lines, think of the right of the batterer to defend himself.[154] Take the *Skalaski* case. Lisa attacked Jim with a knife while he was asleep; unlike some cases (such as *Norman*), he had not beaten her before he fell asleep, and had not threatened to beat her upon waking (he had done just the opposite, informing her that he might leave her). Is Jim entitled to defend himself forcefully from Lisa's attack? If the answer is "yes," then Lisa's attack simply cannot be justified. If the answer is "no," then we have given Lisa a license to kill her husband without his being allowed to defend himself, even though he poses no present or near-future danger. Surely the criminal law cannot bestow such a privilege, though precisely this result is entailed in the arguments of those who claim Lisa acted justifiably. Thinking about the right of people such as Jim Skalaski to defend themselves adds weight to the contention that BWS is about incapacity excuse rather than justification. The matter might have differed had Jim threatened Lisa upon falling asleep, and Lisa had had good reason to believe that there was "no way out." We will address this type of scenario in the concluding chapter.

To be sure, the woman's special knowledge about the batterer will most likely not be shared by the outsider, *and the justification for acting should take this special knowledge into consideration.* Again, this is because the battered woman might know more about what constitutes imminence or impending harm than the third party does. If there is no imminent danger from any reasonable perspective, then a third person will never be justified in acting with deadly force.

Acknowledging that the battered woman can possess special insight into the presence of deadly harm provides a better basis from which to reconsider the above discussion of PTSD in the comparative contexts of battered women and war veterans. The criminal cases involving veterans and PTSD are almost invariably incapacity excuse–oriented for the simple reason that the spouse or boss whom the vet targets is not really the Viet Cong. But what if the vet is still in Vietnam and under the influence of PTSD or a related highly charged mental state? Various scenarios could take place: 1) he "freaks out" and thinks his sergeant is the Cong. This is clearly a state of delusion, of incapacity and excuse; 2) he encounters a Vietnamese villager, whom he mistakenly thinks is a Cong soldier. Given the objective situation in Vietnam, this mistake of fact might be reasonable. Villagers did act as soldiers, but not all the time. Factors pertaining to the villagers' appearances, demeanors, and behavior will influence how we construe the soldier's behavior; 3) he sees the real Cong but mistakenly believes he is under attack because he "freaks out" at the sight of the Cong, so he jumps to a factually mistaken conclusion or is hyperalert given what he perceives and simply misreads the danger; 4) he correctly sights a Cong soldier coming toward him and ascertains the need to defend himself with deadly force.

The battered woman's situation is normally similar to the third and fourth examples in the previous paragraph. She does not attack someone out of the delusion that he is her batterer. That case would be akin to the vet who thinks his boss is the Cong.[155] *Instead, she attacks her tormentor. So the real question is whether: a) she is deluded, b) simply mistaken about the presence of danger; or c) correct about the nature of the danger that she confronts.* Of course, real situations might well involve a mixture of these possibilities.

State v. Manning dealt with a proffered instruction that involved these judgments. The defendant argued that BWS should be defined as "whenever a battered woman experiences a sudden flashback triggering an immediate fear of danger causing her to respond instinctively in self-defense." But the court rejected this definition that points to excuse, holding that BWS is designed to assist the trier of fact in determining whether the defendant acted out of honest belief that she was in imminent danger at the time.[156] *Manning* represents a court's effort to keep BWS honest—it assists in determining justification or determining excuse. It cannot do both.

But it might make sense to limit BWS to precisely these claims, freeing self-defense law from its influences. More importantly, it should be possible to reconstrue the "flashback" argument in a manner that stresses the potential reasonableness and acuity of the battered woman's perceptions. Her flashback involves the history of abuse that informs her that she is in danger. *Outsiders (third parties or observers) who have not participated in the relationship are less likely to perceive what impends than she is. Recognizing this difference in perception is the Archimedean point around which the entire debate about battered women and self-defense cases pivots* (unless we extend the right to use lethal force beyond situations of actual imminent harm, which we should be loath to do for reasons we will articulate in the concluding chapter). From the vantage point of her victimization, the battered woman might indeed be in danger; but even if she is not endangered in this particular incident, her belief might still be reasonable because of what she knows. The issue should go to the jury to decide: the magnitude of the present danger will affect the jury's judgment of the reasonableness of the "flashback" or perception. *Rather than dismissing the flashback as "delusion" or "incapacity" (the excuse model) or elevating it to the status of conclusive evidence of present danger (the BWS model bent to fit justification), the flashback and the objective status of the present threat are dialectically related. The flashback might or might not be reasonable, depending on the facts at hand.* But the facts concerning the present threat cannot be isolated from the background of the relationship.

When Walker talks about "opinions" being as important as "facts" and the need to appreciate the pattern of the relationship, this is what she must mean. But the point of this *gestalt* logic is that it represents a true state of affairs that the battered woman ascertains with informed reason. The logic of "syndrome" undercuts this point at every turn, for it points to unreason, not reason. Although BWS can serve pragmatic interests by fudging reality as a "legal fiction" (see the previous chapter), it does so at a precious price. As presently conceptualized, BWS is inextricably impaled on a dilemma. In attempting to prove reason by using the discourse of unreason, it is forced to jump over hurdles that it places in its own path.

What if a battered woman's judgment is rational but still mistaken? In some cases, we would have a "reasonable mistake of fact," which, interestingly, is seldom addressed in the literature, perhaps because such cases are weeded out by prosecutorial discretion. More interesting cases arise when the woman is clearly mistaken from the perspective of a reasonable person. Are such cases manslaughter (intentional killing driven by heat of passion), imperfect self-defense (unreasonable mistake of fact concerning the presence of imminent danger or the need to employ deadly, rather than some lesser. force), or "accident?"

The battered woman will normally fathom the cues of her batterer. After being presented with evidence of the relationship and the things that trigger attacks, if the jury is convinced that his behavior presents such a cue given her knowledge, then self-defense can be reasonably derived. At least it should go to the jury for consideration. For example, if he beats her a "majority" of the time after pounding his fist, she might be entitled to self-defense if she shot him after he pounded his fist in a similar fashion: even if this particular time he did not intend to carry out the act. Her judgments in this case are presumptively more reasonable than in the cases of "delusion" discussed above.

The debate over BWS and justification boils down to this point: that battered women possess special knowledge of their abuser's actions, forged in the bonds of love, so their "reason" or perceptions of the meanings of his actions are more highly tuned than those of outside observers. This is why Walker, Dutton, Blackman, Schneider, and other advocates of battered women entreat us to think in terms of the overall relationship, not just specific incidents. Thus, our determination of what constitutes imminent or impending danger should take the battered woman's view very seriously. Julie Blackman underscores this argument, which is the strongest and most reliable argument of all:

> [These sources] explain the reasonableness of a battered woman's perception of danger as an alternative form of reasonableness. That is, battered women are construed as reasonable in a relational framework and with a sense of history that is quite explicitly different from the traditional, legal standard of reasonableness. . . . Careful attention to the battered woman's past experiences with her husband's or partner's violence enhances one's capacity to understand her attack against him as reasonable or not. A true standard of reason is best approximated when all relevant factors that bear on good judgment are considered.[157]

But do not be misled: this is an argument of reason and necessity, not incapacity excuse, compassion, or vengeance in the name of higher substantive justice. Indeed, to the extent that advocates of battered women and BWS rely on arguments of incapacity excuse, they do Blackman's argument a disservice by compromising it with arguments of excuse that are often tenuous. Just as bad, they commit a disservice to the women involved by portraying them as incapable of being reasonable.

So, the baggage of incapacity "excuse," baggage that attends BWS, including the concept of learned helplessness, is at best irrelevant and at worst harmful to the determination of legal justice. Being helpless does not mean that the woman is deluded or unable to see the facts or control her actions. And it certainly does not mean that she does not possess special insights into the batterer's behavior; indeed, my interviewees construed such special knowledge as an example of agency, contra BWS. Given the need to be true to the facts and to maintain intellectual integrity to draw just lines of responsibility, the very concept of learned helplessness, the centerpiece of BWS's edifice, should be abandoned.

The Most Appropriate Framework

We need to address the enormity of battering from the perspective of reason and common sense, not from the syndrome that is so laden with questionable science and the victimization worldview. And in criminal law, as in all public law, we must not compromise our obligation to deal with the uniqueness of each case and the need to take seriously the rebuttable presumption of individual responsibility. This obligation cannot hide behind the comforting tentative conclusions of science or pseudoscience. The questions of our responsibilities toward battered women and of battered women's legal (and moral) responsibility and obligations to the law cannot be answered by reliance on the syndrome, for such questions are ultimately moral and anguished. We must make our decisions on the grounds of our considered normative judgements. Attempting to provide easy answers for us, BWS and other syndromes in criminal defense spare us anguish at the price of our freedom, which depends upon personal responsibility.[158] Conversely, to ignore real victimization is to escape the anguish of judgment through denial. As George Fletcher holds, we must be open to certain types of excuse because of the need to achieve and accommodate individual justice, but we must not abandon the presumption of responsibility. "In order to defend the criminal law against the determinist critique, we need not introduce freighted terms like 'freedom of the will.' Nor need we 'posit' freedom as though we were developing a geometric system on the basis of axioms. The point is simply that the criminal law should express the way we live. Our culture is built on the assumption that, absent valid claims of excuse, we are accountable for what we do. If that cultural presupposition should someday prove to be empirically false, there will be far more radical changes in our way of life than those expressed in the criminal law." [159]

BWS is not necessary to an appreciation of the pressures that a battered woman encounters, and it inexorably embraces the logic of incapacity excuse, which it too often places in the service of justification. BWS seems most suitable to excuses like insanity or partial excuses like diminished capacity, and imperfect self-defense/manslaughter. But why focus on mental condition when justice can be done by focusing on the situation battered women face?

In an essay critical of the concept of diminished capacity, Morse brings into relief a difference between *pressures that partially negate or compromise responsibility from within the psyche and pressures that compromise responsibility due to the influence of external pressures*. Thus, the provocation doctrine of manslaughter differs from the diminished-capacity doctrine. Pointing to the *doctrine of "hard choices,"* in which the law, in the name of fairness and justice, takes account of the difficult choices individuals confront (as in necessity), Morse remarks,

> At some point along the continuum of choice, society and the law are ready to grant that a choice was too hard—it was too difficult for the actor to choose to behave otherwise—and that the actor's conduct should be morally and legally excused . . .
>
> The heat of passion reduction is premised on the view that some provocations are so powerful that they may enrage even a reasonable person, depriving him or her of usual self-control, and consequently reducing the person's culpability. Cases where the ability to conform to law is impaired by provocation and passion therefore may seem like cases where it is impaired by mental abnormality. There is a difference, however.

The provocation-passion formula is based on the reaction of persons to engaging *external* stimuli: it is assumed that even fully normal persons can be impassioned by certain sufficiently provocative circumstances (legally adequate provocation). By contrast, the law typically does not allow mitigation to manslaughter in those cases where the ability to conform to law was allegedly weakened by *internal* causes.[160]

As she was serving as the co-chair in the *Richardson* retrial, Ann Jacobs expressed the choice the defense team confronted in language congruent with Morse's logic. "We know that [psychologist] Hutchinson did not have much impact on the jury. And so you can analyze Ronda as a normal person in a bad situation, or as a mentally ill person who fits a psychiatric diagnosis. And the more I know Ronda, the more I know she is not crazy." [161]

Morse's distinction between the doctrines of diminished capacity and provocation delivers a way out of our dilemma. The doctrines of self-defense, necessity, duress, and related doctrines embrace elements of excuse and justification. But they are premised on similar tenets: the notion of external necessity and overwhelming pressure. In thinking about responsibility in this context, we can apply similar standards to all citizens that are congruent with the larger enterprise of criminal law, taking account of individual plight while acknowledging the necessity and validity of community standards of right and wrong.

Syndromes and Political Theory: The Twilight of Considered Judgment and Citizenship

Common standards are absolutely indispensable to a democratic society. Societies organized around hierarchy of privilege can afford multiple standards, but a democracy cannot. Double standards mean second-class citizenship. . . . As Hannah Arendt has pointed out, the Enlightenment got it backward. It is citizenship that confers equality, not equality that creates a right to citizenship.—CHRISTOPHER LASCH, *The Revolt of the Elites*

The reputed leniency that women receive with respect to death sentencing supports the view widely held in our society that women are incapable of achieving, nor are they in fact held to, the same standards as are men. . . . [E]qual democratic citizenship can proceed from no other premise than that of equal personal responsibility for decisions and actions. . . . There is, from a feminist point of view, an invidious subordination of the interests of women involved in the failure of the statutes to attach our society's most profound condemnation to crimes that destroy the domestic peace. . . . The supposition that predatory violence is more reprehensible than domestic violence is a symptom or effect of the ancient family privacy doctrine that has supported male domestic authority, and the parental authority of both sexes, at the price of tolerating if not encouraging a culture of domestic violence.—ELIZABETH RAPAPORT, "The Death Penalty and Gender Discrimination"

In this chapter I present a critique of the syndrome society from the perspectives of political theory and citizenship. My concern is with the impact of syndrome logic on society and criminal law in general, not with the disposition of actual or specific cases, though in the next chapter Gerstmann and I will be more specific. As I have emphasized throughout this work, criticism of syndrome defenses is not the same thing as criticism of battered women or other victims of abuse. The broader process of syndromization involves a host of phenomena and assumptions that are problematic in their own right, independent of concern for the situations of abuse victims.

The ultimate question we confront is this: how to serve the demands of responsibility and empathy at the same time. Both demands are crucial to justice and constitutional freedom. Syndromes seem to open our eyes to empathy, but not in a way that is conducive to the equal respect that leads to equal citizenship. As I will show below, a society that values political freedom has no choice but to take the principle of responsibility seriously. This is so not simply because of some transcendent quality of persons, but because of the requirements of constitutional equality and freedom. Syndrome logic in the service of criminal defense severs the connection between empathy and responsibility. In so doing, it undermines respect for its would-be beneficiaries, leading to their marginalization and "othering." This result is a function of the fact that citizenship ultimately confers equality, not the other way around.

Criminal law is one important aspect of political life and obligation, though, of course, the criminal law possesses its own standards and criteria of validity that distinguish it from politics and other important practices in society. Indeed, I will argue, law and politics must be construed as separate enterprises, however much they overlap. This said, not enough attention has been paid to the ways in which the standards of criminal law reflect judgments that are important to constitutional and political citizenship more broadly defined. First, rules in criminal law involve the codification of our moral judgments, even though such rules are interpreted and applied according to legal standards (in particular, the norm of due process) that exist independently of particular moral judgments.[1] Second, criminal law standards are important aspects of citizenship for the simple reason that they embody common standards of community judgment that are forged out of social and political interaction. As I will show, the making of such judgments constitutes a crucial obligation of democratic politics and political freedom. How we construe responsibility in the criminal law has important implications for how we envision citizenship and the self in society, and the making of deliberate judgments about responsibility engages us in an active form of thinking that may educate and enrich citizenship. But not just any standards will contribute in this way, and the concept of responsibility cuts more way than one.

In addressing the criminal law debate over reliance upon objective versus subjective standards of responsibility, I proceed from the vantage point of liberal communitarian political theory that emphasizes the importance of active citizenship. I draw from theorists who stress the attributes of citizenship from a variety of angles, including Hannah Arendt, Alexis de Tocqueville, Jean Bethke Elshtain, Mary Midgley, and Christopher Lasch, among others.[2] Most defenses of objective standards of right or truth derive from either the natural law or "moral realism" tradition that goes back to Aristotle and other conservative sources, or from modern positivistic methods that emphasize technical and mathematical precision within a narrow range of questions. According to the natural law view, objective standards are products of the discernment of a higher standard of truth that is independent of the judgments that arise from social or political interactions. The methodological school emphasizes the proper method as the way to discover truth. Though I do not disavow the validity of objective standards (see below), my approach differs in that I want to show how common standards of right conduct in criminal law can be defended on other grounds: as forms of a constantly challenged consensus about justice that results from deliberate political interaction and obligation. This approach is similar to twentieth-century pragmatism and *praxis* theory, which eschew certainty in favor of a reasoned discourse that proceeds provisionally toward truth; such understanding entails a politically oriented discourse that consists "of assertions that command provisional assent even though they lack unimpeachable foundations and are therefore subject to revision."[3] But my main emphasis is to show how judgments concerning responsibility are relative to the communal judgments we make (or must make) as citizens in a constitutional democracy. Thus, the analysis is both empirical and normative: I argue not only that we *do take* the concept of responsibility seriously, but that the norms and principles associated with political freedom *require us* to take responsibility seriously.[4] Indeed, the more syndrome logic permeates society, the more the normative argument contrasts with the empirical argument, for syndrome logic undermines the presumption of responsibility. If so, syndrome logic is detrimental to constitutional freedom.

Aristotle also treated justice from this type of political and constructivist perspective, as more commentators are coming to emphasize. That is, Aristotle often portrayed justice not only as a matter of transcendent truth, but also as a product of practical communal judgment which is embedded in responsible political participation.[5] While commitment to truth independent of politics is necessary to keep politics honest, politics is the domain in which considered common judgments are made. Democratic deliberation involves a tension between truth and skepticism, and particularity and generality. The reader will find that I have assumed the right to use both objectivist and constructivist logics at different points of the analysis. I hope that this juxtaposition is a product of the nature of political and legal judgment rather than one of conceptual confusion.

Political community requires commonly shared purposes, but the citizens who engage in the making of such consensus come from different backgrounds and possess different perspectives, experiences, claims, and interests. Citizenship entails a delicate balance of self-assertion, perspectivism, and commitment to the good of the whole. Self and "other" are distinct yet dialectically related. As Jessica Benjamin and Michelle Masse showed in chapter 4, personal and political interactions are driven by the tensions and conflicts surrounding the quest for mutual recognition. Consequently, common norms are always tentative and subject to the whims of self-interest, subconscious desires, ideology, and history. Yet they are something for which we must strive, for community is impossible without them. But a constitutional order also values dissent that exists for its own sake and for the purpose of challenging and improving what is held in common.[6] Indeed, the protection of freedom of speech is the litmus paper test by which any provisional method of truth-seeking proves its good faith. Responsible politics embodies the pursuit of the common good without forsaking due respect for those who are situated outside of one's own experience, presenting both an opportunity and a threat. The standards of criminal law (and the debate surrounding them) are important aspects of this politics and citizenship, for deciding what is forbidden and what is permitted is one of the most important tasks of any political community. At the same time, however, each case bears its own complexion and controversies, making it sometimes difficult to apply the general law to the specific case. Sound political and legal judgments require (and bring out in us) the capacity to think through difficult issues and claims. As Mary Midgley declares in *Can't We Make Moral Judgments?*

> *Judging* is not in general simply accepting one or two ready-made alternatives as the right one. It cannot be done by tossing up. It is seeing reason to think and act in a particular way. It is a comprehensive function, involving our whole nature, by which we direct ourselves and find our way through a whole forest of possibilities. No science rules here; there is no given system of facts which will map our whole route for us. We are always moving into new territory.[7]

This approach allows me to defend "*contextual objective" standards* concerning personal legal responsibility on grounds of responsible political and practical judgment rather than pure notions of transcendent right or metaphysical free will. Nietzsche (the arch critic of transcendent notions of right and free will) indicated how equal respect is tied to the capacity to assume responsibility. In addition, authors like Marion Smiley (see below) have laid new pragmatic grounds for the analysis of responsibility. Here, this new way of understanding responsibility is applied to the political theory of citizenship in relation to the criminal law, and an effort is made to salvage a defense of the basic presumption in favor of personal responsibility in the face of postmodern tenets, which disavow a foundational basis to truth. The means by which to accomplish this end is *the discourse of citizenship*, which justifies holding citizens to demanding yet just standards without resorting to metaphysical arguments. The resurrection of the discourse of citizenship is crucial to achieving justice without forsaking political freedom. The discourse of citizenship does two things. First, it provides a justification for taking responsibility seriously. Second, in the area of gender relations and politics, it furnishes a common ground upon which woman and man might come together from their different perspectives to forge standards through political agreement and conflict. As I will show, citizenship embodies a tension and dialectic between perspectivism and common ground, particularity and generality. The concept of citizenship, therefore, presents the best way of thinking about gender relations, since it makes room for difference (difference is one reason that the standards of citizenship are "provisional" rather than "absolute") at the same time that it points us toward common understanding.

Syndrome logic furthers the evisceration of citizenship that is already taking place, for syndrome logic (as seen in the previous chapter) forsakes the standards that make up sound, difficult judgment in favor of a logic that provides no standards by which to draw lines. Recognizing the brutality of domestic violence in a manner that is removed from the syndrome connection promises better results, because it opens our minds to the plights of others without presuming that they lack any responsibility for their actions or that they lack will.

The concepts of citizenship and responsibility obligate the state and society as well. The legal order depends on the state fulfilling its promise to protect citizens from violence. If it fails in this obligation, as it has so often when it comes to battered women, the obligation to obey the law is undermined. The social contract begins with the promise of equal protection of the law. A similar logic applies to civil society. We must be our brother's and sister's keepers. The claims of citizenship fall on us all.

Throughout this book we have seen the ways in which knowledge of the nature of domestic violence sharpens our awareness of the effects of domestic violence and contributes to justice. We have also seen how the syndromization of this knowledge blurs or undermines normative and empirical distinctions that are important to moral and legal judgment on several fronts. *The understanding that emerges out of the interconnected discussions of this chapter sets the stage for anchoring victimization defenses in a reformed version of the traditional law of self-defense.*

Equal Standards, Judgment, and Citizenship

Before we plunge into the major ways in which syndrome logic harms citizenship, some caveats and introductory remarks are in order. First, the reader must recognize that the analysis of this chapter is couched largely in universal or general terms. It does not in itself tell us how to draw the specific lines of culpability that must be drawn. Equally important, this analysis in no way undermines the culpability of batterers and other victimizers for what they do. If the concept of responsibility begins anywhere, it begins here.

The analysis is intended only to address the consequences of syndromizing the question of culpability, even in cases of oppression, and of attaching labels like

BWS to women in such situations. Though it might help avoid the label of "criminal" by leaning on incapacity excuses, BWS "labels" women in its own right. Labels like "mental illness" lead to stigmatization and redefinitions of the self. "The label tends to redefine the whole person."[8] (Recall the "redefinition" of Lisa Skalaski).

The discussion of the disposition of custody cases in chapter 5 proves to be pivotal. There we witnessed how justice to battered women, children, and society in general incorporates knowledge of domestic and gendered violence at the same time that it eschews or seriously downplays the cycle and learned helplessness theories without which BWS cannot stand. One reason for this twist of fate for the syndrome is that the concept of responsibility is in important respects (if not all) indivisible.

In addition, such responsibilities should be shared equally among those who make claims to equal treatment. Equal standards concerning rights and duties are important elements of equal citizenship for at least three reasons. First, equal standards furnish a foundation for community by providing common norms of responsibility under which all citizens live. As seen, different philosophical perspectives vie over the sources of these shared values. Many theorists (including this author) take intermediate positions between moral realism and constructivism, seeing social norms as either an evolving product of social conflict and a dialectic between constructivist and realist understandings, or as a result of practical reasoning, *praxis* and political participation.[9] The danger lies in relying too heavily upon either pole. Taken to extremes, constructivism leads to the belief that all normative positions are nothing but masks of ideology, thereby turning all arguments into questions of power that never transcend politics or particularism.[10] And unblinking constructivism runs into epistemological dead ends in dark alleys. For example, if all truth is nothing but constructive, there is no solid basis for refuting those who deny that the Holocaust occurred. On the other hand, realism can lead to dogmatism or "absolutism" if it is not tempered by self-doubt and commitment to the rights of those who disagree.

Second, equal standards of citizenship necessarily require noninvidious treatment, for invidious discrimination is a hallmark of unequal respect and the "othering" of citizens. Equal protection includes the protection of law enforcement, which is the most elemental function of the state. We have already seen how this principle should protect battered women and make batterers fully culpable for their violence. As so many supporters of battered women have emphasized, it makes no sense to talk about the legal obligation of battered women to obey the law if society and the state refuse to provide the protection they need.

The third element of equal standards involves the value of what de Beauvoir calls transcendence: equal persons or groups must share in carrying the burdens of personal responsibility and citizenship. At this level of citizenship, rights and responsibilities are reciprocally related. The libertarian psychiatrist Thomas Szasz indicts the insanity plea for severing this vital connection. "Central to the contemporary argument favoring the general idea that insanity annuls responsibility—and in particular the idea that the insanity defense is morally desirable and practically necessary—is the denial that liberty and responsibility are two sides of the same coin. In fact, it is not possible to increase or diminish the one without increasing or diminishing the other." [11] This logic leads inescapably to another proposition: double standards are a recipe for second-class citizenship.

These tenets support the conclusion that equal citizens should be protected by and comply with equal legal standards. This does not mean, however, that the law should never provide different standards for men and women that are justified by demonstrable differences between the sexes. Women are generally less physically powerful and less criminally violent than men, though this difference does not invariably hold. Yet the gender difference is prevalent enough to justify reconsideration of the law concerning women and self-defense, or *using battered women's experiences to reform the standards or understandings of self-defense in a manner that all victims of sustained abuse (men or women) may use.* As Martha Minow points out in *Making All the Difference,* different standards for the genders and races can compromise equal citizenship if they reinforce differences that were the basis for past discrimination. But they can also further justice if they deal with actual differences or effects of discrimination that justly call for recognition. Distinguishing between these two possibilities can be very difficult, but worth the effort. [12]

So *different* standards are not necessarily the same thing as *unequal* standards. Unequal standards can never be justified. But Catharine MacKinnon's keen questioning of the gendered test of reasonable self-defense in *Wanrow* raises concerns which should lead us to strive for as consistent a set of standards as possible. Any different standards must be justified by precise arguments that bear the burden of proof:

> Equality apparently means that men are judged against a reasonable man standard, women against a reasonable woman standard. But is this two rules or one? This is more than a superficial semantic or inconsequentially symbolic concern. Double standards have often been a legal means for disadvantaging women, as well as for rationalizing women's social exclusion and denigration. Many feminists believe, not without cause, that *any* rule "for women only" stigmatizes women in a sexist society. Such rules also tend not to address women to whom the female stereotype does not apply and not to challenge, beyond reflective accuracy, the content of the male standard as applied to men. [13]

Despite its importance, this concept of personal responsibility is as charged as it is obligatory. In "Particularity and Generality," Elizabeth Schneider argues that the legal system needs to go beyond the binary poles of "agency" and "nonagency" in order to do justice for battered women, especially in such contexts as omissions and custody cases.[14] In other words, the very concept of responsibility needs reconsideration. Schneider foreshadows something even deeper: the concept of responsibility in the West is gendered and ridden with normative, political and ideological tensions. It is tied (as I present it below) to the realm of transcendence (the realms of obligation, achievement, production, and public participation), over which men have predominated, as de Beauvoir's paradigmatic analysis in *The Second Sex* reveals. Transcendence requires the opportunity to act in the world, but it carries with it a strong responsibility to tackle opportunity and to accept responsibility for the consequences of one's actions. In other words, transcendence is a form of power and accountability which men *have been privileged—yet burdened*—to accept. Power is a privilege, but ask anyone who possesses it in a responsible manner how easy it is to sleep at night. From this vantage point, the very essence of sexism and racism lies in the belief that women and racial minorities are incapable of bearing the burdens of responsibility. The coexistence of privilege and burden is too often ignored by schools of thought that focus on only one side of the equation.[15]

Among other things, this book has shown the collision between two normative perspectives: the discourse of personal responsibility and the discourse of victimhood. Nietzsche saw into the heart of this tension near the end of the nineteenth century, especially in *The Genealogy of Morals*, which I will draw on below. Anticipating Freud's analysis in *Civilization and Its Discontents* by several decades, Nietzsche depicts the rise of the conscience and the concept of responsibility in the West as a struggle within society and the self to obtain a measure of self-control over the inclinations, so that individuals could make good on their promises, debts, and obligations to others (the ties that bind citizens in community). This internal struggle, which Nietzsche, and later Freud, depict as "the internalization" of humans' aggressive instincts (and about which Nietzsche and Freud were ambivalent but ultimately supportive), was painful and difficult; but it led to a new kind of freedom based on the ability to exercise self-control and to sublimate one's instinctual energy into cultural and social achievements—the process that de Beauvoir and Sartre would later portray as transcendence.[16] This realm is also the realm of judgment that holds individuals accountable for falling short of the ethic of responsibility.

The debate concerning the syndromization of criminal law is one manifestation of a deeper tension in the West between the discourse of personal responsibility (which is a discourse of self-reliance and judgment) and the discourse of suffering and victimhood, which is uncomfortable with making judgmental distinctions concerning personal responsibility, except when the subject is someone identified as an oppressor. This latter discourse arose as a reaction to the discourse of responsibility, especially in the post-Enlightenment era, which has sought to eliminate suffering and qualitative distinctions among individuals (what Tocqueville called the ethic of "equality of condition").[17] Both discourses constitute their own forms of judgment, and each is subject to its own form of cruelty and violence.

In a sense, this book is dedicated to finding an alternative to these two poles, though I have maintained consistently that the ethic of responsibility must be the presumption upon which justice and community exist. Analogously, compromise not guided by an overarching principle is meritless. Though all politicians must compromise in democratic polities, we all know the difference between compromise in service of principle and compromise in service of something less admirable or for its own sake. Similarly, judgment needs to be guided by the presumption of responsibility or it proceeds without a compass.

But severe judgments on the part of each discourse are uncaring about the suffering of those outside the sanctified group (the "other"). A more democratic form of responsibility requires compassion and caring about others who suffer. On the one hand, democratic "political freedom" (Tocqueville's term of art for self-reliance and meaningful democratic participation) requires a willingness to look beyond one's own horizon and to deal constructively with those in society who are different from oneself. Democratic politics is predicated on the ability to assert one's interests and views, but also on the ability to listen, to struggle creatively with the tensions that exist between the self and others in the incessant struggle for mutual recognition in personal, social, and political interactions.[18] Self and other must never completely merge. Nor may they become completely separate.

On the other hand, victim ideology (the discourse attached to syndromizing the question of responsibility) and the political correctness to which it is attached are uncaring about those outside the community of victimhood, and dismissive of the importance of exercising responsibility and making strong yet considered judgments that apply to all. Political freedom requires meaningful interaction by citizens and the sustaining of institutions and laws that support personal responsibility and the assumption that citizens are capable agents, not victims without wills. As I will soon show, holding individuals presumptively responsible for their criminal actions is necessary to protect victims from the predations of others. And at a deeper level, political freedom depends on the presumption of personal responsibility because if individuals do not rule themselves, then external authority (which will always be present in some form) will fill the void. Authority must come from somewhere. Tocqueville, whose perceptions of what is at stake in this chapter are as acute as anyone's, puts the matter this way:

> A principle of authority must then always occur, under all circumstances, in some part or other of the world. Its place is variable, but a place it necessarily has. The independence of individual minds may be greater, or it may be less: unbounded it cannot be. Thus the question is, not to know whether any intellectual authority exists in the ages of democracy, but simply where it resides and by what standard it is to be measured.[19]

Political freedom, therefore, requires that we take the ethic of responsibility seriously. But the ethic of responsibility has two aspects: upholding the standards of responsibility upon which freedom and achievement (transcendence) rest, and caring about the opportunities and suffering of others (empathy for others that broadens the connections and interactions of the community).[20] Political freedom and justice cannot do without the right balance of compassion and judgment.

Aristotle speaks of judgment consisting of the right balance of sympathy and standards. "What is called judgement, in virtue of which men are said to 'be sympathetic judges' and to 'have judgement,' *is the right discrimination of the equitable.* This is shown by the fact that we say the equitable man is above all others a man of sympathetic judgement, and identify equity with sympathetic judgement about certain facts. . . . [C]orrect judgement is that which judges what is true."[21] Sympathy in this context does not mean surrendering one's judgment to whatever the claimant urges. It means putting oneself in the claimant's shoes in order to ascertain and fathom the choices the claimant had to make. But then the "equitable" woman must apply the knowledge or consciousness gained to the broader standards of law. She must exercise the "right discrimination" to judge "what is true." If she does not take this step, she commits two harms. First, judgment cannot take place, for judgment consists of an honest attempt to decide correctly, which means by standards independent of the claimant. Second, democracy would be harmed, for she would be ignoring the law that the democratic political order produced. To be sure, jury and prosecutorial discretion (in deciding how to apply the law or whether to apply it at all) is part of legal practice and judgment. But even such departures must be justified by reference to general norms (legal or otherwise) embedded in the legal system. Without such reference and justification, discretion degenerates into favoritism.[22]

A key point emerges out of this discussion: all particular conclusions must be challenged by and ultimately reconciled with more general standards, and vice versa. For example, if a battered woman is presumptively entitled to kill her husband in a situation without any imminent danger, someone like Bernard Goetz must also be entitled to kill if the situation is similar. Unless one is willing to accept double standards, one must either grant a similar right to Goetz, or find factual or related differences that justify differential treatment of the two cases. And this latter move must justify itself on grounds that transcend the case (so if Goetz found himself in a similar circumstance, he could exercise self-defense, etc.). Take another example: if syndrome defense X is available in case A, another syndrome defense should be available in case B if the syndrome meets the same standards of reliability as syndrome X. As seen, BWS is admissible in many courts, but PMS is not, even though PMS's scientific pedigree is more sound. For obvious reasons, we are reluctant to open the syndrome door too far, especially given the explosive growth in syndrome claims in recent years (see chapter 2). And though PTSD is admissible in war veteran cases, it appears to fare less well than BWS. Compare this state of affairs to the insanity defense, which is narrower yet potentially available to any defendant. The insanity defense comes closer to satisfying the norm of generality, whereas syndrome defenses do not. Paradoxically, the insanity defense makes itself more subject to generality by virtue of its being more limited in scope. Below I will discuss how the differential treatment among BWS, PMS, and other syndromes is explained—perhaps even justified—on pragmatic grounds. But such results are troubling in a democratic order that inescapably values equal treatment under the law because they suggest that syndrome defenses are subject to partisan pressures, in this case those of political correctness. In a different but equally troubling sense, syndrome defenses reinforce the "otherness" of their would-be beneficiaries, for they consist of personal attributes (e.g., will-lessness) that cannot be tied to the attributes of common citizenship. As the discussion of the custody cases in chapter 5 showed, the rights that accrue to citizenship are negated by syndrome logic and legal determination.

Thus, judgment requires a process whereby empathy and common standards inform one another. Without empathy and mature compassion, we cannot listen to the truths of differently situated others; we lose any chance of fathoming the empirical truth. Without judgment that takes responsibility seriously, we cannot defend right and wrong. We lose any chance of defending the moral truth.

Along these lines, we must be careful to avoid letting compassion degrade into pity, which dehumanizes its recipients and represents a moral cop-out. The ultimate goal of meaningful equality must be mutual respect, which is a psychologically and socially subtle concept that requires renewal with each day. Respect is not manna from heaven. It has to be earned, and it can be lost once it is earned. Respect is intimately linked to judgment and standards. Compassion without respect surrenders the judgment that unites equal citizens. It means that its beneficiaries are worthy only of sentiment, not serious thinking. Sentiment is easy. Thinking is hard. And, as Christopher Lasch observes, "A misplaced compassion degrades both the victims, who are reduced to objects of pity, and their would-be benefactors, who find it easier to pity their fellow citizens than to hold them up to impersonal standards, attainment of which would entitle them to respect." [23]

Finally, my approach differs from those who are willing to attribute legal responsibility only to individuals with fairly highly developed moral capacities. Peter Arenella, for example, depicts what it might mean to go beyond liberal theories of moral blameworthiness in a thoughtful article. One approach entertains the notion that a "threshold conception of moral agency" for *mala in se* (evil) crimes must include

> the capacity to care for the interests of other human beings; the internalization of others' normative expectations, including self-identification as a participant in the community's blaming practices; the ability to engage

in moral evaluation of one's character and acts, the capacity to respond to moral norms as a motivation for one's choices; and the power to control those firmly entrenched aspects of character that impair one's ability to act in accordance with one's moral judgments.[24]

The model of moral capacity that Arenella portrays is problematic. The standards would disarm society from protecting itself, for the legal culpability of psychopaths like Ted Bundy would be weakened under such an approach. Criminal law should not simply reflect what we are (our actual mental states), but what the polity reasonably determines we should not do (or do, in the case of omissions). It is a set of normative standards concerning conduct. For example, as we saw earlier, many batterers lack the character capacity to truly appreciate their spouses' needs and humanity, and many feel that they cannot control their explosive rage. But surely these characteristics should not excuse their victimizations. Also, many women who remain in battering relationships feel extraordinary empathy for their batterers. Thus, under the moral character capacity theory, batterers would be more excusable than their victims when it comes to criminal culpability!

Once character becomes a relevant ground for attributing criminal responsibility, such incongruent results inexorably arise. We have seen that battered women's culpability for criminal acts should depend on the nature of their circumstances, not their capacities for moral character. Character should not be made part of criminal liability because culpability should depend on what we do, not who we are. Battered women who resort to lethal force to protect themselves should be able to claim self-defense regardless of their capacities or incapacities for moral empathy. As seen, BWS unfortunately brings character distinctions in the back door because the syndrome logic creates a profile that legitimates some types of coping over others. Finally, we saw in the previous chapter that no evidence supports any kind of link (positive or negative) between "craziness" or mental disorder and the ability to control one's behavior. In the absence of such evidence, it is problematic indeed to build a culpability theory based on the even vaguer tenets of character capacity.

My contention that equal citizenship entails equal capacity to abide by legal obligations parallels the demanding standards of criminal law. Stephen Schulhofer pointed out above that criminal law is premised on three "organizing assumptions" or principles that can be difficult to meet: *criminal law is "judgmental," "demanding," and "pacifist."*[25] If equal citizenship and respect are based on equal capacities to bear the burdens of citizenship, then Schulhofer's logic links obligation to obey the law to the psychology of equal respect. Indeed, one critique of criminals is that they "cheat" on those who abide by the law, seeking the "easy way" to get what they want. Consequently, one theory of punishment maintains that we need to punish criminals in order to honor the sacrifices of those who choose to abide by the law's sometimes difficult requirements.[26] I discussed similar social judgments about syndrome excuses in the critique of BWS above.

It should be noted, however, that this normative position does not tell us what sanction to apply. We saw in chapter 5 that BWS and the new knowledge about domestic violence have justifiably affected the nature and extent of punishment in certain cases. My points in this chapter are more basic: that the criminal law must take personal responsibility and common standards of culpability seriously, and that syndrome logic thwarts these standards.

The Subjectification of Criminal Law: Judgment, Politics, and Community Standards

Syndrome defenses present us with the ultimate subjectivization of criminal law, for they replace concern for objective standards of conduct with deterministic assumptions about mental states and action. And they do so in a manner that has much greater scope than such traditional defenses as insanity. Constitutional citizenship and criminal law generally require appropriate common standards of reason and accountability, as opposed to purely subjective standards. In substantive criminal law, "subjectivity" pertains to the actual mental states of individual defendants, whereas "objectivity" refers to mental states that a reasonable man or woman would (or should) have possessed under the circumstances. The distinction between objective and subjective standards of culpability in the determination of *mens rea* (criminal intent) is important because objective standards incorporate community norms and expectations that purely subjective standards lack. In a self-defense case, for example, the subjective test would ask only if the defendant subjectively believed she faced imminent danger; the reasonableness of the belief would be immaterial. Under an objective test, the jury would be instructed that this belief must also be what a reasonable or typically constituted person (or man or woman) would have believed under the circumstances. Objective tests foster citizenship by incorporating community standards of reason and care. Criminal law standards are "objective" not in terms of any universal transcendent essence, but in terms of considered social judgments reached in thinking, participation in legal institutions, and other interactions of a social or political nature. They constitute community judgment about the appropriateness of conduct in particular contexts, about doing the right thing. In this sense, the term "objective" is a misnomer if it denotes a scientific or positivistic assessment. These standards typically also take heed of individual experiences such as fear, anger, and circumstance, yet in a manner which does not abandon the commitment to reason.

Today the debate over subjectivity and objectivity in law is heated, especially in gender politics. Some feminists and others deride "objectivity" as a social construction designed to reinforce oppressive male notions of truth, or question the validity of the term. As Genevieve Lloyd declares, "[T]he maleness of the Man of

Reason . . . is no superficial linguistic bias."[27] This critique is useful if it challenges dogmatic notions of objectivity, which serve as shields from painful confrontation with reality or as weapons in ideological wars.

But the critique is problematic if it reduces all notions of objectivity to ideology, politics, and power. It is too simplistic to dismiss objective, universal standards across the board as simply partisan. Antonio Gramsci, Arendt, and others have shown that while ideologies are necessarily limited to their circumstances, they must also speak to universal claims beyond their particularity if they wish to be successful. These broader claims form the common grounds upon which community develops. As Lasch puts the matter, "The need to argue on this common ground—not universal agreement on epistemological foundations—is what creates the possibility of a common culture."[28] The tension between particularity and generality is a cardinal attribute of both thinking and political freedom. In discussing judgment, which she depicts as a "community sense," Arendt remarks, "the chief difficulty in judgment is that it is 'the faculty of thinking the particular"; but to *think* means to generalize, hence it is the faculty of mysteriously combining the particular and the general."[29]

We need to note that politics embodies a paradox. On the one hand, politics and political obligation are necessary for meaningful community. We need politics in order to get along and to construct public standards. The democratic *polis* is the cradle of both freedom and individual development. On the other hand, the power which inextricably accompanies politics threatens to devour our moral and intellectual consciences. As Arendt, the erstwhile champion of "the political," has shown in a classic essay that is strangely forgotten, truth and political power are often at odds; Arendt's career was dedicated to exploring the many implications of this question, as is the career of former Czech president Vaclav Havel, a rare philosopher king. Political power of whatever persuasion strives to corral the truth to serve its own ends. Recognition of this fundamental historical fact "brings us back to our suspicion that it may be in the nature of the political realm to be at war with truth in all its forms, and hence to the question why a commitment even to factual truth is felt to be an anti-political attitude."[30] Political freedom maintains a severe tension between truth and politics—a paradox that is one element of Socratic irony (the product of the polis who took the polis's hemlock as the law required because he refused to abandon his pursuit of truth and freedom of speech, as the polis demanded).[31]

The essential problem of politics has always been how to make agreement and justice out of the many voices, interests, and viewpoints that exist in the polity.[32] Appropriately self-critical objective standards express such judgments about proper conduct in our relations with one another and in public life. Objective standards of reason in law are associated with responsibility, rationality, the ability to exercise free will, and the capacity to act nobly—in other words, the very qualities that define citizenship.[33] The issue is whether the community norms that give content to the objective values are fair and sensible. Case law offers many examples of unfair and dogmatic application of legal standards, as well as undue relaxation of the standards of reason.

In criminal law, justice requires balancing objective (in the sense defined) standards of reason with appreciation of the individual circumstances and characteristics of defendants.[34] A "contextual objective" approach (developed in the concluding chapter) offers the best way to balance individuation and community standards of the right thing to do. This blend suggests that those who dismiss objectivity across the board as a fraud or an imposition of power either treat the concept in stereotypical terms, or do not adequately appreciate its subtle relationship to citizenship and communal standards of care and appropriate conduct. By the same token, those who dismiss individual reality retreat behind a formalism that shields them from the anguish of seeking justice for real individuals and real communities. They also trumpet consensus where such consensus might not exist because of subjective differences, different understandings of what counts, and differences based on inevitable social experiences and inevitable conflicts. Although the law points to standards of conduct to which citizens should conform, it is highly subject to different interpretations and ideological manipulation.[35] For this reason, justice necessitates never abandoning critical reason as we assume the responsibility of judging in a discriminating fashion.

As society grows more complex, the criminal law and punishment take on a complex set of functions that abound in controversy and conflict. According to David Garland, "[P]enality communicates meaning not just about crime and punishment but also about power, authority, legitimacy, normality, morality, personhood, social relations, and a host of other tangential matters. . . . Penality is thus a cultural text—or perhaps better, a cultural performance—which conveys an extended range of meanings."[36] But acknowledging this "extended range" does not trump reason. On the contrary, reason calls for recognizing the ambiguities and complexities of social life and existence. Without complexity, mystery, and the constant presence of the unknown, there could be no philosophy. Acknowledgment of complexity occasions a call to reason, not relativism.

Those who would disparage objective community standards in the name of protecting women would do well to consider the famous rape case *Regina v. Morgan* (1976). *Morgan* dealt with the issue of whether the court should instruct the jury with subjective or objective standards of "mistake of fact." Four male members of the Royal Air Force in Britain repeatedly raped the wife of an RAF officer because, they claimed, they ostensibly fell for the husband's story that his wife longed for group sex and that her protestations to the contrary were simply her way of making it more fun. But Ms. Morgan desired no such intercourse, so the defendants had to resort to a mistake-of-fact defense: since they believed she really consented to the act, they could not be guilty of rape. Unfortunately for them, their mistake of fact was patently unreasonable under the circumstances, so their only hope lay in a purely subjective test for mistake of fact: that their simple belief that she wanted such sex was enough to excuse them, however unreasonable that belief may have been according to contemporary community standards.

The judge, however, instructed the jury that the mistake of fact had to be honestly held (the subjective component) and reasonable (the objective component): "[H]is belief must be a reasonable belief; such a belief as a reasonable man would entertain if he applied his mind and thought about the matter." Finding their alleged belief implausible or unreasonable, the jury convicted the defendants. On appeal, however, the House of Lords held that the test of belief of fact should have been purely subjective. This reversal triggered a wave of protest, culminating in legislation that made it an offense to make a reckless mistake of fact concerning consent in rape cases.[37]

Consider also *People v. Casassa,* a 1980 case in which the New York Court of Appeals ruled that the defendant was not entitled to the expanded manslaughter defense based on "extreme emotional disturbance" just because he flew into a fit of jealousy when he brutally murdered a woman whom he obsessively loved. In sustaining the trial court's preclusion of the defense, the Court of Appeals stated that the trial court "recognized that in exercising its function as trier of fact, it must make a further inquiry into the reasonableness of that disturbance. In this regard, the court considered each of the mitigating factors put forward by the defendant, including his claimed mental disability, but found that the excuse offered by defendant was so peculiar to him that it was unworthy of mitigation."[38] This case was a response to the controversial result in the famous Richard Herrin case, in which a New York jury found Herrin guilty of manslaughter rather than murder because of the "emotional disturbance" he suffered when the victim, Bonnie Garland, cut off the relationship.[39] Such separation killing is a major component of the danger battered women and women in general confront, and too many men have received relatively minor prison time because juries have accepted such "excuses" or mitigating circumstances.[40]

Among other things, *Morgan* and *Casassa* illustrate how "objective" community standards of reasonable conduct derived from practical reason and judgment are meant to protect victims of crime from unreasonable acts by others. There is no substitute for reason in law.[41] The objective instruction in the *Morgan* trial court (which legislation reinstated in modified form) embodies communal norms that reinforce standards of care toward others. Certainly it would be wrong to excuse an honest but patently absurd belief of consent based on, say, a rabid ideology of misogyny. At some point the unreasonableness of the belief must not shield culpability, independent of the fact that defendants are unlikely to entertain such belief in the first place. The abandonment of objective standards entirely would disempower the community from mandating such care and protection. *Morgan* demonstrates that standards of reasonable conduct furnish tools for protecting women from victimization; they are not invariably legal devices for sustaining subjugation of whatever form.[42]

Lenore Walker's role in *Gordon* (the "woman without a will" confession case discussed above) and the House of Lords' logic in *Morgan* represent a kind of Balkanization of the standards of responsibility, but in the service of different ends. Although *Morgan* fosters individual permissiveness perhaps typical of that era, Walker's *Gordon* logic caters to the culture of victim ideology. The common denominator between the cases is a distrust of community standards forged out of the struggle to sustain a political community. Both reflect flip sides of the larger retreat from political obligation and the ability to sustain the tensions of judgment.

Universal Justice and Group Justice

Syndrome defenses' contributions to the subjectivization of criminal law leads to a related problem: the Balkanization of law. Balkanization of legal justice ineluctably accompanies subjective standards, especially in an environment that witnesses the centrifugal pull of interest group liberalism, group-based identity politics, and the politics of victimhood.

To be sure, consciousness of the impact of law and policy on certain groups is mandatory in contexts where invidious and illegal forms of discrimination exist or are suspected. Sometimes group-based justice is necessary to achieve universal justice. The best use of BWS, as we have seen, is to counter illegitimate stereotyping of the defendant. Race consciousness can accomplish the same end in countering racism. After all, racists are the ones who invented race consciousness in the first place by asserting that race determines the person rather than individual choice or transcendence.[43] In such cases, special judicial scrutiny or other specially tailored legal actions are mandated in the name of equal protection and other basic constitutional norms.[44] But we must be careful whenever we adopt double standards or legal policies of non-universal application. Though the norm of equal standards is flexible, its moral and legal pull grows stronger as legal policies move further away from its center of gravity.

Syndrome defenses raise the spectre of double standards (because they are not available to everyone who has a syndrome, let alone people without one), and should be avoided so long as equal justice can be achieved by policies available to all citizens. In the end, Holly Maguigan's treatment of the law of self-defense points us in the right direction, because it holds out the possibility of achieving justice by equal standards that are cognizant of particular women's circumstances better than Walker's syndrome approach.[45] Rather than drawing on insightful new forms of feminist jurisprudence that seek to account for the subtlety and complexity of reality and gender relations, BWS, for example, is associated with forms of identity politics that view women as fundamentally alike.[46] The general merits or demerits of such thinking aside, severe problems arise when criminal justice incorporates such thinking into the process by which criminal responsibility is determined. As Maguigan declares, "Guilt is personal."[47] Individuals are not more or less guilty because of the groups to which they belong (or to which we ascribe them); nor are they more or less guilty because of such qualities in their victims. And, as discussed in chapter 6, there is no demonstrated link between mental defect and criminal culpability or behavior. The entire edifice of criminal procedure and evidence rules (a set of principles derived from deep constitutional principles) is designed to prevent giving vent to prejudice against the defendant or victim based on the defendant's or victim's character, ascriptive qualities, beliefs, or political standing. This set of principles is a manifestation of the principle of freedom, whereby one has the freedom to develop whatever type of character one chooses without legal interference (thus, punishments based on character or belief threaten the First Amendment). We have seen that battered women should not be judged on their character when we consider whether they deployed lethal force in a justifiable manner. To the extent that BWS counters such prejudice, it is a good thing. Unfortunately, we have also seen that BWS's logic encourages such improper judgments in other ways (see chapter 6). Only the actions and specific *mens rea* (criminal intent) of the defendant are relevant under the law. When we punish or excuse because of factors pertaining to the character of defendants or victims, we make a Faustian pact with partiality and, ultimately, thought control. Inflicting capital punishment because of the race of the victim is certainly wrong; and character or political status is as illegitimate a basis for such differential treatment as race.[48]

The lack of public standards embodied in the syndrome defenses encourages this process. Syndrome logic has thrived in this selective environment, especially to the extent that it reinforces abstract binary oppositions (men/women; parent/child; will/will-lessness). Jessica Benjamin and Michelle Masse portrayed the alternatives in our analysis of the battering relationship above: accept the tensions of responsible citizenship that embroil us in the struggle of intersubjectivity, or retreat into the securities of domination (or reverse domination), othering, favoritism, and selective justice. Self-determination and the construction of objective knowledge and justice are forged in the struggle that characterizes intersubjective relations with others. Steven B. Smith shows how this dialectical process is essential to self-development in Hegel's philosophy of citizenship:

[W]e come to know ourselves not through isolated introspection in the manner of Descartes but only through interaction with others. . . . "Self-consciousness," [Hegel] writes, "exists in and for itself . . . by the fact that it so exists for another self-consciousness: that is to say, it is only by being acknowledged or 'recognized.' " . . .

This desire for recognition is, for Hegel, the quintessentially human desire . . .

[Society is] seen not as mere restrictions on the will's activities but as providing the moral context within which freedom is possible. Only from within the concrete forms of ethical life is mutual recognition possible . . . [49]

Mutual respect emerges only out of honest and ethical participation in community—a participation that pits individuals and groups against and with one another in the effort to establish common understandings and standards of justice. Provisionally, universal rule of law (whose standards apply equally to every differently situated individual) is one of the important products of this struggle. The relationships of individuals and groups in a community—unless they are at war—are dialectical, not binary or unitary. But the dialectic is driven by the quest for universal justice and community. Without this transcendent element, law and judgment dissolve into partisanship and power, and community is impossible. Midgley observes that "[i]f we did not have, at some level, a common mental structure with other people, we could not live with them at all, and we rightly assume that, in spite of their diversity, in principle, strangers are people with whom it is eventually possible to live. . . . This is part of our general assumption of inhabiting a single world which is in principle coherent and intelligible—an assumption that is needed as much for science as for morals, and is indeed the basis of all thought." [50]

A final issue related to the debates over objective/subjective standards and universal/group justice concerns respecting the rights of all citizens—even batterers, whose status in our society is justifiably very low. Batterers have rights, *not in spite* of the fact that they are fully responsible for their brutal actions, *but because* we rightly hold them responsible. If responsibility is the flip side of rights, as I have stressed throughout this book, rights are the flip side of responsibility. Battered women have the right to be protected by the state against their victimizers and to use lethal force when necessary to protect themselves; and batterers have the right not to be killed except when they truly endanger their victims, as the discussion of Jim Skalaski's self-defensive rights in the previous chapter brought into relief. Recall that Lisa Skalaski attacked him with a knife while he slept, and that—unlike the *Norman* case—he had not threatened her before he fell asleep. To not allow him to defend himself in this situation would be inconsistent with any plausible notion of self-defense law; but such a conclusion is implicit in the claim that Lisa's act was justified. Acknowledging rights can be disturbing when it comes to immoral and dangerous people like batterers. But constitutional freedom rests upon such counterintuitive understandings.

This appreciation is related to the type of character that the Constitution is meant to foster: self-control and deliberateness that are conducive to the restraints of law and due process for all citizens, as opposed to impulsive emotionalism and moralism that tempt us to bestow such rights selectively. In defending freedom of speech of extremist groups, for example, the First Amendment compels us to control our impulse to censor, which is the ultimate jerking knee. The hope is that this restraint will then contribute to the type of deliberation and judgment upon which constitutional political freedom depends. First, listening to such groups provides us with politically relevant knowledge about the dangerous world (the anti-ostrich principle). Second, by controlling such impulses, we objectify threats and thereby subject our fears (and the stereotyping and scapegoating that are the social and cultural manifestations of fear) to more deliberate thinking.[51] We learn to distinguish the crying of "wolf" from the actual presence of a wolf. If constitutionalism means anything, it lies in compelling us to distinguish rational from irrational fear, much as in the law of self-defense.

It is perhaps a sign of the decline of *civitas* and judgment that the mental process of "objectification" finds itself so universally condemned in political and intellectual circles today. Objectification taken to extremes certainly does contribute to thoughtlessness and an alienated sense of reality. Uncritical objectification and false moral universals result in what Hegel called "unreal abstractions."[52] But a certain degree of objectification is necessary to thinking, and to subjecting fear to reason. It is also necessary to establishing the distance between one's emotions and between selves that preserves individualism and civility. Reflexive condemnation of objectification arises from a failure to take dialectical thinking seriously. This point applies to citizenship. Astute thinkers on citizenship and *civitas* have shown how civility (the way we treat others outside the private realm of home and friendship) is enhanced by a respectful distancing of people based on manners and standards of respect. Indeed, manners contribute to both individualism and common standards, because the common standards of civility they require protect, in turn, the integrity, self-respect, and autonomy of people with whom we deal. Manners support individualism rather than compromise it. In exercising self-control in the form of manners, we show that we respect similar attributes in others. Manners are a form of internal personal governance. It is no accident that Tocqueville considered manners to be essential to political freedom and the "forms of liberty."[53]

In a sense, the norms of civility require that we treat others in the public realm as if they represented public roles consisting of agency and self-control. Such roles protect individuals from the vicissitudes of emotions and psychological quirks such as narcissism and dependency. They presuppose and reinforce the autonomy and mental capacity of the other. According to Richard Sennett, who advocates this type of distancing and civility as an essential attribute of "public man," the therapeutic ethic and state have eroded such citizenship by sanctioning the display of inner psychic states in all forums of interaction and by personalizing relationships to an unbalanced extent.[54] It is for this reason that pity and undue expansion of the psychology of "self-esteem" in the schools are so destructive: at their core they deprive the sources of their caring of the respect that comes from being assumed to be responsible agents capable of mastering demanding tasks. In the end, such treatment leaves its beneficiaries wondering if they could ever live up to such standards, thereby undermining the very confidence the ethic of self-esteem ostensibly championed in the first place. As Hegel and other students of the psychology of citizenship understand, self-confidence and true equal respect come from overcoming struggle (inner and outer) and meeting the call of responsibility. Failure to meet this call entraps the self in dependency and self-doubt, the domains of existential fear.[55]

The broader assumptions associated with the "syndrome society" eviscerate citizenship and civility along these lines by construing the self as so overwhelmed by forces outside of the self that it is too weak to be responsible and to be subject to public, common standards of law.

This logic also applies to constitutionalism. Lee E. Bollinger shows how the self-restraint encouraged by limiting censorship inculcates constitutional character. Such self-restraint "seeks to induce a *way of thinking* that is relevant to a variety of social interactions, from the political to the professional. . . . [It contributes to the] capacity to distance ourselves from our beliefs, which is so important to various disciplines and professional roles. . . . Free speech in this sense, then, is not inconsistent with what we do toward speech in other areas, like juries. There we seek means of controlling the impulse just as we do with the principle of free speech, though in each case in a different way."[56] Attorney Stephen Hurley of Madison represented this principle in his interview. Hurley personally does not believe that one is ever justified in using lethal force outside situations of strictly imminent danger. "There are always other options available unless the danger is immediate."[57] But as a legal advocate, Hurley puts this belief aside and defends battered women defendants with dedication, even when they have resorted to using force in situations in which the danger was not imminent.

Extending First Amendment rights to extremists disturbs many people. But who would deny such individuals or groups a fair trial governed by normal standards of proof when they are charged with crime? Would it be acceptable to allow a guilty verdict based on the lower evidentiary standard of a "preponderance of the evidence" rather than the more demanding "beyond a reasonable doubt?" Would it be proper for their defense attorneys to work less rigorously on their behalf? If the answer is "no," then we confront a powerful example of how equal and universal standards in criminal law embrace a valid expectation.

Yale Kamisar and others stress that the new "abuse excuses" too often constitute justifications for vigilante justice and scapegoating.[58] This certainly appears to be the case in *Menendez*. As we saw often above, most battered women who resort to deadly force have good reason to. But if this is so, why should they need a syndrome to make their case? Employing a syndrome in the clear absence of any imminent danger or captivity certainly raises the spectre of vigilante justification; and it spuriously undermines the claims of battered women who really do confront danger.

Vigilante justice is always among the major threats to fairness and due process. On a deeper psychological level, it unhinges the moral and intellectual restraints that temper the impulse to rush to moral judgment.[59] After the state's failure or refusal to protect citizens equally, the next major threat to the social contract lies in moralism unrestrained by public standards and public definitions of justice. In the classic portrayals of Aeschylus, Hobbes, and Locke, the violence of the state of nature or private justice is not simply a matter of unrestrained selfishness, but also a product of irreconcilable private notions of justice; rather than being a domain of amorality and selfishness, the state of nature is alive with untamed moral anger.[60] Along these lines Jack Katz shows how many homicides in the domestic context are motivated by "righteous slaughter."[61]

But if batterers and other immoral individuals deserve fair trials, they also presumptively deserve the other protections provided by the law, including the laws pertaining to self-defense. If Bernard Goetz was not justified in his resort to deadly force in the New York subway because of a lack of imminent danger, then a battered woman is not justified when she acts in a similar preemptive fashion.[62] *The factual dangers battered women confront will often result in drawing this line in a considerably different place than for Goetz, as we will make clear in the final chapter. As seen in chapters 3 and 4 above, batterers can be extremely dangerous, often flying into uncontrollable rage which presents imminent danger sooner than in other cases. And battered women might indeed reasonably believe there "is no way out." But these are factual differences, not categorical differences based on political or moral judgments about the respective characters or ascriptive status of the aggressors.* As formulated and practiced, syndrome logic is an open vessel into which such improper judgments can be poured.

No society dedicated to equal justice and the sanctity of life can accept this underlying logic for two basic reasons. First, society is fundamentally concerned with preventing the spiral of violence. As the California Court of Appeals declared in *People v. Aris*, "It is fundamental to our concept of law that there be no discrimination between sinner and saint solely on moral grounds. Any less exacting definition of imminence fails to protect every person's right to live."[63] We already live in a too-violent world in which, in Bob Dylan's words, everything is broken.[64] Although the law needs to be more cognizant of the dilemmas that plague victims of abuse, it must not forsake its duty to discourage vigilante violence.

In a related sense, organized society needs to abide by fundamental interdicts or taboos such as the prohibition against murder and unjustifiable use of self-defensive lethal force. One of the disturbing things about the *Menendez* case in Beverly Hills was the way in which the supporters of the Menendez brothers came across as insouciant to the interdict against murder, and how the alleged past deeds of the brothers' parents seemed to justify (fully or partially) the killings in such supporters' eyes.[65]

Common Sense, Judgment, and Politics

So *Morgan, Menendez*, and similar logic that focuses only on the psychological states of the individual without consideration of responsibility represents questionable subjectivization of the criminal law. In so doing, it compromises the basic *protective function* of the criminal law, as well as the universality of justice. And it does something more. It undermines the discriminating common judgment that makes community standards and responsible politics possible. Estimations of criminal responsibility must stem from the community's considered normative judgments, not simply from empirical determinations or estimations of actual mental states. According to George Fletcher, subjectivism

> misconstrues the foundation of criminal responsibility. The basis for all blaming is not the offender's thoughts, but our judgment about whether he could and should have acted otherwise under the circumstances. . . . That this confusion exists in the academy as well as in the courts tells us something about our cultural condition. We have lost confidence in the very notion of guilt based on self-control or "free will." It is hard for us to understand the individuals' having the capacity to act other than as they have acted. . . . In an age in which psychology has nearly displaced moral philosophy, this is a tempting way out.[66]

Undue subjectivization of criminal law stems from a lack of faith in *the capacity* of individuals to be responsible for their actions, and a lack of faith in citizens' capacity for common judgment. One aspect of this lack is the twilight of common sense that seems to grip us. Common sense is a *political* virtue because it arises from sense perceptions and judgments held in "common." The prevalence of common sense is a sign of political health and the ability to make credible moral and legal distinctions. To be sure, like anything valuable in this world, common sense has potential drawbacks. It has reinforced the prosaic, and lent support to the cultural "tyranny of the majority," as well as oppression of a more blatant sort. If truth and politics are separate, common sense must always be judged by an independent standard of validity. Constructive social change is sometimes moved to reject common sense in favor of claims and values that transcend the given (say, to reject what passed for "common sense" in Nazi Germany). But responsible advocates of common sense hardly countenance uncritical deference to its claims.

Sometimes common sense supplies a critical edge for constructive change (to wit, Thomas Paine's call to revolution in *Common Sense* or George Orwell's and Vaclav Havel's appeals to judgment and universal human sense in their resistance to communism). And abdication of allegiance to common sense disempowers resistance to spurious or nefarious claims of authority draped in the seductive guise of intellectual sophistication (the "opium of the intellectuals" that cloaked Marxist-Leninism in intellectual immunity).[67] Consequently, the responsible practice of common sense is a political virtue of a high order, as Arendt remarks:

> The only character of the world by which to gauge its reality is its being common to us all, and common sense occupies such a high rank in the hierarchy of political qualities because it is the one sense that fits into reality as a whole our five strictly individual senses and the strictly particular data they perceive. It is by virtue of common sense that the other sense perceptions are known to disclose reality and not merely felt as irritations of our nerves or resistance sensations in our bodies. *A noticeable decrease in common sense in any given community and a noticeable increase in superstition and gullibility are therefore almost infallible signs of alienation from the world . . .*
>
> [R]eason and faith in reason depend not upon single sense perceptions . . . but upon the unquestioned assumption that the senses as a whole—kept together and ruled over by common sense, the sixth and the highest sense—fit man into the reality which surrounds him.[68]

This observation indicts the widespread gullibility that has attended the most specious forms of victimization allegations discussed earlier in this book. These cases highlight the links between the disrespect of objectivity and evidence, vigilante justice, and the compromise of constitutionalism. Arendt stresses that her political notion of common sense is antithetical to what she calls purely "introspective" notions of reality, or the undue subjectivization of social and individual meaning. She speaks of the "nightmare of non-reality" that this subjectivization brings about. "Nothing could prepare our minds better for the dissolution of matter into energy, of objects into a whirl of atomic occurrences, than this dissolution of objective reality into subjective states of mind or, rather, into subjective mental processes."[69] Modern forms of knowledge based on the "triumph of the therapeutic," in which individual and human reality are defined in terms of psychological processes that overwhelm the self and common sense, pose problems for citizenship along these lines. A tension emerges between the "homo politicus" and the "homo psychologicus."[70]

In their most extreme incarnations, the various victimization syndromes have exacerbated the blurring of fact and fantasy. The "Remembering Satan" case in Olympia, Washington, united victimization syndrome and the memory recovery movement in a communal ritual of demonic fantasy, false accusation, self-flagellation, and confession.[71] Ofshe and Watters compare the widespread acceptance of the most extreme versions of recovered memory to Holocaust denial as portrayed in Deborah Lipstadt's excellent book on the subject. "The growing acceptance of these groups and their theories, [Lipstadt] believes, shows a fragility of reason within our society and dangerous relativism that makes it impossible to say that something is nonsense. . . . This is the story of the recovered memory movement. . . . When reading the literature surrounding the topic of MPD [multiple personality disorder], one sometimes feels the ground of reality crumbling away."[72] In 1990 Elizabeth Loftus participated as an expert witness for the defense in the George Franklin murder trial in San Francisco, a case premised on the recovered memory of George's daughter Eileen. As she testified about the problems associated with the theories of recovered memory and repression, Loftus observed that "[t]he courtroom was awash in credulity, the jurors' and spectators' opinions seemed predetermined, and my carefully researched scientific studies were just an old-fashioned irritation, a necessary but inconsequential detour on the road to confirming Eileen Franklin's memory and finding George Franklin guilty of murder."[73] Similar observations have recently gained widespread public attention concerning the famous child abuse prosecutions in the McMartin and Amirault day care cases in California and Massachusetts, and, more recently, the outbreak of false accusations in Wenatchee, Washington.[74] These extremely publicized cases amounted to nothing less than witch-hunts supported by societal moral hysteria. In these cases high-level state authorities refused to intervene and restore due process despite conspicious evidence of hysteria. As Garry Wills has stated, "The learned have their superstitions, prominent among them a belief that superstition is evaporating."[75]

Such instances are not yet commonplace (though noted intellectual authorities such as Judith Herman treat memory recovery and victimization syndrome as inseparable). But the syndromes' excessive mixing of incapacity excuse and justification (see chapter 6) in the context of group justice poses a danger for justice that cannot be ignored, for this mixture by definition blurs the line between reason and unreason. Recall that Walker has maintained that "opinions" are as valid as "facts" in the adjudication of cases of battered women who kill.[76]

Responsibility and Citizenship

There are some powerful theories of responsibility in relation to citizenship. The frameworks provided by these theories serve us in at least two ways. First, they provide us with a picture of citizenship that casts light on the circumstances of battered women. The inner logic and typical consequence of battering compromise women's capacities to take on the responsibilities of citizenship, so we gain a sense of the profound inequities that battering engenders by looking through these theo-

retical lenses. Second, these theories provide a means of distinguishing constructive from nonconstructive legal remedies to battering, including the question of
how to deal with battered women who kill or commit other serious crimes.

We use the word "responsibility" in many different but interrelated senses,
including role responsibility, causal responsibility, liability responsibility, and capacity responsibility.[77] And within these domains, the concept of responsibility
takes on different meanings in different contexts. But having different usages does
not mean that the term is meaningless or uselessly vague. It signifies similar capacities in each context; and its widespread usage in a variety of contexts is a sign
of its universal appeal. As Hanna Pitkin remarks in defending the concept of representation from its critics, " 'A varied usage is not the same thing as a vague usage;'
quite the opposite: 'the need for making distinctions is exactly contrary to the
vagueness which results from failure to distinguish.' "[78] I am concerned primarily
with a version of capacity responsibility because this notion is most relevant to
equal citizenship and the psychology of equal respect. And this notion is linked
to liability responsibility in criminal law, for only those with the requisite mental
capacity (however broadly understood) are subject to liability. Role and causal responsibility are subsets of these more encompassing categories. Hart delineates
capacity responsibility in a manner that highlights its centrality to the capacity for
citizenship: "In most contexts . . . the expression 'he is responsible for his actions'
is used to assert that a person has certain normal capacities. . . . The capacities in
question are those of understanding, reasoning, and control of conduct: the ability to understand what conduct legal rules or morality require, to deliberate and
reach decisions concerning these requirements, and to conform to decisions when
made."[79]

This portrayal of capacity responsibility points to the characteristics of equal
citizens, including the capacity to abide by the sometimes difficult strictures of law.
The insanity defense operates when such capacity is lacking. It is based on "a
shared Western conception of personal responsibility," and the concomitant notion
that a person is "blameless" if he or she is incapable of "individual autonomy."[80]
Autonomy is not a simple concept, for the self is influenced by many external and
internal factors throughout life. Freedom is never an unproblematic principle or
term. And criticism and deconstruction of autonomy abound. But the fact remains
that autonomy remains an essential attribute of the self in a liberal polity.[81] Being
responsible for one's actions is another way of saying that one is capable of the self-
determining action upon which political freedom is built. Sartre defines responsibility "in its ordinary sense as 'consciousness (of) being the incontestable author
of an event or of an object.' "[82] For example, in response to those who warned that
politicians had better be cautious in accusing First Lady Hillary Clinton of financial improprieties, Harriet Woods, the head of the National Woman's Political Cau-
cus, told the press in January 1994, "The change that she has brought about to

evaluating the wife of a president . . . is that she is accountable to herself. We [women] seek the glory, but we also have to take the consequences when we make mistakes. I don't know if she has made mistakes, but if she has I hope she would be equally accountable."[83] Similarly, Elizabeth Rapaport presents the argument that women should be as subject as men to the death penalty.[84] One could not find more poignant statements highlighting the relationship between accountability for one's acts and equal citizenship.

As Schneider points out, while portrayals of incapacity might help individual woman defendants in criminal cases, such portrayals can harm women in other contexts which place a premium on being capable of handling responsibility, including termination of parental rights, child custody cases, and considerations of capacity for citizenship. Schneider observes,

> The "dysfunctional portrait of battered women" that has emerged in cases involving battered women on trial for the killing of their assailant, has created a legal stereotype. When a battered woman decides to identify her abuse in the context of a custody suit, courtroom professionals, many of them trained in family systems theory, may shunt that woman into a stereotypical category, one that characterizes her as weak, passive, victimized, and therefore unable to properly care for her children.[85]

The moral and legal status of battered women who commit crimes reflect these tensions. On the one hand, battered women often are victimized in ways that reduce them to immanence, an oppressive evil. One interviewee told me "I was a trained dog. I no longer had a real self that was my own." Another interviewee, Ronda Richardson, had no meaningful sense of time, no real grasp of past and future after years of abuse, so to conduct a defense her advocates had to investigate and piece together incidents of abuse for her to recall. According to the defense attorney and the main investigator in the case, this defendant's lack of a sense of time paralleled her lack of independent self-consciousness at that time in her life, an attribute that is essential to rational freedom.[86] On the other hand, interviewees often accepted responsibility for their crimes based on the particular facts in their cases. Their sense of self involved transcending incapacity victimhood. One accepted her responsibility for killing her abusive boyfriend, as well as her fifteen-year sentence for first-degree reckless homicide: "I'm not blaming no one for what happened that night. . . . I'm the one that pulled the trigger. . . . I should have been more in control of myself." Asked if she thought that justice was done in her case, she said, "I think so. Because I did take a life . . . a life was involved."[87]

The presumption of responsibility is not absolute, and ambiguity about responsibility persists, as evidenced by the traditional "excuses" the criminal law provides, such as insanity, diminished capacity, duress, and necessity. The presumption of responsibility makes sense only if we harbor a comparative notion of when the capacity to be responsible does not exist; thus, we must acknowledge the insanity defense if we are committed to the capacity to be responsible.[88] As seen above, BWS is a species of this type of incapacity defense, so it should be used only there. But the ultimate source of our actions and intentionality (our free will or some other "cause") is not fully graspable. Conclusive knowledge about the well-springs of our actions eludes us because we are alienated from our souls, and because we are simultaneously influenced by our socialization and our capacity to act freely.[89] Criminal law requires delicate moral considerations like those Melville portrays in *Billy Budd:* "those intricacies involved in the question of moral responsibility." [90]

Recent critical scholarship has shown that particular constructions or interpretations of responsibility and free will are not simply rooted in conclusions derived from universal human nature or objective findings of free will. They are shaped to significant extents by political, social, and legal considerations. For example, what is the extent of our assurance that Lorena Bobbitt was "temporarily insane" when she cut her husband's manhood with that knife, edgy and dull? When we consider particular applications of responsibility in concrete cases, we become aware of the normative and social factors that influence such judgments.

In *Moral Responsibility and the Boundaries of Community,* Marion Smiley has recently shown how the attribution of responsibility depends more than we commonly admit on social and political criteria. Smiley's analysis does not directly address the constructivism/moral realism debate (though her work has implications for this debate), but the debate between free will and determinism. Smiley criticizes modern moral philosophy for holding that one possesses moral responsibility only if one's actions or thoughts are not "caused" by forces or sources beyond the sphere of one's free will. She entreats us to go beyond the free will versus determinism debate.

Smiley argues that this effort to locate responsibility in "contra-causal freedom" is misguided for at least two reasons. First, we simply cannot determine the absence or presence of free will or contra-causal freedom in the objective way many modern philosophers assume. The free will/determinism debate remains fundamentally irresolvable.[91] Second, the search for contra-causal freedom ignores the ways in which political and social points of view and normative value judgments influence assessments of moral responsibility. Smiley explains:

> Since we generally view our judgments of responsibility as purely factual, we might, understandably, be taken aback by any insinuation that these judgments are shaped by the exercise of political power. But once we explore them in detail, we are forced to acknowledge two things. One is that our judgments of causal responsibility often depend not only on our

configuration of social roles and the boundaries of our community, but on the distribution of power between those suffering and those being held responsible. The other is that when our judgments of causal responsibility change over time, they do so not only because of new causal discoveries, but because we as a community have come to alter our expectations of particular individuals on the basis of shifts in social and political power.

While competing expectations and the wielding of power make such changes possible, they would not be effective if we were not also able to incorporate our judgments of causal responsibility into our social practice of blaming.[92]

The respective failures and successes of different syndrome defenses and insanity tests (e.g., PMS and Vietnam veteran's syndrome compared to BWS, and the return to more restrictive insanity tests in the 1980s) that I discussed in previous chapters provide supporting evidence of Smiley's thesis, for these differences are functions of political and social concerns, not changes in the field of psychiatry and psychological science. The law of manslaughter presents another example. We saw above that the New York Court of Appeals ruled in 1980 that the defendant in *People v. Casassa* was not entitled to a manslaughter defense because of the unreasonableness of the disturbance that influenced the killing. But courts have been more tolerant of the defense when a spouse discovers his or her mate in an act of adultery.[93] Different judgments associated with the social practice of blaming explain the divergence between such cases, not causal psychological analysis.

Smiley shows how power and social values not only influence these decisions but are part and parcel of them. Modern medical and psychological science, heirs of the Enlightenment project, have transformed our understanding of the mind. Rather than imputing spiritual or other transcendent qualities to the self, we look for positivistically grounded sources of psychological states and motivation, including intentional, biological, environmental, and emotional factors. We have come a long way since the days when courts looked to divine intervention to determine guilt or innocence in criminal trials, and when many societies held criminal trials for animals and insects (medieval practices that displayed human projection and social construction in their purest forms).[94] Today the practice of blaming must deal with scientific and individualist or humanistic understandings. Yet Smiley shows how blaming is still properly affected by social judgments, politics, and normative values that cannot be reduced to science and pure determinations of causation.

Our approach to culpability must account for the complex judgments and assessments that properly characterize the social practice of blaming. This is one reason that attorneys in such cases are reluctant to generalize, and ask to "see what all the facts are like" in the case at hand.[95] But this does not mean that *any* conditions will do.

Even though context, relationships, political power, social psychology, and social need influence the attribution of criminal responsibility, the criminal law's assumption of individual responsibility is not meaningless or illegitimate. *Indeed, a constructivist perspective tied to an understanding of citizenship can lead to a greater appreciation of the importance of responsibility than metaphysical or positivistic orientations.* In the famous Second Essay of *The Genealogy of Morals*, Nietzsche develops a constructivist theory of the psychology of respect that is central to my understanding of the social and political meaning of responsibility. Nietzsche is no democrat; but few thinkers have matched the acuity of his insights into the nature of the human psyche, especially concerning moral phenomena. (He defines himself as the first major philosophical psychologist, and claims that his goal is to remind us that psychology is "the queen of the sciences." By "psychology," Nietzsche means a philosophical awareness that probes human motivation and character, not something therapeutic.) [96] As seen, Nietzsche eschews a metaphysical notion of free will, but values the personal capacities associated with its genealogical and historical developments. Nietzsche's portrayal in his major work on responsibility resembles de Beauvoir's concept of transcendence: responsibility is a product of one's ability to exercise self-control and take on obligations and other difficult tasks. In a painful struggle over time, humans had to chisel the capacity of being responsible for their actions out the self. But this struggle opened up a new kind of freedom:

This precisely is the long history of how *responsibility* originated. The task of breeding an animal with the right to make promises evidently embraces and presupposes as a preparatory task that one first makes men to a certain degree necessary, uniform . . .

If we place ourselves at the end of this tremendous process, where the tree at last bears fruit . . . we discover that the ripest fruit is the *sovereign individual,* like only to himself . . . in short, the man who has his own independent, protracted will and the *right to make promises*—and in him a proud consciousness, quivering in every muscle, of *what* has at length been achieved and become flesh in him, a consciousness of his own power and freedom. . . . This emancipated individual, with the actual right to make promises, this master of a *free will,* this sovereign man— how should he not be aware of his superiority over all those who lack the right to make promises and stand as their own guarantors. . . . The proud awareness of the extraordinary privilege of *responsibility,* the consciousness of this rare freedom, this power over oneself and one's fate, has in his case penetrated to the profoundest depths and become instinct. [97]

Nietzsche presents several important insights about the capacity to be responsible in this remarkable statement. First, such capacity is an important ingredient of self-determination and citizenship. It is tied to the capacity to make promises to others, which is a quintessential aspect of political community. Arendt pinpoints the importance of this insight for political theory: "The sovereignty of a body of people bound and kept together, not by an identical will which somehow magically inspires them all, but by an agreed purpose for which alone the promises are valid and binding, shows itself quite clearly in its unquestioned superiority over those who are completely free, unbounded by any promises and unkept by any purpose. . . . Nietzsche, in his extraordinary sensibility to moral phenomena . . . saw in the faculty of promises (the 'memory of the will,' as he called it) the very distinction which marks off human from animal life." [98]

Second, the capacity for responsibility is a necessary if not sufficient condition for attaining self-respect and the respect of others. However we make adjustments for compassion or pity, the truths of the psychology of respect remain: we ultimately extend less respect to those unable to bear the capacity for responsibility (or who do not strive to live up to their potential, however limited). Third, Nietzsche's understanding of responsibility is linked to his evaluation of the importance of exercising discriminating judgment.[99] Finally, his portrayal of the genealogy and psychology of responsibility (and the respect that attends its exercise) captures a paradox that supports the liberal political freedom that Nietzsche otherwise disparaged: limiting one's inclinations and desires in the name of responsibilities to society and others can increase one's freedom in the longer run. The same principle applies to political freedom: we attain a qualitatively and quantitatively enhanced freedom by binding ourselves to constitutional limits and the obligations of citizenship (recall the discussion of manners). As I have elucidated throughout this chapter, these obligations include sympathetic judgment.[100] In judging we stretch ourselves by learning about others (putting ourselves in their shoes) and increasing our mental capacities (by then struggling to make sense of what we have learned in relation to common standards of right). As Midgley remarked, judgment "is a comprehensive function, involving our whole nature, by which we direct ourselves and find our way through a whole forest of possibilities." [101] By upholding the presumption of responsibility, the criminal law seeks to protect us from violators of our rights and contributes to the fostering of self-control and judgment in the citizenry.

Many victimized individuals refuse to view themselves as incapacity victims because their sense of dignity hinges on feeling appropriately responsible for their lives. The most telling was one interviewee who was sexually abused as a teenager by her stepfather, who told us that she respected the psychologist who dealt with her after she reported her abuse because he did not treat her like a label. "I was victimized, but I am not a 'victim.' He [the psychologist] treated me with respect, as a person, not a 'victim.' The others, especially the nurses and social workers, treated me condescendingly, with pity. It was like I was being abused again. They just couldn't understand it." [102] In addition, several therapists who work with war veterans told us that they eschew therapies based on tenets or concepts that allow patients to hide from their responsibilities for themselves. Two pinpointed PTSD as a problem in this regard because "it provides a label behind which the patient can hide." [103]

Susan Brownmiller pinpoints the link between responsibility and citizenship in her dramatization of the actual case in New York in which Joel Steinberg killed his daughter while Hedda Nussbaum, his battered and cocaine-addicted wife, stood by. Brownmiller, the author of the paradigm-shifting analysis of rape *Against Our Will,* draws a line between being raped and certain ways of being battered. She calls for appropriate distinctions and moral discrimination. Brownmiller's commentary recalls the discussion in chapter 5 about how certain crimes of omission highlight the meaning of the attribution of responsibility:

> Feminist analysis of the Steinberg-Nussbaum case must center on moral responsibility for the death of six-year-old Lisa. The battery of Hedda Nussbaum cannot be denied, but her complicity must also be acknowledged. The movement to aid battered women does the cause of feminism a disservice when it supports unquestioningly the behavior and actions of all battered women. The movement must drop its simplistic attitude toward batterers, and cease to view them as giant suction machines with the power to pull in any woman who crosses their path. It must also cease to excuse every battered woman who engages in criminal behavior, with the argument that she is, after all, merely a victim of patriarchy.
>
> The point of feminism is to give women the courage to exercise free will, not to use the "brainwashed victim" excuse to explain away the behavior of a woman who surrenders her free will. Victimhood must no longer be an acceptable or excusable model of female behavior. Unlike rape, which is an isolated act of violence committed by an aggressive assailant who may or may not be known to his victim, battery defines a sustained relationship over many years between two people.[104]

As I have emphasized throughout, victim ideology and doing justice for victims of abuse are not the same thing. I have chronicled the extent and nature of domestic violence, and have shown how such abuse must be taken very seriously. Victim ideology, however, amounts to the abandonment of any meaningful norms of responsibility when it comes to assessing the actions of victims of abuse, thereby forsaking the difficult judgments that make for justice. Citizenship and judgment require dialectical thinking that wrestles with the relationship between individual circumstance and common standards, whereas syndrome logic eschews this tension in favor of simplistic abstraction and psychological speculation.

Feminist scholar Ruth Leys shows how the nondialectical thinking that characterizes victim ideology harms citizenship across the board. Leys decries the non-dialectical thinking of such feminists as Herman, MacKinnon, and Jeffrey Masson. Drawing on the logic of Jacqueline Rose, Leys criticizes these theorists and others who "rejecting the notion of unconscious conflict, embrace instead a rigid dichotomy between the internal and the external such that violence is imagined as coming to the subject *entirely* from the outside—a point of view that inevitably reinforces a politically retrograde stereotype of the female as a purely passive victim. . . . [Such thinking] in effect denies the female subject of all possibility of agency."[105] Of course, violence does often "come from the outside in a manner that violently victimizes," as Brownmiller remarked just above. The key to Leys's critique lies in the word "entirely," which accentuates the fact that victim ideology portrays women as presumptively lacking in agency, and that it is ultimately nondialectical in logic. We saw in chapter 4 how some models of the battering relationship fall into this simplistic way of thinking, and how they fail to adequately grasp the nature of the will in oppressive situations.

Foucaultian understanding of the links between knowledge claims and social forces can be turned on the general logic of the "syndrome society" itself. Victimization syndromes arise from two milieus: the empirical truth of domestic violence, sexual abuse, warlike conditions in society, and the larger culture and politics of values that determine which truths to emphasize over others. To the extent that the new syndromes represent *more* than the truth of abuse, the mentality behind victimization syndromes represents deeper social and historical trends about which one can only speculate.

America has become a violent, disordered society in which abuse is widespread. A breakdown of community and economic security has created a state of victimhood for too many citizens (though earlier forms of coherent community also hid abuse from public recognition). The economic vise that is squeezing the middle class has enormous consequences for citizenship and the state of domestic tranquility (familial and national), and is worthy of serious attention in its own right.[106] In *addition,* Tocqueville's bleak vision also could be unfolding. In *Democracy in America,* Tocqueville feared that Americans would lose their political virtue by turning away from public responsibilities and, concomitantly, by moving toward too great a reliance upon the administrative-welfare state. Tocqueville understood that meaningful community and self-reliance are dialectically related, and that as political obligation dwindles, the self becomes imperial yet ever more fragile (this is another paradox of political freedom). As noted above, we can gain strength when we open ourselves to political and social interaction with others, when we bind ourselves by obligations, so long as such pursuits are not means to escape from the existential burdens of individuality.[107] When the process of evisceration unfolds, the weakened, embattled self is shaken by all sorts of risky actions and speech "fraught with death." Courage is the first casualty of the process. Courage is "the political virtue par excellence," because it is the attribute that makes us unafraid to speak our minds and enter the public realm, which is the realm of the "other" and judgment.[108] The public realm and other beings constitute a threat and an opportunity for growth. If we retreat into excessive individualism, thoughtless conformity, or identity politics (uniting with groups of only the like-minded, turning the "me-other" into the "us-them"), the sense of threat tightens its grip. Tocqueville was the first to recognize that democratic regimes dedicated to individualism and equality of condition are threatened by an undercurrent of paranoia, which is kept at bay only by institutions, practices, and assumptions conducive to political freedom. Book Two of *Democracy in America* is dedicated to diagnosing the problem and recommending remedies. The overall solution lay in promoting "self-interest rightly understood," in which self-interest and concern for the good of society exist in a creative tension. Today the politics of paranoia appears to have gained headway, affecting groups across the political spectrum. From the politically correct to the militias, the politics of distrust and othering reigns.

In today's world, courage seems the most forgotten of all virtues. Other major casualties of this process are the confidence and character needed to exercise discerning judgment, as Elshtain discloses in a recent article showing how the inability to make substantive, discriminating judgments represents a manifestation of Tocqueville's fears. Judgment is risky, requiring sufficient belief in the validity of common standards—that is, belief in the validity of a public world. In such a society, Tocqueville foresaw:

> The will of man is not shattered, but softened, bent, and guided: men are seldom forced by it to act, but they are constantly restrained from acting; such a power does not destroy, but it prevents existence; it does not tyrannize, but it compresses, enervates, extinguishes, and stupefies a people, till each nation is reduced to be nothing better than a flock of timid and industrious animals, of which government is the shepherd.[109]

Notions of the shriveled self are prevalent in many circles today. Psychological and social sciences have lost faith in reason and will.[110] So has postmodern philosophy and social theory. In the influential intellectual universe spawned by Foucault's epigones, for example, the opposite of the presumption of responsibility governs because the self is envisioned as a porous vessel through which various forms of power flow. This construction of the self turns the self into a presumptive victim (recall the discussion of William Ryan in chapter 2), giving birth to the politics and art of blame which drown out the meaningful and credible blaming that is conducive to justice.[111]

Foucault's sometimes undifferentiated treatment of power provides a background for the assumptions that attach to the syndrome society. For example, in

Foucault's universe, the exercise of power in the prison becomes emblematic of the effects of power in society as a whole.[112] We are all prisoners. The line between the exceptional or extreme case and the typical case blurs. This move is dangerous for citizenship in general and for those who become the real victims of abuse. If distinctions cannot be made between qualitatively different phenomena, just moral claims get lost in the din. This lack of differentiation (which I have portrayed as a lack of judgment) is the *sine qua non* of syndrome logic, which also fails to provide meaningful standards of differentiation. Syndrome logic obfuscates the traditional distinction between sanity and insanity. So does Foucault. Foucault began his career as a great student of marginality. His brilliant treatment of madness in *Madness and Civilization* is paradigmatic, since madness is almost by definition something that lies in the darkness on the edge of town, beyond the polis in which agency and freedom reign.[113] But Foucault concludes that madness dwells paradoxically at the very heart of the world of reason, an understanding of coexisting contradiction and negation. This subtle, nuanced perception opens up profound theological, poetic, psychological, and philosophical insights into the contingencies, vicissitudes, and adventures of human existence.[114] But its imperialistic extension to the realms of politics and law poses significant problems. Foucault's philosophy is many worthy things; but a philosophy of citizenship it is not. Foucault's followers view agency and constructive will as a myth, forgetting that Nietzsche, Foucault's ultimate mentor, viewed the will as the essence of the self, and personal responsibility as a mark of accomplishment and the will to power. Nietzsche consistently drew a telling line between the flourishing will and the languishing will. One prominent commentator understands this distinction to be Nietzsche's major contribution to modern thought.[115] Unfortunately, Nietzsche feared that the twentieth century would be characterized by descendant life, not ascendant. The general assumptions of the syndrome society that I have examined travel the path indicated by Nietzsche's fears.

Two broader social phenomena contribute to the minimalization of the self and risk-taking. First, we live in an entitlement society that offers dispensations by the state if the individual can pigeonhole himself or herself into the appropriate category. We label ourselves in various shades of victimhood in order to gain passive benefits from the provider (the explosion of Social Security Disability Insurance in recent decades is a prime example). Second, an actuarial logic prevails in many domains, especially insurance (the major provider of psychiatric costs). This logic bears the same form as the syndrome, since it construes individual variance in terms of patterns and tendencies, not distinctiveness.[116]

Transcendence, Equality, and Citizenship

In order to do justice in difficult cases of criminal law, the ethics of citizenship and political freedom must be reborn. The inroads that syndrome logic and discourse have made in society are a sign of how difficult this renewal will be. The place to start this renewal of democracy is with the state and society meeting their obligation to protect us from violent predators, and for all of us to face the facts about domestic violence and other dark aspects of our society. We have seen that this effort has grown in the area of domestic violence, though it has a long road to travel. If we turn our backs on the victims of abuse, such actions (or omissions) cannot help but be very relevant to the victims' claims that they confronted a situation of dangerous necessity in which there was no reasonable way out. But as the state and society come to honor their obligations and promises, citizens must reassume responsibility. Those who deny the importance of personal responsibility fail to appreciate its centrality to any viable conception of democratic freedom. There is nothing hypocritical or contradictory about wanting to do justice for victims of domestic abuse without abandoning the principle of responsibility, but such a position does commit its defenders to work out how justice and responsibility can be achieved. The reader will find one such attempt in the following chapter.

Some thinkers have criticized the understanding of the public realm and citizenship articulated here for being "masculinist."[117] Others point out (correctly) that conceptions of the public realm are subject to reformulation as historical consciousness and power relations change.[118] Nonetheless, it is not evident that the emphasis on common sense, responsibility, courage, and common standards is gendered per se. The phenomenology of transcendence is somewhat universal; we constantly make judgments about individuals based on their wills, courage, and common sense. Women make such judgments as frequently as men.

Furthermore, the "standpoint epistemology" that posits a chasm between male and female ways of knowing threatens to ghettoize women in the realm of action and politics. Men and women are different in telling ways, and women's entry into the realm of citizenship undoubtedly will change (and is changing) common sense and standards. Changes in the criminal law's treatment of battered women reflect this effect. But the assimilation process cuts two ways, and the elements of transcendence and responsibility give shape and meaning to the new contributions of women. On the one hand, one might view the qualities of reason, autonomy, responsibility, and courage as expressions of masculine character. On the other hand, these qualities might well be attributes that are intrinsic to the very enterprise of transcendence in the form of political participation or any activity to which one commits oneself. Just as true justice incorporates individual and group perspectives as it moves toward universal justice, so does action transcend individual difference. Anyone who strives to achieve something in the realms of art, business, the professions, politics, or homemaking assumes responsibilities and must make decisions that have consequences. When we abandon judgments that take these responsibilities seriously, we not only forsake our responsibilities as citizens, we also risk consigning the "beneficiaries" of such supposed largesse to second-class citizenship. Equally important, we also damage those over whom we are obligated to exercise care, for mature caring (as any parent knows) requires that emotional commitment and love be supplemented by effort and a strong sense of obligation. Like Thomas Edison's portrayal of "genius," relationships based on care entail as much perspiration as inspiration. In parenting, as in other tasks, neglect often occurs when love or other forms of emotional bonding lose their connection to obligation and the right degree of self-denial and self-control. In the end, the ethics of responsibility (and the judgment needed to reinforce it) and care are not enemies, but allies.

Since men have enjoyed a gender monopoly on the avenues of public participation, it is easy to equate the values attached to transcendence to masculinity.[119] But as women assume such responsibilities, they ineluctably find themselves employing the attributes of transcendence and responsibility and looking for such attributes in others. Truth about human qualities is often discovered in the commitment to action, or, as Hans-Georg Gadamer relates, in the acts of play and creation.[120] In the realm of action and care, which is the realm of citizenship, we give part of ourselves over to the requirements of the task. These latter make such ascriptive attributes as race, gender, and physical appearance comparatively less relevant. In the days before the advent of "identity politics" (the victim group-basis of which contributes to syndrome logic), King and other civil-rights leaders asked us to judge people by their characters and actions, not by the color of their skins. The realm of action and care is consistent with the psychology of equal respect because the obligations associated with the task constitute the basis of judgment, not skin color, gender, or the quality of one's victimization. This understanding exposes the dangers that lurk in the ideology of identity and victimization politics, for such ideologies emphasize deterministic attributes rather than achievement. In so doing, they cannot help but compromise responsibility, care, creativity, and the only kind of equality that can endure.[121]

Conclusion

Compliance with contextualized objective norms is an important element of citizenship and equal respect. Equally important, as seen in the discussions of the *Morgan* and *Casassa* cases above, objective standards provide one modest way to protect individuals from the irrational predations of others. Of course, such standards are mere rhetoric if the state does not enforce them and protect its citizens from violence. But the criminal law should not be concerned simply with the actual empirical mental states and knowledge of individuals; it should uphold certain standards of reasonable conduct, for such requirements support constructive citizenship and social norms of self-control, and promote the protection of others by holding individuals blameworthy for unreasonable acts that seriously harm others.

Self-control is not antithetical to political freedom. Political freedom is premised on it.[122]

For these reasons, we must be reluctant to subjectivize the basic tenets of criminal law, including cases of battered women who kill or commit other crimes. One problem with the model of BWS deployed in the courts is that it caters to such tendencies. Driven by determinism, battered women are portrayed under BWS's sway as lacking the very attributes that make citizenship possible. But the syndrome picture is only a partial truth whose tenets countermand the norms of a viable political community. Battered women and justice deserve better.

Like homosexuals in relation to the APA, the women's movement was intended to give women the opportunity to demonstrate their ability to bear the burdens of citizenship in a context of nondiscrimination. Abiding by the law of self-defense represents this ability, for this law is premised on the capacity to act with reason under pressure. We will see in the next chapter that the law of self-defense properly gives leeway to the targets of original aggressors. In cases of domestic violence, the leeway should be flexible in a principled fashion.

Especially in the context of the criminal law, objective standards of responsibility must be educated by the often unique pressures that battered women endure. *The law must frame the standard of reasonableness with this reality in mind.* This contextualization is perhaps the most important issue in the law governing the legal and moral responsibility of battered women, as Julie Blackman portrayed near the end of chapter 6, where she declared, "*Careful attention to the battered woman's past experiences with her husband's or partner's violence enhances one's capacity to understand her attack against him as reasonable or not. A true standard of reason is best approximated when all relevant factors that bear on good judgment are considered.*"[123]

Blackman hits the bull's eye. Recall the remark of Ann Jacobs in the penultimate paragraph of the last chapter in which Jacobs emphasized Ronda's "bad situation" over her "mental illness." Another example of how we should stress situation over craziness is Lieutenant William Calley. Calley certainly confronted extraordinary danger and violence in Vietnam. Nonetheless, the law had no choice but to hold him up to common standards of right and reason in his trial for the My Lai massacre. *Just judgment required appreciating the awful realities of war while honoring the standards that require doing the right thing under these circumstances.* This logic is also the way to adjudicate difficult "necessity" cases such as *Dudley v. Stephens,* the cannibalism case discussed in chapter 5. Similarly, juries should be presented with evidence that brings the nature of the battering relationship in the case to life. In this way, we can avoid the pitfall of a double standard in favor of a single standard that is attuned to the complexity and subtlety of reality. Justice for battered women defendants comes down to a "true standard of reason," which entails empathetic understanding applied to common standards of judgment. Honestly contextualized objective standards are the only reliable vehicles to take us down the difficult road of justice. In the next chapter Evan Gerstmann and I will call for a new type of situational expert testimony in lieu of the expert psychological testimony that has confused the worlds of reason and unreason. Let us turn to the policy prescription.

PART **IV** *Conclusion*

A New Framework for Battered Women: Self-Defense and the Necessity of the Situation

by Donald A. Downs and Evan Gerstmann

> While the recognition of the battered woman's syndrome revised the law
> of self-defense for a limited class of women . . . a new stereotype of the
> battered woman is created once again placing women outside the pur-
> view of the reasonable. Thus battered women have been placed in a
> double bind of two stereotypes: if an abused woman's responses in the
> relationship did not conform exactly to the legal stereotype of a woman
> suffering from battered woman syndrome, courts could find her, by defi-
> nition, to be neither battered nor reasonable.—SHIRLEY SAGAW, "A Hard
> Case for Feminists: *People v. Goetz*"

> Who in the rainbow can show the line where the violet tint ends and the
> orange tint begins? Distinctly we see the difference of colors, but when
> exactly does the one first blendingly enter into the other? So with sanity
> and insanity. In pronounced cases, there is no question about them. But
> in some supposed cases, in various degrees supposedly less pronounced,
> to draw the exact line of demarcation few will undertake.—HERMAN
> MELVILLE, *Billy Budd*

This chapter is meant to further the long-overdue debate (initiated recently by
Maguigan) about whether the law of self-defense should be modified to respond to
the situation of battered women—debate which has been thwarted by the courts'
reliance on the red herring of BWS. We will suggest that the law of self-defense,
clarified and adjusted in some places, provides a more appropriate framework for
society to make the difficult choices that bedevil us in situations in which a battered woman resorts to lethal force. This approach will result in fairer treatment of
such women because it addresses their individual situations and does not rely on
pseudo-scientific stereotypes of helplessness and lack of will. In some respects, our
proposals are similar to the "necessity" defenses proffered by Rosen, Schulhofer,
and others. Like these writers, we ask courts and juries to consider the balance of

equities in a deliberate fashion. Nonetheless, we believe that our proposals go further by providing more detail and specificity than the inherently vague necessity defense. Such specificity contributes to drawing the lines that balance responsibility and empathy. By providing more concrete standards, we increase the tools by which to make the difficult judgments at stake. It is said that God resides in the details. The proposition is true in this issue. By being more concrete and specific, our proposals actually compel us to provide examples of who might be culpable and who not.

In responding to battered women's claims to justice, society has certain obligations. *First and foremost, society must get tougher with batterers.* We agree with Elizabeth Rapaport that the failure to treat domestic battery as seriously as battery in other contexts constitutes illegitimate discrimination.[1] On July 1, 1994, Colorado became the sixteenth state to pass legislation requiring mandatory arrest of batterers. It also stiffened the penalties for batterers who violate judicial restraining orders to stay away from their victims, and established a statewide registry of batterers to help detect recidivists. Such steps and other reforms (lawsuits against indifferent police, reasonable state policies concerning parental rights and divorce settlements, etc.) are highly recommended.

States are struggling with the question of whether batterers are chronic "dangerous" offenders who merit harsher treatment by the law because of their failure to rehabilitate themselves. We make no psychological judgment about batterers other than those rendered above, yet all the evidence about batterers confirms the claim that once battering develops as a *modus operandi*, it is reasonable to assume that it will happen again. Accordingly, penalties for recidivism should be stiff.

Sometimes it appears that BWS was propounded in part to "cover" the legal system's original sin of letting batterers have their way with their victims. Tougher treatment of batterers in the first place is a better way to atone for this sin. If we shirk this responsibility, nothing else we do will amount to much.

Society must also continue to recognize the pains, fears, and needs of battered women by providing meaningful shelter opportunities and related measures to promote their and their children's safety and well-being. Information about shelters and legal remedies should be disseminated as fully as possible. We need to realize that spending our scarce resources in this domain pays both immediate and long-term dividends. It helps protect women who are in agonizing need.

By prosecuting batterers and offering shelter, succor, and justice to battered women who are in danger, we can limit the number of cases in which these women resort to deadly force. To deal properly with such unfortunate cases, however, society must clearly demarcate the bounds within which violent self-help is legally permissible. We must struggle to ensure that these laws are not tinged with sexism, and we must enforce them equally and fairly, judging each person's actions in context.

In addition, society must not abandon its commitment to the sanctity of life. As the California Court of Appeals declared in *People v. Aris*, "[I]t is fundamental to our concept of law that there be no discrimination between sinner and saint solely on moral grounds. Any less exacting definition of imminence fails to protect every person's right to live."[2] Legal reforms that take this value cavalierly or insouciantly portend unfathomable consequences. An indiscriminate use of BWS as an excuse would effectively embrace an implicit death sentence for persons who commit domestic violence—an extreme position that we reject. In the end, self-defense law ineluctably embodies a balancing of equities. Albert Dicey portrays the tensions at stake in his classic work *Law of the Constitution:*

> The rule that fixes the limit of the right of self-help must, from the nature of things, be a compromise between the necessity, on the one hand, of allowing every citizen to maintain his rights against private wrongdoers, and the necessity, on the other hand, of suppressing private warfare. Discourage self-help, and loyal subjects become the slaves of ruffians. Over-stimulate self-assertion, and for the arbitrament of the courts you substitute the decision of the sword or the revolver.[3]

Recap: The Case against BWS

Meeting none of these obligations, BWS defenses undermine many of the central tenets of the American legal system and of equal citizenship. One of these tenets is that the legal system must judge a person's *acts*, not the person. Once the status of being a battered woman is established, these defenses draw no line between justified and unjustified acts of lethal force. Walker's willingness to apply a BWS defense in *Buhrle* (see Chapter 6), the case in which the defendant sought out her husband and killed him at a motel, provides a telling example. Yet the status of being battered should not, in and of itself, be tantamount to a legal defense. As Dawson puts it: "We can't allow violence to occur when it is not purely self-defense by anybody. . . . [W]e have to sort out whether this person's actions were justified."[4]

All citizens must be held accountable to certain standards of conduct, standards surely violated by the Buhrle killing. Without clear standards to guide them, juries are left to rely solely on their subjective sense of justice. In a case such as *Buhrle*, Walker's proposed testimony boils down to an invitation to jury nullification. Indeed, several authors have noted the relatively frequent accounts of jury nullification in cases involving battered women who kill.[5]

Of course, jury nullification is often appropriate to venture beyond the letter of the law. But it can amount to judgment about the person rather than the person's action. As Susan Murphy points out in her work on expert testimony, leaving such questions solely to the jurors' subjective weighing of equities will often lead to judgments grounded in common prejudice rather than common wisdom.[6] The sympathies of the jury can be swayed by racial and gender prejudices, as we saw in the previous chapter.

Obviously, that a woman has been battered is extremely relevant to the question of whether her use of lethal force was justified. Under certain circumstances, women who have suffered from repeated battery can be entirely justified in killing their tormentor. Yet these determinations must be made on an individual, not a group, basis. BWS defenses seek clemency for battered women as a group. In *People v. Aris,* for example, Walker proposed to testify about Aris's shooting her sleeping husband as follows: "In my professional opinion . . . [defendant] had a reasonable perception of danger."[7] This testimony, if accepted, leaves no further decision to the jury. Nothing in Walker's writings indicates how we or a jury could divine when a battered woman's perception of danger is not reasonable. This lack of individuation suggests that Walker's understanding of BWS is group justice rather than individual justice. In other words, it is not justice.

Schneider alleges that BWS defenses promote stereotypes and nonindividuation:

> Despite the recognition in [the case law] of the value of expert testimony dealing with battered women in general, expert testimony not clearly tied to the individual woman defendant's circumstances and perspective should be used with care. Such testimony may suggest to the trier of fact that there is a "battered women's syndrome" defense which would encourage sexual stereotyping. Thus, the use of expert witnesses is often prudently forgone, especially where the defendant is credible and articulate.[8]

It is easy to see why Schneider fears the stereotyping prowess of BWS. The whole vocabulary of BWS terms such as "syndrome," "authentic voice," "learned helplessness," and "loss of will" is one of stereotype.

BWS speaks the language of justification and situational excuse, although it is at heart a defense based on incapacity excuse. In this respect, BWS furthers a trend away from justification defenses for women defendants. Even before BWS came into vogue, women were being steered away from self-defense claims and toward incapacity excuse defenses that fit better with sexist stereotypes. Schneider argues that "sex-bias increases the probability that the trier of fact will prefer to excuse the woman, seeing her acts as 'unreasonable' self-defense."[9] She cites a study of twenty-seven women convicted of murder or manslaughter which showed "the tendency to use a defense of mental impairment, normally diminished responsibility. Despite circumstances that could well ground a defense of self-defense, in only one case was self-defense argued."[10]

Moreover, the linchpin of BWS, the theory of learned helplessness, is strained.

First, recall that virtually none of our interviewees in the front lines of the battered women's movement—people who see battered women with extraordinary agency and coping skills—agreed that such women suffer from learned helplessness. Second, it is unlikely that a helpless woman would find the agency needed to repel or escape her batterer. BWS advocates reconcile this discrepancy in logic by pointing to the survival instinct and arguing that BWS prevents flight but not fight. Nevertheless, they have no scientific basis for this contention. (It is significant that in *Richardson,* the jury convicted the defendant even though the expert testified that the ability to fight is instinctive and never lost.)[11] Third, BWS invites trouble in predicting that women will somehow be cured of their passivity upon leaving the relationship. This assertion is a mere expedient; without such recovery, women using a BWS defense could lose custody of their children (after all, anyone else with severe PTSD is a poor candidate for parental responsibility). But the assumption of recovery is scientifically baseless. In other forms of PTSD, such as Vietnam veteran's syndrome, the debilitating effects linger long after the exposure to trauma. The dogs upon which Walker generated the theory of learned helplessness did not regain their capacity to act freely.

In the next section we will argue that it is far better to ask whether a battered woman's actions were justified under the circumstances than to seek to explain them as the result of BWS. *The focus should be on battered women's situation, not battered women's syndrome.* There is no need to explain the failure of the woman to leave a violent relationship as a symptom of a "syndrome." Even the most rational woman might decide it is not wise to attempt to leave the relationship under certain circumstances. Many of the women we interviewed related shocking stories of the lengths their batterers went to prevent them from leaving the relationship. And as Schneider writes:

> Women derive no pleasure from battering relationships, but they are unable to see any alternative to continuing, often escalating violence. A woman who leaves her husband may be without employment, child care or adequate housing. There are few shelters for her. The woman often must leave young children behind or uproot her children and separate them from their father, friends and school. The extreme isolation the typical battered woman feels is the result of her shame and her efforts to hide her situation, her husband's active attempts to separate her from her friends and relatives and the unwillingness of the friends and relatives to intervene. The isolation strengthens her belief that she has no alternative to remaining with the violent man, even across state lines, and force her to return.[12]

BWS advocates aver that BWS defenses are necessary to dispel juror myths about how a battered woman could easily leave the relationship if she were really being beaten. Instead of relying on a pseudo-scientific, internally contradictory, and potentially degrading theory of how women act like helpless dogs, however, why not dispel juror myths by presenting jurors with the *truth?* Why not allow women to explain their reasons for not leaving and allow experts to testify—without needlessly "psychologizing" the issue—that many severely battered women often decide to remain for the rational reasons Schneider delineates? Such testimony is already being given, but the syndrome connection muddies the waters. Let experts testify about the facts concerning separation danger and related fears of battered women, and the experts or the defense can show whether the defendant felt such fears.

We believe that in cases in which battered women killed to protect themselves, jurors would be more persuaded by the simple truth: the woman stayed because she had good reason to stay; she killed because she had to kill. Juries are more prepared than ever to fathom these facts because of the dissemination of knowledge about domestic abuse discussed in previous chapters. And thinking along these lines would not be contradicted by all the constructive messages in society that women are as capable of bearing individual responsibility as men. We will suggest the development of clear jury instructions that the decision to remain in a relationship is not to be construed as evidence that the woman was not battered or that she was not acting in self-defense.

The Law of Self-Defense

Rules in criminal law involve the codification of our moral judgments.[13] Though drafters of the law must be as precise as possible, the law remains a cumbersome enterprise that is fraught with tension between general rules and individual cases (hence the inevitability of jury discretion). A rule that satisfies us in one set of cases often disturbs us when it pops up in other sets. A rule that justifies a lethal act by a battered woman can also justify the acts of Bernard Goetz.[14] Consequently, we should tread with caution on the road to reforming the law of self-defense. What is important is that society come out of the cave of the syndrome and discuss the issue in the open light.

The law must be responsive to the situation of battered women, but it must ultimately rest on general principles of proportionality, necessity, and responsibility that are applicable to all. There can be no "law of battered women," only general law that is not myopically sexist or paternalistic in its assumptions. The law should assume, where feasible, the rational agency of defendants. It should ask for justification before it asks for excuse. It should examine the reasonableness of the defendant's actions, not the purity of her victimhood.

The advocates of BWS and other critics of the law of self-defense often argue that the law of self-defense is phallocentric, meaning that it is based upon the experiences of men, not women. The law has unfairly required women to act in a "manly manner";[15] it has failed to take account of any previous history of violence. As Schneider puts the argument: "Sex bias in the law of self-defense prevents battered women asserting self-defense claims from receiving full and fair consideration by juries. The male assumptions contained in legal doctrine and the manifestations of those assumptions in court rulings on exclusions of evidence and jury instructions deny to women an opportunity equal to that of male defendants to present their claims of self-defense."[16] Cynthia Gillespie makes a similar charge, speaking of the law being "far too settled in its masculine assumptions to acknowledge" women's reality.[17]

The law of self-defense might well now be less remiss, however, especially in the wake of adjustments made in the decade and a half since Schneider made this charge. With certain adjustments attuned to our knowledge about domestic abuse, the law of self-defense would treat battered women as fairly as it treats others. *We should recall that the law of self-defense places difficult burdens on all defendants, not just battered women* (even if the typical burden of proof is on the state to disprove self-defense, the standards that make up self-defense are fairly strict for all).[18] Let us begin by looking more closely at the standards of self-defense law.

The Elements of Self-Defense

The law of self-defense sets forth an exemption to the rule that one may not intentionally take the life of another human being.[19] The key standards in the law of self-defense are: imminence, duty to retreat, proportionality, reasonable belief in the necessity of force, and certain "threshold questions."[20] We gratefully draw on Maguigan's pathbreaking and masterful analysis extensively in the following discussion.

1) *Imminence. The use of deadly force must be temporally proximate to the danger.* A claim of self-defense is possible only if some sort of necessity exists, and imminence of harm is the best indication of such necessity.[21] We will see that there are two major ways of defining temporal proximity: "imminence" or "immediacy." The imminence standard tolerates flexibility (depending on how it is defined) more than an immediacy test by virtue of expanding the time frame of justified action and accommodating the introduction of more evidence of past abuse.

The question of temporal proximity and imminence is perhaps the most important issue in the law of self-defense. Accordingly, testimony about the defendant's perceptions of imminence are crucial, and such testimony must include the reasons she feared for her safety. Recall that a battered woman can often read her mate like a book.

The graveness of the danger cannot substitute for temporal proximity, except to some extent in cases of duress (and here the threat must be very specific). If a gangster threatens to kill a local shopkeeper in an effort to receive protection money within a month, the shopkeeper cannot claim self-defense if he kills the sleeping gangster a week later. Nonetheless, we will argue for an equitable understanding the relationship between graveness and imminence.

2) *The duty to retreat.* States vary over this requirement. A minority do not allow resort to deadly force even in the face of imminent danger if the target can retreat in complete safety.[22] Most states that require retreat have exceptions allowing a person to "stand his or her ground" in his or her home or business. A few states require retreat even from the home if the attacker is a cohabitant.[23]

3) *Proportionality.* To discourage the use of deadly force as much as possible, the law stipulates that the amount of force used must be reasonably commensurate with the threatened harm. One may not use lethal force to fend off an attack that does not threaten serious bodily harm.[24] This can be an exacting standard, but we will see that individual differences should be factored into the law in this area.

4) *Reasonable belief in the necessity of force.* The law of self-defense typically requires that a person reasonably believes that deadly force is necessary to prevent harm. The definition of reasonable belief varies among the states and has occasioned a great deal of controversy. The controversy revolves around the use of "objective" or "subjective" standards of reasonableness. But these terms have been used in so many different ways that it is hard to tell whether they clarify or obfuscate the issue.[25]

One way to define "subjective" is simply as the defendant's actual, honestly held belief that deadly force was necessary under the circumstances. All states require at least this kind of honest belief, but in only a few (and in the Model Penal Code) will a claim of self-defense succeed on this ground alone. Most go further and demand that the belief satisfy some type of objective test of reasonableness.[26] A second meaning of "subjective" pertains to the consideration of contextual factors. Obviously, this is a cardinal concern when it comes to battered women. We can grasp this if we first describe what the objective test looks like.

In jurisdictions with a purely objective test, "the jury is told to measure the defendant's belief in the necessity of using defensive deadly force against a generic standard of reasonableness."[27] The standard does not look at the specific characteristics or experiences of the defendant. Instead, the law asks whether the hypothetical "reasonable man" or "reasonable person" would have believed it necessary to use deadly force in the defendant's situation. *We will call this the "noncontextual objective test" of reasonableness.* The majority of states reject the noncontextual objective approach, requiring the jury to consider factors that are "subjective" in the second sense of the word: factors such as whether the defendant is male or female, weak or powerful, timid or rugged. *We will refer to this more common test as the "contextual objective test."*[28]

The dual meanings of "subjective" and "objective" have generated confusion. Commentators refer to statutes as "objective" even though the measures require a subjective (good faith) belief in the necessity of lethal force and allow the jury to consider subjective (contextual) factors in determining the reasonableness of the defendant's actions.[29] As we have seen and will see again, these distinctions are enormously important in the context of battered women who resort to deadly force. It is important to be clear that the majority of states use the contextual objective test that asks whether a reasonable person having the defendant's characteristics would have believed that lethal force was necessary. And virtually every state allows the jury to consider other contextual factors, particularly a history of violence between the defendant and the victim.[30] *Expert testimony in this area should highlight the fact that battered women often develop keen awareness (and tacit knowledge) of their batterer's acts and intentions.*

States are divided over what happens when a person kills out of the honest but unreasonable belief that it was necessary to avoid serious bodily injury. In some states, an unreasonable belief will reduce the crime from murder to manslaughter. In other states, an unreasonable belief has no exculpatory effect at all, and in states that use a purely subjective test it is fully exculpatory.[31]

5) *Threshold questions.* Procedural rules governing evidence in self-defense cases are also important, for not every defendant who wishes to claim self-defense may do so at her trial; she must gain the judge's assent. *Maguigan points out that this decision is as important as the standard of imminence in determining the outcome of the case.*

Judges have great discretion in deciding whether to allow a claim of self-defense at trial, but the standards they are supposed to apply in making this decision vary from state to state. Some states have fairly relaxed rules that require the judge to permit self-defense claims if the defendant can show *any evidence* that she might have been acting in self-defense. Other states are stricter, mandating a more substantial showing from the defendant before the issue goes before the jury.[32] Let us now turn to the crucial question: how responsive is the law of self-defense to the situation of battered women?

Battered Women and the Law of Self-Defense

In this section we will discuss the law of self-defense in confrontational and non-confrontational situations, and propose policies or possible reforms. Before we begin, however, it is worthwhile to remind the reader that the outcomes of self-defense cases also depend on factors beyond the standards of criminal law. Maguigan states the matter succinctly: "The predictors of not-guilty verdicts are many and varied. Few are susceptible to change through legal redefinition." Other relevant factors include the "interplay of sex, race, and class bias in the courtroom, prevailing attitudes about family violence in the community . . . the quality of lawyering on each side, and the resources available in the form of money, expert witnesses, trial consultants, and investigators."[33]

Our interviews with prisoners and others brought a major problem into relief: many women are economically disadvantaged and appear to have been represented by less than fully conscientious counsel. When all is said and done, justice at the trial level depends on the quality of lawyering, and quality depends on money in the form of payments to private counsel or state support for committed public defenders (such as that found in Wisconsin, which is unusually devoted to supporting public defender offices; the Kenosha Public Defender's Office, which defended Ronda Richardson, was a model of conscientiousness, as was the public defender in the *Skalaski* case in Madison). The legal system's growing unavailability to the lower and middle classes, a shameful situation, betrays justice as much as any single factor, and impinges on the issue of criminal defenses of battered women who kill or commit other crimes.[34]

Confrontational Situations

A major question here is whether the law of self-defense is responsive to the situation of battered women who kill. Let us begin by looking at confrontational situations. Before Maguigan's 1991 article, many commentators assumed that battered women typically killed in nonconfrontational situations, such as when the abuser was sleeping or otherwise indisposed, or when there was a lull in the violence.[35] As seen above, this claim is problematic based on Maguigan's searching of the appellate cases. Maguigan believes that, if anything, she probably oversampled nonconfrontation cases because her sample did not include cases that led to acquittal or cases in which the charges were dismissed. Since it is easier to argue self-defense in confrontational cases, these cases are more likely to result in acquittal or dismissal. Maguigan also looked at studies done on this issue by sociologists and criminologists, who concluded that confrontation cases make up somewhere between 70–90 percent of the cases in which battered women kill.[36]

Temporal proximity of danger. Confrontation cases involve imminence by their very nature, so we will postpone our treatment of the imminence standard until the discussion of nonconfrontational cases. The standard of imminence recommended there should also apply to confrontational situations, though the more flexible standard we recommend is less needed in confrontational situations simply because a confrontation presents an immediate danger. Nonetheless, even confrontation cases present different degrees or forms of danger, and the facts concerning the temporal nature of the harm are often in dispute, making the nature of the imminence standard important even in the context of confrontation cases. *A flexible notion of imminence is needed in both confrontation and nonconfrontation contexts.*

Duty of Retreat. This standard presents little problem for most battered women because it does not exist in most states, and most retreat states do not require retreat from one's home.[37] One exception prevails, however: when the attacker is a spouse or cohabitant.[38] This rule is unfair, especially in cases in which the woman has suffered past abuse and believes that fleeing is dangerous. But such laws stipulate that the victim be able to retreat with complete safety, thereby mitigating their potential for mischief.

Nonetheless, raising the question of retreat with complete safety obfuscates the question of necessity, making conviction more likely. And fleeing can exacerbate the danger instead of alleviating it. *We recommend that the minority of states that would require retreat create an explicit exception where there is a situation of ongoing domestic battery.* Rather than constituting a "double standard," this policy takes the rage and relentlessness of domestic battering into consideration. Such an exception would be fully consistent with the general purposes of the law, which is to require retreat only when a person can retreat safely. It is hardly realistic to expect a woman to dash out of her home during an attack and never return, nor is it realistic to assume that she could later return with safety. *Ironically, the "cycle theory" actually reinforces the retreat rationale:* after the batterer's rage is spent, it is safe for her to return home to his contrition. We reject this logic. Reforming the law in this way would make explicit what the policy behind self-defense doctrine implies.

A further danger looms in the retreat requirement in domestic contexts: *juries might misapply the law by confusing the issue of retreat with the issue of whether the woman should have left the relationship.* As seen throughout this book, such confusion or conflation of issues confounds justice. To be sure, no one has found evidence that shows juries are confused in this respect. But Maguigan cites scholars and judges who make such mistakes, so it is reasonable to assume that juries are at least equally vulnerable.[39] *As stressed repeatedly above, no law requires women to leave the battering relationship.* If a woman voluntarily remains in a battering relationship but, upon being threatened with imminent violence, kills the batterer to protect herself, she has not violated the duty to retreat. *The duty to retreat refers to a retreat in the face of an imminent attack, not in anticipation of a possible attack.*

We saw that women stay in violent relationships for a host of reasons, none of which should have legal significance. Consequently, addressing the issue of retreat furnishes us with an occasion to propose what could be our most important reform: a judicial instruction that a battered woman's right of self-defense cannot be waived by virtue of her previous behavior (i.e., her reasons for leaving or not leaving the relationship are irrelevant to her self-defense claim). The instruction should also address the fact that the status of the attacker (e.g., as a family member) is irrelevant to the woman's right to defend herself. The instruction could read as follows:

A person has no legal obligation to leave a violent relationship. . . . The right of self-defense can never be waived, regardless of the status of the attacker. If you find that the defendant killed because she reasonably believed that lethal force was necessary to prevent imminent serious bodily injury to herself, you must find that she acted in self-defense. That the defendant had earlier opportunities to leave the relationship, or that the victim is related to the defendant, does not deny or diminish her claim of self-defense in any way.

This instruction need not undermine a jury's comprehension of the fear that engulfed the relationship, for that would be demonstrated by ample means throughout the trial. *Such an instruction should be made in every state, not just those requiring retreat, for prejudices surrounding the defendant's failure to leave might constitute the most important reason that battered women have trouble getting justice under the law.* Indeed, countering such prejudices is the *raison d'être* of BWS. Why not counter such potential judgments by a simple yet powerful judicial instruction that cuts through the fog of psychological speculation left in BWS's wake?

The rules of evidence should continue to allow expert and non-expert testimony regarding the woman's decision to stay in the relationship, if the defense deems such testimony necessary. This type of expert testimony, which simply informs the jury of a fact (albeit an often complex fact), is quite different from BWS expert testimony, which presents the jury with conclusions about the internal psychological processes of the defendant. Of course, the women themselves should be given significant latitude to explain why they stayed in the relationship. Freed from BWS, such reasons as fear, love, economic dependence, threats by the batterer, etc., would stand out.

The reform we suggest is similar to reforms in the domain of rape law. *Just as it is no longer acceptable for the defense to refer to the victim's sexual behavior in general or with men other than the defendant, so it is improper to impugn a woman's claim of self-defense because she did not leave the relationship.*[40] In cases involving battered women, juries may doubt either that she was abused or that the abuse was deadly or serious because the defendant stayed in the relationship. Too, they may blame her for not taking more decisive and rational action. But we believe that rather than arguing there was something wrong with the woman (BWS), which plays into stereotypes of irrationality, it is better to show the jury that there might have been nothing irrational about the woman's behavior under the circumstances, and, more importantly, that her behavior in the relationship does not negate her right to defend herself. This approach is better suited to a claim of self-defense, which argues that the use of lethal force was a rational response to the situation. *BWS errs in asking the jury to countenance the irrationality of learned helplessness at the same time it must credit the defendant with rationality in the commission of the defensive act.*

Proportionality. The "deadly force" or "like force" rule stipulates that a person may not use lethal force to protect himself or herself from a minor injury. The key question here is whether a person may use a weapon against an unarmed attacker. Schneider and others charge that the rule discriminates against women. "The deadly force rule is particularly troublesome for a battered woman. Although she may have no alternative but to defend herself with a weapon, the traditional interpretation of the deadly force rule can render her use of a deadly weapon unreasonable."[41]

If women were precluded from using a weapon against an unarmed but more powerful male attacker, then the law of self-defense would indeed be skewed against women. Fortunately, this is not the case. "In the overwhelming majority of jurisdictions . . . the rule does not prohibit resort to a weapon against an unarmed aggressor."[42] Proportionality requires only that the person using lethal force is herself threatened with serious injury and has no other way of preventing that injury. "In this area, scholars have posited and then argued against a like force requirement that does not exist. There are no current proposals in any legislature for change in this substantive area, and none are necessary. The appropriate inquiry in this area is one ordinarily conducted: whether the force employed by the defendant was necessary, not whether it was the same as that directed against the actor."[43]

The famous *Wanrow* case in 1979 rejected a like force rule, as did several cases decided years before. This issue arose in 10 percent of Maguigan's cases, and only once did an appellate court rule the level of force used was unreasonable per se because the defendant used a weapon to ward off an unarmed attacker. In the end, issues of proportionality are typically decided on a case-by-case basis, recognizing such factors as size, gender, the violent nature of the attacker, and any violent conduct by the assailant that is known to the defendant.[44]

If a woman has suffered repeated violent assault by a larger, stronger, or more physically aggressive man, there is little doubt that she may use a weapon to defend herself. Far from assuming a one-time encounter between equally matched male adversaries, the law normally takes account of the sizes of the assailant and the defendant, their genders, and the violence of past attacks.[45] Virtually all of the appellate courts that have considered the issue have rejected the argument that a woman may not use a weapon to defend herself against an unarmed male assailant. Still, *it makes sense for the court to instruct the jury clearly on this issue, so that the jury is aware that weaker defendants have a right to use weapons against powerful unarmed attackers.*

A related issue is the level of harm that justifies deadly force. Deadly force is disproportionate to a slap, but might not be to a fist to the jaw. On the question of intermediate assaults, courts have ruled that it is improper to use weapons or react with lethal force against hard slaps, punches, or assaults that amount to misdemeanors.[46] What about more serious harms? Wisconsin law, for example, distinguishes "simple battery" from "aggravated battery."[47] Simple battery causes bodily harm; it involves the infliction of such things as physical pain, a wrenched arm, black eyes, bruises, and injuries that are not permanently disfiguring. Such harms typically occur in battering situations. Aggravated battery is meant to cause great bodily harm, including a substantial risk of death, permanent disfigurement, protracted loss or impairment of any bodily member or organ, or other serious injury. Deadly force and typical self-defense are authorized against these types of acts. Had John Bobbitt woken in time, he could have used deadly force to stymie Lorena's design.

The line between simple and aggravated battery can be thin indeed, however. Acts of simple battery could easily escalate into aggravated battery in the next attack, and the acts themselves could amount to aggravated battery. We read a press report about one case in which a batterer finally broke his wife's jaw. Years later, after liberating herself from his clutches, she underwent a new surgical procedure to correct the lasting damage, but the procedure backfired, compounding the harm.[48] Thus, it seems reasonable to assume that any violent action with a fist or other tool by a more powerful attacker creates a reasonable apprehension of real danger.

In *People v. Williams*, for example, the appellate court ruled that a cab driver was justified in firing a gun at a gang after a gang member threw a brick at his taxi.[49] The social understanding of what "gangs" are about created a reasonable apprehension of serious danger. The same understanding should apply to batterers. *State v. Spaulding* goes even further. The court said that an actual show of deadly force (an overt act) was not needed because the victim had previously stabbed the defendant and in this case had made a threat and stepped toward the defendant with his hand in his pocket.[50] The situation in *Spaulding* closely resembles the situation that battered women often confront. *The law should be clear that reasonable apprehension of serious bodily harm permits lethal force, and that fists to the head or other sensitive areas can result in deadly or serious bodily harm.*

In addition, the stress should be on the apprehension of harm, not "overt acts" per se. The overt act requirement is another "threshold" rule that says that the defendant cannot even raise the issue of self-defense unless she can show that the decedent made some sort of overt threatening act. Though the presence of an overt act is important evidence of imminent danger, it should be a flexible requirement because of the typical power differential between men and women. (See the discussion below of overt acts.)

Many jurisdictions hold that verbal "threats" alone are insufficient to pass the threshold of a self-defense claim.[51] In general, this rule makes sense, but given what we know about domestic battering, such a rule is problematic when applied to threats that are made at the time of the defensive act.[52] Certainly, threatening words accompanied by acts can make one an "initial aggressor" for purposes of self-defense law. Perkins and Boyce claim that words "so vile that they are calculated to result in combat, and do so result" make one an initial aggressor.[53] A verbal threat can be a cue sufficient to actuate a reasonable belief in imminent danger. The overt act rule must take this reality into account by accepting as satisfactory any type of evidence that the threat is meaningful. *Aris* mentions "an apparent design then and there to carry them [previous threats] into effect."[54] This standard appears reasonable in terms of the threshold requirements for a self-defense instruction to the jury. *We endorse a standard that makes "slight" or "any" evidence of the need for self-defense sufficient to take the case to the jury, including "slight" evidence of the seriousness of threats.* The jury will always be able to make judgments about the plausibility of such claims.[55]

In addition, targets of assaults should be permitted to use more force than the attacker uses, so long as such disproportion is well within reason. A strict proportionality test rests on the "communitarian" logic discussed by George Fletcher (see chapter 5), which binds the target of an attack by the rights and interests of the attacker.[56] Certainly this logic must prevail to a large extent; one does not have the right to shoot someone who is going to put gum in one's hair. And as we saw in the last chapter, batterers have rights, too. But what if the attacker is bent on bending one's face out of shape? Kent Greenawalt calls the understanding that brooks some disproportionality the "deontological intuition," which holds that if someone's rights or interests are to be sacrificed, "it should be those of the aggressor. This deontological intuition about rights has two important aspects. One is that the threatened victim should not have to surrender his or her most precious possessions in the absence of wrongdoing; the second is that the transgressor sacrifices rights he or she would otherwise have by the intentional breach of another's rights."[57]

Along similar lines, the law concerning the use of force by third parties or "intervenors" reflects the emphasis on the rights of the target. We typically give greater leeway to the victim than to the intervenor because the victim's rights have been violated and there might be reason to believe that he or she is less amenable to rational calculation under the circumstances than an intervenor.[58] This point refers us back to the discussion in chapter 6 concerning the situational pressure and the interpretation of self-defense and duress as excuses rather than justifications.

On the other hand, the law of self-defense cannot countenance a license to use whatever force one desires to protect one's autonomy (a license that amounts to what Fletcher calls the strict Lockean or Kantian model). Greenawalt remarks that the principles of proportionality and necessity "impose consequentialist constraints" on actions that the deonotological position might justify.[59] If society sets no limits or insufficient limits to proportionality, people will kill each other for minor reasons, as in the Old West legends or in the forsaken neighborhoods of contemporary life.[60] The law of self-defense embodies a mixture of rights-oriented (deontological) and consequentialist principles, which means that measured leeway in favor of the innocent target of aggression is desirable. *The relevant instruction should not encourage jury nullification, but it should clearly state that the amount of force used should be that which a reasonable person believes is necessary to place him or her in complete safety or to repel the attack. In domestic violence contexts, the fear of death is gendered (see chapter 2), so the gender of the defender should be taken into consideration (but in a way that illuminates the mental state of the woman and the power differential between the partners rather than gender per se).* The instruction in *People v. Jones* stated, "the degree of resistance must not be clearly disproportionate to the nature of the injury offered or given; the force used in repelling or resisting the assault or battery must not be clearly greater than is apparently necessary." [61] In light of the general reforms we suggest, an instruction such as *Jones*'s is appropriate.

A final issue regarding the requirement of proportionality is the question of when the defendant must cease using lethal force. Even if the defendant was protecting herself from a serious assault, she violates the proportionality requirement if she continues using lethal force after she has disabled the attacker. Such continuance also exposes the possibility that self-defense was but a pretext for revenge. For example, if she keeps firing a gun after the assailant has clearly been disabled, this could bar her claim of self-defense. Of the small number of appellate cases where the woman's conviction was upheld on grounds of proportionality, this was often the issue.

The question of when a defendant must break off a lethal counter-attack often comes up as a threshold issue. If the judge decides that no reasonable juror could conclude that the defendant's continued use of lethal force was necessary to avoid serious bodily injury to herself, the judge can decide not to give the jury an instruction on self-defense at all.

These cases present tough judgment calls. Deciding in the heat of the moment when one has overstepped the bounds of self-defense is difficult and defendants should be given leeway on this issue. One or two further shots is different from several, and there is a difference between deliberate furtherance of force and furtherance based on adrenalin. However, we do not recommend wholesale changes in this area of the law. Where the defendant has clearly overstepped the bounds of necessity and is continuing the attack for vengeance rather than self-defense, the defendant should not get a self-defense read to the jury. There are situations where the line is crossed. For example, in the *Goetz* case, one teenager, who had already been shot once by Goetz, was sitting down and bleeding from the previous bullet. Goetz deliberately went up to him and remarked, "You seem to be [doing] all right; here's another," and fired a further shot (his fifth of the encounter, and second at this particular victim). [62] This is not self-defense.

Similarly, we believe that a battered woman who kills her attacker in a situation when the attacker has already *clearly* been disabled should not get a self-defense instruction. The question is whether *any* reasonable juror, taking into account the history of violence and the fact that the defendant was acting in the heat of the moment, could conclude that the defendant reasonably believed that she was acting in self-defense. If self-defense is ruled out, heat of passion manslaughter might be an appropriate instruction or option.

In sum, the law as presently constituted appears to provide sufficient opportunities for contextualization to serve battered women, as well as other defendants who plead self-defense. Fairly applied in light of our suggestions, the law of self-defense would afford battered women the same opportunities it affords to all other citizens: the chance to put her use of deadly force into its full context and to explain rationally why its use was necessary. But the law must allow the defendant to present as much evidence as necessary to apprise the jury of the reasons she feared her attacker at that particular time. Also, the law must make the jury aware that fists can lead to aggravated harms. This addresses the need for a persuasive narrative, which we discuss in the next section.

Reasonable Belief in the Necessity of Force. Before a woman may use lethal force in self-defense, she must have a reasonable belief that deadly force is necessary to avoid serious bodily injury. Schneider and other commentators contend that this rule disadvantages women because it persuades courts to limit or preclude evidence of past attacks on the woman by the decedent, thereby making it more difficult for her to convey the reasonableness of her belief. When the woman is precluded from presenting such evidence, "the jury is unable to understand why the woman believed herself to be in danger."[63]

We agree that such exclusion would be patently unfair. Fortunately, no state excludes it. Maguigan, who conducted her unprecedentedly thorough survey of cases in every state more than a decade after Schneider issued her charge, found that "evidence regarding the decedent's violence toward the defendant ['history of abuse'] and toward third persons ['history of other violence'] is admissible in every jurisdiction."[64] Still, in some jurisdictions BWS has served to open the evidentiary door further than traditional self-defense law provided in the past. This door should remain open. There is no reason that the door should be kept open only by the prop of psychological expertise. *Defendants should be allowed to present sufficient evidence of the abuse they suffered and how the abuse factored into their perceptions of danger.*

This is another area where much criticism has been levelled at a nonexistent rule. Judging from Schneider's citations, she may be confusing the issue of admitting the history of past violence with the "overt act" requirement that exists in some states. However, even in those states with such a requirement, once an overt threatening act is shown, a history of past violence is admissible.

There are sound reasons for the overt act requirement. Someone should not be able to raise a claim of self-defense without any evidence of a threat to her by the decedent. A defendant who, for example, killed a young black man on a dark city street simply because the defendant had some strong prejudices about the danger posed by young black males at night in the city should not be able to even get to the jury with a self-defense claim.

However, some degree of reform is needed in this area. *In those states that have an overt act as a threshold requirement, the requirement should be waived when there is a substantial history of violence between the parties.* While society is entitled to prohibit a person from gunning down a stranger who is advancing toward him or her with a nasty look in his eye, society must also recognize that when there is a history of past violence between the parties, the defendant might well have seen that look before and may have good reason to fear it. The defendant in that situation should at least get to tell her story to the jury. *This reform addresses those who criticize self-defense doctrine for not taking relevant aspects of long-standing relationships into account. And it is the most practicable way to account for the special knowledge of the batterer forged in the bonds of love.*

A classic example deals with the typical batterer's explosive rage. Suppose a battered woman hears the car door slam, looks out her front window, and sees her spouse walking onto the porch in a fit of anger that echoes those that have preceded previous attacks. Though she cannot know for sure what his intentions are, it would hardly be unreasonable for her to believe that she is in imminent danger. Recall that she is excused even if her belief turns out to be mistaken, so long as her belief was reasonable in the first place. Her recollections of previous beatings are the crucial determinant that should entitle her claim of self-defense to be heard by the jury. Consider another example, one that is more of a stretch: a woman whose husband beats her severely if she refuses to perform a humiliating act like barking on the floor like a dog (as in the *Norman* case or the case of some of our interviewees). One day he tells her to perform this act, but takes no further action. She can tell by the tone of his voice that he is serious. Must she actually refuse and await the likely attack before she defends herself with lethal force? Note that she has no legal obligation to perform the task in order to ward off the attack (just as she has no legal obligation to retreat or leave the relationship). It seems to us that requiring proof of overt acts in order to get the case to the jury in a case like this is harsh. The *substantial history of abuse* gives the woman an arguably good reason to believe that she is a step away from a severe beating if she does do what she has a right to do (refuse to comply), and waiting to use force until he goes further might well disable her defense. Arguably good reason should be enough to cross the threshold and get the claim of self-defense before the jury. Eliminating the overt act requirement in the context of a substantial history of abuse is also consistent with our treatment of imminence and kidnapping in the following pages.

However, it should be emphasized that, in general, a history of prior violence is admissible in every jurisdiction. Allowing the defendant to rely on the history of prior violence in lieu of showing that the decedent made some sort of overt act against her merely brings the overt act rule into sync with the rest of self-defense.

Other critics have attacked the notion of "reasonableness," arguing that it is biased for not taking women's subjective characteristics into account. Shirley Sagaw summarizes such arguments:

> The unfairness of applying the "reasonable man" standard to the narrow class of particularly sympathetic cases, battered women who kill their batterers, prompted feminists to consider the overall inadequacy of the common law self-defense standard. Feminists have recognized that merely revising statutory language to read "reasonable person" rather than "reasonable man" is insufficient. Instead they have advocated reconceptualizing the meaning of reasonableness to consider individual differences among defendants. . . . The individualized standard, while objective, would allow the finder of fact to consider the defendant's sex and other factors giving a clearer and fairer picture of whether her actions should be condemned.[65]

This criticism applies most readily to the "noncontextual objective" standard of reasonableness, which does not look at such factors as the gender or other subjective or individualized characteristics of the defendant. *We concur with this criticism. The proper inquiry should be whether a reasonable woman who was in the abusive relationship would have believed that lethal force was necessary to prevent serious bodily injury to herself at the time she used lethal force.* It serves no purpose to ask what a de-contextualized, genderless, hypothetical reasonable person would have done at the moment that the defendant resorted to the lethal force.

Still, we must emphasize that only a few states use the noncontextual objective standard. Only seven states unambiguously apply this standard to battered women; in six other states, the standard is ambiguous.[66] One questions why the critics focus so intensely on this minority standard. Perhaps the confusing terminology and the different ways that courts and commentators have used the terms "subjective" and "objective" make it appear that many states actually use the troublesome standard. The test used in New York State, which New York courts refer to as "objective," is clearly a contextual standard. It asks the jury to "decide whether a reasonable person in the defendant's circumstances, including his or her history with the decedent, and his or her perceptions," would have believed that lethal force was necessary.[67] But the confusion cited above has led some commentators to champion the creation of a separate "reasonably prudent battered woman" standard.[68] Some jurisdictions have adopted or endorsed such a standard in self-defense or manslaughter contexts.[69] Yet it is not self-evident that such a standard would improve matters all that much in those states that give full effect to a contextualized standard of reason. Maguigan contends that the reasonably prudent battered woman standard "does not differ significantly from the [contextual objective] standard currently in use in the majority of jurisdictions."[70] Also, there is no such thing as a "reasonably prudent war veteran" or the like.

Reform efforts would be better spent in lobbying for the adoption of the contextual objective standard. For all the reasons discussed in the earlier chapters, law that applies the same standards to all adults is preferable to law that subjects men and women to different standards of rationality. It is better to apply a single standard to all, which can incorporate situational differences and demands placed on battered women's shoulders. This is the best way to reconcile difference with equal treatment.[71]

Jurors must see and feel what the woman saw and felt at the time of the deadly encounter, and to do this they must see the relationship and his actions through her eyes. *Accordingly, the test of reason must be contextual, and testimony about her reasons for fearing him must be extensive without being syndromized.* Good lawyering is necessary to convey the reality she confronted. But the law should facilitate justice by *letting her tell her story,* as we saw in the discussion of the narrative of abuse in chapter 5. And she should be able to tell her story without resorting to expert psychological testimony in the form of the syndrome.

Advocates of BWS contend that BWS is necessary to counter myths and to contextualize the woman's situation. Yet the ideology of BWS is built on myths—among others, the myth that law is abstract and not cognizant of context. And in many cases BWS is less cognizant of overall context than the law of self-defense, because it fits every battered woman into the same box of symptomology: passivity, loss of will, and helplessness. As Sagaw observes with telling accuracy:

> While the recognition of the battered woman's syndrome revised the law of self-defense for a limited class of women . . . a new stereotype of the battered woman is created once again placing women outside the purview of the reasonable. Thus battered women have been placed in a double bind of two stereotypes: if an abused woman's responses in the relationship did not conform exactly to the legal stereotype of a woman suffering from battered woman syndrome, courts could find her, by definition, to be neither battered nor reasonable.[72]

In sum, when the woman kills in a confrontational situation, BWS hinders rather than helps the quest for a justice that treats women equally and with a full appreciation of the context of their individual situations. *We can do the right thing if the law of self-defense honestly and fairly allows the battered woman defendant to tell her story with the jury being apprised of her right to defend herself regardless of her past decisions and the status of the person against whom she uses deadly force.*

Nonconfrontational Situations

Cases in which battered women kill in nonconfrontational situations pose greater difficulties for the law of self-defense because imminence is less present. Some nonconfrontational cases illustrate how rigid adherence to a narrow notion of imminence can lead to injustice. In an article advocating reform of the imminence requirement, Richard Rosen relates the plight of Judy Norman in North Carolina:

> J. T. Norman's abuse of his wife was prolonged and vicious. Over the years, whenever he was drunk, he brutally beat her, often inflicting serious injuries. He used his fists, bottles, ashtrays, and even a baseball bat. Mr. Norman forced his wife to prostitute herself to support him. When she was pregnant he kicked her down the stairs, causing the premature birth of her child. When she ran away, he tracked her, caught her, and beat her. He frequently threatened to kill her.
>
> In the days immediately preceding the killing, the abuse Ms. Norman suffered became more constant and vicious, and the threats to kill became more frequent and, by all accounts, more believable. . . . During the day [on which she killed him], he threatened twice to cut off her breast, and his threats to kill her continued until he took a nap late that afternoon, forcing her to lie on the floor by the bed.[73]

The judge in Norman's case would not let her present a defense of self-defense because the law in North Carolina deems a sleeping batterer incapable of posing an imminent danger. The jury convicted Norman of manslaughter and sentenced her to six years in prison.

It is difficult to conclude that justice was served in *Norman*. Accordingly, Rosen proposes reforming the law of self-defense. His reforms raise many questions, demonstrating the complexity of attempts to alter seriously the imminence requirement. Rosen argues that "[i]n self-defense, the concept of imminence has no significance independent of the notion of necessity."[74] The law requires that the harm be imminent because it assumes that there is no necessity without imminence. A person always has other ways to avoid the harm short of killing the would-be assailant.

There can be times when killing might be necessary to prevent a nonimminent harm, however. Rosen presents the example of kidnapping in which the kidnapper tells his hostage he will kill him, but not yet. Clearly, if the hostage seizes an opportunity to kill the kidnapper and escape, he may do so even in the absence of imminent harm. Most jurisdictions allow the use of lethal force to prevent a kidnapping from happening at all. Along these lines, Rosen advocates modifying the law of self-defense by giving judges the discretion to supplement the imminence standard with the standard of necessity. The jury would have to decide whether the defendant's use of lethal force was necessary to avoid serious bodily harm, regardless of the imminence of the danger.[75]

In his estimable *Criminal Law Defenses,* Paul H. Robinson addresses cases involving (or akin to) kidnap situations and shows how the strict imminence requirement fails to provide justice in them:

> Suppose A kidnaps and confines D with the announced intention of killing him one week later. D has an opportunity to kill A and escape each morning as A brings him his daily ration. Taken literally, the *imminent* requirement would prevent D from using deadly force in self-defense until A is standing over him with a knife, but that outcome seems inappropriate. If the concern of the limitation is to exclude threats of harm that are too remote to require a response, the problem is adequately handled by requiring simply that the response be "necessary." The proper inquiry is not the immediacy of the threat but the immediacy of the response necessary in defense. If a threatened harm is such that it cannot be avoided if the intended victim waits until the last moment, the principle of self-defense must permit him to act earlier—as early as is required to defend himself effectively.[76]

Rosen analogizes Ms. Norman to the hypothetical hostage. Her attempts to escape her husband were frustrated when he tracked her down and forced her to return. She knew that she faced grave danger if she attempted to flee again. She killed her husband because she believed it was the only way to avoid yet more serious physical abuse. For these reasons, argues Rosen, the law should consider her actions necessary even if the danger is not imminent. Schulhofer develops a similar line of thought: whether, given all the circumstances, "such a person would have considered deadly force the only reasonably available remedy." The burden would be on the defendant to show that, unlike other battered women who do leave the relationship, she was unable to do so for reasons that are excusable. He maintains that "[s]uch a standard, applied with genuine sensitivity to the full texture of the battered spouse situation, should be adequate to produce acquittal in those cases involving both truly serious abuse and tangible barriers to flight," including fear, being pursued, fear for the safety of children, etc.[77] These reasons are similar to those that are relevant to duress defenses. In other words, the woman is trapped.

Unfortunately, not every situation is as straightforward as Judy Norman's, and the test of Rosen's suggested reforms is not only whether they would have brought justice to her, but whether they would make the law more just in dealing with the universe of nonconfrontational situations in which battered women kill. Rosen acknowledges that his move carries the risk of leaving too much discretion in the hands of the jury, although he accepts the stakes in order to reach cases like *Norman:*

One reasonable concern is that a jury would be encouraged to make ad hoc decisions based upon its estimation of the relative worth of the individuals involved. The danger also exists that increasing the discretion given to jurors will simultaneously increase the opportunity for bias, arbitrariness, or discrimination to influence the jurors' decision making. After all, it arguably was the Crown's distrust of jurors' proclivities in homicide cases that led to the medieval development of strict rules for self-defense.[78]

A switch to vaguer standards is tempting in a situation in which the more specific standards encourage a harsh result, but it is important to remember that vague standards can produce harsh results in their own right. Vague standards leave the door open for racial discrimination and other insidious factors to influence the jury. For example, the standards determining whether the death penalty should be applied are among the vaguer standards in criminal law, often calling for the consideration of all "mitigating" and "aggravating" circumstances.[79] Not surprisingly, jury decisions regarding the death penalty rank among the decisions most plagued by racial discrimination.[80] We also saw in chapter 6 that the inherent vagueness of BWS also opens the door to discrimination based on race and character.

To limit jury discretion, Rosen proposes a two-stage process that incorporates some judicial control. The burden lies with the defendant to produce substantial evidence that the killing was necessary even though the state of danger fell short of imminence. If she met this burden, the judge would then instruct the jury to apply the standard of necessity in lieu of the standard of imminence. Otherwise, the judge would instruct the jury to apply the standard of imminent harm.

Rosen's proposal is thoughtful and powerful, but he fails to ask a crucial question: what standards should the judge or jury apply in determining whether the woman's action was necessary? Throughout his article, Rosen obviously has Ms. Norman's case in mind. Applying the standard of necessity to her case is appropriate because her actions were necessary under any conceivable definition of that term.[81] Any reasonable person would have perceived impending danger.

In more difficult cases, however, people's understandings of when a killing is necessary can vary drastically. For example, Loraine P. Eber, in an article criticizing the imminence standard, imagines the following situation:

> Suppose a woman has been subjected to physical and sexual abuse during the course of a twenty year marriage. The woman's husband leaves her but continues to threaten to kill her and often follows her. On the day in question, the woman sees her estranged husband standing outside her apartment building and kills him. The husband is found to be unarmed.[82]

Eber's scenario amply demonstrates that the presence of necessity lies in the eye of the beholder. The husband made no threat or move against the wife, was in no position to harm the wife, had committed no act of violence against his wife since moving out, and might have been coming merely to talk to her. Compare this situation to the hypothetical case presented above, in which the woman sees her husband coming into the house in an explosive rage. In this case, there are factual cues that more definitively signal danger. The facts in Eber's example differ substantially from those in this hypothetical case, as well as from those in *Norman*. To claim that Eber's woman acted in self-defense is to stretch the law of self-defense far beyond its traditional and accepted moorings. Would Eber be willing to extend this logic to everyone who espies a previous tormentor? If not, she endorses a double standard and elevates the status of being battered to the level of being a defense in itself, rather than being highly relevant evidence concerning the perception of danger. Moreover, how would Eber deal with the facts of the *Buhrle* case? What if *Mr.* Buhrle had shot and killed *Ms.* Buhrle as she approached his motel room? (Assume for the moment that she was unarmed.) Would Eber deem *him* entitled to a necessity defense?

In Eber's case, there is really no way for the jury to know why she killed her husband. She might have killed him because she thought there was no other way to prevent violence (Eber's position). She might also have killed him because she wanted him to stop following her or because she hated him. Accordingly, reliance upon a necessity defense is problematic. The vagaries of the term "necessity" invite subjectivity and subject the defendant to the sympathies and prejudices of the jury. These problems show another reason why some sort of imminence standard is so useful: *because in the absence of imminence outside the context of actual kidnapping or captivity, motives other than self-defense (and necessity) too easily enter into the set of reasons for lethal force.*

Another problem is related to the reforms we propose: *replacing or supplementing a temporal closeness requirement with a necessity standard entails reviving judgments about why the woman did not leave the relationship.* This is the major problem with Schulhofer's recommended approach, which requires the defendant to show why she could not leave as other battered women have done.[83] This problem is especially acute when we think of being battered as being kidnapped. Under a kidnap model, the law would have to ask when it is appropriate to demand that a woman do her best to leave the relationship, for if she could have left fairly readily during her captivity (and the standard concerning this possibility would have to be objective), it would be hard to construe her as being kidnapped or held hostage.[84] The law would slip back into the position of arguing that some reasons for staying in the relationship are more eligible for the defense against kidnapping than others. Physical threats certainly constitute captivity, but financial dependence or emotional dependence cannot, unless we unwisely stretch the *legal* notions of captivity and being kidnapped. *Since making the battered woman's reasons for leaving irrelevant is essential to doing justice in homicide cases, any standards that return our focus to her reasons for not leaving are inherently problematic.*

On the other hand, it is clear that some cases do involve kidnapping or captivity, and the marital relationship does not turn such captivity into something else (just as marital status does not diminish a woman's right to defend herself). Accordingly, battered women who are kidnapped or held captive should be able to use deadly force to escape such situations if necessary. The question is how this right should be expressed. Rosen and Robinson would frame such defenses as general necessity defenses, and it appears that Schulhofer's model is a variation of this defense. But we have seen that such defenses should be the exception. As Leo Katz declared earlier in the discussion of necessity, it might be wise to resist the necessity defense as Odysseus resisted the Sirens.[85]

What about a separate instruction about the right to defend oneself in kidnapping situations? Such an instruction would focus clearly on the factors that constituted being kidnapped or held captive, including the use of physical force and meaningful threats against the woman. Her fear of leaving due to death or serious bodily harm against her or her children (not her emotional or financial dependence, etc.) would have to be demonstrated. There is nothing wrong in principle with such an instruction/defense for such cases as *Norman*. Such an instruction would supplement, or be offered in lieu of, the typical self-defense instructions. "Kidnapping" seems to provide a more coherent standard than "necessity."

We emphasize that all we are suggesting is that the law of kidnapping be applied to the domestic sphere. Where a person is being kept against her will by force and threats, she should not lose her right to defend herself simply because the kidnapper is her spouse or cohabitant.

However, this reform would affect only the most extreme cases. The criminal law cannot afford the luxury of such writers as Herman and Walker, who use the concept of captivity loosely, rendering it applicable to many or most battering relationships. In order to reach those cases that are somewhat less extreme, but where a conviction for murder would still be an injustice, we suggest a second reform. We believe that the minority of states that require that the harm be "immediate" adopt the standard of "imminence" rather than immediacy, and that the term imminent be made more flexible by acknowledging that "imminent" and "immediate" are not synonyms.

Given that fear builds throughout many battering relationships, the standard of immediacy (which is how the *Norman* court defined imminence) is myopic and unjust.[86] *We strongly urge that the imminence test replace immediacy tests. The test for imminence should be that of the Oxford English Dictionary rather than something more restrictive: "Impending threateningly, hanging over one's head; ready to befall or overtake one; close at hand in its incidence; coming on shortly."*[87] This notion of imminence is close to the standard in the Model Penal Code, which says that the defensive act must be against an attack "on the present occasion." In a handful of other jurisdictions, the defendant must believe that he is "about to be attacked," or that defensive force must be "immediately necessary." [88]

As we have seen, the main reason for an imminence standard is to provide good evidence of actual necessity, and a certain flexibility should prevail in the law of self-defense. To be sure, some sort of imminence test is necessary because, as the California court stressed in *Aris,* any other notion presents a slippery slope indeed. This said, the interpretation of imminence should not be as restricted as in *Aris.* The *Aris* court articulated what amounts to an immediacy test and spoke favorably of the *Norman* ruling as well as the overt acts requirement in Kansas law.[89] We have seen that a contextual understanding suggests that victims of aggressors are often very aware of the intentions of their attackers, especially if they know them well. When the target is weaker and less violent than the aggressor, requiring too much in terms of "overt acts" or similar actions that indicate immediacy sets the balance too much in favor of the aggressor.

As Greenawalt illustrates, the standards of self-defense should take into consideration the special circumstances of the targets who bear no legal responsibility for bringing on the attack. Granting them some principled, controllable leeway is fair because they are blameless and because the choices they make are often difficult and pressured. The logics of justification and excuse are at play in such cases.[90] Unlike BWS, which frames this issue in terms of psychological disability and helplessness, our recommendation accounts for a balance of the equities by reference to the norms of self-defense law and the common judgments of the community (Oxford dictionary, Model Penal Code, new knowledge about battered women's situation, etc.). *Thus, we recommend a standard that interprets imminence as "about to befall" or "coming on shortly," especially in cases in which the target has been attacked by the aggressor before.*

Judy Norman's situation would satisfy any of these broader notions of temporal proximity. She suffered serious and escalating violence in the days preceding her homicidal act. She had good reason to believe that her husband's nap was only a brief lull in the storm of abuse. And she had ample reason to believe that she was trapped as a captive. Continued serious violence against her was "impending threateningly" or "coming on shortly." *Accordingly, evidence of captive situations should constitute relevant evidence in the determination of imminence. Rather than constituting a separate defense based on necessity or the kidnap analogy, the case for self-defense should simply use evidence of being trapped in this manner to buttress the claim that harm was imminent in terms of being impending or "about to befall," or that leaving was fraught with danger.*

Courts should apply the "imminence" standard using the word in its ordinary sense. A woman who reasonably believes that she will be attacked when her husband wakes up, and (as in Schulhofer's model) has no other options at that time (her previous reasons for not leaving are irrelevant) to defend herself, *is* in imminent danger, as is a woman who kills in a lull in the relationship. *Recall that she has no obligation to retreat from the home.* If the facts are murky in this regard, then it is up to the jury to decide which way the pendulum swings.

Thus, when there is a history of abuse, the fact that the husband was asleep or had his back turned should not in itself prevent a battered woman from getting an instruction on self-defense read to the jury. The courts' approaches in *Norman, Aris,* and similar cases, therefore, should be rejected.[91] In *State v. Hennum,* the trial court did not rule out as a matter of law a self-defense plea by a battered woman who killed her sleeping husband. The Minnesota Supreme Court let this ruling stand without comment when it addressed the admissibility of BWS testimony on appeal.[92] We endorse this approach. In like situations, the threshold decision must be based on the facts of each case. Surely if a battered woman sought her husband out across town and killed him as he slept, no reasonable person could find imminent harm. Our policy follows our recommendation concerning threats, in which we maintain that meaningful threats should be sufficient grounds for getting a self-defense instruction before the jury.

Still, a battered woman would still have to convince the jury that she reasonably believed an attack was "coming on shortly," perhaps because the husband was drunk and angry and had a long history of severe violence whenever he fell into that state or, as in *Norman,* because of the severe and escalating violence from which she was suffering that very day. Given that the future is always impossible to predict with certitude, such claims will present the jury with tough questions. We ask that a self-defense claim in such contexts go before the jury, and that the common notion of imminence govern the jury's consideration. *With testimony about the defendant's fears of the batterer, the dangers attendant to separation, and the battered woman's ability to "read" her batterer, this standard of imminence provides a fair hearing on the issue of necessity.*

What about "contract" or related cases? Since most of these cases embody situations falling well outside the realm of imminence as we define it, such cases are losers on the facts. But it appears that such cases will often fall short of the self-defense threshold in the first place, thereby justifying judicial refusal to offer self-defense instructions. Contract cases often involve third parties who could protect the woman in any event. Similarly, cases like *Buhrle* do not merit self-defense instructions. The line has to be drawn somewhere, and cases outside the context of impending harm simply do not meet the test of necessity.

To be sure, the standard of imminence we support has its own vagueness that leaves much to jury discretion. But no standard will be perfect, and too rigid a standard simply cannot do justice to the balance of equities and complexities in such cases. Our notion of imminence, linked to the other reforms we suggest, provides more guidance than a simple necessity standard and gives the jury background facts with which to put the notion of imminence in proper context.

Finally, *if the defendant's fears were reasonable under the circumstances of the case (which include the nature of the relationship as well as the activities of the time in question), then she has a right to defend herself even if the jury believes she factually misjudged the situation. Evidence of her previous beatings do not justify her actions at the time at issue, but it shows why her perceptions of danger might have been reasonable under the circumstances. All of our recommendations are designed to bring this understanding to light. Accordingly, instructions about imminence and contextualized reason should include references to the exculpatory nature of reasonable mistakes of fact.*

BWS and questions relating to her reasons for staying in the relationship are not necessary to illuminate what is ultimately a matter of reasonable judgment within the context of this unusual reality. During Judy Norman's trial an expert offered substantial testimony on BWS;[93] the Supreme Court of North Carolina did not dispute this testimony, but it found that Norman was not entitled to a jury instruction on self-defense because she did not confront imminent danger. *Norman* demonstrates the inability of BWS-based defenses to help women who kill in non-confrontational situations. In these situations, BWS-based defenses are little more than a plea for jury nullification, which in the long run is a thin reed upon which to rest.

Conclusion

This book was written to move the focus of battered women defenses away from the discourse of psychological syndrome and toward more just and responsible ways to deal with batterers that are consistent with the discourses of reason, informed common sense, and individual responsibility. In a broader sense, this work stands as a critique of those conceptualizations of the self and citizenship that are threatening politics and the quest for public judgment. Issues of criminal law and political theory are spun in the same seamless web. It is hoped that this book will contribute to doing justice in individual cases while reinforcing the norms of public judgment that make political freedom possible.

The book therefore concludes with a dedication to those thinkers like Hannah Arendt who have sought to foster a discourse of politics and citizenship that satisfies the thirst for justice and humaneness without sacrificing the critical reason and responsibility upon which political intelligence must rest.

NOTES

Chapter One

1. See, e.g., George Fletcher, *A Crime of Self-Defense: Bernard Goetz and the Law On Trial* (Free Press, 1988), chap. 2.

2. LaFave and Scott, *Criminal Law* (West Publishing Co., 1986), 2d ed., pp. 432–33.

3. See, e.g., Cynthia Gillespie, *Justifiable Homicide: Battered Women, Self-Defense, and the Law* (Ohio State University Press, 1989).

4. See, e.g., Cathryn J. Rosen, "The Excuse of Self-Defense: Correcting a Historical Accident on Behalf of Battered Women Who Kill," 36 American University Law Review 11 (1986), p. 43.

5. Judith Herman, *Trauma and Recovery: The Aftermath of Violence—From Domestic Abuse to Political Terror* (Basic Books, 1992), p. 119.

6. The most prominent test today is based on the famous *M'Naughten's* case, 8 Eng. Rep. 718 (1843), which stresses the complete lack of cognitive capacity to distinguish right from wrong. The other major test, the Model Penal Code test, focuses on the lack of substantial cognitive or volitional capacity. Model Penal Code, Sect. 4.01.

7. State v. Martin, 666 S.W. 2d 895 (Mo. Ct. App. 1984), at 900.

8. *Diagnostic and Statistical Manual* (DSM-III; American Psychiatric Association, 1980), p. 236.

9. Lenore Walker, *Terrifying Love: Why Battered Women Kill and How Society Responds* (Harper Collins, 1989), p. 36. See also Mary Ann Dutton, *Empowering and Healing the Battered Woman: A Model for Assessment and Intervention* (Springer, 1992), chap. 4.

10. Julie Blackman, "Potential Uses for Expert Testimony: Ideas toward the Representation of Battered Women Who Kill," 9 Women's Rights Law Reporter 227 (1986), p. 231. People v. Torres, 488 N.Y. S. 2d 358 (Sup. Ct. 1985). See also Blackman, *Intimate Violence: A Study of Injustice* (Columbia University Press, 1989).

11. Angela Browne, *When Battered Women Kill* (Free Press, 1987), p. 182.

12. Interview with Nora Cashen, Wisconsin Coalition against Domestic Violence.

13. *Webster's Second International Dictionary* (D. C. Merriam and Co., 1961).

14. Many courts do treat BWS and related syndromes as medical or pathological conditions, though some prefer a definition less indebted to scientific psychology. Whereas the Supreme Court of Kentucky defines the word "syndrome" as "a characteristic pattern of behavior . . . a set of characteristics regarded as identifying a certain type" in speaking of BWS, the Supreme Court of Pennsylvania remarked that "battered women are terror-stricken people whose mental state is distorted." Commonwealth v. Craig, 783 S.W. 2d 387 (Ky. 1990), at 388; Commonwealth v. Stonehouse, 555 A. 2d 772 (Pa. 1989), at 783, fn. 6.

15. Sharon Angella Allard, "Rethinking Battered Woman Syndrome: A Black Feminist Perspective," 1 U.C.L.A. Women's Law Journal 191 (1991), pp. 193–94, 206. Emphasis added. Quoting Sagaw, "A Hard Case for Feminists: People v. Goetz," 10 Harvard Women's Law Journal 253 (1987), p. 256, note 21.

16. See, for example, Elizabeth Schneider, "Particularity and Generality: Challenges of Feminist Theory and Practice in Work on Woman-Abuse," 67 New York University Law Review 520 (1992).

17. See, for example, Alan Dershowitz, *Abuse Excuse* (Little, Brown, 1994), p. 54.

18. Interview with Patti Seeger, Dane County Advocates for Battered Women.

19. George Fletcher, *Rethinking Criminal Law* (Little, Brown, 1978), p. 759. On the difficulty of drawing lines, see Kent Greenawalt, "The Perplexing Borders of Justification and Excuse," 84 Columbia Law Review 1897 (1984).

20. David Faigman, "The Battered Woman Syndrome and Self-Defense: A Legal and Empirical Dissent," 72 Virginia Law Review 619 (1986).

21. Hannah Arendt, "Judging," in *The Life of the Mind* (Harcourt Brace Jovanovich, 1978), pp. 269, 271 (quoting Kant's *Critique of Judgment*).

22. Mary Midgley, *Can't We Make Moral Judgments?* (St. Martin's Press, 1993), p. 25. Emphasis in original.

23. Simone de Beauvoir, *The Second Sex* (Vintage, 1989), pp. xxv–xxvi, xxxiv–xxxv.

24. See Shirley Sagaw, "A Hard Case for Feminists: People v. Goetz," 10 Harvard Women's Law Journal 253 (1987), p. 266.

25. Interview with Kathleen Kreneck, policy coordinator, Wisconsin Coalition against Domestic Violence.

26. See, e.g., Frederick Crews, "The Revenge of the Repressed," I and II, New York Review of Books, November 17 and December 1, 1994; Elizabeth Loftus and Katherine Ketcham, *The Myth of Repressed Memory: False Memories and Allegations of Sexual Abuse* (St. Martin's Press, 1994); Richard Wright, *Remembering Satan: A Case of Recovered Memory and the Shattering of an American Family* (Knopf, 1994); Richard Ofshe and Ethan Watters, *Making Monsters: False Memories, Psychotherapy, and Sexual Hysteria* (Scribner's, 1994).

27. Judith Herman, *Trauma and Recovery*.

28. On Wenatchee, see Dorothy Rabinowitz, "Wenatchee: A True Story," The Wall Street Journal, September 29, 1995. See also the HBO movie *Indictment* (1995), and Ruth Shalit, "Witch Hunt," The New Republic, June 19, 1995, pp. 14–16. See

also Wright, *Remembering Satan;* Mark Pendergast, *Victims of Memory: Incest Accusations and Shattered Lives* (Upper Access, 1995).

29. Eventually, Walker did not testify because her work was not deemed relevant to the question of Simpson's guilt.

30. Kathleen O'Donovan, "Law's Knowledge: The Judge, the Expert, the Battered Woman, and Her Syndrome," 20 Journal of Law and Society 427 (1993), pp. 429–30. R. v. Lavelle [1990] 1 S.C.R. 852.

31. State of Wisconsin v. Richardson, No. 94-0105-CR (November 23, 1994).

Chapter Two

1. Richard W. Jaeger, "Son Sentenced to 9 Years for Killing Dad," *Wisconsin State Journal,* July 10, 1993, p. 1A.

2. Premenstrual syndrome (PMS) and gambler's syndrome are two well-known ones that have had little influence in the criminal law, for reasons I will discuss below.

3. American Psychiatric Association, *Diagnostic and Statistical Manual of Psychiatric Disorders,* vol. 3 (DSM-III; American Psychiatric Association, 1980), p. 236. See also DSM-IIIR (American Psychiatric Association, 1987), sect. 309.89; and DSM-IV (American Psychiatric Association, 1994), sect. 309.81.

4. Sigmund Freud, *Dora: An Analysis of a Case of Hysteria* (Macmillan, 1963).

5. See, e.g., Alice Miller, *The Untouched Key: Tracing Childhood Trauma in Creativity and Destructiveness* (Doubleday, 1990); *Banished Knowledge: Facing Childhood Injuries* (Doubleday, 1990); *Prisoners of Childhood* (Basic Books, 1981) (republished as *The Drama of the Gifted Child* (Basic Books, 1982).

6. Jeffrey Masson, *The Assault on Truth: Freud's Suppression of the Seduction Theory* (Farrar, Straus, and Giroux, 1984).

7. Allen Esterson, *Seductive Mirage: An Exploration of the Work of Sigmund Freud* (Open Court, 1993).

8. See Note, "Unequal and Inadequate Protection under the Law: State Child Abuse Statutes," 50 George Washington Law Review 243 (1982).

9. In *The Order of Things* (Vintage, 1970), Michel Foucault discusses how certain background assumptions or *epistēmēs* make particular forms of knowledge possible in the first place.

10. Wright, *Remembering Satan: A Case of Recovered Memory and the Shattering of an American Family* (Knopf, 1994). George Rosen discusses other historical incidents of "social madness" in *Madness and Society: Chapters in the Historical Sociology of Mental Illness* (University of Chicago Press, 1968).

11. Ofshe and Watters, *Making Monsters: False Memories, Psychotherapy, and Sexual Hysteria* (Scribner's, 1994); Loftus and Ketcham, *The Myth of Recovered Memory: False Memories and Allegations of Sexual Abuse* (St. Martin's Press, 1994).

12. See David Ramsay Steele, "Partial Recall," Liberty, March 1994, pp. 37–47.

13. See, e,g, John Taylor, "The Lost Daughter: How One American Family Got Caught Up in Today's Witches' Brew of Sexual Abuse, the Sybil Syndrome, and the Perverse Ministrations of the Therapy Police," Esquire, March 1994, pp. 76–87.

14. Henry Kempe, Frederic N. Silverman, Brandt F. Steele, William Droege-

mueller, and Henry K. Silver, "The Battered Child Syndrome," 181 Journal of the American Medical Association 17 (1962); Murray Straus, David Gelles, and Suzanne Steinmetz, *Behind Closed Doors: Violence in the American Family* (Sage, 1980).

15. See generally, Ian Hacking, *Rewriting the Soul: Multiple Personality and the Sciences of Memory* (Princeton University Press, 1995), chaps. 3 and 4.

16. DSM-III, p. 257.

17. Hacking, *Rewriting the Soul*, p. 51.

18. Hacking, *Rewriting the Soul*, p. 19; *Diagnostic and Statistical Manual* (American Psychiatric Association, 1994), p. 487.

19. See Daniel Keyes, *The Minds of Billy Milligan* (Bantam, 1982). Corbett Thigpen and Hervey M. Cleckey, *The Three Faces of Eve* (McGraw Hill, 1957). Flora Rheta Schreiber, *Sybil* (Regnery, 1973). For strong critiques of the concept, see Ofshe and Watters, *Making Monsters*, esp. chap. 10.

20. Hacking, *Rewriting the Soul*, chap. 4.

21. The problem of differential diagnosis is frequently encountered in cases involving syndromes and post-traumatic stress disorder (PTSD). See C. B. Scrignar, *Post-Traumatic Stress Disorder: Diagnosis, Treatment, and Legal Issues* (Bruno Press, 1988), 2d ed., pp. 117–46. Several interviewees agreed that this was a major problem, especially in determining the cause of crime. John Greist, psychiatrist. Carol Kraft and Bob Donohoo, district attorneys, Milwaukee.

22. Ronald Summit, "The Child Sexual Abuse Accommodation Syndrome," 7 Child Abuse and Neglect 177 (1983), p. 181.

23. See Joelle Anne Moreno, "Killing Daddy: Developing a Self-Defense Strategy for the Abused Child," 137 University of Pennsylvania Law Review 1281 (1989), pp. 1303–4.

24. See Philip Rieff, *The Triumph of the Therapeutic: Uses of Faith after Freud* (Harper, 1966). On feminism's critique of Freud's followers for their desire to "ratify traditional roles, and to validate temperamental differences," see Kate Millet, *Sexual Politics* (Doubleday & Co., 1970).

25. Lenore Walker, *Terrifying Love: Why Battered Women Kill and How Society Responds* (HarperCollins, 1989), p. 7.

26. James R. Acker and Hans Toch, "Battered Women, Straw Men, and Expert Testimony: A Comment on State v. Kelly," 21 Criminal Law Bulletin (1985), p. 153.

27. William Ryan, *Blaming the Victim* (Vintage, 1976), revised edition. Reviewed in New York Times, January 26, 1971.

28. Christopher Lasch, *The Minimal Self: Psychic Survival in Troubled Times* (Norton, 1984), p. 67.

29. Galanter Lexis search, presented to me in February 1994.

30. Bob Golic on ESPN; McLaughlin Group, January 16, 1994. Coach Ron Meyer on CNN, January 30, 1994.

31. See, e.g., Michael Andrew Tesner, "Racial Paranoia as a Defense to Crimes of Violence: An Emerging Theory of Self-Defense or Insanity?" 11 Boston College Third World Law Journal 307 (1991).

32. Nexis and Lexis searches performed by research assistant Evan Gerstmann,

February 1994. See also the extensive "Glossary of Abuse Excuses" in Dershowitz's *Abuse Excuse* (Little, Brown, 1994), pp. 321–41.

33. Richard E. Vatz, "Blanket Mental Health Coverage-Crazy," Wall Street Journal, April 14, 1993, editorial page. See also Wall Street Journal, April 25, 1994, p. 1: drugs for "compulsive and obsessive personalities" are now being developed.

34. Vatz, "Attention Deficit Delirium," Wall Street Journal, July 27, 1994, p. A14. See DSM-IV, sects. 314.00, 314.01, 314.9.

35. Stuart A. Kirk and Herb Kutchins, *The Selling of DSM: The Rhetoric of Science in Psychiatry* (Aldine De Gruyter, 1992), pp. 8–9. For a more extensive treatment of the socioeconomic transformation of modern psychiatry, see Robert Castel, Francoise Castel, and Anne Lovell, *The Psychiatric Society* (Columbia University Press, 1982).

36. Elizabeth Schneider, "Particularity and Generality: Challenges of Feminist Theory and Practice in Work on Woman-Abuse," 67 New York University Law Review 520 (1992), p. 537.

37. David McCord, "Syndromes, Profiles and Other Mental Exotica: A New Approach to the Admissibility of Nontraditional Psychological Evidence in Criminal Cases," 66 Oregon Law Review 19 (1987), pp. 24–25.

38. Dyas v. U.S., 376 A. 2d 827 (D.C. 1977), at 832.

39. Frye v. U.S., 293 F. 1013 (D.C. Cir. 1923), at 1014.

40. See *McCormick's Handbook on the Law of Evidence* (West Publishing Co., 1978), Edward W. Cleary, ed., chap. 16.

41. Daubert v. Merrell Dow Pharmaceuticals, Inc., 61 LW 4807–8 (1993).

42. See McCord, "Syndromes, Profiles and Other Mental Exotica"; compare: "Evidence of Syndromes: No Need for a 'Better Mousetrap,'" 32 South Texas Law Review 37 (1990); and James T. Richardson et al., "The Problems of Applying *Daubert* to Psychological Syndrome Evidence," 79 Judicature 1995, pp. 10–16.

43. See also the discussion of MPD and dissociative identity disorder, above.

44. American Humane Association, Highlights of Official Child Neglect and Abuse Reporting 1986, at 23 (1988), cited in John E. B. Myers, "The Child Sexual Abuse Literature: A Call for Greater Objectivity," 88 University of Michigan Law Review 1709 (1990), at 1709–10.

45. McCord, "Syndromes, Profiles, and Other Mental Exotica," p. 43. See, e.g., Commonwealth v. Baldwin, 502 A. 2d 253 (Pa. 1985), at 257–58.

46. See Jahnke v. State, 682 P. 2d 991 (Wyo. 1984). See, e.g., "Menendez Case Fascinates Court-Watchers Nationwide," Los Angeles Times, October 12, 1993, Part A, page 1, col. 5.

47. See People v. Cruickshank, 105 A.D. 2d 325 (N.Y. 1985); case of Sociz "Johnny" Junatanov, in Chambers, "Children Citing Self-Defense in Murder of Parents," New York Times, October 12, 1986, sect. 1, p. 38, col. 3.

48. "Battered Child Syndrome Recognized as Self Defense," National Public Radio, Morning Edition, June 22, 1993 (Lexis).

49. "When a Child Kills a Parent, Does Abuse Forgive the Act?" Chicago Tribune, June 17, 1993, page 1.

50. Anastasia Toufexis, "When Kids Kill Abusive Parents; Once Seen as Evil or

Ill, These Desperate Youngsters are Gaining New Sympathy," Time magazine, November 23, 1992, page 60. On the Rush Springs case, see Doras Quan, "Relatives Rally Support for Boys Who Killed Father . . . Lawyers Plan Battered Child Defense." On another case, see Dallas Morning News, August 18, 1993, page 1A.

51. Gordon Black, reporter: "Battered Child Syndrome Recognized as Self Defense," National Public Radio, Morning Edition, June 22, 1993 (LEXIS)

52. "Rape Trauma Syndrome," 131 American Journal of Psychiatry 981 (1974).

53. David McCord, "The Admissibility of Expert Testimony Regarding Rape Trauma Syndrome in Rape Prosecutions," 26 Boston College Law Review 1143 (1985), pp. 1155–56, 1168.

54. State v. Saladana, 324 N.W. 2d 227 (Minn. 1982), at 230. For a contrary result in this regard, see State v. Huey, 699 P. 2d 1290 (Ariz. 1985).

55. On these and related issues, see Tracy E. Watson, " 'Rape Trauma Syndrome' and Inconsistent Rulings on Its Admissability Around the Nation: Should the Washington Supreme Court Reconsider Its Position in State v. Black?" 24 Willamette Law Review 1011 (1988).

56. See, e.g., State v. Saldana, 324 N.W. 2d 227 (1982) (not admissible); State v. Marks, 647 P. 2d 1292 (Kan. 1982) (admissible).

57. People v. Bledsoe, 681 P. 2d 291 (Cal. 1984), at 298. See also, e.g., Commonwealth v. Zamarriripa, 549 A. 2d 980 (Pa. Super. Ct. 1988); People v. Taylor, 552 N.E. 2d 131 (N.Y. 1990). Overall, see the excellent article by Susan Murphy, "Assisting the Jury in Understanding Victimization: Expert Psychological Testimony on Battered Woman Syndrome and Rape Trauma Syndrome," 25 Columbia Journal of Law and Social Problems 277 (1992).

58. DSM-IIIR (American Psychiatric Press, 1987), p. 247, sect. 309.89.

59. Menachim Student, *In the Shadow of War: Memories of a Soldier and Therapist* (Temple University Press, 1991), pp. xvi, 10, 145.

60. Interview with T. M., Madison.

61. Interview with Nora Cashen, Dane County Advocates for Battered Women.

62. Herman, *Trauma and Recovery: The Aftermath of Violence—From Domestic Abuse to Political Terror* (Basic Books, 1992), p. 32.

63. Mardi Jon Horowitz, *Stress Response Syndromes* (Aronson, 1986), second edition. On cognitive adjustment problems, see interview with Morey Bernstein, psychologist at the Veterans Administration Hospital in Milwaukee, Wisconsin, and interview with John Greist, nationally acclaimed expert on psychiatric disorders with Dean Clinic, Madison, Wisconsin.

64. Mary Ann Dutton, *Empowering and Healing the Battered Woman* (Springer, 1992), p. 53.

65. For a set of essays that include cognitive and physiological perspectives, often in combination, see Bessel A. van der Kolk, ed., *Post-Traumatic Stress Disorder* (American Psychiatric Press, 1984).

66. See McCord, "Syndromes, Profiles and Other Mental Exotica," p. 65.

67. Peter Erlinder, "Paying the Price for Vietnam: Post-Traumatic Stress Disorder and Criminal Behavior," 25 Boston College Law Review 305 (1984), p. 311.

68. See Richard A. Kulka et al., *Trauma and the Vietnam War Generation: Report of Findings from the National Vietnam Veterans Readjustment Study* (Brunner/Mazel, 1990). In 1983 the *Journal of Behavioral Science and Law* dedicated an entire journal to PTSD and Vietnam vets. The authors were the major pro-vet researchers in the field of PTSD and vets.

69. Interviews with Bob Cook and Tom Dietz, social work psychologists at Community Vet Center in Madison, Wisconsin; interview with Dr. Morey Bernstein at Veterans Administration Hospital, Milwaukee, Wisconsin.

70. Erlinder, "Paying the Price for Vietnam," pp. 308–9.

71. See Michael R. Trimble, "Post-traumatic Stress Disorder: History of a Concept," in Charles R. Figley, ed., *Trauma and Its Wake.* vol. I. *The Study and Treatment of Post-traumatic Stress Disorder* (Brunner/Masel, 1985). p. 8.

72. People v. Gilberg, 240 P. 1000 (1925), at 1004.

73. Erlinder, "Paying the Price for Vietnam," p. 314.

74. People v. Walker, 201 P. 2d 6 (1948), at 11. For a similar case, see People v. Danielly, 202 P. 2d 18 (1949); Commonwealth v. Logan, 63 A. 2d 28 (1949).

75. On the matters discussed in this paragraph, see Erlinder, "Paying the Price for Vietnam," p. 315.

76. Lifton's book *Home from the War: Learning from Vietnam Veterans* (Beacon, 1973; revised in 1992) is a product of his activism in this area.

77. Wilbur J. Scott, "PTSD in DSM-III: A Case in the Politics of Diagnosis and Disease," 37 Social Problems 294 (1990).

78. Scott, "PTSD in DSM-III," pp. 305–6. See Lifton, *Death in Life: Survivors of Hiroshima* (Random House, 1968). See also Henry Krystal's powerful book, *Massive Psychic Trauma* (International Universities Press, 1968).

79. See brochure on Ist Annual PTSD & The Law Symposium in Lakewood, Colorado, February 18 and 19, 1993; Illinois Mental Health Association, packet on PTSD.

80. DSM-IV, sect. 308.3.

81. Erlinder, "Paying the Price for Vietnam."

82. See, e.g., Edwards v. State, 540 S.W. 2d 641 (1976). The discussion of the following cases is based on Erlinder's reporting and Geraldine L. Brotherton, "Post-Traumatic Stress Disorder—Opening Pandora's Box?" 17 New England Law Review 91 (1981); Elizabeth J. Delgado, "Vietnam Stress Syndrome and the Criminal Defendant," 19 Loyola of Los Angeles Law Review 473 (1985).

83. Erlinder, "Paying the Price for Vietnam," pp. 320–21. Emphasis added. State v. Heads, No. 106, 126 (1st Jud. Dist. Ct. Caddo Parish, La. Oct. 10, 1981). See also People v. Wood, No. 80–7410 (Cir. Ct. Cook County, Ill. May 5, 1982). Wood also involved a situation in which the "discovery" of PTSD made a difference in the process of the adjudication.

84. For similar changes in retrials due to the intervening advent of PTSD, see U.S. v. Tindal (action addiction PTSD leading to drug smuggling) and State v. Gregory (PTSD leading to false imprisonment in a bank). See Erlinder, "Paying the Price for Vietnam," pp. 325–26. State v. Gregory, No. 19205 (Cir. Ct. Montgomery County, Md. 1979).

85. Interview with Carol Kraft, assistant D.A., Milwaukee, Wisconsin. See also interview with Bob Donohoo, assistant D.A., Milwaukee.

86. People v. Babbitt, 755 P. 2d 253 (Cal. 1988), at 274–75.

87. People v. Babbitt, 755 P. 2d 253 (Cal. 1988), at 267. Emphasis added.

88. People v. Babbitt, 755 P. 2d 253 (Cal. 1988), at 281–94.

89. For excellent discussions of PMS on many fronts, including medical, legal, ethical, and social, see Benson E. Ginsburg and Bonnie Frank Carter, eds., *Premenstrual Syndrome: Ethical and Legal Implications in a Biomedical Perspective* (Plenum Press, 1987).

90. R. v. Smith, No. 1/A/82 (Crim App. April 27, 1982). For the latter case, see "British Legal Debate: Premenstrual Tension and Criminal Behavior, New York Times, December 29, 1981, p. C3, col. 5. For a critique of these cases on feminist grounds, see Valerie Hey, "Getting Away with Murder: PMS and the Press," in Sophie Laws, Valerie Hey, and Andrea Eagan, *Seeing Red: the Politics of Premenstrual Tension* (Hutchinson, 1985), chap. 3. The widely cited *People v. Santos* was the first American case to consider PMS in a criminal case. Authorities charged Santos with child battering. The judge ruled during the motions that PMS is admissible as evidence; but the defendant ended up pleading guilty to the lesser charge of harassment, so the PMS issue did not get addressed. People v. Santos, No. 1KO46229 (Crim. Ct. N.Y. Nov. 3, 1982). See Robert Mark Carney and Brian D. Williams, "Premenstrual Syndrome: A Criminal Defense," 59 Notre Dame Law Review 252 (1983). For cases in which PMS was deemed irrelevant to negating the presumption of voluntariness in making a guilty plea, a revocation of a license due to failure to take a breath test, and a relinquishing of parental rights, see State v. Lashwood, 384 N.W. 2d 319 (S.D. 1986); Commonwealth Department of Transportation v. Grass, 595 A. 2d 789 (Pa. Cmwlth. 1991); Hensman v. Parsons, 458 N.W. 2d 199 (Neb. 1990); Wentzel v. Montgomery General Hospital, Inc., Md., 447 A. 2d 1244.

91. Dershowitz, *Abuse Excuse,* p. 54.

92. Joann D'Emilio, "Battered Woman's Syndrome and Premenstrual Syndrome: A Comparison of Their Possible Use as Defenses to Criminal Liability," 59 St. John's Law Review 559 (1985).

93. Elizabeth Holtzman, "Premenstrual Symptoms: No Legal Defense," 60 St. John's Law Review 712 (1986), p. 715.

94. See Richard T. Oakes, "PMS: A Plea Bargain in Brooklyn Does Not A Rule of Law Make," 9 Hamline Law Review 203.

95. Interview with Dale Cobb, attorney-at-law, Charleston, South Carolina, March 1993.

96. Former professional quarterback Art Schlichter received a plea-bargained two-year sentence on January 27, 1995, for stealing (through fraud) $500,000 from friends and associates to fuel his gambling habit. Wisconsin State Journal, January 28, 1995, p. 4B.

97. DSM-IIIR, Section 312.31 (American Psychiatric Association, 1987), pp. 324–25.

98. U.S. v. Lewellyn, 723 F. 2d 615 (1983), at 619.Q

99. Zarin v. Commissioner, 92 T.C. 1084 (1989). See Daniel Shaviro, "The Man Who Lost Too Much: Zarin v. Commissioner and the Measurement of Taxable Consumption," 45 Texas Law Review 215 (1990).

100. Matter of Lobbe, 539 A. 2d 733 (N.J. Super. A.D. 1987), at 731–32. See also unpublished opinion, Matter of John Shorter, Court of Appeals of the District of Columbia, 1990 D.C. App. Lexis 28.

101. Interview with Coramae Mann, Institute of Criminal Justice, Indiana University, Bloomington, Indiana.

102. See Kulka et al., *Trauma and the Vietnam War Generation.* See also Marion E. Wolf and Aron D. Mosnaim, *Posttraumatic Stress Disorder: Etiology, Phenomenology, and Treatment* (American Psychiatric Press, 1990).

103. Bruce Boman, "Are All Vietnam Veterans Like John Rambo?" in Wolf and Masnaim, eds., *Posttraumatic Stress Disorder,* p. 87, and, generally, chap. 6. The study Boman refers to is Nace et al., "The Prognosis for Addicted Returnees: A Comparison with Civilian Addicts," 15 Comparative Psychiatry 49 (1974).

104. See, e.g., Alexander C. McFarlane, "Vulnerability to Posttraumatic Stress Disorder," in Marion E. Wolf and Aron D. Mosnaim, *Posttraumatic Stress Disorder,* chap. 1.

105. Sanford Kadish and Stephen Schulhofer, *Criminal Law and Its Processes* (Little, Brown, 1989), p. 864. State v. Wanrow, 559 P. 2d 548 (1977); State v. Kelly, 478 A. 2d 364 (1984).

106. Susan Murphy, "Assisting the Jury in Understanding Victimization: Expert Psychological Testimony on Battered Woman Syndrome and Rape Trauma Syndrome," 25 Columbia Journal of Law and Social Problems 277 (1992), p. 281.

107. Murphy, "Assisting the Jury in Understanding Victimization," p. 297.

108. U.S. v. Gordon, 638 F. Supp. 1120 (W.D. La. 1986), at 1148. On the normative conflict between psychiatric and legal notions of causation and responsibility, see Seymore L. Halleck's classic treatment in *Psychiatry and the Dilemmas of Crime: A Study of Causes, Punishment and Treatment* (University of California Press, 1976), chap. 15, "The Psychiatrist and the Legal Process."

109. On the new syndromes' relationship to "soft" science rather than "hard," see McCord, "Syndromes, Profiles and Other Mental Exotica," pp. 29–30.

110. Arthur Kleinman, *The Illness Narratives: Suffering, Healing, and the Human Condition* (Basic Books, 1988), chap. 1, "The Meaning of Symptoms and Disorders," p. 26.

111. McCord, "Syndromes, Profiles and Other Mental Exotica," pp. 27–35.

112. Thomas Kuhn, *The Structure of Scientific Revolutions* (University of Chicago Press, 1962); Foucault, *The Order of Things.*

113. See Susan C. Smith, "Comment: Abused Children Who Kill Abusive Parents: Moving toward an Appropriate Legal Response," 42 Catholic University Law Review 141 (1992), p. 141. DeShaney v. Winnebago County Department of Social Services, 109 S. Ct. 998 (1989).

114. Michel Foucault, *Power/Knowledge: Selected Interviews and Other Writings* (Pantheon, 1980). See Murray Edelman's excellent chapter on the rhetoric and symbolic

politics of the helping professions in *Politics and Language* (University of Wisconsin, Inst. for Poverty, 1977).

115. Charles Krauthammer, "Defining Deviancy Up: The New Assault on Bourgeoisie Life," The New Republic, November 22, 1993, pp. 22–23. For a fine piece on the need to maintain balance against the exaggerated claims and critiques of both sides, see Myers, "The Child Sexual Abuse Literature: A Call for Greater Objectivity."

116. See, e.g., Linda Gordon, *Heroes of Their Own Lives: The Politics and History of Family Violence* (Penguin, 1988), esp. Introduction.

117. Joseph Gusfield, *The Culture of Public Problems: Drinking—Driving and the Symbolic Order* (University of Chicago Press, 1981), pp. 3–6.

118. H. L. A. Hart and A. M. Honoré, *Causation in the Law* (Oxford University Press, 1959), p. 61.

119. See Morton J. Horwitz, *The Transformation of American Law: 1780–1860* (Harvard University Press, 1977).

120. These and related factors are discussed in Joseph A. Amato's insightful *Victims and Values: A History and a Theory of Suffering* (Praeger, 1990).

121. Amato, *Victims and Values*, p. xvii, xix. On the proliferation of victim ideology as a form of "radical egalitarianism," see Aaron Wildavsky, *The Rise of Radical Egalitarianism* (American University Press, 1991), esp. Preface: "The Search for the Oppressed."

122. Aristotle, *Nichomachean Ethics* (Oxford University Press, The World's Classics, 1954), p. 3. See also Mary Midgley's illuminating discussion of the differences between hard scientific, moral, and normative truths in *Can't We Make Moral Judgments?* (St. Martin's Press, 1993), chap. 4.

123. See Karl Jaspers, *General Psychopathology* (University of Chicago Press, 1963), pp. 301–3.

124. See Peter R. Breggin, *Toxic Psychiatry: Why Therapy, Empathy, and Love Must Replace the Drugs, Electroshock, and Biochemical Theories of the 'New Psychiatry'* (St. Martin's, 1991).

125. See, e.g., Gregory Zilboorg, *A History of Medical Psychology* (Norton, 1941). For a recent declaration of the resurgence of bio-psychiatry, see Philip A. Berger and H. Keith H. Brodie, *American Handbook of Psychiatry*, vol. 8, *Biological Psychiatry* (Basic, 1986), p. xiv. See also Deborah W. Denno, "Human Biology and Criminal Responsibility: Free Will or Free Ride?" 137 University of Pennsylvania Law Review 615 (1988).

126. Paul R. McHugh and Phillip R. Slavney, *The Perspectives of Psychiatry* (Johns Hopkins University Press, 1986), p. 23. John Searle develops the relationship between consciousness and biology with acuity in *The Rediscovery of the Mind* (M.I.T., 1992). Searle eschews the reduction of consciousness to sheer biological or nonpsychical qualities (monism), but also eschews dualism.

127. McHugh and Slavney, *Perspectives of Psychiatry*, p. 20.

128. Paul Ricoeur, *Freud and Philosophy: An Essay on Interpretation* (Yale University Press, 1970), p. 151.

129. Ricoeur, *Freud and Philosophy*, p. 190.

130. Herman, *Trauma and Recovery*, pp. 17–18.

131. Lynn Payer, *Medicine and Culture: Varieties of Treatment in the United States, England, West Germany, and France* (Penguin, 1988). The medical profession has also managed to frame the meaning of disease because of its institutional power. See Paul Starr, *The Social Transformation of American Medicine: The Rise of a Sovereign Profession and the Making of a Vast Industry* (1982). On how the framing of physical disease is interpretive, see Charles E. Rosenberg and Janet Golden, *Framing Disease: Studies in Cultural History* (Rutgers University Press, 1992).

132. *International Classification of Diseases* (World Health Organization, 1992), pp. 151–61. See Hacking, *Rewriting the Soul*, p. 10.

133. See Ronald Bayer, *Homosexuality and American Psychiatry: The Politics of Diagnosis* (Princeton University Press, 1987).

134. Indeed, the entire reformulation of psychiatry in DSM-III was driven by political and social considerations. See Kirk and Kutchins, *The Selling of DSM*.

135. In August 1993 I interviewed a psychiatrist who asked to remain anonymous. He steadfastly maintained that this politicization posed severe problems for the practice of psychiatry. See also the numerous similar claims by sources in Bayer, *Homosexuality and American Psychiatry*, and Kirk and Kutchens, *The Selling of DSM*.

136. For a penetrating analysis of the negative effects of psychiatric labeling that supplants previous social and personal narratives or roles with a medical one, see Erving Goffman, *Asylums: Essays on the Social Situation of Mental Patients and Other Inmates* (Anchor, 1961). Goffman holds, however, that the key transition occurs when the individual becomes hospitalized rather than simply labeled (see, e.g., p. 128).

137. There is copious literature on the issue of the relationship between culture and the framing of physical and mental illness. See Edward Shorter, *From Paralysis to Fatigue: A History of Psychosomatic Illness in the Modern Era* (Free Press, 1992); Susan Sontag, *AIDS and Its Metaphors* (Farrar, Straus and Giroux, 1988).

138. Shorter, *From Paralysis to Fatigue*, p. 164.

139. "Culture Wars: Political Correctness on Campus," aired on Public Broadcasting System nationwide in fall 1993.

140. See Henry Krystal, *Massive Psychic Trauma* (International Universities Press, 1968); Robert Jay Lifton, *Death in Life: Survivors of Hiroshima* (Random House, 1968).

141. John Irving, *The World According to Garp* (Ballantine Books, 1990), p. 147. On Springsteen, see New York Times, July 3, 1994, sect. H, p. 1, "How Pop Music Surrendered the Melody to a Raucous Clatter." Irving, "Pornography and the New Puritans," New York Times Book Review, March 1992, p. 1. See also New York Times Book Review, May 3, 1992, "Pornography and the New Puritans: Letters from Andrea Dworkin and Others." See also Oates, *Solstice* (Berkeley, 1985), where her main character and other characters are portrayed and defined as "survivors."

142. See Helen Epstein, *Children of the Holocaust* (Putnam, 1979).

143. Catharine MacKinnon, "Pornography, Civil Rights, and Speech," 20 Harvard Civil Rights-Civil Liberties Law Review 1 (1985). See also *Only Words* (Harvard University Press, 1993), pp. 82–83.

144. Joseph A. Amato, *Victims and Values: A History and a Theory of Suffering*

(Praeger, 1990), esp. chap. 8, "Universal Victims." Ayn Rand's essay "Faith and Force: The Destroyers of the Modern World" portrays the development of victim ideology with acuity. In Rand, *Philosophy: Who Needs It* (Signet, 1984).

Chapter Three

1. Caroline Walker Bynum, *Holy Feast and Holy Fast: The Religious Significance of Food to Medieval Women* (University of California Press, 1987), p. 287. See also chaps. 9 ("Woman as Body and as Food") and 10 ("Women's Symbols").

2. Hegel, *The Phenomenology of Mind* (Harper, 1967), pp. 229–32.

3. Angela Browne, *When Battered Women Kill* (Free Press, 1987), pp. 9–10.

4. David Coleman, "An Elusive Picture of Violent Men Who Kill Mates," New York Times, January 15, 1995, p. 13.

5. Martin Wolfgang, *Patterns in Criminal Homicide* (University of Pennsylvania Press, 1958). On males as much more violent than women, see James Q. Wilson and Richard J. Herrnstein, *Crime and Human Nature* (Simon and Schuster, 1985), chap. 4. See also Uniform Crime Reports, 1983.

6. Planned Parenthood of Southeastern Pennsylvania v. Casey, 112 S.Ct. 2791 (1992). In a comparison of surveys conducted in 1975 and 1985, respectively, Murray A. Straus and Richard Gelles found that the level of severe violence was about the same in each period, though slightly lower in 1985. In 1975, 38 out of every 1,000 husbands and 46 out of every 1,000 wives engaged in "severe violence," while the figures for 1985 are 30 out of every 1,000 husbands and 44 out of every 1,000 wives. See Straus and Gelles, "Societal Change and Change in Family Violence from 1975 to 1985 as Revealed by Two National Surveys," in Straus and Gelles, *Physical Violence in American Families: Risk Factors and Adaptations to Violence in 8,145 Families* (Transaction, 1992), chap. 7, pp. 118–21.

7. Lucy Berliner, "Domestic Violence: A Humanist or Feminist Issue?" Journal of Interpersonal Violence, March 1990, p. 128.

8. Straus, Gelles, and Steinmetz, *Behind Closed Doors: Violence in the American Family* (Sage, 1980); Susan Steinmetz, "The Battered Husband Syndrome," 2 Victimology 499 (1977).

9. Steinmetz herself received death and bombing threats. See Katherine Dunn, "Truth Abuse," The New Republic, August 1, 1994. Academic feminists ostracized the woman expert on gender who testified against the feminist argument in the famous Equal Employment Opportunity Commission lawsuit against Sears for sexism in job advancement practices. See Thomas Haskell and Sanford Levinson, "Academic Freedom and Expert Witnessing: Historians and the Sears Case," 66 Texas Law Review 1629 (1988). EEOC v. Sears, Roebuck, & Co., 628 F. Supp. 1264 (N.D. Ill. 1986), aff'd, 839 F. 2d 302 (7th Cir. 1988).

10. See Susan Schechter, *Women and Male Violence: The Visions and Struggles of the Battered Women's Movement* (South End Press, 1982). Telephone interview with Coramae Mann, Indiana University Criminal Justice Program.

11. See many of the articles in Emilio Viano, ed., *Intimate Violence: Interdisciplinary Perspectives* (Hemisphere, 1992), esp. Coramae Richey Mann, "Female Murderers

and Their Motives: A Tale of Two Cities," and Alfred DeMaris, "Male Versus Female Initiation of Aggression: The Case of Courtship Violence." And Sharon Angella Allard, "Rethinking Battered Woman Syndrome: A Black Feminist Perspective," 1 U.C.L.A. Women's Law Journal 191 (1991), pp. 193–94, 206.

12. Interview with inmate at Taycheetah Correctional Inst., Fond du Lac, Wisconsin.

13. Katherine Dunn, "Truth Abuse," p. 16.

14. R. I. McNeely and Coramae Mann, "Domestic Violence Is a Humanist Issue," Journal of Interpersonal Violence, March 1990, p. 130. See also many of the articles in Viano, ed., *Intimate Violence,* esp. Mann, "Female Murderers and Their Motives" and DeMaris, "Male Versus Female Initiation of Aggression."

15. See, e.g., Daniel G. Saunders, "When Battered Women Use Violence: Husband-Abuse or Self-Defense?" 1 Violence and Victims 47 (1986).

16. Jan E. Stets and Murray A. Straus, "Gender Differences in Reporting Marital Violence and Its Medical and Psychological Consequences," in Straus and Gelles, *Physical Violence in American Families,* p. 161. On Straus and Gelles's recent research, see also John Leo, "Is It a War against Women?" U.S. News and World Report, July 11, 1994, p. 22

17. R. Emerson Dobash and Russell Dobash, *Violence against Wives: A Case against the Patriarchy* (Free Press, 1979), pp. 15, 27. See also Del Martin, *Battered Wives* (Volcano, 1976); Kersti Yllo and Michele Bograd, *Feminist Perspectives on Wife Abuse* (Sage Publications, 1988), for a major compilation of more recent feminist perspectives on research issues.

18. Interview with Gerry Mueller, public defender, Kenosha, Wisconsin; interview with Stephen Hurley, Madison attorney.

19. Shawn Sullivan, "Wife-Beating N the Hood," Wall Street Journal, July 6, 1993, editorial op-ed page. See also "Boy Meets Girl, Boy Beats Girl," Newsweek, December 13, 1993, pp. 66–68.

20. "8 Die Despite Court Orders," The Capital Times (Madison), October 10, 1994, p. 1A.

21. Interview with boyfriend of murdered woman, Madison, Wisconsin. The press reported this killing, but, at my source's request, I must refrain from citing the reports. State v. Simpson, 393 S.E. 2d 774 (1990). On the Milwaukee case, see interview with Carol Craft, Milwaukee D.A. office. See also cases cited in Richard A. Rosen, "On Self-Defense, Imminence, and Women Who Kill Their Batterers," 71 North Carolina Law Review 371 (1993), pp. 372–73, fn. 2. See also Martha Mahoney, "Legal Images of Battered Women: Redefining the Issue of Separation," 90 Michigan Law Review 1 (1991).

22. Interview with inmate at Taycheedah Correctional Institution.

23. Walker, *The Battered Woman Syndrome* (Springer, 1984), p. 34.

24. Stets and Straus, "Gender Differences in Reporting Marital Violence," p. 163.

25. It is also possible that some forms of violence against women are due to the *breakdown* of patriarchy as a system of social control. Feminists forget that patriarchy is as much about the control of sons' sexuality as it is about controlling women (see,

e.g., Freud's *Totem and Taboo*, Norton, 1950). For example, the history of the censorship of pornography is the history of patriarchs like Anthony Comstock striving to eliminate pornography from society in order to control the sexuality of the young—a fact that confounds the view that pornography is a patriarchal conspiracy against women alone. Though violence against women transcends class lines, many observers note greater misogyny and battering in communities without fathers, where patriarchy as a system of control is lacking.

26. MacKinnon, "Toward Feminist Jurisprudence," 34 Stanford Law Review 703 (1982), pp. 717–18, fn. 73. Emphasis added.

27. See Julia Kristeva's critique of those women who form a "counter-society" that inflicts its own form of injustice and othering in her essay "Women's Time," in Toril Moi, ed., *The Kristeva Reader* (Columbia University Press, 1986), p. 202. For a brilliant and disturbing analysis of scapegoating in relation to the onset of social othering and forms of knowledge that dissolve individual differences in favor of systemic patterns, forms, and profiles, see Rene Girard, "The Plague in Literature and Myth," in *To Double Business Bound: Essays on Literature, Mimesis, and Anthropology* (Johns Hopkins University Press, 1978).

28. For examples of Manicheanism, see, e.g., MacKinnon, "Feminism, Marxism, Method, and the State: Toward Feminist Jurisprudence," 8 Signs 635 (1983); Ann Scales, "The Emergence of Feminist Jurisprudence: An Essay," 95 Yale Law Journal 1373 (1986).

29. Katharine Bartlett, "Feminist Jurisprudence," 103 Harvard Law Review 829 (1990), p. 851. See also Simone de Beauvoir on the links between accepting the "ambiguity" of the world and existential responsibility in *The Ethics of Ambiguity* (Philosophical Library, 1948); and Charles Anderson, *Pragmatic Liberalism* (University of Chicago Press, 1990).

30. Interview with inmate at Taycheedah Correctional Institution. See also Crisis Letter, Dane County Advocates for Battered Women, March 23, 1994. Interview with Nicole Johnston, Dane County Advocates for Battered Women.

31. Julie Blackman, "Emerging Images of Severely Battered Women and the Criminal Justice System," 8 Behavioral Sciences and the Law 121 (1990), p. 127. See also Blackman, *Intimate Violence: A Study of Injustice* (Columbia University Press, 1989).

32. See Mardi Jon Horowitz, *Stress Response Syndromes* (Aronson, 1986), 2d. edition, chap. 6. Interview with John Greist, psychiatrist, Madison, Wisconsin. Greist is a nationally renowned forensic and clinical psychiatrist dealing with these issues.

33. Mary Ann Dutton, *Empowering and Healing the Battered Woman: A Model for Assessment and Intervention* (Springer, 1992), pp. 4, 6.

34. Dobash and Dobash, *Violence against Wives*, p. 157.

35. Much of the discussion of psychological effects is drawn from Dutton, *Empowering and Healing the Battered Woman*, chap. 4, though other sources are used as well.

36. Interview with inmate at Taycheedah Correctional Inst.

37. Dutton, *Empowering and Healing the Battered Woman*, chap. 4.

38. Elaine Hilberman and Kit Munson, "Sixty Battered Women," 2 Victimology 460 (1977–78), p. 464; Bessel A. van der Kolk and Charles Ducey, "Clinical Implica-

tions of the Rorschach in Post-Traumatic Stress Disorder," in van der Kolk, ed., *Post-Traumatic Stress Disorder: Psychological and Biological Seuelae* (American Psychiatric Press, 1984), pp. 30–31; Dutton, *Empowering and Healing the Battered Woman*, p. 61.

39. State v. Norman, 378 S.E. 2d 8 (N.C. 1989). Browne, *When Battered Women Kill*, p. 68. Dutton, *Empowering and Healing the Battered Woman*, p. 63. Interviews with inmates at Taycheedah Correctional Inst.

40. Martin Symonds, "Victims of Violence: Psychological Effects and After-effects," 35 The American Journal of Psychoanalysis 19 (1975), p. 24. Interview with inmate at Taycheedah Correctional Institution.

41. Interviews with inmates at Taycheedah Correctional Institution.

42. In general, see Charles Silberman, *Criminal Violence, Criminal Justice* (Vintage, 1980), chap. 1, on the need for a sense of social order and "communality," and how violent crime destroys this sense.

43. Hilberman and Munson, "Sixty Battered Women," p. 464

44. Interview with Nora Cashen. In chapter 1 of *Seductions of Crime: Moral and Sensual Attractions in Doing Evil* (Basic Books, 1988), Jack Katz portrays many homicides as moments of transcendent truth for the killer.

45. Anthony Giddens, *Modernity and Self-Identity: Self and Society in the Late Modern Age* (Polity Press/Basil Blackwell, 1991), pp. 53–54. R. D. Laing, *The Divided Self* (Penguin, 1969).

46. Interviews with Gerry Mueller and Cindy Kollath, Public Defenders' Office, Kenosha, Wisconsin.

47. Browne, *Battered Women Who Kill*, pp. 128–29. M. Sherif and C. Hovland, *Social Judgment* (Yale University Press, 1961).

48. See Daniel Jay Sonkin, Del Martin, and Lenore E. A. Walker, *The Male Batterer: A Treatment Approach* (Springer, 1985), esp. chaps. 2 and 4.

49. Hans Toch, *Violent Men: An Inquiry Into the Psychology of Violence* (American Psychological Association, 1992), p. 179.

50. Interview with inmate at Taycheedah Correctional Inst.

51. Interview with inmate at Taycheedah Correctional Inst.

52. Interviews with Patti Seeger, Dane County Advocates for Battered Women, and Kathleen Kreneck, Wisconsin Coalition against Domestic Violence.

53. Anne Ganley has developed a "power and control wheel," which lays out several types of abuse which we will be covering as we proceed. See Ganley, *Court Mandated Treatment for Men Who Batter* (Center for Women Policy Studies, 1981); E. Pence and M. Paymar, *Power and Control: Tactics of Men Who Batter: An Educational Curriculum* (Minnesota Program Development, Inc., 1986).

54. State v. Norman, 378 S.E. 2d 8 (N.C. 1989), at 10.

55. State v. Norman, 378 S.E. 2d 8 (N.C. 1989), at 11.

56. For an interesting discussion of the importance of attaining "upright posture" in the evolutionary process, see E. W. Straus, "The Upright Posture," 26 Psychiatric Quarterly 529 (1952). See also Heinz Kohut, *The Restoration of the Self* (International Universities Press, 1977), pp. 111–15. Interviews with inmates at Taycheedah Correctional Inst.

57. See Bynum, *Holy Feast and Holy Fast,* esp. chap. 9, "Woman as Body and as Food," and chap. 10, "Women's Symbols." Camille Paglia, *Sexual Personae: Art and Decadence from Nefertiti to Emily Dickinson* (Yale University Press, 1990), chap. 1. De Beauvoir, *The Second Sex* (Vintage, 1989), esp. chap. IX. See also the discussion below about "dark hearts."

58. Francine Hughes, quoted in Faith McNulty, *The Burning Bed: The Story of an Abused Wife* (Avon Books, 1980), p. 181.

59. Interview with Darald Hanusa, psychotherapist, Madison. See also Daniel D. Saunders and Darald Hanusa, "Cognitive-Behavioral Treatment of Men Who Batter: The Short-Term Effects of Group Therapy," 1 Journal of Family Violence 357 (1986).

60. Interviews with inmates at Taycheedah Correctional Inst.; interview with Ronda Richardson, Taycheedah Correctional Inst.

61. Interview with inmate at Taycheedah Correctional Inst.

62. Angela Browne, *Battered Women Who Kill,* pp. 153–54.

63. Interview with inmate at Taycheedah Correctional Inst.

64. Interview with inmate at Taycheedah Correctional Inst.

65. G. Bernard, H. Vera, M. Vera, and G. Newman, "Till Death Do Us Part," 10 Bulletin of the American Academy of Psychiatry and the Law (1982), pp. 271–80.

66. Martha Mahoney, "Legal Images of Battered Women: Redefining the Issue of Separation," 90 Michigan Law Review 1 (1991), p. 3.

67. Interview with Darald Hanusa, psychotherapist, Madison.

68. On the potential compatibility of political and psychological models of battering, see Michelle Bograd, "Feminist Perspectives on Wife Abuse: An Introduction," in Yllo and Bograd, *Feminist Perspectives on Wife Abuse,* p. 17.

69. Thomas Szasz, *Insanity: The Idea and Its Consequences* (Wiley, 1987), p. 263.

70. Interview with Ken Streit, Wisconsin LAIP. See also the portrayal of this effect in Linda Lovelace and Michael Grady, *Ordeal* (Bell Publishing Co., 1980).

71. See James Ptacek, "Why Do Men Batter Their Wives?" in Yllo and Bograd, *Feminist Perspectives on Wife Abuse,* p. 152, and, generally, pp. 133–56. See also Walker, *The Battered Woman* (Harper and Row, 1979); J.R. Lion, "Clinical Aspects of Wifebattering," in M. Roy, ed., *Battered Women: A Psychosociological Study of Domestic Violence* (Van Nostrand Reinhold, 1977).

72. Ptacek, "Why Do Men Batter Their Wives?" p. 151.

73. Thomas Schelling, *The Strategy of Conflict* (Oxford University Press, 1963), pp. 16–18.

74. A researcher in 1987 remarked that "no empirical research has at this date been completed to address that issue" (of the common personality structure of batterers). Anne L. Ganley, "Perpetrators of Domestic Violence: An Overview of Counseling the Court-Mandated Client," in Daniel Jay Sonkin, ed., *Domestic Violence on Trial: Psychological and Legal Dimensions of Family Violence* (Springer, 1987), p. 161. In 1985, Sonkin, Del Martin, and Lenore Walker published *The Male Batterer: A Treatment Approach.*

75. See, e.g., Renata Vaselle-Augenstein and Annette Ehrlich, "Male Batterers:

Evidence for Psychopathology," in Emilio C. Viano, *Intimate Violence*, pp. 139–54; and Richard M. Tolman and Larry W. Bennett, "A Review of Quantitative Research on Men Who Batter," 5 Journal of Interpersonal Violence 87 (1990), pp. 87–118.

76. Edward Gondolf, *Battered Women as Survivors: An Alternative to Treating Learned Helplessness* (Lexington Books, 1988), pp. 65–66.

77. Interview with inmate at Taycheedah Correctional Inst.

78. Alexandra Symonds, "Violence against Women—The Myth of Masochism," XXXIII American Journal of Psychotherapy 161 (1979), p. 165–66.

79. Symonds, "Violence against Women," p. 171.

80. Stets and Straus, "Gender Differences in Reporting Marital Violence," p. 161.

81. See, e.g., Straus et al., *Behind Closed Doors*; Steinmetz, "The Battered Husband Syndrome."

82. Susan Hanks, "Translating Theory into Practice: A Conceptual Framework for Clinical Assessment, Differential Diagnosis, and Multi-Modal Treatment of Maritally Violent Individuals, Couples, and Families," in Viano, ed., *Intimate Violence*, pp. 165–68.

83. Interview with inmate at Taycheedah Correctional Inst.

84. Interview with inmate at Taycheedah Correctional Inst.

85. Understanding this splitting function may explain why Walker found that her sample of battered women had more self-esteem than her control group of nonbattered women—a fact that is largely ignored in the literature and in court cases discussing BWS. See Walker, *The Battered Woman Syndrome*, pp. 80–82.

86. Hanks, "Treatment of Maritally Violent Individuals," pp. 166–67.

87. Loren E. Pedersen, *Dark Hearts: The Unconscious Forces That Shape Men's Lives* (Shambhala, 1991); Toch, *Violent Men*, pp. 185–92. See also Talcott Parsons, "Certain Primary Sources and Patterns of Aggression in the Social Structure of the Western World," 10 Psychiatry (1947), pp. 167–81.

88. Nancy Chodorow, *Feminism and Psychoanalytic Theory* (Yale University Press, 1989), pp. 51–52. See also Alexander Mitscherlich, *Society without the Father* (Schocken, 1970). On the ways in which boys' relations with the mother and the father influence political theories of masculine *virtu* and affect political relationships, see Hanna Fenichel Pitkin, *Fortune Is a Woman: Gender and Politics in the Thought of Niccolo Machiavelli* (University of California Press, 1984).

89. Such alienation of self leads to rage. See Kohut, *The Restoration of the Self*, p. 117. On destructive rage generally, see pp. 111–31. On oral rage, see the pioneering work of Melanie Klein, e.g., *The Psycho-Analysis of Children* (Hogarth Press, 1932).

90. Ronda Richardson interview, Taycheedah Correctional Inst. Interview with Gerry Mueller.

91. See, e.g., Seymore L. Halleck, *Psychiatry and the Dilemmas of Crime: A Study of Causes, Punishment, and Treatment* (University of California Press, 1967), p. 103.

92. For interpretations of de Sade and other dark thinkers as acts of rebellion against the rationalized, bureaucratized logic of the Enlightenment, see Max Horkheimer and Theodor W. Adorno, *Dialectic of Enlightenment* (Herder and Herder, 1972),

pp. 81–119 ("Excursus II, Juliette or Enlightenment and Morality"), and p. 231. See also Peter Shaffer, *Equus* (Penguin, 1974), which pits the deeper, darker needs of the self against the presumptions of psychiatry as the heir to the Enlightenment.

93. Walker, *The Battered Woman*, pp. 125–26.

94. Interview with A. V. W., Madison, Wisconsin.

95. Dorothy Allison, *Bastard out of Carolina* (Plume, 1992), pp. 306–7.

Chapter Four

1. Martin Orne, review of Reiter, *Antisocial or Criminal Acts and Hypnosis: A Case Study*, 46 American Bar Association Journal 81 (1960), in Kadish and Schulhofer, *Criminal Law and Its Processes* (Little, Brown, 1989), p. 193.

2. Walker, *The Battered Woman* (Harper and Row, 1979).

3. Del Martin, *Battered Wives* (Volcano, 1976); Erin Pizzey, *Scream Quietly or the Neighbors Will Hear You* (Penguin, 1974).

4. Susan Schechter, *Women and Male Violence: The Visions and Struggles of the Battered Women's Movement* (South End Press, 1982), pp. 1, 3, 29.

5. Buhrle v. State, 627 P. 2d 1374 (Wyo. 1981).

6. State v. Thomas, 423 N.E. 2d 137 (1981), at 139.

7. The major accounts of these trials are Faith McNulty, *The Burning Bed: The Story of an Abused Wife* (Avon, 1980); and Steven Englund, *Manslaughter* (Doubleday, 1983).

8. State v. Wanrow, 559 P. 2d 548 (1977). Quoting Frotniero v. Richardson, 411 U.S. 677 (1973), at 684.

9. See, e.g., State v. Bailey, 591 P. 2d 1212 (Wash. App. 1979). State v. Dokken, 385 N.W. 2d (S.D. 1986).

10. Schulhofer, "The Gender Question in Criminal Law," 7 Social Philosophy and Policy 105 (1990), p. 120.

11. Ibn-Tamas v. U.S., 407 A. 2d 626 (D.C. 1979), at 639.

12. State v. Anaya, 438 A. 2d 892 (Me. 1981), esp. at 894.

13. State v. Dozier, 255 S.E. 2d 552 (W.Va. 1979).

14. State v. Baker, 424 A. 2d 171 (1980).

15. Smith v. State, 277 S.E. 2d 678 (981); see also Chapman v. State, 386 S.E. 2d 129 (1989).

16. State v. Kelly, 655 P. 2d 1202 (1982); State v. Ciskie, 751 P. 2d 1165 (1988).

17. State v. Leidholm, 334 N.W. 2d 811 (N.D. 1983).

18. People v. Minnis, 455 N.E. 2d 209 (1983).

19. State v. Kelly, 478 A. 2d 364 (1984); State v. Frost, 577 A. 2d 1282 (N.J. 1990).

20. Terry v. State, 467 So. 2d 761 (Fla. Dist. Ct. App. 1985).

21. State v. Hundley, 693 P. 2d 475 (1985); State v. Stewart, 763 P. 2d 572 (1988).

22. People v. Aris, 215 Cal. App. 3d 1178 (1989).

23. Commonwealth v. Craig, 783 S.W. 2d 387 (Ky. 1990).

24. State v. Williams, 787 S.W. 2d 308 (Mo. Ct. App. 1990).

25. See Schmitz, "S.C.C. Allows 'Battered Woman Syndrome Defense,' " Lawyer's Weekly, May 25, 1990, p. 1, col. 1. Cited in Hugh Breyer, "The Battered Woman

Syndrome and the Admissibility of Expert Testimony," 1992 Criminal Law Bulletin, p. 110.

26. State v. Buhrle, 627 P. 2d 1374.

27. State v. Necaise, 466 So. 2d 660 (La. Ct. App. 1985), at 664–65.

28. State v. Martin, 712 S.W. 2d 14 (Ct. App. Mo. 1986). See also State v. Martin, 666 S.W. 2d 895 (Mo. App. 1984), at 899–900. State v. Anderson, 785 S.W. 2d 596 (Mo. App. 1990).

29. State v. Moore, 695 P. 2d 985 (1985).

30. See Breyer, "The Battered Woman Syndrome and the Admissibility of Expert Testimony," p. 112.

31. State v. Koss, 551 N.E. 2d 970 (Ohio 1990), at 972.

32. State v. Koss, 551 N.E. 2d 970, at 973–74. Quoting State v. Kelly, 478 A. 2d 364 (1984), at 378. Emphasis in Koss opinion.

33. State v. Hennum, 441 N.W. 2d 793 (Minn. 1989), at 798.

34. See Comment, "Battered Wives Who Kill: Double Standard Out of Court, Single Standard In?" 2 Law and Human Behavior 133 (1979), p. 164.

35. See State v. Poling, 1991 Ohio App. Lexis 2294; State v. Hennum, 441 N.W. 2d 793 (Minn. 1989); Chapman v. State, 386 S.E. 2d 129 (Ga. 1989); State v. Norman, 378 S.E. 2d 8 (N.C. 1989); State v. Manning, 1991 Ohio App. Lexis 2111; State v. Stewart, 763 P. 2d 572 (Kan. 1988); Commonwealth v. Dollman, 541 A. 2d 319 (Penn. 1988); State v. Aucoin, 756 S.W. 2d 705 (Tenn. Crim. App. 1988); State v. Briand, 547 A. 2s 319 (Pa. 1988); Hill v. State, 507 So. 2d 554 (Ct. Crim. App. Ala. 1986).

36. See, e.g., State. v. Walker, 700 P. 2d 1168 (Wash. Ct. App. 1985), at 1172 (presence of BWS alone, without presence of aggressive act by husband, does not require self-defense instruction); and cases to be discussed below.

37. See, e.g., Commonwealth v. Stonehouse, 555 A. 2d 772 (Pa. 1989), at 784. See also Fiedler v. State, 683 S.W. 2d 565 (Tex. Ct. App. 1985), at 595, rev'd, 765 S.W. 2d 309 (Tex. Crim. App. 1988).

38. Chapman v. State, 386 S.E. 2d 129 (Ga. 1989), at 131.

39. Fielder v. State, 683 S.W. 2d 565 (Tex. App. 2 Dist. 1985), at 588.

40. State v. Anderson, 785 S.W. 2d 596 (Mo. App. 1990), at 600.

41. State v. Norman, 378 S.E. 2d 8 (N.C. 1989), at 13. For similar logic, see State v. Stewart, 763 P. 2d 572 (Kan. 1988), at 577.

42. State v. Manning, 1991 Oh. App. Lexis 2111, at *20–21.

43. See Lenore Walker, R. K. Thyfault, and Angela Browne, "Beyond the Juror's Ken: Battered Women," 7 Vermont Law Review 1 (1982). In *The Battered Woman*, pp. 19–31, Walker lists twenty-one myths BWS is designed to counter. I have discussed the most important ones.

44. Walker, *Terrifying Love: Why Battered Women Kill and How Society Responds* (Harper Collins, 1989), pp. 256–7. See also pp. 10–14.

45. Note, "Battered Women's Syndrome and Premenstrual Syndrome: A Comparison of Their Possible Use as Defenses to Criminal Liability," 59 St. John's Law Review 558 (1985), pp. 563–65.

46. Walker, *The Battered Woman*, pp. 49–50. Emphasis added. See also Jane Tot-

man, *The Murderess: A Psychological Study of Criminal Homicide* (R. & E. Research Associates, 1978), pp. 49 and 55.

47. Walker, *Terrifying Love,* p. 50. Seligman, *Helplessness: On Depression, Development, and Death* (W. H. Freeman, 1975).

48. See People v. Aris, 264 Cal. Rptr. 167 (Cal. App. 4 Dist. 1989), which describes BWS as a form of PTSD in contradistinction to a "mental illness."

49. Walker, *The Battered Woman Syndrome,* (Springer, 1948), chap. 10.

50. Walker, *The Battered Woman Syndrome,* pp. 82–85.

51. Walker, *The Battered Woman Syndrome,* p. 84

52. Walker, *The Battered Woman Syndrome,* p. 85.

53. Walker, *The Battered Woman Syndrome,* p. 80.

54. Such pleasing is an inherent problem in all such surveys and laboratory experiments with human subjects. See Stanley Milgram, *Obedience to Authority* (Harper & Row, 1974).

55. Walker, *The Battered Woman Syndrome,* pp. 81–82.

56. Walker, *The Battered Woman Syndrome,* pp. 78–79.

57. Walker, *The Battered Woman Syndrome,* p. 79.

58. Herman, *Trauma and Recovery: The Aftermath of Violence—From Domestic Abuse to Political Terror* (Basic Books, 1992), pp. 118–19.

59. Herman, *Trauma and Recovery,* p. 121.

60. Herman, *Trauma and Recovery,* p. 92–93.

61. DSM-IV (American Psychiatric Association, 1994), sect. 308.3.

62. People v. Day, 2 Cal. App. 4th 405 (1992).

63. Gondolf, *Battered Women as Survivors: An Alternative to Treating Learned Helplessness* (Lexington Books, 1988), pp. 16, 37, 21–22. See also Lee Bowker, *Beating Wife Beating* (Lexington Books, 1983).

64. Gondolf, *Battered Women as Survivors,* p. 16; T. Mills, "The Assault on the Self: Stages in Coping with Battering Husbands," 8 Qualitative Sociology 103 (1985). Interview with inmate, Taycheedah Correctional Inst.

65. Jessica Benjamin, *The Bonds of Love: Psychoanalysis, Feminism, and the Problem of Domination* (Pantheon, 1988), pp. 9–10.

66. See, e.g., Karen Horney, *Feminine Psychology* (Norton, 1967), p. 214; de Beauvoir, *The Second Sex* (Vintage, 1989), pp. 397ff.

67. Natalie Shaines, *Sweet Suffering: Woman as Victim* (Bobbs-Merrill, 1984), p. 127. See also Sheila Isenberg's discussion of the self-defeating patterns of women who love men imprisoned for murder in *Women Who Love Men Who Kill* (Dell, 1991), pp. 11, 13.

68. Michelle A. Masse, *In the Name of Love: Women, Masochism, and the Gothic* (Cornell University Press, 1992), pp. 44–51. Masse quotes Benjamin, *Bonds of Love,* p. 31. On how the powerless and oppressed seek power and esteem through subversive (often symbolic) acts which are products of their situation, see James Scott, *Weapons of the Weak: Everyday Forms of Peasant Resistance* (Yale University Press, 1985).

69. See Edward Shorter, *From Paralysis to Fatigue: A History of Psychosomatic Illness in the Modern Era* (Free Press, 1992). On mental illness as a function of social

condition in terms of etiology and construction, see Michel Foucault, *Mental Illness and Psychiatry* (University of California Press, 1987).

70. Morse Peckham, *Art and Pornography* (Basic Books, 1969), p. 216. Roger Scruton depicts mild forms of masochism and sadism as normal forms of sexuality, so long as they are integrated into a larger humanistic sexuality. See Scruton, *Sexual Desire: A Moral Theory of the Erotic* (Free Press, 1986), pp. 298–301. In *The Ego and the Mechanisms of Defense* (International Universities Press, 1942), Anna Freud provides several interesting examples of children who "reverse" a power relation in fantasy in order to ward off anxiety and threats to the ego. This reversal is similar to the inner vision of masochism. See also Pauline Reage, *Story of O* (Grove Press, 1965); and Horney, *Feminine Psychology*, "The Problem of Feminine Masochism," pp. 228–29 (feminine masochism as a weak form of the will to power).

71. Rene Girard, *Violence and the Sacred* (Johns Hopkins, 1977), esp. chapter 1.

72. Nietzsche's Zarathustra teaches that "the pure spirit is a pure lie." In other words, the pure motive can also be a pure lie. *Thus Spoke Zarathustra*, in Walter Kaufmann, ed., *The Portable Nietzsche* (Viking, 1954).

73. Don Dutton and Susan Lee Painter, "Traumatic Bonding: The Development of Emotional Attachments in Battered Women and Other Relationships of Intermittent Abuse," 6 Victimology 139 (1983), p. 139.

74. Interview with inmate, Taycheedah Correctional Inst.

75. Dutton and Painter, "Traumatic Bonding," pp. 145–46.

76. Ibn-Tamas v. U.S., 407 A. 2d 626 (1979); U.S. v. Hearst, 412 F. Supp. 889 (1976). See Edith Greene, Allan Raitz, and Heidi Lindblad, "Juror's Knowledge of Battered Women," 4 Journal of Family Violence 105 (1989), pp. 106–7.

77. Dee L. R. Graham, Edna Rawlings, and Nelly Rimini, "Survivors of Terror: Battered Women, Hostages, and the Stockholm Syndrome," in Yllo and Bograd, *Feminist Perspectives on Wife Abuse*, (Sage Publications, 1988), pp. 218–19. U.S. v. Kozminski, 821 F. 2d 1186 (6th Cir. 1987), at 1194. See application in State v. Dunn, 758 P. 2d 718 (Kans. 1988), at 727 (defense denied because defendant went along for the murderous ride).

78. A. Freud, *The Ego and the Mechanisms of Defense* (International Universities Press, 1942), chap. 9. See also Krystal, *Massive Psychic Trauma* (International Universities Press, 1968), pp. 29, 65, 85, 333, 343–44.

79. Dutton and Painter, "Traumatic Bonding," pp. 150–51.

80. Herman, *Trauma and Recovery*, p. 92. Emphasis added.

81. Foucault, "Truth and Power," in *Power/Knowledge: Selected Interviews and Other Writings* (Pantheon, 1980), p. 119. See also Stanton Peele, with Archie Brodsky, *Love and Addiction* (Taplinger Publishing Co., 1975).

82. Interview with inmate, Taycheedah Correctional Inst.

83. Interview with John Burr, Assistant Dane County D.A. For Richardson, David Sherman was a vehicle of transcendence and esteem.

84. Virginia Woolf, *A Room of One's Own* (Harcourt Brace Jovanovich, 1957), p. 35.

85. Benjamin, *The Bonds of Love*, p. 12. On the interdependency of individuals

and love as getting "lost in the other," see Julia Kristeva, *Tales of Love* (Columbia University Press, 1987), p. 4.

86. Benjamin, *The Bonds of Love*, p. 21.

87. Benjamin, *The Bonds of Love*, pp. 31–32. See Hegel, *The Phenomenology of Mind* (Harper, 1967), pp. 229–32.

88. See Jacques Lacan, *The Four Fundamental Concepts of Psycho-Analysis* (Norton, 1981), concept of the "lack," esp. pp. ix, 203–5, 214–15.

89. Julia Kristeva, *Tales of Love*, p. 15. Jean-Paul Sartre, *Being and Nothingness*, (Washington Square, 1966), part three, chapter 3, "Concrete Relations with Others," discusses the inevitability of sadomasochistic feelings in relationships because of the nature of human relations. Interview with Ronda Richardson, Taycheedah Correctional Inst.

90. Model Penal Code, sect. 3.09(2).

91. See, e.g., State v. Kutchara, 350 N.W. 2d 924 (Minn. 1984); compare, Faulkner v. State, 458 A. 2d 81 (Md. Ap. 1983).

92. Interview with Nora Cashen.

93. Rosen, "On Self-Defense, Imminence, and Women Who Kill Their Batterers," 71 North Carolina Law Review 371 (1993), p. 398.

Chapter Five

1. Interview with inmate, Taycheedah Correctional Inst.

2. Gerry Mueller interview. Ann Jacobs, co-chair of the Richardson retrial, agreed with this assessment. Interview with Ann Jacobs. Interviews with jurors. State v. Richardson, Marion Hutchinson, psychologist. Transcript of hearing, February 11, 1993. File no. 92-CF-574.

3. Dennis Burke interview. Bob Donohoo interview. See also Patti Seeger interview, Nora Cashen interview, Linda Dawson interview . And interview with Deirdre Wilson Garton, Assistant D.A., Dane County.

4. Interview with Dennis Burke; Evan Gerstmann, comment to me.

5. Dale Cobb telephone interview.

6. Patti Seeger interview.

7. Schulhofer, "The Gender Question in Criminal Law," 7 Social Philosophy and Policy 105 (1990), p. 120.

8. Bennett and Feldman, *Reconstructing Reality in the Courtroom: Justice and Judgment in American Culture* (Rutgers University Press, 1981), p. 66.

9. Bennett and Feldman, *Reconstructing Reality in the Courtroom*, pp. 6, 10, 32. See also Kenneth Burke, *A Grammar of Motives* (University of California Press, 1969).

10. Bennett and Feldman, *Reconstructing Reality in the Courtroom*, p. 59. See also 57–59, 152–54. Willard Gaylin depicts the success of a psychological victimization narrative vis-à-vis competing narratives in *The Killing of Bonnie Garland: A Question of Justice* (Penguin, 1983), pp. 111–12. "The killing of Bonnie Garland was a tragedy, but a different tragedy when viewed from the different perspectives of religion, psychiatry, and the law. . . . Bonnie and Richard's story was to be the subject of four different and contradictory tellings—from the perspective of religion, psychiatry, prosecution, and defense."

11. Walker, *Terrifying Love: Why Battered Women Kill and How Society Responds* (Harper Collins, 1989), pp. 14–15.

12. McNulty, *The Burning Bed: The Story of an Abused Wife* (Avon, 1980).

13. Nightline, February 4, 1994 ABC, Lisa Kelmer statement.

14. Prof. Charles Weisselberg, U.S.C. Law School, quoted in "Bobbitt Verdict: Service of Justice or Media Circus? Jurors May Feel Pressured in High-Profile Court Cases," Boston Globe, Saturday, January 22, 1994, p. 6.

15. David G. Myers, *Social Psychology* (McGraw Hill, 1993), p. 84. Fifth Edition.

16. Closing Argument by Defense, State v. Richardson, February 1993.

17. Interview with Prof. Walter Dickey, U.W. Madison Law School. Dickey is the former Warden of the Corrections System for the state of Wisconsin, and a contributor to the Wisconsin legal code.

18. Stephen Hurley interview. I should also note that Hurley personally disagrees with the syndrome, particularly because he believes that self-defensive force is never justified outside the context of imminent danger. Of course, as a lawyer he uses it for his clients without qualifications. I will discuss Hurley's view in the next chapter. For critical commentary of this use, see Acker and Toch, "Battered Women, Straw Men, and Expert Testimony: A Comment on State v. Kelly," 21 Criminal Law Bulletin 125 (1985).

19. See Jean-Paul Sartre, *Being and Nothingness* (Washington Square Press, 1966), part 4, esp. pp. 707–11.

20. Myers, *Social Psychology*, p. 83. See generally, pp. 78–79, 82–86.

21. See Mark Kelman, "Interpretive Construction in the Substantive Criminal Law," 33 Stanford Law Review 591 (1981). Or, in Kalven and Zeisel's terms, the jury simply exercises a moral judgment that transcends any particular legal standards (the "nullification hypothesis"). Harry Kalven, Jr. and Hans Zeisel, *The American Jury* (Little, Brown, 1966).

22. See Alan Chaikin and John M. Darley, "Victim or Perpetrator? Defensive Attribution and the Need for Order and Justice," 25 Journal of Personality and Social Psychology, p. 268. Nietzsche had keen insight into how the psychology of blaming is related to notions of justice.

23. George Fletcher, *A Crime of Self-Defense: Bernard Goetz and the Law on Trial* (Free Press, 1988), p. 27. Self-defense cases also provide classic opportunities for what Kalven and Zeisel call the "liberation hypothesis" (i.e., when the jury feels entitled to go beyond or against the written law). Kalven and Zeisel, *The American Jury*, pp. 231–36. On how all standards of criminal law are subject to narrow or broad interpretations, see Kelman, "Interpretive Construction in the Substantive Criminal Law."

24. MacKinnon, "Toward Feminist Jurisprudence," 34 Stanford Law Review 703 (1982), p. 726.

25. Leo Katz, *Bad Acts and Guilty Minds: The Conundrums of Criminal Law* (University of Chicago Press, 1987), p. 49. See Polanyi, *Personal Knowledge: Towards a Post-Critical Philosophy* (University of Chicago Press, 1962), esp. chap. 5, "Articulation."

26. State v. Kelley, 478 A. 2d 364 (1984), at 377. On BWS and RTS as means to counter such misconceptions, see Susan Murphy, "Assisting the Jury in Understanding Victimization: Expert Psychological Testimony on Battered Woman Syndrome

and Rape Trauma Syndrome," 25 Columbia Journal of Law and Social Problems 277 (1992), p. 298.

27. People v. Torres, 488 N.Y. S. 2d at 358. Emphasis added.

28. See, e.g., Julie Blackman, *Intimate Violence: A Study of Injustice* (Columbia University Press, 1989). For other cases based on this notion, see Smith v. State, 277 S.E. 2d 678 (Ga. 1981), at 683; State v. Allery, 682 P. 2d 312 (Wa. 1984), at 316; State v. Anaya, 438 A. 2d 892 (Me. 1981), at 894.

29. People v, Aris, 264 Cal. Rptr. 167 (Cal. App. 4 Dist. 1989), at 177.

30. People v, Aris, 264 Cal. Rptr. 167 (Cal. App. 4 Dist. 1989), at 177.

31. Commonwealth v. Stonehouse, 555 A. 2d 772 (Pa. 1989), at 774, and fn. 1.

32. Commonwealth v. Stonehouse, 555 A. 2d 772 (Pa. 1989), at 779–80.

33. Commonwealth v. Stonehouse, 555 A. 2d 772 (Pa. 1989), at 783.

34. Commonwealth v. Stonehouse, 555 A. 2d 772 (Pa. 1989), at 784. Emphasis in original.

35. Commonwealth v. Stonehouse, 555 A. 2d 772 (Pa. 1989), at 783. Quoting State v. Hundley, 693 P. 2d 475 (1985), at 479.

36. Commonwealth v. Craig, 783 S.W. 2d 387 (Ky. 1990), at 388.

37. Commonwealth v. Watson, 431 A. 2d 949 (Pa. 1981), at 951–52. Emphasis added. Cited in Commonwealth v. Stonehouse, 555 A. 2d 772 (Pa. 1989), at 783. Quoting State v. Hundley, 693 P. 2d 475 (1985), at 781–82.

38. People v. Yokum, 302 P. 2d 406 (Cal. Ct. App. 1956), at 416.

39. See Kalven and Zeisel, *The American Jury*; Mortimer R. Kadish and Sanford H. Kadish, *Discretion to Disobey: A Study of Legal Departures from Legal Rules* (Stanford University Press, 1973).

40. Lon Fuller, *Legal Fictions* (Stanford University Press, 1967), pp. 10–11. See also pp. 70–71. Timothy Litton of Capital Law School in Columbus, Ohio, alerted me to the connections between BWS and Fuller's notion of legal fictions during a talk I gave at Ohio State Law School in Spring 1993.

41. People v. Aris, 264 Cal. Rptr. 167 (Cal. App. 4 Dist. 1989), at 174.

42. Aristotle, *Nichomachean Ethics* (Oxford University Press, The World's Classics, 1954), pp. 132–36, 152–53.

43. Interview with Dennis Reilly, Domestic Crimes Bureau, Madison Police Department.

44. Interview with John Burr, Assistant District Attorney, Dane County.

45. Linda Dawson interview.

46. Herbert Wechsler and Jerome Michael, "A Rationale for the Law of Homicide," 37 Columbia Law Review 701 (1937), p. 740.

47. See Mira Mihajlovich, "Does Plight Make Right: The Battered Woman Syndrome, Expert Testimony and the Law of Self-Defense," 62 Indiana Law Journal 1253 (1987), p. 1274.

48. On the way in which too strong a reliance on "equity" and substantive justice undermines the integrity of legality, see Roberto Mangabiera Unger, *Law in Modern Society* (Free Press, 1977), chap. 3. Unger underscores how such reliance compromised the integrity and equal protection of the law in Weimar and Nazi Germany.

49. See Arthur Kleinman, *The Illness Narratives: Suffering, Healing, and the Human Condition* (Basic Books, 1988), chap. 1, "The Meaning of Symptoms and Disorders," p. 26.

50. Schulhofer, "The Gender Question in Criminal Law,"; Rosen, "On Self-Defense, Imminence, and Women Who Kill Their Batterers," 71 North Carolina Law Review 371 (1993).

51. LaFave and Scott, *Criminal Law* (West Publishing Co, 1986), Second Edition., p. 444.

52. MPC, 3.02

53. State v. Moe, 24 P. 2d 638 (1933) (economic necessity); People v. Whipple, 279 P. 1008 (1929) (prison escape); Dempsey v. U.S., 283 F. 2d 934 (5th Cir. 1960) (prison escape); U.S. v. Dorrell, 758 F. 2d 427 (9th Cir. 1985) (entry and painting of military base); Cleveland v. Municipality of Anchorage, 631 P. 2d 1073 (Alaska, 1981) (trespass at abortion clinic).

54. See LaFave and Scott, *Criminal Law*, p. 444 and cases cited therein.

55. See, generally, LaFave and Scott, *Criminal Law*, pp. 445–50, from which I draw the analysis in this paragraph.

56. Fletcher, *Rethinking Criminal Law* (Little, Brown, 1978), p. 795. Emphasis added.

57. Fletcher, *Rethinking Criminal Law*, p. 780. In American jurisprudence, Ronald Dworkin's notion of legal "principle" comes close to this understanding. See *Taking Rights Seriously* (Harvard University Press, 1977).

58. Fletcher, *Rethinking Criminal Law*, pp. 786–88.

59. Kant, *Introduction to the Science of Right* (N. Hastie, trans. 1887), discussed in Fletcher, *Rethinking Criminal Law*, p. 819. Fletcher, *Rethinking Criminal Law*, p. 820.

60. Regina v. Dudley and Stephens, 14 Q.B.D. 273 (1884), at 287. See also U.S. v. Holmes, 1 Wall Jr. 1, 226 Fcd. Cas. 360 (No. 15, 383) (3d Cir., 1842), for a similar case.

61. Katz, *Bad Acts and Guilty Minds*, pp. 13, 41, 61.

62. Rosen, "On Self-Defense," p. 380.

63. Prof. Charles Weisselberg, U.S.C. Law School, quoted in "Bobbitt Verdict: Service of Justice or Media Circus? Jurors May Feel Pressured in High-Profile Court Cases," Boston Globe, Saturday, January 22, 1994, p. 6.

64. On the significance of informal justice, see Arthur Rosett and Donald R. Kressey, *Justice by Consent: Plea Bargains in the American Courthouse* (J. B. Lippincott, 1976).

65. Interview with Beverly Brickford, Domestic Violence Unit, Dane County Prosecutor's Office.

66. Interview with Dale Cobb.

67. Interview with Linda Dawson.

68. Interview with Dennis Reilly, detective in Domestic Crimes Bureau.

69. Story from Nora Cashen interview.

70. Interview with Stephen Hurley.

71. Interview with John Burr.

72. Interview with Jeff Hook, Madison Police Officer.

73. As reported by Cindy Kollath and Gerry Mueller.

74. U.S. v. Homick, 964 F. 2d 899 (9th Cir. 1992), at 905.

75. U.S. v. Gregory, 1988 WL 93949 1 (N.D. Ill), p. 2.

76. U.S. v. Johnson, 965 F. 2d 894 (9th Cir. 1992), at 898–902.

77. U.S. v. Johnson, 965 F. 2d 894 (9th Cir. 1992), at 898.

78. U.S. v. Johnson, 965 F. 2d 894 (9th Cir. 1992), at 899.

79. U.S. v. Johnson, 965 F. 2d 894 (9th Cir. 1992), at 900.

80. U.S. v. Gaviria, 804 F. Supp. 476 (1992), at 477.

81. U.S. v. Gaviria, 804 F. Supp. 476 (1992), at 478.

82. U.S. v. Gaviria, 804 F. Supp. 476 (1992), at 478. See also U.S. v. Whitetail, 956 F. 2d 857 (8th Cir. 1992), at 863–64. For a federal battered woman decision that seems harsh and goes the other way on this issue, see U.S. v. Santos, 932 F. 2d 244 (1991).

83. Strickland v. Washington, 466 U.S. 668 (1984).

84. People v. Day, 2 Cal. Rptr. 2d 916 (Cal. App. 5 Dist. 1992), at 923–24.

85. People v. Romero, 10 Cal. App. 4th 1150 (1992), at 1159–60.

86. Neeley v. State, 1993 Ala. Crim. App. LEXIS 908, *44 (p. 17).

87. See, e.g., State v. Baker, 1992 WL 168842 (Ohio App. 3 Dist.), p. 2.

88. U.S. v. Sebresos, unpublished opinion, 972 F. 2d 1347 (9th Cir. 1992), p. 3.

89. Schneider, "Particularity and Generality: Challenges of Feminist Theory and Practice in Work on Woman-Abuse" 67 New York University Law Review 520 (1992), p. 556. See also Phyllis Chesler, *Mothers on Trial: The Battle for Children and Custody* (1986); "Report of the New York Task Force on Women in the Courts," 15 Fordham Urban Law Journal 1 (1986–87), pp. 105–7.

90. See, e.g., Naomi R. Cahn, "Civil Images of Battered Women: The Impact of Domestic Violence on Child Custody Decisions," 44 Vanderbilt Law Review 1041 (1991). Linda R. Keenan, "Domestic Violence and Custody Litigation: The Need for Statutory Reform," 13 Hofstra Law Review 407 (1985).

91. On Texas and other state legislation, see Lewelling v. Lewelling, 796 S.W. 2d 164 (Tex. 1990); Texas Statutes, 14.01 (c) (2). On the Congressional resolution, see Knock v. Knock, 1993 WL 54358 (Conn.), *5; H.R. Con. Res. 172, 101st Congress, 2d Sess. (1990). See also "Family Violence Project, Family Violence: Improving Court Practice," 41 Juvenile and Family Court Journal (1990), pp. 19–20.

92. Santosky v. Kramer, 455 U.S. 745 (1982), at 753.

93. Lewelling v. Lewelling, 796 S.W. 2d 164 (Tex. 1990), at 167–68.

94. Walker, *Terrifying Love*, p. 7.

95. 1995 Wisconsin Senate Bill 138. Interview with Nichole Burgess, legislative assistant to Senator Brian Burke. Burgess also sent me a packet of materials on this issue that Burke is using.

96. Press Release, Senator Paul Wellstone, March 9, 1995, p. 1.

97. American Political Network, Inc. Health Line, March 9, 1995. Emphasis added.

98. Robinson v. California, 370 U.S. 660 (1962).

99. Lewelling v. Lewelling, 796 S.W. 2d 164 (Tex. 1990), at 165.

100. In re Int. of J.B. and A.P., 453 N.W. 2d 477 (Neb. 1990). T.P. was later found guilty of murder and child neglect.

101. In re Interest of C.P., 455 N.W. 2d 138 (Neb. 1990), at 144.

102. In re Interest of C.P., 455 N.W. 2d 138 (Neb. 1990), at 145.

103. In re Interest of C.P., 455 N.W. 2d 138 (Neb. 1990), at 145.

104. In Interest of Betty J.W., 371 S.E. 2d 326 (W.Va. 1988), at 330. West Virginia passed an improvement period statute in 1984: W. Va. Code, 44–6–2 (b), 1984.

105. In Interest of Betty J.W., 371 S.E. 2d 326 (W.Va. 1988), at 331.

106. In Interest of Betty J.W., 371 S.E. 2d 326 (W.Va. 1988), at 332.

107. Knock v. Knock, 1993 WL 54358 (Conn.), *6.

108. See Schiro v. Clark, 963 F. 2d 962 (1992).

109. For a critique of this "misuse" of MacKinnon's logic, see my former student, Martin Jay Sweet, "Blocking the Backlash: Against the Pornography Defense," 4 Kansas Journal of Law and Public Policy 23 (Fall, 1994). I predicted such disingenuous use of MacKinnon's logic in *The New Politics of Pornography* (University of Chicago Press, 1989), p. 158. Sweet and I agree on the illegitimacy of the "pornography defense," but Sweet contends that its logic betrays MacKinnon's logic.

110. Marion Smiley, *Moral Responsibility and the Boundaries of Community: Power and Accountability from a Pragmatic Point of View* (University of Chicago Press, 1992), chap. 7.

111. People of the State of Illinois v. Elijah Stanciel, Supreme Court of Illinois, Springfield, 73097, 73184 cons. Emphasis added.

112. Minn. Stat. sec. 609.378 (1984) See also, e.g., Iowa Code Ann. sect. 726.6.1e (West Supp. 1986); Okla. Stat. Ann. tit. 21, sec. 852.1.a (Supp. 1990).

113. Anne T. Johnson, "Criminal Liability for Parents Who Fail to Protect," 5 Law and Inequality 395 (1987), p. 397.

114. Schneider, "Particularity and Generality," pp. 553–54.

115. See, e.g., Lott v. State, 686 S.W. 2d 304 (Tex. App. 1 Dist. 1985); Phelps v. State, 439 So. 2d 727 (Ala. Ct. App. 1983); State v. Williams, 670 P. 2d 122 (N.M. App. Ct. 1983); Commonwealth v. Cardwell, 515 A. 2d 311 (Pa. Super. 1986); Commonwealth v. Howard, 402 A. 2d 674 (Pa. Super. 1979); State v. Willaquette, 385 N.W. 2d 145 (Wisc. 1986); Commonwealth v. Lazorich, 574 N.E. 2d 340 (Mass. 1991).

116. See, e.g., Worthington v. State, 409 N.E. 2d 1261; State v. Kamel, 466 N.E. 2d 860 (Ohio 1984); State v. Portiga, 481 A. 2d 534 (N.H. 1984).

117. See Herbert C. Kelman and V. Lee Hamilton, *Crimes of Obedience: Toward a Social Psychology of Authority and Responsibility* (Yale University Press, 1989).

118. State v. Willaquette, 385 N.W. 2d 145 (Wis. 1986), at 150, 151.

119. Neeley v. State, 1993 Ala. Crim. App. LEXIS 908, *44 (p. 17).

Chapter Six

1. Cathryn J. Rosen, "The Excuse of Self-Defense: Correcting a Historical Accident on Behalf of Battered Women Who Kill," 36 American University Law Review 11 (1986), p. 43.

2. Holly Maguigan, "Battered Women and Self-Defense: Myths and Misconceptions in Current Reform Proposals," 140 University of Pennsylvania Law Review 379 (1991), pp. 388–89.

3. Maguigan, "Battered Women and Self-Defense: Myths and Misconceptions in

Current Reform Proposals," 140 University of Pennsylvania Law Review 379 (1991), p. 397.

4. See Rosen, "On Self-Defense, Imminence, and Women Who Kill Their Batterers" 71 North Carolina Law Review 371 (1993).

5. Blackstone, *Commentaries on the Laws of England* (R. Welch & Co., 1897), p. 1602.

6. Ann Jones, *Women Who Kill* (Fawcett Crest, 1980), chap. 3.

7. Gillespie, *Justifiable Homicide: Battered Women, Self-Defense, and the Law* (Ohio State University Press, 1989), pp. 48–49. Williams v. State, 70 S.W. 756 (Tex. Cr. App. 1902). The other two cases are Cotten v. State, 9 So. 287 (Ala. 1891); Bowman v. State, 20 S.W.

8. Interestingly, the creator of BWS, Lenore Walker, and two compatriots mention Jones's finding in an article designed to show the need for BWS in trials. But the literature on the whole is largely silent about this fact. See Lenore E. Walker, R. K. Thyfault, and Angela Browne, "Beyond the Juror's Ken: Battered Women," 7 Vermont Law Review 1 (1982), p. 2.

9. Defense Strategy meeting after preliminary hearing in State v. Richardson, August 1992. See also interviews with Gerry Mueller and John Moyer, Public Defenders, Kenosha, Wisconsin. And Moyer note to Mueller, Kollath, and Peters, November 3, 1992, on self-defense.

10. See, e.g., George Fletcher, "Convicting the Victim," New York Times, February 7, 1994, p. A11; and John Taylor, "Irresistible Impulses, Why America Has Lost Its Capacity to Convict the Guilty," Esquire, April 1994, pp. 96–98.

11. Law and Order, NBC, March 9, 1994.

12. See, e.g., Ralph Slovenko, "The Insanity Defense in the Wake of the Hinckley Trial," 14 Rutgers Law Journal 373 (1983); Kadish and Schulhofer, *Criminal Law and Its Processes* (Little, Brown, 1989), chap. 8.

13. The success of books like Robert Hughes's *Culture of Complaint: The Fraying of America* (Oxford University Press, 1993) and Charles Sykes's *A Nation of Victims: The Decay of the American Character* (St. Martin's, 1992) show that the claim of omnipresent victimization is now highly contested.

14. See Martin Jay Sweet, "Blocking the Backlash: Against the Pornography Defense," 4 Kansas Journal of Law and Public Policy (1994).

15. See the discussion of Herman in the following chapter. Herman, *Trauma and Recovery: The Aftermath of Violence—From Domestic Abuse to Political Terror* (Basic Books, 1992); Miller, *Banished Knowledge: Facing Childhood Injuries* (Doubleday, 1990). MacKinnon and Dworkin's claim that most heterosexual sex is tantamount to rape points to the same destination.

16. See, e.g., Bayer, *Homosexuality and American Psychiatry: The Politics of Diagnosis* (Princeton University Press, 1987); Scott, "PTSD in DSM-III: A Case in the Politics of Diagnosis and Disease," 37 Social Problems 294 (1990).

17. See Gerald L. Klerman, "Classification and DSM-III-R," in *The New Harvard Guide to Psychiatry* (Harvard University Press, 1988), pp. 70–87.

18. See Peter Berger, "Towards a Sociological Understanding of Psychoanalysis," 32 Social Research 26 (1965).

19. A similar problem of legitimacy accompanied the expansion of the modern administrative state, one might add. See Harvey C. Mansfield, Jr., *America's Constitutional Soul* (Johns Hopkins, 1991). The growth of the state has also fed the growth of psychiatry as a field—public money and authority have financed and legislated broad use of psychiatry to maintain order and public health. See, e.g., Castel et al, *The Psychiatric Society* (Columbia University Press, 1982).

20. Kirk and Kutchens, *The Selling of DSM: The Rhetoric of Science in Psychiatry* (Aldine de Gruyter, 1992), p. 30.

21. Kirk and Kutchens, *The Selling of DSM*. See also Robert Spitzer's Introduction to DSM-III (American Psychiatric Press, 1980).

22. George Vaillant, "The Disadvantages of DSM-III Outweigh Its Advantages," in "A Debate on DSM-III," 141 American Journal of Psychiatry 539 (1984), pp. 543–44.

23. Stephen Morse, "Crazy Behavior, Morals, and Science: An Analysis of Mental Health Law," 51 Southern California Law Review 527 (1978), p. 553.

24. The tension between reliability and validity is the key theme of Kirk and Kutchens, *The Selling of DSM*.

25. For an excellent discussion of the problem of conflating epistemology and ontology, see John R. Searle, *The Rediscovery of the Mind* (M.I.T. Press, 1988), esp. chap. 1. For a careful analysis of the relationship between social construction and reality that is independent of such construction, see Searle, *The Construction of Social Reality* (Free Press, 1995).

26. See W. W. Meissner, "Theories of Personality," in *The New Harvard Guide to Psychiatry*, pp. 171–99.

27. See, e.g., "On Being Sane in Insane Places," 179 Science 250 (1973). In this study, pseudo-patients were able to pass themselves off as "crazy" in mental hospitals in an experiment.

28. Commonwealth v. Grimshaw, 576 N.E. 2d 1374 (Mass. App. Ct. 1991), at 1375.

29. Morse, "Crazy Behavior, Morals, and Science," p. 565. Frederick Schauer calls the predisposing type of causation "proximate" or "multiple" causality. See Frederick Schauer, "Causation Theory and the Causes of Sexual Violence," in 1987 American Bar Foundation Research Journal, Symposium on the 1986 Attorney General's Commission on Pornography.

30. Morse, "Crazy Behavior, Morals, and Science," pp. 565, 571.

31. Lacan, "The Freudian Unconscious and Ours," in *The Four Fundamental Concepts of Psycho-Analysis* (Norton, 1981), p. 21: "Kant comes [close] to understanding the gap that the function of cause has always presented to any conceptual apprehension. . . . [Kant more or less states] that cause is a concept that, in the last resort, is unanalyzable."

32. Stephen J. Morse, "Failed Explanations and Criminal Responsibility: Experts and the Unconscious," 68 Virginia Law Review 971 (1982), p. 991. On the hermeneutic nature of psychoanalysis, see Ricoeur, *Freud and Philosophy: An Essay on Interpretation* (Yale University Press, 1970).

33. Even in *Psychopathology of Everyday Life*, the work that comes the closest to

making "causal" arguments about the unconscious, Freud does not make a case for psychological causation of serious acts like murder: minor acts of omissions or accidents are subject to this analysis, but even here Freud does not excuse the actors from responsibility. Freud, *Psychopathology of Everyday Life* (Norton, 1965).

34. See, e.g., Elliott Leyton, *Compulsive Killers-The Story of Modern Multiple Murder* (New York University Press, 1986); Colin Wilson, *A Casebook of Murder* (Cowles Book Co., 1069); "The Serial Killer," unpublished paper by Kristyn M. Aceto, May 1992. Dostoyevski, *Crime and Punishment* (Random House, 1950).

35. David L. Faigman, "The Battered Woman Syndrome and Self-Defense: A Legal and Empirical Dissent," 72 Virginia Law Review 619 (1986), pp. 631–32. The case Faigman focuses on is State v. Martin, 666 S.W. 2d 895 (Mo. Ct. App. 1984).

36. See, e.g., the many essays in Yllo and Bograd, *Feminist Perspectives on Wife Abuse* (Sage, 1988) and the debate between feminism and humanism in Journal of Interpersonal Violence, March 1990, discussed in chapter 3 above.

37. Polanyi, *Tacit Knowledge: Towards a Post-Critical Philosophy* (University of Chicago Press, 1958), part 1.

38. Buhrle v. Wyoming, 627 P. 2d 1374 (1981), at 1376.

39. Buhrle v. Wyoming, 627 P. 2d 1374 (1981), at 1377.

40. Walker, *Terrifying Love: Why Battered Women Kill and How Society Responds* (Harper Collins, 1989), p. xv.

41. Walker, *Terrifying Love*, p. 98. Emphasis added.

42. Walker, *Terrifying Love*, p. 175.

43. U.S. v. Gordon, 638 F. Supp. 1120 (W.D. La. 1986), at 1148. Emphasis added.

44. Elizabeth Schneider, "Describing and Changing: Women's Self-Defense Work and the Problems of Expert Testimony on Battering," cited in Charles Patrick Ewing, *Battered Women Who Kill: Psychological Self-Defense as Legal Justification* (Lexington Books, 1987), p. 56. See also Sara Lee Johann and Frank Osanka, eds., *Representing . . . Battered Women Who Kill* (Charles C. Thomas, 1989), p. 97.

45. Walker, *Terrifying Love*, p. 194.

46. Walker, *Terrifying Love*, p. 198.

47. See Walker's commentary on State v. Martin in *Terrifying Love*, pp. 286–93.

48. Morse, "Crazy Behavior, Morals, and Science," p. 627.

49. Interview with John Burr.

50. Walker, *Terrifying Love*, pp. 11, 14, 256–57. Emphasis added.

51. Maguigan, "Battered Women and Self-Defense," pp. 403, 407. For a pre-BWS case that provided for such evidence, see People v. Yokum, 302 P. 2d 406 (Cal. Ct. App. 1956), at 416.

52. See Susan Estrich, "Defending Women," 88 Michigan Law Review 1430 (1990), p. 1436.

53. *In a Different Voice: Psychological Theory and Women's Development* (Harvard University Press, 1982). For a series of pieces on Kohlberg's work, critical and supportive, see 92 Ethics, April 1982, Special Issue on Moral Development.

54. I draw heavily from a research piece provided by Evan Gerstmann in this listing of flaws in Gilligan's research.

55. Lawrence Walker, "Sex Differences in the Development of Moral Reasoning: A Critical Review," 55 Child Development 677 (1984), pp. 670, 688.

56. C. Greeno and E. Macoby, "How Different is the 'Different Voice'?" 11 Signs 310 (1986), p. 312. See also Zella Luria, "A Methodological Critique," 11 Signs 316 (1986).

57. Carol Stack, "The Culture of Gender: Women and Men of Color," 11 Signs 321 (1986), pp. 322–23.

58. See Randall Kennedy, "Racial Critiques of Legal Academia," 102 Harvard Law Review 1745 (1989), esp. 1816–17, footnote 303.

59. Interview with Nora Cashen.

60. Much of my discussion of the problems of the cycle theory is drawn from Faigman, "Battered Woman Syndrome," pp. 636–40.

61. Faigman, "Battered Woman Syndrome," p. 637.

62. Faigman, "Battered Woman Syndrome," p. 638. See also T. Cook and D. Campbell, *Quasi-Experimentation: Design and Analysis Issues for Field Settings* (1979), p. 66.

63. David J. Rothman, *The Discovery of the Asylum: Social Order and Disorder in the New Republic* (Little, Brown, 1970), pp. 70–71.

64. E. L. Quarantelli, " An Assessment of Conflicting Views on Mental Health: The Consequences of Traumatic Events," in Charles R. Figley, ed., *Trauma and Its Wake*, vol. I: *The Study and Treatment of Post-traumatic Stress Disorder* (Brunner/ Mazel, 1985), chap. 9. See also Murray Edelman, *Politics and Language*, (University of Wisconsin, Inst. for Poverty, 1977).

65. John P. Jendusa, "Stress Managment and Mental Health Clinics," Report to Kathryn Bemman, M.D., Re: Lisa Skalaski, October 18, 1992. Case # CF 1114.

66. Patricia A. Jens, M.D., Dodge County Department of Human Resources, Report on Lisa Skalaski, presented to William Foust, District Attorney of Dane County. Case # 92 CF 1114, p. 8.

67. Patricia A. Jens, M.D., Report on Lisa Skalaski, pp. 14–15. On how the supporters of MPD tend to have less training and credentials than those who maintain skepticism about the disorder, see Hacking, *Rewriting the Soul: Multiple Personality and the Sciences of Memory* (Princeton University Press, 1995).

68. Faigman, "Battered Womam Syndrome," p. 638.

69. Faigman, "Battered Womam Syndrome," p. 638.

70. Faigman, "Battered Womam Syndrome," p. 640. Interviews with Richardson jurors.

71. Faigman, "Battered Womam Syndrome," pp. 639–40.

72. See R. Emerson Dobash and Russell Dobash, "The Nature and Antecedents of Violent Events," 24 British Journal of Criminology 269 (1984), pp. 280–81: only 14 percent of their sample experienced the full cycle—loving contrition was often absent. See also interviews with Maria Santos and A. V. W.

73. Martin F. P. Seligman, Steven F. Maier, and James H. Geer, "Alleviation of Learned Helplessness in the Dog," 73 Journal of Abnormal Psychology 256 (1968), pp. 260–61.

74. Faigman, "Battered Womam Syndrome," pp. 640–41.

75. Walker, *Battered Woman Syndrome*, (Springer, 1984), p. 33; see also pp. 86–94.

76. *Terrifying Love*, p. 50.

77. Interview with Maria Santos.

78. See Susan Schechter, *Women and Male Violence: The Visions and Struggles of the Battered Women's Movement* (South End Press, 1982), chaps. 3, 4, 9.

79. Interview with Patti Seeger, Dane County Advocates for Battered Women.

80. Interview with Nora Cashen. Szasz, *Insanity: The Idea and Its Consequences* (Wiley, 1987); Browne, *When Battered Women Kill* (Free Press, 1987).

81. Interview with Kathleen Kreneck, Policy Coordinator, Wisconsin Coalition against Domestic Violence.

82. Browne, *When Battered Women Kill*, in general and esp. p. 182.

83. See also State v. Poling, 1991 WL 84229 (Ohio App.). See also *Buhrle* case discussed above.

84. Walker, *Terrifying Love*, p. 91. Emphasis added.

85. In the analysis of motives and murder for hire cases, I draw extensively on research done by my excellent research assistant Ann S. Jacobs. Ann is presently a public defender in Kenosha, Wisconsin. I am indebted to Ann's work and initiative. An unpublished paper she prepared for me is entitled "Battered Woman's Syndrome: A Factual Dissent." Ann's intellectual disagreement with BWS would not compromise her advocacy in trial. It is fair to say that any battered woman who needs a defense lawyer could do no better than give Ann a call. In January 1995, Ann became co-chair in the *Richardson* retrial.

86. Interview with inmate of Taycheedah Correctional Inst.

87. I say alleged because the reality of abuse was questionable in some cases. See Jacobs, "Battered Woman's Syndrome" (see note 85), p. 6, fn. 14.

88. State v. Clark, 377 S.E. 2d 54 (N.C. 1989).

89. Walker, *Terrifying Love*, p. 284.

90. People v. Yaklich, 1991 Colo. App. Lexis 357 (Colo. 1991).

91. People v. Jackson, 535 N.E. 2d 1086 (Ill. App. 1989).

92. State v. Daniels, 734 P. 2d 1888 (Mont. 1987).

93. State v. Leaphart, 673 S.W. 2d 870 (Tenn. Crim. App. 1983). See also Martin v. State, 712 S.W. 2d 14 (Ct. App. Mo. 1986), discussed above.

94. Walker, *Terrifying Love*, p. 285.

95. People v. Yaklich, 1991 Colo. App. Lexis 357 (Colo. 1991), at 1.

96. Ann Jacobs, "Battered Woman's Syndrome," pp. 21–22, 27, 28.

97. See State v. Vigil, 794 P. 2d 728 (N.M. 1990), where an ensuing scuffle led to the shooting of the husband and a first-degree murder conviction; State v. Manning, 1991 OH App. Lexis, where a woman killed her sleeping husband for retributive reasons after finding out he had molested their daughter.

98. See State v. McClain, 591 A. 2d 652 (N.J. Sup. A.D. 1991), in which the defendant flew into a rage when her boyfriend told her he never intended to marry her or anyone, and shot him in a bar. Over a relationship of many years, he had assaulted her

twice, the last time being a few years before the fatal shooting; State v. Walker, 700 P. 2d 1168 (Ct. App. Wash. 1985).

99. State v. Pascal, 736 P. 2d 1065 (Wash. 1987). Jacobs, "Battered Woman's Syndrome," p. 32.

100. See, e.g., Yale Kamisar, American Bar Association Journal, June 1994, p. 41, cited in Alan M. Dershowitz, *The Abuse Excuse* (Little Brown, 1994), Introduction.

101. See State of Wisconsin v. Jennifer Patri, Unpublished Slip Opinion, No. 78–187-CR, Court of Appeals, District IV, December 19, 1980.

102. Englund, *Manslaughter* (Doubleday, 1983).

103. Gillespie, *Justifiable Homicide: Battered Women, Self-Defense, and the Law* (Ohio State University Press, 1989), p. 10; Jones, *Women Who Kill* (Fawcett Cress, 1980), pp. 312–14.

104. Katherine Dunn, "Fibbers: The Lies Journalists Tell," The New Republic, June 21, 1993, p. 19. See also The Wall Street Journal, "Football's Day of Dread," February 5, 1993, editorial.

105. Ewing, *Battered Women Who Kill*, p. 62. See also Kohut, *The Restoration of the Self* (International Universities Press, 1977), pp. 103–5; R. D. Laing, *The Divided Self* (Pelican, 1970), pp. 39–43.

106. See Benjamin, *The Bonds of Love: Psychoanalysis, Feminism, and the Problem of Domination* (Pantheon, 1988).

107. Perhaps because of the intensity, couples bound by battered love live on the emotional edge where sensations are often very acute—contra the notion of "learned helplessness," which assumes emotional deadening. See, e.g., Dutton and Painter, "Traumatic Bonding: The Development of Emotional Attachments in Battered Women and Other Relationships of Intermittent Abuse," 6 Victimology 139 (1983), p. 139. McNulty, *The Burning Bed: The Story of an Abused Wife* (Avon Books, 1980).

108. Jack Katz, *Seductions of Crime: Moral and Sensual Attractions in Doing Evil* (Basic Books, 1988) pp. 14, 20.

109. For further critiques, see Stephen J. Morse, "The Misbegotten Marriage of Soft Psychology and Bad Law: Psychological Self-Defense as a Justification for Homicide," 14 Law and Human Behavior 595 (1990), p. 603.

110. For a critique of Chicago's victim ideology, see Andrew Patner, "Judy Chicago's New-Age Holocaust: Exhibit Blends Meat-Eating, Patriarchy, Nuclear Weapons, and the Nazis," Forward, December 24, 1993, p. 9. In general, see Robert Hughes's *Culture of Complaint*.

111. Ewing, "Psychological Self-Defense: A Proposed Justification for Battered Women Who Kill," 14 Law and Human Behavior 586 (1990), p. 591.

112. See Kalven and Zeisel, *The American Jury* (Little, Brown, 1966), pp. 231–36. One controlled study found that an instruction on Ewing's concept secured "not guilty" verdicts in lieu of manslaughter verdicts by juries not given the instruction. But this begs the question of the justice of such decisions. See Jessica P. Greenwald, Alan J. Tomkins, Mary Kenning, and Denis Zavodny, "Psychological Self-Defense Jury Instructions: Influence on Verdicts for Battered Women Defendants," 8 Behavioral Sciences and the Law 171 (1990).

113. In October 1993 she participated in a major panel on defending battered women at the annual Wisconsin State Public Defender Criminal Defense Conference (Mueller was on another of the major panels): 1993 SPD Criminal Defense Conference, October 21 & 22, Oconomowoc, WI.

114. State v. Richardson, Transcript, File No. 92-CF-574, February 11, 1993, Testimony of Marilyn Hutchinson, p. 56.

115. Marilyn A. Hutchinson, Ph.D., Hutchinson and Associates, Psychological Evaluation of Ronda Richardson, Report date November 16, 1992, pp. 8–10.

116. Hutchinson Report, op. cit., pp. 12–13.

117. Allard, "Rethinking Battered Woman Syndrome: A Black Feminist Perspective," 1 U.C.L.A. Women's Law Journal 191 (1991), pp. 193–4, 206. Emphasis added. Quoting Sagaw, "A Hard Case for Feminists: People v. Goetz," 10 Harvard Women's Law Journal 253 (1987), p. 256, note 21.

118. Schneider, "Describing and Changing," p. 79.

119. There is an interesting literature on the sociological and psychological implications of being labeled as deviant or less than rational. See, e.g., Irving Goffman, *Asylums: Essays on the Social Situation of Mental Patients and Other Inmates* (Anchor, 1961); Howard Becker, *Outsiders: Studies in the Sociology of Deviance* (Macmillan, 1963); Edwin Schur, *Labeling Deviant Behavior* (Harper and Row, 1972).

120. U.S. v. Whitetail, 956 F. 2d 857 (1992), at 859–60.

121. Interviews with inmates, Taycheedah Correctional Inst.

122. Interviews with Richardson jurors.

123. MacKinnon, "Toward Feminist Jurisprudence," 34 Stanford Law Review 703 (1982), p. 726.

124. Mihajlovich, "Does Plight Make Right: The Battered Woman Syndrome, Expert Testimony and the Law of Self-Defense," 62 Indiana Law Journal 1253 (1987), pp. 1265–66.

125. Acker and Toch, "Battered Women, Straw Men, and Expert Testimony: A Comment on State v. Kelly" 21 Criminal Law Bulletin (1985), pp. 138–39, quoted in Mihajlovich, "Does Plight Make Right," p. 1266, emphasis by Mihajlovich.

126. Charles Ewing and Moss Aubrey, "Battered Women and Public Opinion: Some Realities and the Myths," 2 Journal of Family Violence 257 (1987).

127. Mary Dodge and Edith Greene, "Juror and Expert Conceptions of Battered Women," 6 Violence and Victims 271 (1991).

128. Ewing and Aubrey, "Battered Woman and Public Opinion," p. 261.

129. Edith Greene, Alan Raitz, and Heidi Lindblad, "Jurors' Knowledge of Battered Women," 4 Journal of Family Violence 105 (1989), p. 108.

130. Greene et al., "Jurors' Knowledge of Battered Women," p. 120.

131. Dyas v. U.S., 367 A. 2d 827 (1977). Dodge and Greene, "Juror and Expert Conceptions of Battered Women," p. 271.

132. Dodge and Greene, "Juror and Expert Conceptions of Battered Women." See Table 3a, p. 278.

133. Interview with Stephen Hurley. On this general point about expert versus lay views concerning responsibility, see, e.g., Morse, "Crazy Behavior, Morals, and Science"; "Failed Explanations and Criminal Responsibility."

134. See the discussion of the differences between "reliability" and "validity" in Kirk and Kutchens, *The Selling of DSM,* pp. 29–32.

135. Dodge and Greene, "Juror and Expert Conceptions of Battered Women," pp. 280–81. Emphases added.

136. Another syndrome has emerged in popular culture, which I will call the "Oprah syndrome." This "syndrome" refers to the impact that television shows such as the *Oprah Show* and *Geraldo,* which showcase domestic trauma, have had on popular understanding, for better or for worse. The triumph of the therapeutic in the simulacrum of mass culture was confirmed in early 1994, when Roseanne Barr's book, *My Lives* (Ballantine Books, 1994) reigned on best-seller lists. The book is a long victimization narrative and rumination on the psychological self of the popular comedian. As I browsed through the book at a local bookstore on April 1 of that year, two sales clerks struck up a conversation with me about what the book's reception meant for social psychology.

137. Gerry Mueller interview. Actually, the burden of proof (to show no self-defense) lies with the prosecution in all but two states (Ohio and South Carolina). The Supreme Court upheld this allocation of the burden of proof (by a preponderance of the evidence) in Martin v. Ohio, 480 U.S. 228 (1987).

138. Interview with Stephen Hurley, Madison attorney.

139. Schulhofer, "The Gender Question in Criminal Law," 7 Social Philosophy and Policy 105 (1990), pp. 112–15. On rotten background, see Richard Delgado, "'Rotten Social Background': Should the Criminal Law Recognize a Defense of Severe Environmental Deprivation?" 3 Law and Inequality 9 (1985).

140. State v. Shroeder, 261 N.W. 2d 759 (Neb. 1978). Shulhofer, "The Gender Question in Criminal Law," p. 115. For other "tough verdicts" against men in self-defense or related contexts, see also State v. Collins, 306 So. 2d 662 (La. S.Ct. 1975); State v. Dill, 461 So. 2d 1130 (La. App. 5 Cir. 1984), at 1137; State v. Flory, 276 P. 458 (Wyo. 1929).

141. George Fletcher, *Rethinking Criminal Law* (Little, Brown, 1978), p. 759. On the difficulty of drawing lines, see Greenawalt, "The Perplexing Borders of Justification and Excuse," 84 Columbia Law Review 1897 (1984).

142. Leo Katz, *Bad Acts and Guilty Minds: The Conundrums of Criminal Law* (University of Chicago Press, 1987), p. 65. See also MacKinnon, "Toward Feminist Jurisprudence," pp. 717–18, fn. 73.

143. David Creach, "Partially Determined Imperfect Self-Defense: The Battered Wife Kills and Tells Why," 34 Stanford Law Review 615 (1982), p. 632.

144. See, e.g., Kadish, "Respect for Life and Regard for Rights in Criminal Law," 64 California Law Review 871 (1976).

145. See Kent Greenawalt, "Violence—Legal Justification and Moral Appraisal," 32 Emory Law Journal 437 (1983), pp. 453–60.

146. Katz, *Bad Acts and Guilty Minds,* p. 65.

147. Schneider, "Describing and Changing."

148. Mihajlovich, "Does Plight Make Right," p. 1278.

149. DSM-IV (American Psychiatric Association, 1994). Sect. 308.3.

150. People v. Aris, 264 Cal. Rptr. 167 (Cal. App. 4 Dist. 1989).

151. State v. Poling, 1991 WL 84229 (Ohio App.), at 5.

152. See Fletcher, *Rethinking Criminal Law*, p. 830.

153. People v. Yaklich, 833 P. 2d 758 (Colo. Ct. App. 1992). Interview with Barb Miller, Taycheedah Corrections Inst., June 1993.

154. Fletcher also deals with this permutation in terms of duress in *Rethinking Criminal Law*, p. 830.

155. It is not clear to me that delusion is completely present in even these cases. Perhaps the vet "really" knows the difference, but in the depths of his or her mind the boss is a substitute for the Cong, or ultimately deserving of death or harm because of his or her insensitivity to the vet, or whatever. I am suggesting that even such cases might involve a rationality and objectivity on the part of the vet that is framed in the narrative of revenge or some other motive. It seems to me to be too simplistic and escapist to simply declare such cases "delusion," and be done with it.

156. State v. Manning, 1991 OH App Lexis 2111, at *20, *21.

157. Blackman, "Potential Uses for Expert Testimony: Ideas Toward the Representation of Battered Women Who Kill," 9 Women's Rights Law Reporter 227 (1986), p. 231. People v. Torres, 488 N.Y. S. 2d 358 (Sup. Ct. 1985). See also Blackman, *Intimate Violence: A Study of Injustice* (Columbia University Press, 1989).

158. Freud argued against leaving psychoanalysis to the doctors because their narrow training did not prepare them to fathom the human dimension of the psyche. Freud sought humanists because true knowledge requires a broad, deep education that defies the simplicities of narrow professions. "[A]nalytic instruction would include branches of knowledge which are remote from medicine and which the doctor does not come across in his practice: the history of civilization, mythology, the psychology of religion, and the science of literature. Unless he is at home in these subjects, an analyst can make nothing of a large amount of his material. By way of compensation, the great mass of what is taught in medical schools is of no use to him for his purposes." *The Question of Lay Analysis* (Norton, 1978), pp. 93–94.

159. Fletcher, *Rethinking Criminal Law*, pp. 801–2. See also Fletcher, "The Individualization of Excusing Conditions," 47 Southern California Law Review 1269 (1974).

160. Stephen J. Morse, "Diminished Capacity: A Moral and Legal Conundrum," 2 International Journal of Law and Psychiatry 271 (1979), pp. 290, 297 (note 121). Emphasis in original.

161. Interview with Ann Jacobs, Kenosha Public Defender, co-chair in Richardson case retrial.

Chapter Seven

1. On how criminal law embodies moral judgments, see Greenawalt, "Violence—Legal Justification and Moral Appraisal," 32 Emory Law Journal 437 (1983), pp. 445–47.

2. There are two common interpretations of Arendt, whose understanding I draw on the most. One construes Arendt as contextualizing Kant's view of freedom by plac-

ing it in a political context of citizenship. The other interprets Arendt as a strict Kantian. I endorse the former view, and will draw on this view throughout the analysis of this chapter.

3. Christopher Lasch, *The Revolt of the Elites and the Betrayal of Democracy* (Norton, 1995), pp. 188–89. See also Richard Bernstein, *Beyond Objectivism and Relativism: Science, Hermeneutics, and Praxis* (University of Pennsylvania Press, 1983), esp. part 4.

4. In "Free Speech and Its Relation to Self-Government," Alexander Meiklejohn treats "political freedom" and free speech as normative commands that derive from the very logic of self-government itself. Meiklejohn, *Political Freedom* (Oxford University Press, 1965).

5. See, e.g., Bernard Yack, *The Problem of a Political Animal: Community, Justice, and Conflict in Aristotelian Political Thought* (University of California Press, 1993); J. G. A. Pocock, *The Machiavellian Moment: Florentine Political Thought and the Atlantic Republican Tradition* (Princeton University Press, 1975).

6. On the protection of voices of dissent as a cardinal First Amendment free speech principle, see Steven H. Shiffren, *The First Amendment, Democracy, and Romance* (Princeton University Press, 1990), esp. chap. 3.

7. Midgley, *Can't We Make Moral Judgments?* (St. Martin's Press, 1993), p. 25. Emphasis in original. See also Jean Bethke Elshtain, "Judge Not?" First Things, October 1994, pp. 36–40, p. 40.

8. Larry J. Siegel, *Criminology* (West Publishing Co., 1989), 3d ed., p. 204. On how the images of persons and rights bearers encoded in the law have consequences for citizenship and society, see Mary Ann Glendon, *Rights Talk: The Impoverishment of Political Discourse* (Free Press, 1991), esp. p. 67.

9. For an example of "realism," see John Finnis, *Natural Law and Natural Rights* (Oxford University Press, 1980). For examples of constructionism, see Michael Sandel, *Liberalism and the Limits of Justice* (Cambridge University Press, 1982). See also Charles Anderson, *Pragmatic Liberalism* (University of Chicago Press, 1990).

10. For a powerful portrayal of the way deconstructionist tenets lead to this problem, see David Lehman's book on the Paul de Man scandal, *Signs of the Times: Deconstruction and the Fall of Paul de Man* (Poseidon Press, 1992). On how much of the social world is constructed by conventions which ultimately refer to an independent external reality, see John R. Searle, *The Construction of Social Reality* (Free Press, 1995).

11. Szasz, *Insanity: The Idea and Its Consequences* (Wiley, 1987), p. 274.

12. Martha Minow, *Making All the Difference: Inclusion, Exclusion, and American Law* (Cornell University Press, 1990), esp. p. 47.

13. MacKinnon, "Toward Feminist Jurisprudence," 34 Stanford Law Review 703 (1982), pp. 724–25.

14. Schneider, "Particularity and Generality: Challenges of Feminist Theory and Practice in Work on Woman-Abuse," 67 New York University Law Review 520 (1992).

15. A book could be written about this question alone. Science, literature, philosophy, technology, buildings, airplanes, etc., didn't "just appear" out of nothing, but rather due to the efforts and sacrifices of previous generations. What constitutes "the

world" took effort. On the difference between the ethic of responsibility (which is also an ethic of gratitude) and an unreflective ethic of rights that takes such efforts for granted, see Jose Ortega y Gasset's great work *The Revolt of the Masses* (Norton and University of Notre Dame Press, 1985). Ortega stresses the links between liberty and responsibility.

16. Nietzsche, *The Genealogy of Morals* (Vintage, 1967), esp. Essay 2, sect. 16. Walter Kaufman, trans. and editor. Freud, *Civilization and Its Discontents* (Norton, 1961). Simone de Beauvoir, *The Second Sex* (Vintage, 1989). Sartre, *Being and Nothingness* (Washington Square, 1966), pp. 238–98.

17. See Joseph A. Amato, *Victims and Values: A History and a Theory of Suffering* (Praeger, 1990), esp. chap. 4.

18. See Benjamin, *The Bonds of Love: Psychoanalysis, Feminism, and the Problem of Domination* (Pantheon, 1988). Accordingly, freedom of speech—which embodies these aspects of social existence *par excellence*—is crucial to democratic politics.

19. Tocqueville, *Democracy in America,* vol. 2 (Schocken, 1961), book 1, chap. 2, pp. 9–10. Meiklejohn states: "Under actual conditions, there is no freedom for men except by the authority of government. Free men are not non-governed. They are governed—by themselves. *Political Freedom,* p. 19.

20. On "responsibility" as a wider net of concern for the plights of others, see Timothy D. Lytton, "Responsibility for Human Suffering: Awareness, Participation, and the Frontiers of Tort Law," 78 Cornell Law Review 470 (1993). In general, see Marion Smiley, *Moral Responsibility and the Boundaries of Community: Power and Accountability from a Pragmatic Point of View* (University of Chicago Press, 1992).

21. Aristotle, *Nichomachean Ethics,* (Oxford University Press, The World's Classics, 1954), p. 152. See also pp. 132–36, 153. Emphasis added.

22. For a book that explores these questions insightfully and systematically, see Mortimer R. Kadish and Sanford Kadish, *Discretion to Disobey: A Study of Lawful Departures from Legal Rules* (Stanford University Press, 1973).

23. Lasch, *The Revolt of the Elites,* p. 105.

24. Peter Arenella, "Convicting the Morally Blameless: Reassessing the Relationship Between Legal and Moral Accountability," 39 UCLA Law Review 1511 (1992), p. 1525.

25. Schulhofer, "The Gender Question in Criminal Law," 7 Social Philosophy and Policy 105 (1990), pp. 112–15.

26. Variations of this argument are discussed in Richard A. Wasserstrom, "The Obligation to Obey the Law," in Joel Feinberg and Hyman Gross, *Law in Philosophical Perspective: Selected Readings* (Dickenson, 1977), pp. 102–5. See also Herbert Morris, *On Guilt and Innocence: Essays in Legal Philosophy and Moral Psychology* (University of California Press, 1976), pp. 33–34.

27. Genevieve Lloyd, *The Man of Reason: "Male" and "Female" in Western Philosophy* (University of Minnesota Press, 1984), p. ix.

28. Lasch, *The Revolt of the Elites,* p. 191.

29. Arendt, "Judging," in *The Life of the Mind* (Harcourt Brace Jovanovich, 1977),

p. 271 (quoting Kant's *Critique of Judgment*). Hegel provides one of the more penetrating discussions in his treatment in *The Phenomenology of Mind* of the tension between reason, which strives for universality, and moral action or concrete sensibility, which by its very nature is plural and individual. Hegel, *The Phenomenology of Mind* (Harper, 1967), pp. 618–19, 638–39.

30. Arendt, "Truth and Politics," in Laslett and Runciman, eds., *Philosophy, Politics and Society* (Basil Blackwell, 1967), esp. p. 113. See also Havel, "Politics, Morality, and Civility," in *Summer Meditations* (Vintage, 1992), pp. 1–20.

31. See John Burnet, ed., *Plato's Euthyphro, Apology of Socrates and Crito* (Oxford: Clarendon Press, 1924).

32. See Arendt, *The Human Condition* (University of Chicago Press, 1958), p. 57.

33. See, e.g., Elmo Schwab, "The Quest for the Reasonable Man," 1982 Texas Bar Journal 178, p. 181. Aristotle, *Nichomachean Ethics*.

34. On this balance, see George Fletcher, "The Individualization of Excusing Conditions," 47 Southern California Law Review 1269 (1974).

35. See Murray Edelman, "Crime, Politics, and Symbolism," The August C. Backus Lecture, University of Wisconsin Law School, April 14, 1994. And Edelman, *The Symbolic Uses of Politics* (University of Illinois Press, 1964).

36. David Garland, *Punishment and Modern Society: A Study in Social Theory* (University of Chicago Press, 1990), pp. 252–53.

37. Regina v. Morgan, House of Lords [1976] A.C. 182. 1976 Sexual Offenses (Amendment) Act, sect. 1 (1).

38. People v. Casassa, 404 N.E. 2d 1310 (N.Y. Ct. App. 1980).

39. See Willard Gaylin's excellent treatment of the issues in this case in *The Killing of Bonnie Garland: A Question of Justice* (Penguin, 1983).

40. ABC's "Journal" show presented a segment on such cases on July 19, 1994, and related that the O. J. Simpson defense team at that time might have been considering a jealous rage defense. A former client of Simpson's lead lawyer, Robert Shapiro, spent only a few years in prison for killing his wife, and admitted that the defense in a good lawyer's hands was a partial license to kill.

41. For an insightful article on how Justice Blackmun's constitutional jurisprudence was wounded and rendered less effective by a lack of reasoning power in favor of result-oriented sentiment, see Jeffrey Rosen, "Sentimental Journey: The Emotional Jurisprudence of Justice Blackmun," The New Republic, May 2, 1994, pp. 13–18.

42. This is one of Camille Paglia's critiques of radical feminist theory: that law and society in patriarchal states are established for the purpose of suppressing women. Paglia points to the violence and rapine committed against women in conditions of social breakdown (wartime, civil unrest, etc.) when law and the state disappear to show that this view is either suspect or, at least, incomplete. Paglia, *Sexual Personae* (Norton, 1990), chap. 1.

43. See Albert Memmi, *The Colonizer and the Colonized* (Beacon Press, 1965).

44. For a defense of judicial activism on these grounds, see John Hart Ely, *Democracy and Distrust* (Harvard University Press, 1980).

45. Maguigan, "Battered Women and Self-Defense."

46. For a feminist critique of this type of binary approach and an articulation of a subtle, contextually rich form of feminist jurisprudence, see Katharine T. Bartlett, "Feminist Legal Methods," 103 Harvard Law Review 829 (1990). For an example of binary feminism, see Ann Scales, "The Emergence of Feminist Jurisprudence: An Essay," 95 Yale Law Journal 1373 (1986). For a broader perspective on feminist viewpoints, see Virginia Sapiro, *A Vindication of Virtue: The Political Theory of Mary Wollstonecraft* (University of Chicago Press, 1992).

47. Maguigan, "Battered Women and Self-Defense," p. 444.

48. See Samuel R. Gross and Robert Mauro, *Death and Discrimination: Racial Disparities in Capital Sentencing* (Northeastern University Press, 1989).

49. Steven B. Smith, *Hegel's Critique of Liberalism: Rights in Context* (University of Chicago Press, 1989), pp. 114, 115, 116, 122. Quoting Hegel, *Phenomenology of Mind*, p. 229.

50. Midgley, *Can't We Make Moral Judgements?*, p. 80.

51. On the individual psychology of scapegoating and prejudice, see the classic by Gordon Allport, *The Nature of Prejudice* (Allsion-Wesley, 1979), esp. p. 430. For a brilliant and disturbing analysis of the social psychology of scapegoating in relation to the onset of social crisis and disintegration, social othering, and forms of knowledge that dissolve individual differences in favor systemic patterns, forms, and profiles, see Rene Girard, "The Plague in Literature and Myth," in *To Double Business Bound: Essays on Literature, Mimesis, and Anthropology* (Johns Hopkins University Press, 1978).

52. Hegel, *Phenomenology of Mind*, p. 638.

53. See Harvey Mansfield, Jr., "The Forms and Formalities of Liberty," 1983 The Public Interest, p. 121.

54. Richard Sennett, *The Fall of Public Man* (Knopf, 1977), esp. chaps. 11–13.

55. Hegel's depiction of the master-slave encounter in *The Phenomenology of Mind*, pp. 229–33, is still the starting point for this understanding. Consciousness must risk itself and prove itself in the eyes of the other to gain "freedom" or "independent self-consciousness." Both de Beauvoir and Benjamin are indebted to this passage (*The Second Sex, Bonds of Love*). Psychoanalysis is relevant, too: failure to achieve transcendence entraps us in the throes of Oedipal fears and related primitive emotions. Transcendence toward independence and responsibility is the only way out of the trap.

56. Lee E. Bollinger, *The Tolerant Society: Freedom of Speech and Extremist Speech in America* (Oxford University Press, 1986), pp. 120. 140, 142. Emphasis in original. Justices Douglas and Black gave perhaps the finest judicial expressions of this logic in their famous dissents to the Supreme Court's upholding of the convictions of the leaders of the Communist Party during the McCarthy era. See Dennis v. U.S., 341 U.S. 494 (1951), dissenting opinions.

57. Interview with Stephen Hurley.

58. Yale Kamisar, American Bar Association Journal, June 1994, p. 41.

59. Vigilante justice is always driven by unreflective moral impulses: "Was it not Freud who revealed the power of the destructive forces working against the ethical, and

even worse, *within the ethical?*" Ricoeur, *Freud and Philosophy: An Essay on Interpretation* (Yale University Press, 1970), p. 326. Emphasis added. In psychoanalytic topography, the superego derives its instinctual energy and drive from the id. Hence the punitive fury to which the superego is subject. See Freud, *The Ego and the Id* (Norton, 1960).

60. Moral anger is essential to any notion of justice, as Walter Berns shows in *For Capital Punishment: Crime and the Morality of the Death Penalty* (Basic Books, 1979). But such anger is dangerous when it is not channeled and controlled by public law and due process.

61. Locke, *Second Treatise of Government*, in *Two Treatises of Government*, ed. Peter Laslett (Cambridge University Press, 1967); Hobbes, *Leviathan*, ed. M. Oakeshott (Blackwell, Oxford); Jack Katz, *Seductions of Crime: Moral and Sensual Attractions in Doing Evil* (Basic Books, 1988), chap. 1. See also Aeschylus's *The Oresteia*, ed. Harold Bloom (Chelsea House, 1988), on how the rule of law ameliorates the "moral furies."

62. See Shirley Sagaw, "A Hard Case for Feminists: People v. Goetz," 10 Harvard Women's Law Journal 253 (1987).

63. People v. Aris, 264 Cal. Rptr. 167 (Cal. App. 4 Dist. 1989), at 174. In *Violence and the Sacred*, Rene Girard shows how the primordial concern and fear of every society (ancient, traditional, or modern) lies in preventing acts of violence from spiraling out of control. Law or ritual are designed to stop the spiral by providing a publicly sanctioned means of satisfying the passion of vengeance. Girard, *Violence and the Sacred* (Johns Hopkins University Press, 1977).

64. Bob Dylan, "Everything Is Broken," in *Oh Mercy* (Columbia Records, 1989).

65. On the importance of interdicts and unspoken morality to society, see Philip Rieff, *Fellow Teachers* (Delta, 1973).

66. George Fletcher, *A Crime of Self-Defense: Bernard Goetz and the Law on Trial* (Free Press, 1988), p. 61.

67. See Ramond Aron, *The Opium of the Intellectuals* (Greenwood Press, 1977), originally published in 1957.

68. Arendt, *Human Condition*, pp. 208–9, 274. Emphasis added.

69. Arendt, *Human Condition*, p. 282.

70. See Jean Bethke Elshtain, "Freud and the Therapeutic Society: Homo Politicus or Homo Psychologicus?" in Elshtain, *Meditations on Modern Political Thought: Masculine/Feminine Themes from Luther to Arendt* (Penn State Press, 1992).

71. Wright, *Remembering Satan: A Case of Recovered Memory and the Shattering of an American Family* (Knopf, 1994).

72. Ofshe and Watters, *Making Monsters: False Memories, Psychotherapy, and Sexual Hysteria* (Scribner's, 1994), pp. 203, 224. See Deborah Lipstadt, *Denying the Holocaust: The Growing Assault on Truth and Memory* (Free Press, 1993).

73. Loftus and Ketcham, *The Myth of Repressed Memory: False Memories and Allegations of Sexual Abuse* (St. Martin's Press, 1994), p. 64. The jury found Franklin guilty of murder. The case is being retried after an appeals court found procedural violations unrelated to the evidence on memory recovery.

74. See the HBO movie *Indictment* (1995). And Ruth Shalit, "Witch Hunt," The New Republic, June 19, 1995, pp. 14–16. See also the series of articles on the Wenatchee hysteria by Dorothy Rabinowitz in the Wall Street Journal.

75. Garry Wills, quoted in Ofshe and Watters, *Making Monsters*, p. 177. These episodes are contemporary versions of the outbreaks of "social madness" that occur throughout history, often conjoined with religion. See George Rosen, *Madness in Society: Chapters in the Historical Sociology of Mental Illness* (University of Chicago Press, 1968).

76. Herman, *Trauma and Recovery: The Aftermath of Violence—From Domestic Abuse to Political Terror* (Basic Books, 1992), chap. 9. Walker, *Terrifying Love: Why Battered Women Kill and How Society Responds* (Harper Collins, 1989), p. 257.

77. See H. L. A. Hart, "Responsibility," in Joel Feinberg and Hyman Gross, *Philosophy of Law* (Wadsworth, 1991), p. 492.

78. Hanna Fenichel Pitkin, *The Concept of Representation* (University of California Press, 1967), pp. 8–9. Quoting Harvey Pinney, "Government—By Whose Consent?" 13 Social Science 298 (1938).

79. Hart, "Responsibility," p. 499.

80. Fletcher, *Rethinking Criminal Law* (Little, Brown, 1978), pp. 843, 846.

81. Diana T. Myers analyzes the various aspects of autonomy, showing its centrality to any coherent notion of the self in *Self, Society, and Personal Choice* (Columbia University Press, 1991).

82. Sartre, *Being and Nothingness* (Washington Square, 1966), p. 707.

83. Harriet Woods, quoted in "Hillary Clinton's Role in Whitewater Flap Poses Difficulties for Both Republicans and Democrats," Wall Street Journal, January 13, 1994, p. A20.

84. Elizabeth Rapaport, "The Death Penalty and Gender Discrimination," 25 Law and Society Review 367 (1991), pp. 367–68.

85. Schneider, "Particularity and Generality," pp. 556–57.

86. Interview with Ronda Richardson, Taycheedah Correctional Inst.; interviews with J. L., Gerry Mueller and Cindy Kollath. On time horizons as important to personal narratives, see Giddens, *Modernity and Self-Identity: Self and Society in the Late Modern Age* (Polity Press/Basil Blackwell, 1991), pp. 53, 77–87. In Kant's philosophy, time is an essential category of rational thought.

87. Interview with inmate, Taycheedah Correctional Inst.

88. Fletcher, *Rethinking Criminal Law*, pp. 835–46.

89. John Searle says that all human action and communication depend upon what he calls the "Background," which is, among other things, a set of presumptions about how the world works, and without which we would not be able to act. No one can "prove" or locate the Background, but all human action and intentionality presuppose its presence. See Searle, *The Rediscovery of the Mind* (M.I.T. Press, 1992), esp. chap. 8.

90. Melville, *Billy Budd* (Signet, New American Library, 1961), p. 38.

91. On the different incarnations in the history of philosophy of determinism in relation to freedom, see Richard Taylor, "Determinism," 2 Encyclopedia of Philosophy 359 (1967).

92. Smiley, *Moral Responsibility and the Boundaries of Community*, p. 13. For a "practical reason" model of responsibility that also eschews the free will/determinism distinction, but is less politically and socially contingent than Smiley's approach, see Michael Moore, "Causation and the Excuses," 73 California Law Review 1091 (1985), pp. 1148, 1136.

93. Compare People v. Casassa, 404 N.E. 2d 1310 (N.Y. Ct. App. 1980), with Scroggs v. State, 93 S.E. 2d 583 (1956) (wife who killed the other woman entitled to manslaughter defense).

94. For a fascinating account of how medieval societies attributed blame and punished animals in criminal trials, see E. P. Evans, *The Criminal Prosecution and Capital Punishment of Animals* (Faber and Faber edition, 1987; first published by William Heinemann Limited, 1906).

95. Interviews with Stephen Hurley, defense attorney; Linda Dawson, assistant district attorney, Dane County, Wisconsin; and John Burr, assistant district attorney, Dane County.

96. Nietzsche, *Beyond Good and Evil* (Vintage, 1966), sect. 23. Walter Kaufman, translator. Nietzsche continues: "For psychology is now again the path to the fundamental problems." Of course, Nietzsche is the great precursor of Freud (but whereas Freud teaches us *to understand* the riddle of the Sphinx, Nietzsche teaches us how to *be* the Sphinx).

97. Nietzsche, *The Genealogy of Morals*, trans./ed. Walter Kaufman (Vintage, 1967), Second Essay, section 2. Emphasis in original.

98. Arendt, *The Human Condition*, pp. 243–45. See also Hegel's master-slave discussion, *The Phenomenology of Mind*, pp. 229–33: the distinction between "Person," which is essentially an aspect of nature (natural consciousness), and "independent self-consciousness," which is an aspect of rational freedom.

99. See Nietzsche, *Ecco Homo*, "The Case of Wagner: A Musician's Problem," sect. 4. In *The Portable Nietzsche* (Vintage, 1967). The capable individual is the one who "makes *distinctions*." In Aristotle's words, "sympathetic judgment is judgment which discriminates what is equitable and does so correctly" (Aristotle, *Nichomachean Ethics*, p. 152).

100. Stephen Holmes portrays the paradox of limits and freedom with acuity in *Passions and Constraint: On the Theory of Liberal Democracy* (University of Chicago Press, 1995). See also the incisive review of this work by Alan Wolfe, "The Good, the Bad, and the Gingrich: Liberalism Against Its Enemies—And Its Friends," The New Republic, May 1, 1995, pp. 35–41, in which Wolfe accentuates the importance of paradox to constitutional liberty.

101. Midgley, *Can't We Make Moral Judgments?* p. 25.

102. Interview with J.J., Madison, Wisconsin.

103. Interviews with Bob Cook and Tom Dietz, social work psychologists at Community Vet Center in Madison, Wisconsin. And interview with Dr. Morey Bernstein at Veterans Administration Hospital, Milwaukee, Wisconsin.

104. Susan Brownmiller, *Waverly Place* (Signet, 1989), p. 349.

105. Ruth Leys, "The Real Miss Beauchamp: Gender and the Subject of Imita-

tion," in J. Butler and J. Scott, eds., *Feminists Theorize the Political* (Routledge, 1992), pp. 168, 204. Emphasis added.

106. See, e.g., Simon Head, "The New, Ruthless Economy," *The New York Review of Books,* February 29, 1996, pp. 47–52; William Julius Wilson, *The Truly Disadvantaged: The Inner City, the Underclass, and Public Policy* (University of Chicago Press, 1987).

107. One of the most perceptive aspects of Hegel's *Phenomenology of Mind* is the way in which Hegel shows how the desires and thinking are never static. A mental posture or stand can be enlightening and liberating for a while, but turn into a trap at a later time. Individualism can lead to a fear of others, whereas absorption in the community can be a means of escape from the self. Each stage of the dialectic journey can become a dead end. Desire is never static. As Dylan puts it, "he not busy being born is busy dying." "It's All Right, Ma (I'm Only Bleedin')," in *Bringing It All Back Home* (Columbia Records, 1965).

108. Arendt, *The Human Condition,* p. 12, generally, p. 36.

109. Tocqueville, *Democracy in America,* vol. 2 (Schocken, 1961), p. 381, from book 4, chapter 6, "What Sort of Despotism Democratic Nations Have to Fear." Elshtain ties these themes together in "Judge Not?" First Things, October 1994, pp. 36–40.

110. For a critique of this, see Mansfield, *America's Constitutional Soul,* chap. 1, "Political Science and the Constitution."

111. See Robert Hughes's best-selling *Culture of Complaint: The Fraying of America* (Oxford University Press, 1993).

112. *In Discipline and Punish: The Birth of the Prison* (Vintage, 1979), Foucault assumes that the repression of the prison is indicative of the repression of society as a whole. For a critique of this reductionism, see Garland, *Punishment and Modern Society,* chap. 7.

113. Michel Foucault, *Madness and Civilization: A History of Insanity in the Age of Reason* (Vintage, 1973).

114. See, e.g, the analysis of Jacques Derrida's notion of "inversion" and coexistent negation in J. M. Balkin, "Deconstructive Practice and Legal Theory," 36 Stanford Law Review 127 (1984).

115. "In this connection Nietzsche was the foremost of all seers. . . . I refer to his distinction between ascendent and descendent life, between life as a success and life as a failure." Ortega y Gasset, *The Modern Theme* (Norton and Company, 1933), p. 75.

116. See Jonathan Simon, "The Ideological Effects of Actuarial Practices," 22 Law and Society Review 771 (1988).

117. See, e.g., Kathleen B. Jones, "Citizenship in a Woman-Friendly Polity," 15 Signs 781 (1990).

118. Carole Pateman, *The Disorder of Women: Democracy, Feminism, and Political Theory* (Stanford University Press, 1989), p. 3.

119. Jean Bethke Elshtain and others have shown how women achieved substantial responsibilities and influence in private and domestic spheres before the second wave of feminism in the 1960s. It is not the case that women were pure immanence before

recent times. But it is clear that many avenues were largely cut off, including economic power and major public roles. Elshtain, *Public Man/Private Women: Women in Social and Political Thought* (Princeton University Press, 1981).

120. Hans-Georg Gadamer, *Truth and Method,* trans. Garrett Barden and John Cumming (Seabury Press, 1975), pp. 92–110.

121. Another aspect of this issue is the psychology of the "inner child," which is the background for the memory recovery movement. Such psychology looks backward rather than forward, grounding the self on the shores of regression and immanence. Like the psychology of "self-esteem," the recovery movement enchains those whom it promises to liberate. The best psychological therapy comes to terms with the past from the vantage point of teleology, which is developmental or transcendent. The healthy will looks forward, while the sick will is enchained to the past.

122. In his renowned defense of absolute First Amendment protection for political speech, *Political Freedom* (or *Free Speech and Its Relation to Self-Government*), which is ultimately an essay on citizenship and political obligation, Alexander Meiklejohn proclaims, "Political freedom does not mean freedom from control. It means self-control." *Political Freedom,* p. 13.

123. Blackman, "Potential Uses for Expert Testimony: Ideas Toward the Representation of Battered Women Who Kill," 9 Women's Rights Law Reporter 227 (1986), p. 231. Emphasis added. People v. Torres, 488 N.Y. S. 2d 358 (Sup. Ct. 1985). See also Blackman, *Intimate Violence: A Study of Injustice* (Columbia University Press, 1989).

Chapter Eight

1. Elizabeth Rapaport, "The Death Penalty and Gender Discrimination," 25 Law and Society Review 367 (1991), pp. 377–82.

2. People v. Aris, 264 Cal. Rptr. 167 (Cal. App. 4 Dist. 1989), at 174.

3. Dicey, quoted in Irving J. Sloan, *The Law of Self-Defense: Legal and Ethical Principles* (Oceana Publications, 1987), p. 52.

4. Interview with Linda Dawson, assistant district attorney, Dane County, Wisconsin.

5. Richard A. Rosen, "On Self-Defense, Imminence, and Women Who Kill Their Batterers" 71 North Carolina Law Review 371 (1993), p. 410; S. Graff, "Battered Women, Dead Husbands: A Comparative Study of Justification and Excuse in American and West German Law," 10 Loyola Los Angeles International and Comparative Law Journal 1 (1988), p. 23; M. Marcus, "Conjugal Violence: The Law of Force and the Force of Law," 69 California Law Review 1657 (1981), p. 1725.

6. Susan Murphy, "Assisting the Jury in Understanding Victimization: Expert Psychological Testimony on Battered Woman Syndrome and Rape Trauma Syndrome" 25 Columbia Journal of Law and Social Problems 277 (1992), pp. 279–80, and fn. 17.

7. People v. Aris, 264 Cal. Rptr. 167 (4 Dist. 1989), at 179.

8. Elizabeth Schneider, "Equal Rights to Trial for Women: Sex Bias in the Law of Self-Defense," 15 Harvard Civil Liberties–Civil Rights Law Review 623 (1980), p. 646.

9. Schneider, "Equal Rights to Trial for Women," p. 638.

10. Schneider, "Equal Rights to Trial for Women," fn. 82.

11. State v. Richardson, 92-CF-574, 1993, testimony of Marilyn Hutchinson, February 11, 1993.

12. Schneider, "Equal Rights to Trial for Women," pp. 626–27.

13. See Greenawalt, "Violence—Legal Justification and Moral Appraisal," 32 Emory Law Journal 437 (1983), pp. 445–47.

14. See Sagaw, "A Hard Case for Feminists: People v. Goetz," 10 Harvard Women's Law Journal 253 (1987).

15. Nancy Fiona-Gormally, "Battered Wives Who Kill: Double Standard Out of Court, Single Standard In?" 2 Law and Human Behavior 133 (1978), p. 158.

16. Schneider, "Equal Rights to Trial for Women," p. 402, fn. 80.

17. Gillespie, *Justifiable Homicide: Battered Women, Self-Defense, and the Law* (Ohio State University Press, 1989), p. 41.

18. Schulhofer, "The Gender Question in Criminal Law," 7 Social Philosophy and Policy 105 (1990), pp. 112–15.

19. For simplicity's sake, we deal with cases in which the defendant actually killed. But the law of self-defense applies to cases in which the defendant uses deadly force that falls short of homicide. Its gravamen is that the defendant was forced to use deadly or lethal force to fend off an attack.

20. In general, see LaFave and Scott, *Criminal Law* (West Publishing Co., 1986), 2d. ed., p. 454; Maguigan, "Battered Women and Self-Defense: Myths and Misconceptions in Current Reform Proposals" 140 University of Pennsylvania Law Review 379 (1991). See also chapter 6, above.

21. Fletcher, *Rethinking Criminal Law* (Little, Brown, 1978), p. 795.

22. LaFave and Scott, *Criminal Law*, p. 659.

23. Maguigan, "Battered Women and Self-Defense," pp. 419–20.

24. LaFave and Scott, *Criminal Law*, pp. 455–56.

25. Maguigan, "Battered Women and Self-Defense," p. 409 et seq.

26. LaFave and Scott, *Criminal Law*, pp. 457–58.

27. Maguigan, "Battered Women and Self-Defense," p. 409.

28. See, e.g., State v. Leidholm, 334 N.W. 2d 811 (N.D. 1983), at 817–18, in which the court uses the language of the subjective test, but actually employs a balanced contextualized objective logic.

29. Maguigan, "Battered Women and Self-Defense," p. 409 et seq. and accompanying footnotes.

30. Maguigan, "Battered Women and Self-Defense," pp. 420–21.

31. ALI Model Penal Code and Commentaries, Sect. 3.04 (1985).

32. Maguigan, "Battered Women and Self-Defense," pp. 439–42.

33. Maguigan, "Battered Women and Self-Defense," p. 406 and fn. 93. See also Elizabeth Bochnak et al., eds., *Women's Self-Defense Cases: Theory and Practice* (Michie Co., 1981).

34. The classic statement condemning the legal system on these and related grounds is Jerold Auerbach's *Unequal Justice* (Oxford University Press, 1976). See also Gerry Spence, *With Justice for None* (Penguin, 1989).

35. Maguigan, "Battered Women and Self-Defense," p. 388, fn. 22 for citations of articles making this claim. See, e.g., Ewing, *Battered Women Who Kill: Psychological Self-Defense as Legal Justification* (Lexington Books, 1987), p. 34; McCord, "Syndromes, Profiles, and Other Mental Exotica: A New Approach to the Admissibility of Nontraditional Psychological Evidence in Criminal Cases" 66 Oregon Law Review 19 (1987), p. 49.

36. Maguigan, "Battered Women and Self-Defense," pp. 384, 397–401 and accompanying notes. See, e.g., Marvin Wolfgang's famous study, *Patterns in Criminal Homicide* (University of Pennsylvania Press, 1958), p. 252.

37. See Vanderbraack, "Limits on the Use of Defensive Force to Prevent Intra-marital Assaults," 10 Rutgers-Camden Law Journal 635, pp. 654–55.

38. See Thomas Katheder, "Criminal Law—Lovers and Other Strangers: Or, When Is a House a Castle?—Privilege of Non-Retreat in the Home Held Inapplicable to Legal Co-Occupants—State v. Bobbitt, 415 So. 2d 724 (Fla.1982) (1983)," in Johann and Osanka, eds., *Representing . . . Battered Women Who Kill* (Charles C. Thomas, 1989).

39. Maguigan, "Battered Women and Self-Defense," p. 419, fn. 136.

40. See, e.g., J. Alexander Tanford and Anthony J. Bocchino, "Rape Victim Shield Laws and the Sixth Amendment," 128 University of Pennsylvania Law Review 544 (1980); Susan Estrich, *Real Rape* (Harvard University Press, 1987), chaps. 5 and 6.

41. Schneider, "Equal Rights to Trial for Women," p. 633. For similar views, see Phyllis L. Crocker, "The Meaning of Equality for Battered Women Who Kill Men in Self-Defense," 8 Harvard Women's Law Journal 121 (1985); Victoria M. Mather, "The Skeleton in the Closet: The Battered Women's Syndrome, Self-Defense and Expert Testimony," 39 Mercer Law Review 545 (1988).

42. Maguigan, "Battered Women and Self-Defense," p. 417.

43. Maguigan, "Battered Women and Self-Defense," p. 450.

44. Maguigan, "Battered Women and Self-Defense," pp. 417–19. Lafave and Scott, *Criminal Law*, p. 457. State v. Wanrow, 559 P. 2d 548 (Wash. 1977).

45. LaFave and Scott, *Criminal Law*, p. 457.

46. See, e.g., People v. Jones, 12 Cal. Rptr. 777 (1961), at 780.

47. Wisconsin Code, Sect. 940.19.

48. This article on the dilemmas of a new form of jaw surgery appeared in the Wall Street Journal sometime in 1993.

49. People v. Williams, 205 N.E. 2d 749 (1965).

50. State v. Spaulding, 257 S.E. 2d 391 (1979).

51. See, e.g., People v. Aris, 264 Cal. Rptr. 167 (Cal. App. 4 Dist. 1989), at 173. U.S. v. Peterson, 483 F. 2d 1222 (D.C. Cir. 1973), at 1230.

52. See, e.g., People v. Lucas, 324 P. 2d 933 (1958), at 936.

53. Ronald N. Perkins and Rollin M. Boyce, *Criminal Law* (Foundation Press, 1982), 3d. ed., p. 1132. Discussed also in Kit Kinports, "Defending Battered Women's Self-Defense Claims," 67 Oregon Law Review 393 (1988), p. 436, note 179.

54. People v. Aris, 264 Cal. Rptr. 167 (Cal. App. 4 Dist. 1989), at 173.

55. For a comparison in terms of the quantum or magnitude of evidence necessary

to take the case to the jury in cases of battered women who killed sleeping husbands, compare State v. Leidholm, 334 N.W. 2d 811 (N.D. 1983), with State v. Stewart, 763 P. 2d 572 (Kan. 1988).

56. Fletcher, *A Crime of Self-Defense: Bernard Goetz and the Law on Trial* (Free Press, 1988), pp. 33–34.

57. Greenawalt, "Violence—Legal Justification and Moral Appraisal," pp. 453–54. See the discussion in chapters 4 and 6 about attribution theory in psychology and moral philosophy.

58. Greenawalt, "Violence—Legal Justification and Moral Appraisal," pp. 459–60.

59. Greenawalt, "Violence—Legal Justification and Moral Appraisal," pp. 455–56.

60. Jack Katz calls such retaliations the "ways of the bad ass" in *Seductions of Crime: Moral and Sensual Attractions in Doing Evil* (Basic Books, 1988), chap. 3.

61. People v. Jones, 12 Cal. Rptr. 777 (1961), at 779.

62. Fletcher, *A Crime of Self-Defense*, p. 1.

63. Schneider, "Equal Rights to Trial for Women," p. 634–35. See Fletcher, *A Crime of Self-Defense.*

64. Maguigan, "Battered Women and Self-Defense," pp. 421 and fn. 145.

65. Sagaw, "A Hard Case for Feminists," pp. 263–64.

66. Maguigan, "Battered Women and Self-Defense," table on pp. 464–67.

67. Maguigan, "Battered Women and Self-Defense," p. 410. See People v. Goetz, 497 N.E. 2d 41 (N.Y. 1986). See the instruction in the trial court, People v. Goetz, Trial Record, pp. 9218–19, cited in Maguigan, p. 410, fn. 108. See also State v. Wanrow, 559 P. 2d 548 (Wash. 1977).

68. See, e.g., Kinports, "Defending Battered Women's Self-Defense Claims," p. 416; Fiona-Gormally, "Battered Wives Who Kill."

69. State v. Stewart, 763 P. 2d 572 (Kan. 1988), at 579 (self-defense); State v. Felton, 329 N.W. 2d 161 (Wis. 1983), at 173 (manslaughter). See also Maguigan, "Battered Women and Self-Defense," p. 411, fn. 111.

70. Maguigan, "Battered Women and Self-Defense," p. 412.

71. See Martha Minow, *Making All the Difference: Inclusion, Exclusion, and American Law* (Cornell University Press, 1990).

72. Sagaw, "A Hard Case for Feminists," p. 266.

73. Rosen, "On Self-Defense," pp. 393–94.

74. Rosen, "On Self-Defense," p. 380.

75. Schulhofer also presents a kind of necessity alternative which we will discuss below.

76. Paul H. Robinson, *Criminal Law Defenses* (West Publishing Co., 1984), chap. 4, sect. 131(c).

77. Schulhofer, "The Gender Question in Criminal Law," p. 129.

78. Rosen, "On Self-Defense," p. 404.

79. See, e.g., Lockett v. Ohio, 438 U.S. 586 (1978); Eddings v. Oklahoma, 455 U.S. 104 (1982) (evidence of child abuse syndrome at sentencing hearing).

80. See Samuel R. Gross and Robert Mauro, *Death and Discrimination: Racial Disparities in Capital Sentencing* (Northeastern University Press, 1989). Despite all the evidence of racial discrimination in capital sentencing, the Supreme Court rejected such grounds for invalidating capital punishment in McClesky v. Kemp, 481 U.S. 279 (1987).

81. Rosen, "On Self-Defense," pp. 392–93.

82. Loraine P. Eber, "The Battered Wife's Dilemma: To Kill or Be Killed," 32 Hastings Law Journal 895 (1981), p. 927.

83. Schulhofer, "The Gender Question in Criminal Law," p. 129.

84. Pattie Hearst's ability to leave the SLA for substantial periods of time thwarted her Stockholm syndrome claim. U.S. v. Hearst, 412 F. Supp. 889 (1976).

85. Katz, *Bad Acts and Guilty Minds: The Conundrums of Criminal Law* (University of Chicago Press, 1987), p. 41. See also pp. 13 and 61.

86. State v. Norman, 378 S.E. 2d at 113.

87. O.E.D., Second Edition.

88. LaFave and Scott, *Criminal Law*, p. 458, footnote 36.

89. People v. Aris, 264 Cal. Rptr. 167 (Cal. App. 4 Dist. 1989), at 172–75. State v. Stewart, 763 P. 2d 572 (Kan. 1988), at 577.

90. Greenawalt, "Violence—Legal Justification and Moral Appraisal," pp. 453–60.

91. People v. Aris, 264 Cal. Rptr. 167 (Cal. App. 4 Dist. 1989), at 172–75; State v. Norman, 378 S.E. 2d 8 (N.C. 1989), at 13–16; State v. Stewart, 763 P. 2d 572 (Kan. 1988), at 577.

92. State v. Hennum, 441 N.W. 2d 793 Minn. 1989.

93. State v. Norman, 378 S.E. 2d, at 11–12.

Court of Criminal Appeals of Alabama, 129
Crews, Frederick, 13

D.C. Court of Appeals, 91
Daubert v. Merrell Dow Pharmaceuticals, 28
Dawson, Linda, 117, 123, 225
D'Emilio, Joann, 37
Dershowitz, Alan, 37
Diagnostic and Statistical Manual (DSM),
    25, 26, 34, 85, 143; first ed. (DSM-I),
    34, 142; second ed. (DSM-II), 34, 142,
    143; third ed. (DSM-III), 4, 19, 21, 26,
    38, 46, 70, 142, 143, 175; (DSM-IIIR),
    31, 143, 175; fourth ed. (DSM-IV), 21,
    35, 85, 143, 175; fifth ed. (DSM-V), 21
Dicey, Albert, 225
diminished capacity excuse, 4, 18, 69, 78,
    129, 141, 157, 175.
Dissociative Identity Disorder (DID), 21,
    22, 26, 35, 154. *See also* multiple per-
    sonality disorder
Dobash, R. Emerson, 55, 57, 60
Dobash, Russell, 55, 57, 60
Dodge, Mary, 170–73
domestic abuse. *See* battering
Donnerstein, Edward, 135
Donohoo, Robert, 104–5
Down's syndrome, 25
Doyle, James, 123
Dunn, Katherine, 162
duress, 3, 9, 17, 23, 77, 78, 109, 119, 122,
    127, 128, 137, 150, 174, 181, 208, 237,
    244
Dutton, Don, 90, 92
Dutton, Mary Ann, 32, 60, 61, 62, 96, 179
Dworkin, Andrea, 49
Dyas v. United States, 27, 28, 171
Dylan, Bob, 203

Eber, Loraine P., 245, 246
Eighth Circuit Court of Appeals, 167
Eisenberg, Alan, 60, 108, 161
Elshtain, Jean Bethke, 183, 215
Englund, Steven, 161, 162
Erlinder, Peter, 33, 35, 39

Esterson, Allen, 20
Ewing, Charles, 162, 163, 164, 169–70

Faigman, David L., 145, 152, 154
False Memory Recovery Foundation, 48
False Memory Recovery Syndrome, 21
Federal Bureau of Investigation (FBI), 20,
    54, 124
Federal Rules of Evidence, 28
Feldman, Martha S., 106, 107
feminism, 21, 42, 45, 46, 48, 58, 73, 77, 81,
    87, 123, 145, 150, 158, 162, 194, 199,
    213, 241
Fielder v. State, 80
Fletcher, George, 109, 120, 180, 204, 237
Foucault, Michel, 42, 93, 97, 149, 214, 215,
    216
Franklin, George, 206
Freud, Anna, 91
Freud, Sigmund, 19–20, 42, 45, 94, 144,
    189; criticism of, 19–20; and Freudian
    neurosis, 33; and Freudian theory, 21–
    23, 87
Frye v. United States, 27, 28, 38
Fuller, Lon, 115, 116

Gadamer, Hans-Georg, 218
Galanter, Marc, 24
gambler's syndrome, 4, 27, 38
Garland, David, 196
Gelles, David, 54
Gerstmann, Evan, 15, 105, 174, 182, 200,
    220
Giddens, Anthony, 62
Gillespie, Cynthia, 140, 162, 229
Gilligan, Carol, 151, 152
Girard, Rene, 89
Goetz, 238; and Goetz, Bernard, 109, 191,
    203, 228
Goldman, Ron, 15
Gondolf, Edward, 70, 86
Gramsci, Antonio, 195
Greenawalt, Kent, 237, 248
Greene, Edith, 170–73
Gusfield, Joseph, 42, 43

Sartre, Jean-Paul, 96, 189, 207
Schelling, Thomas, 69
Schneider, Elizabeth, 132; and battered woman syndrome, 167, 226; and battered women and custody cases, 129; and battered women's situation, 227, 228; and child abuse defense, 135; and citizenship and responsibility, 147–48, 188, 189; and concept of battering, 26; and self-defense, 229, 235, 239; and stereotype of battered women, 208
Schreiber, Flora Rheta, 22
Schulhofer, Stephen, 118–19, 223; and defenses for battered women, 121; and development of battered woman syndrome, 77, 106; and expert testimony, 39; and legal standards, 193; and self-defense, 173–74, 244, 246, 249
Seeger, Patti, 8, 9, 64, 105, 138, 156–57. *See also* Advocates for Battered Women
self-defense, 3, 4, 55, 57, 58, 71, 77, 80, 83, 96, 97, 120, 137, 139, 144, 170, 172, 173, 200, 203, 228, 248, 249; in battered woman cases, 119, 178, 188, 243; and battered woman syndrome, 138; and *Buhrle v. Wyoming*, 146; and early cases involving women, 140; and Charles Ewing, 162, 163, 164; and Bernard Goetz, 191; and Catherine MacKinnon, 169; and Holly Maguigan, 198; and *People v. Jackson*, 160; recommended changes in law of, 79, 121, 198, 223, 231–42, 249; and Elizabeth Schneider, 226; standards of, 8, 79, 98, 194, 201, 219, 236, 239, 241, 244; use of, 9, 12, 26, 29, 30; and *State v. Shroeder*, 174; and Lenore Walker, 147, 148, 149, 150, 151, 159; and *Whitetail*, 167, 168. *See also* battered woman syndrome; imminence; syndrome
Seligman, Martin, 82, 155, 156, 168
Sennett, Richard, 201
Shaines, Natalie, 87
Shatan, Chaim, 34
shelter movements, 77

Sherman, David, 96
Shorter, Edward, 47
Simpson, O. J., 15, 76
situational excuse, 145, 226
Sixth Circuit Court of Appeals, 91
Skalaski, 159, 176, 232; and Lisa Skalaski, 104, 105, 153, 154, 187, 200
Slavney, Phillip, 45
Smiley, Marion, 135, 185, 209, 210
Smith, Steven B., 199
Spitzer, Robert, 46
Springsteen, Bruce, 49
Stack, Carol, 152
State v. Anderson, 80
State v. Daniels, 160
State v. Heads, 35–36
State v. Hennum, 249
State v. Hundley, 113
State v. Kelly, 39, 111, 167, 169
State v. Koss, 78–79
State v. Leaphart, 160
State v. Manning, 177
State v. Norman, 246, 247, 248; compared with *Skalaski*, 176, 200; and court's approach, 249; facts of case, 64–65, 240, 243; and hostage syndrome, 98; and Judy Norman, 64–65, 80, 96, 243, 244, 245, 248, 250; relationship between Normans, 98; and Richard Rosen, 243–45; and self-defense, 80, 250
State v. Pascal, 161
State v. Poling, 175
State v. Richardson: background of, 16; and battered woman syndrome, 104, 105, 154, 164–66, 168–69, 227; and defense strategy, 108, 140, 181. *See also* Richardson, Ronda
State v. Saldana, 30
State v. Shroeder, 173–74
State v. Simpson, 56
State v. Spaulding, 236
State v. Thomas, 77, 78
State v. Wanrow, 39–40, 77, 147, 169, 188, 235
State v. Willaquette, 136

131, 210, 227. *See also* post-traumatic
stress disorder